WOMEN IN ULSTER POLITICS

Women in Ulster Politics
1890–1940
A History Not Yet Told

Diane Urquhart

IRISH ACADEMIC PRESS
DUBLIN • PORTLAND, OR

First published in 2000 by
IRISH ACADEMIC PRESS
44, Northumberland Road, Dublin 4, Ireland
and in the United States of America by
IRISH ACADEMIC PRESS
c/o ISBS, 5804 NE Hassalo Street,
Portland, OR 97213-3644

Website: www.iap.ie

British Library Cataloguing in Publication Data
Urquhart, Diane
Women in Ulster politics, 1890–1940: a history not yet told. – (Women in Irish history)
1. Women in politics – Northern Ireland 2. Women – Suffrage – Northern Ireland 3. Ulster (Northern Ireland and Ireland) – Politics and government 4. Northern Ireland – Politics and governments.
I. Title
320'.082'09416
ISBN 0–7165–2627–1

Library of Congress Cataloging-in-Publication Data
Urquhart, Diane.
Women in Ulster politics, 1890–1940: a history not yet told / Diane Urquhart.
p. cm.—(Women in Irish history)
Includes bibliographical references and index.
ISBN 0–7165–2627–1
1. Ulster (Northern Ireland and Ireland)—Politics and government. 2. Women in politics—Ulster (Northern Ireland and Ireland)—History—20th century. 3. Women in politics—Ulster (Northern Ireland and Ireland)—History—19th century. 4. Women—Ulster (Northern Ireland and Ireland)—Politics and government. I. Title. II. Series.

DA 990.U46 U76 2000
320.9'0082'09416—dc21 99–089205

Typeset in 11 pt on 13 pt Sabon
by Carrigboy Typesetting Services, County Cork
Printed by Creative Print and Design (Wales), Ebbw Vale

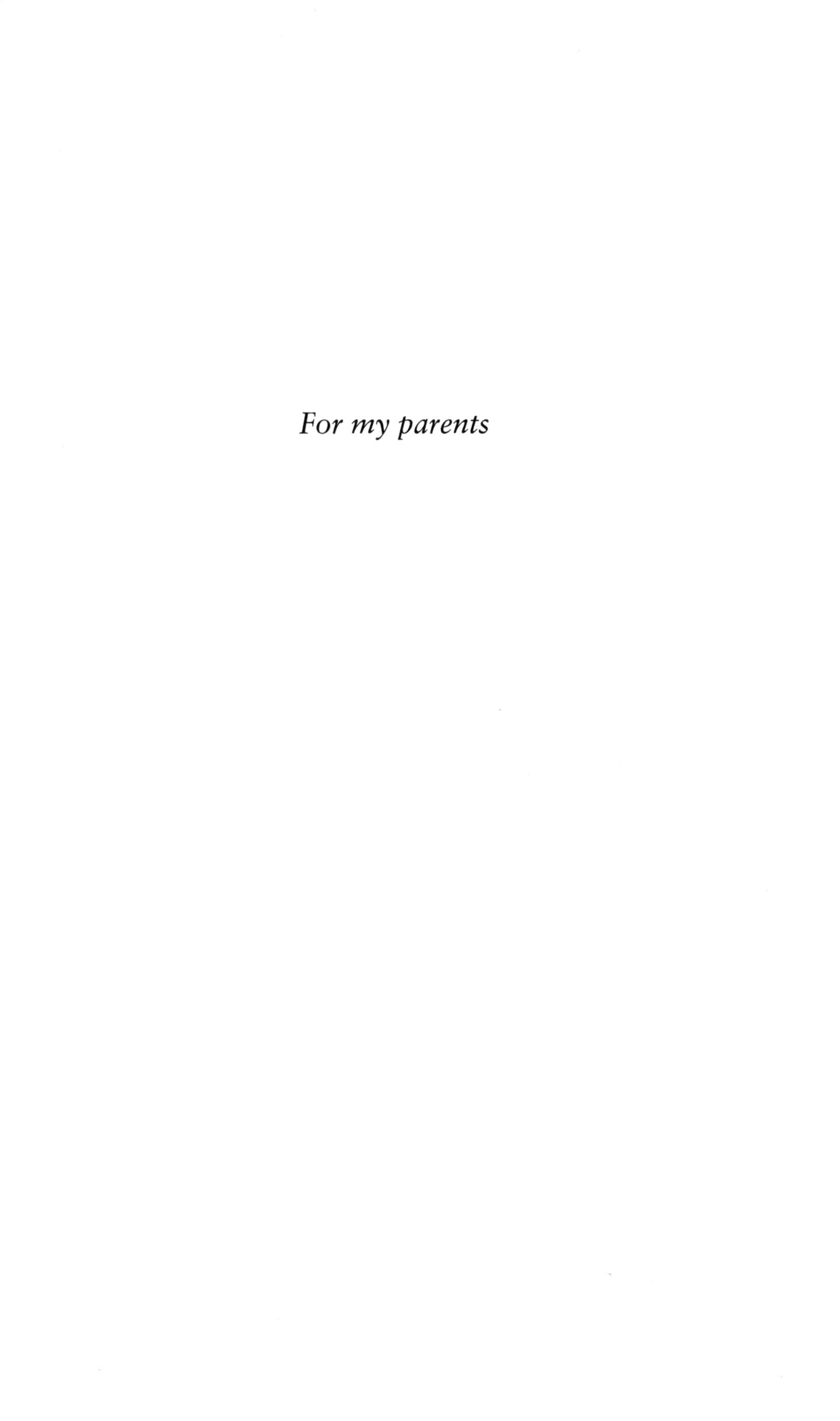

For my parents

Contents

Acknowledgements

I have incurred many debts in the course of my research and it would not be possible to thank all those who have answered letters or offered advice. However, special thanks must go to my PhD supervisor, Dr Mary O'Dowd of the School of Modern History of the Queen's University of Belfast, for her support, enthusiasm and guidance throughout the completion of this work. I also wish to record my thanks to the staff of the following libraries and repositories: the Public Record Office of Northern Ireland (especially Michael Goodall), Council of Trustees of the National Library of Ireland, National Archives, Dublin, Omagh Public Library, the Linen Hall Library, Belfast Central Library, Queen's University Library and Victoria College, Belfast. For permission to consult and quote from the minute books of various boards of guardians I am indebted to Dr David Lammey of the Public Record Office of Northern Ireland and the Record Officer of the Department of Health and Social Services.

On a personal level I would also like to thank the following people for their unfailing support: Gill McIntosh, Gail McMullen, Joseph Braden, Patsy Horton, Elizabeth Rooney, Alyson Urquhart, Caroline Calvert and Martin O'Neill.

I am grateful to the Deputy Keeper of Records of the Public Record Office of Northern Ireland, the National Library of Ireland and the following individuals for granting me permission to publish material: Viscount Craigavon, Lady Mairi Bury, the Marquess of Londonderry and the Ulster Women's Unionist Council, Robert Lowry and H. Montgomery Hyde.

Lists of tables & abbreviations

LIST OF TABLES

LIST OF ABBREVIATIONS

AOH	Ancient Order of Hibernians
IPP	Irish Parliamentary Party
IRA	Irish Republican Army
IRB	Irish Republican Brotherhood
IUA	Irish Unionist Alliance
IWCF	Irish Women's Civic Federation
IWFL	Irish Women's Franchise League
IWSF	Irish Women's Suffrage Federation
IWSLGA	Irish Women's Suffrage and Local Government Association
IWSS	Irish Women's Suffrage Society
NUWSS	National Union of Women's Suffrage Societies
UIL	United Irish League
UUC	Ulster Unionist Council
UVF	Ulster Volunteer Force
UWUC	Ulster Women's Unionist Council
WFL	Women's Freedom League
WSPU	Women's Social and Political Union
WUA	Women's Unionist Association

Introduction

'[I]ndeed it is hard to miss woman as a force if one keeps one's eyes open and seeks . . . the truth about woman . . . if one is not afraid to know her, if one really wants to know her.'[1]

An early work on Irish women's historical role recognised that women had 'exercised a potent . . . influence on society'.[2] This influence was not limited to the private, domestic sphere where female authority as wife, carer and mother was socially accepted, but was also apparent in, perhaps the most male dominated of public preserves, the political arena. In the early twentieth century politically active Irish women were confident that their own contributions would be fully recounted by the historical record. Lady Cecil Craig, president of the Ulster Women's Unionist Council (UWUC) and wife of the first Prime Minister of Northern Ireland, believed the part that she and many other unionist women had taken 'in helping the men in recent troubulous [sic] times would, when the history of those times came to be written, compare favourably with the part played by the women of old'.[3] On the nationalist side of the political spectrum, Countess Constance Markievicz assured the members of Cumann na mBan (Women's Council) that their work would be commemorated through the generations by their 'children and . . . children's children'.[4] These expectations, however, remained unfulfilled. Indeed, the enduring perception that politics was an exclusively male preserve and *terra incognita* for women resulted in little historical attention being directed towards unearthing women's political role.

This study of women in Ulster politics in the period 1890 to 1940 seeks, at least partially, to redress this imbalance and ultimately assess whether gender allowed politically active women to share a common historical experience.[5] By focusing on female affiliation to mainstream nationalist and unionist political associations, on suffragists and women who stood for the elective public positions of MP, poor law guardian and local government councillor, the extent, diversity and significance of the female political role has clearly emerged.[6] Although some pioneering work has been completed on Irish suffragism and female nationalism, the participation of women from Ulster in these movements and the formation of indigenous Ulster associations have not been analysed in any detail.[7] Other areas, such as the work of female unionists and women's participation in municipal and national politics, have not been subject to any in-depth historical scrutiny.[8]

Fernand Braudel's term 'submerged history' can be aptly utilised in the study of women in politics. By transcending the parliamentary perimeters of high politics to encompass popular politics and the methods which women adopted in an attempt to influence policy and events, it becomes apparent that women possessed a role of considerable contemporary and historical importance.[9] From the late nineteenth century, through individual and group momentum, women embarked on a variety of political activities: petitioning, fund-raising, cultivating political allies, subscribing to political associations, attending and addressing political meetings, distributing propaganda, canvassing voters, standing for elective office and, occasionally, committing acts of violence.

Although criticism has been levelled at the 'male-defined conceptual framework' of studying women in politics, it is important to consider this context.[10] Women's political activity never occurred in isolation. Indeed, the specific determinants of women's participation were often directly affected by their relationship with male political associations, as illustrated by the ancillary status of Cumann na mBan and the Ulster Women's Unionist Council in relation to the Irish Volunteers and the Ulster Unionist Council respectively. Moreover, wider considerations, such as the political system, need to be addressed. For instance, even suffragists, who placed their demands for enfranchisement before any party-based concerns, were prompted to campaign for reform through sheer frustration with a male-dominated political system. Suffragists therefore emphasised that women were unable to initiate change by legislative means because of their gender-based exclusion from the decision-making process.

Examining women's contribution to organisations and events also entails an assessment of the 'compensatory' nature of the female political role.[11] However, women's political agenda and the factors responsible for their political participation should also be discussed. Women were encouraged to become politically active by a combination of external and internal factors. The passage of two parliamentary acts in the late nineteenth century had the unintentional effect of facilitating female political participation on an unprecedented scale: the Corrupt and Illegal Practices Act of 1883 forbade the payment of political canvassers and the 1884 Reform Act enfranchised the majority of men in Britain.[12] These changes prompted party organisers to develop pragmatic electoral strategies and consequently to form new organisational networks which harnessed the energies of political volunteers, an increasing number of whom were women. Essentially, women were welcomed as an unpaid source of labour, working in an area which had previously been the exclusive domain of a small number of political wives.[13] By 1900 women were organising electoral campaigns, disseminating propaganda and addressing public meetings. This work became progressively more structured as a result of the establishment of female auxiliary organisations affiliated to the main British political parties: the Conservatives' Primrose League, the Women's Liberal Federation and the Women's Labour League, established in 1883, 1886 and 1906 respectively.[14]

Several branches of the Primrose League and one branch of the Women's Liberal Federation were active in Ulster from the late nineteenth century. The Ulster branches of these associations were, however, quickly usurped by the establishment of indigenous unionist organisations.[15] Indeed, in Ireland the dominance of the diametrically opposed concerns of unionism and nationalism significantly affected the direction of women's political participation in the period 1890 to 1940. As a result, the majority of women who became politically active in Ireland aligned themselves not to Conservative, Liberal or Labour associations, but to unionist and nationalist organisations. Furthermore, as a result of the escalating sense of political crisis that permeated Irish society from the late nineteenth century, both unionism and nationalism became increasingly popular. Female ancillary organisations developed as part of this popularisation process and brought an unprecedented number of women into the political arena.

With increasing levels of female politicisation, the view that politics was wholly incompatible with a woman's designated social role diminished. For instance, the idea that there was 'something repugnant to the ordinary . . . man in the idea of a woman mounting a platform and facing the noisy, gaping, vulgar crowd at an election meeting' gradually declined.[16] As the general public became accustomed to seeing women in such a public capacity, female speakers came to be seen less as a novelty and more as an accepted component of the political process. Amongst those commenting on this change of opinion was the Liberal Prime Minister, H.H. Asquith:

> the stolid masculine audience at political meetings [came] to regard the spectacle of women sitting on the platform – sometimes in the chair –

> moving resolutions and even amendments, not with a silent conventional curtsey and smile, but with flights of rhetoric, flashes of humour, as part of the normal machinery of a 'demonstration' or a 'rally'.[17]

Although the acceptability of women in politics increased, taking the decision to become politically active could still be difficult. It seems that, for many women, addressing a public meeting involved 'much anguish and soul-searching'.[18] The gender-based parameters of social intercourse also lingered and criticism was quickly forthcoming when, for example, suffragettes flouted convention by embracing violence as a means to political ends.[19]

In addition to the external influences affecting women's political activity, internal factors should also be considered. The question of individual motivation is difficult to assess, as the majority of women's lives are not recorded in detail through diaries or private letters. Despite this limitation, some generalisations regarding individual motivation can be made. There are many similarities between British and Irish women's political experiences, but there are also important distinctions. In both countries gender appears not to have been the primary factor in determining women's political affiliation. This is illustrated by the difference in the level of support which was forthcoming for women's suffrage and the auxiliary associations of mainstream political parties like the Primrose League and the Ulster Women's Unionist Council. Suffrage, with its gender focus on women's social and legislative disabilities, failed to mobilise popular support. This suggests that other considerations prompted female activism. Within a British context, both class and community have been suggested as important in encouraging women's political participation, but in Ireland the influence of religion and familial support appear to have been more pervasive.[20]

The influence of religion was apparent in inculcating a sense of Christian duty which led an increasing number of men and women to philanthropy from the middle of the nineteenth century. The execution of charitable work provided some women with the necessary experience and motivation to perform similar duties in a more formal capacity, where they could both exercise and influence policy in the elective positions of poor law guardian and local government councillor. Furthermore, the general identification of the Catholic and Protestant faiths with the dominant political tenets of Irish nationalism and unionism meant that religion was an important factor in shaping political affiliation. The distribution of religious denominations throughout the country, with Protestants concentrated in north-east Ulster, also enabled unionism to become a mass-based movement, whereas nationalism remained less popular in Ulster than was the case throughout the rest of the country.[21] Women's political activity was, therefore, fundamentally influenced by religion in a variety of ways.

The collateral influence of a supportive familial network with common political objectives provided another important stimulus for women and it appears that many women became politically active in order to support their family's traditional political creed. It was also within the familial environment that women first came into contact with conditioning, gender-based social mores. This was especially marked in relation to the treatment afforded to male siblings and the division of domestic responsibilities. Indeed, some women, realising that the public world was as divided as the private, rejected the social and civic positions afforded to their sex by joining campaigns to instigate suffrage and municipal reform.

The extent of female political activity was also controlled by practical considerations of domestic and familial commitments. Theresa, 6th Marchioness of Londonderry, the principal Tory political hostess and president of the Ulster Women's Unionist Council, fully appreciated the impact of these considerations:

> . . . it is impossible for a young wife with a family to take much part in public life, if she does her duty to her husband and children, as I [,] in an old fashioned way, think she ought to do.[22]

Even suffragists, who rejected many of the prescribed social confines, did not challenge the concept that a married woman's first responsibility lay with her husband and children. And, ultimately, the extensive political commitments which went with an elected position or membership of a political association demanded both economic freedom and an abundance of leisure time. This underlines another factor affecting women's political participation – that of class. The majority of working women were prevented from pursuing a more active political role by practical domestic concerns. Limited political involvement, for instance attending a political meeting rather than addressing or organising such an event, should not, therefore, be automatically equated with an individual's level of political commitment.

The majority of women included in this study seem not to have aspired to personal gain, infamy or renown through their political activity, but sought instead to instigate reform, exercise their powers of citizenship, or influence policy. Some women were outstanding individuals, well placed by virtue of an aristocratic background and close familial links with Tory, unionist and nationalist politics to exercise considerable political influence. Others were driven by a belief in their own abilities to instigate change for the greater good of society. Nevertheless, what was common to all these women, regardless of political affiliation, religious denomination, class or familial background, was the overwhelming desire to become actively involved in Ulster politics.

DIANE URQUHART
Belfast
March 2000

CHAPTER ONE

The Campaign for Women's Suffrage

Where the slave ceases, the master of slaves ceases,
Where women walk in public processions in the streets,
the same as the men,
Where they enter the public assembly and take place the
same as men,
Where the city of the cleanliness of the sexes stands,
There the great city stands.[1]

I

All women involved in the suffrage movement across Europe and the Americas had different experiences whilst sharing the same ultimate objective of attaining the right to vote. Distinctions were caused not only by ideological beliefs concerning the merits of constitutional or militant action, but also by geography. In Ireland there were rural, urban and regional variations between the north and south of the country. In addition, the political framework that the women's movement struggled to influence, and operated within, distanced Irish suffragists from many of their contemporaries. The issue of Home Rule effectively alienated many women from joining the Irish suffrage campaign and forced a considerable number of active suffragists to develop different political façades. Indeed, politics ultimately fragmented the tenuous unity of the whole Irish suffrage movement.

Previous histories of Irish suffragism have paid little attention to Ulster and have focused mainly on the militant suffragette campaign of 1913–14. This approach has underestimated the overall complexity of the movement, classing indigenous Ulster suffrage associations as small, non-militant and reticent to comment on the contemporary political situation.[2] Although most suffrage societies throughout Ireland and Britain remained constitutional, militant activity in Ulster pre-dated the arrival of the Pankhursts' English-based organisation, the Women's Social and Political Union (WSPU), in Belfast in 1913. Moreover, the majority of northern suffrage organisations, in parallel with most Irish suffragists, adopted non-party affectations and placed suffrage before any political principle.

It has been argued that:

> Past politics . . . that most traditional of all forms of history, appears at first glance to be almost a totally male preserve. On the rare occasions when women did actively participate in politics, historians have tended to see them as disruptive.[3]

Yet in terms of the suffrage campaign this analysis is apt, as the militant tenets of the movement deliberately used disorderly tactics in an attempt to counter the inertia of both the political system and the general public. But militancy was very much a last resort, embarked upon by Ulster, Irish and British women alike from a sense of frustration and disillusionment. Initially the suffrage movement possessed an air of gentility. From the nineteenth century, middle-class women of leisured affluence became involved in philanthropy and this public volunteerism led some women to more self-orientated issues. Campaigns for educational and property reform gradually aroused interest in the question of women's suffrage. Attaining the vote became the key feminist goal by the early twentieth century, as women collated the liberal arguments of natural rights and equality to their own enfranchisement.[4] Hence the parliamentary vote came to be identified as a fundamental component of citizenship that many suffragists expected to instigate moral and social regeneration.

The suffrage movement was the first sustained political campaign to be conducted by women on their own behalf. Following the 1867 Reform Act's introduction of the term 'man' to define electoral eligibility, the campaign for women's suffrage gradually gained momentum throughout Britain. Although feminism in the 1880s and 1890s was still interpreted as an avant-garde and minority interest, it was apparent that some Irish women actively supported suffrage from the middle of the nineteenth century. There were, for instance, twenty-five Irish women signatories to the suffrage petition which John Stuart Mill presented to the House of Commons in 1866 and Isabella Tod formed the first Irish suffrage association, the North of Ireland Women's Suffrage Society, in 1873.[5]

Tod was a prominent and informed defender of women's rights. Ranked by her contemporaries as one of the 'ablest and certainly the most eloquent speakers' of the late nineteenth century, her support for female enfranchisement was one component of her interest in women's social and moral reform.[6] Given Tod's contemporary reputation it was perhaps not surprising that she was the only woman appointed to give evidence to a select committee on the reform of married women's property law and that she served on the executive of the Married Women's Property Committee in London from 1873–4.[7] In 1871 she also pioneered the establishment of the Belfast branch of the Ladies' National Association, which publicly campaigned for the repeal of the Contagious Diseases Acts.[8] This legislation, passed in three instalments in 1864, 1866 and 1869, permitted the compulsory examination of suspected prostitutes at named military camps in an attempt to curtail the spread of venereal disease. In Ireland these acts were only applicable to Cork, Cobh and Curragh, but members of the Belfast branch of the association actively campaigned to prevent this legislation being extended to the city. As the reform campaign publicised controversial questions pertaining to sexual morality it attracted only minority support and the collective Irish membership was estimated at only fifty women.[9] But Tod's involvement in these early feminist campaigns nurtured her belief that women's suffrage was prerequisite to sexual equality. In pursuit of these ends, in February 1872 she initiated the first Irish suffrage tour: holding meetings in Belfast, Carrickfergus, Coleraine, Londonderry and Dublin. This pioneering endeavour met with considerable success, with the first meeting, held in Belfast on 6 February, attracting an audience of 500. Similar numbers attended a subsequent meeting in Coleraine and, it was claimed, 'everywhere they received good local support and met with much cordial sympathy . . . nowhere opposition'.[10] The tour culminated on 21 February with a meeting held in Dublin that led to the establishment of a suffrage committee. By 1876 this committee had developed into the Dublin Women's Suffrage Society.[11]

In addition to her influential Irish initiatives, Tod was also active in England. She addressed suffrage meetings in London on 6 May 1880, Glasgow on 3 November 1882 and Edinburgh on 22 March 1884 and visited London at least once a year during the parliamentary session 'in order to watch the interests of Irish women'.[12] Her enthusiasm for women's suffrage was also manifested by her writings. As a regular contributor to the *Englishwoman's Journal* and the author of various pamphlets, she often referred to the support which women's suffrage aroused in Ulster in the closing decades of the nineteenth century:

> You know how deep is the conviction of the best women in Ulster, of all religious and political opinions, that the possession of the franchise . . . is an absolute necessity . . . the women of Ireland take a keen interest in politics . . . and their influence is a binding and uniting force in society . . . this claim has reached all parts of the Province, all grades of society, all creeds and classes, serious opposition has gradually disappeared . . . nearly every political Association in Ulster, Liberal and Conservative alike, has expressed its appropriation . . . it is impossible for women to do their duty, and to protect their interests and dignity, without the same weapon men find essential for the same purposes.[13]

As the self-proclaimed 'chief pleader for women's suffrage'[14] and as, perhaps, the most renowned Irish feminist of the nineteenth century, Tod's death in 1896 left a 'wide gap in the ranks of the early workers'.[15] Nevertheless, the organisational foundations laid by her pioneering work enabled and inspired other women to participate in the most active phase of Irish suffragism in the early twentieth century.

II

[T]he varied societies flitter away their power in internecine rivalries and antagonistic methods and principles . . . Suffrage has wandered in a multiplicity of paths that seem to lead nowhere, save to labyrinthine confusion.[16]

From the early twentieth century the Irish suffrage movement gradually gained momentum. This, coupled with a general press boycott of suffrage activities, provided the impetus for the establishment of the *Irish Citizen*, a weekly suffrage paper in May 1912. Under the editorship of Francis Sheehy Skeffington and James Cousins this paper provides the main source for any history of the Irish suffrage movement as it articulated the aggregate suffrage voices in Ireland, from the northern, southern, constitutional and militant constituents of the movement. Indeed, many individual suffrage associations appear not to have maintained organisational records, as the *Citizen* was utilised to record their weekly activities, rally support, comment on contemporary politics and publicise women's position of social and legislative inferiority. The growing interest in female enfranchisement was reflected in the *Citizen*'s circulation figures: by June 1912 it had weekly sales of 3,000, with an estimated readership of 10,000.[17] And as the suffrage movement gained momentum, it also diversified to such an extent that the overall structure of Ulster suffrage societies could only be described as complex.[18] Suffrage associations were established by various means, ranging from individual to group initiative, and in the early twentieth century several existing suffrage organisations were rejuvenated through re-organisation. For instance, the North of Ireland Women's Suffrage Society, established in Belfast by Isabella Tod in 1873, became a branch of the Dublin-based Irish Women's Suffrage and Local Government Association (IWSLGA) in 1896. Led by Anna and Thomas Haslam, the IWSLGA was a constitutional organisation dedicated to securing the vote and greater female representation in the public life of the country. In 1909 there was further re-organisation, as the Belfast branch of the IWSLGA became independent, adopting a new name: the Irish Women's Suffrage Society (IWSS).[19] The IWSS gradually expanded, founding branches in Whitehead and Londonderry and attracting the former Bangor branch of the English-based association, the Women's Freedom League (WFL), into its ranks. As members of the WFL were 'not proselytisers', but sought 'a broad solidarity with progressive Irish forces rather than an organizational conquest', the absorption of its Irish branches into indigenous suffrage societies occurred with apparent ease.[20] Smaller suffrage groups were also established in Ulster: the Belfast branch of the Church League for Women's Suffrage, which combined religious worship with political objectives by holding quarterly communion services in St George's Church in Belfast's High Street, was established in April 1913 and a branch of the Men's Political Union for Women's Enfranchisement was established in Belfast during January 1914, the only all-male suffrage society operative in Ireland.[21]

In addition to Isabella Tod's pioneering work, several Ulster suffragists were also responsible for introducing important initiatives in the early twentieth century. Miss L.A. Walkington, a member of Lisburn Suffrage Society, appears to have been the first to suggest forming an umbrella organisation to co-ordinate the activities of Irish suffragists.[22] In 1911, Walkington, assisted by Lilian Metge, the founder of Lisburn Suffrage Society, wrote to every suffrage society and known suffragist in Ireland to publicise a meeting in Dublin to formally establish the Irish Women's Suffrage Federation (IWSF). Walkington was also responsible for the initiation of a Northern Committee of this body to deal specifically with Ulster suffrage associations.[23] Essentially the establishment of the IWSF provided valuable cohesion for existing suffrage societies throughout Ireland, but it never embraced all, as important organisations like the Irish Women's Suffrage Society remained independent. Nevertheless, the federation was popular, growing from an initial affiliate of four societies to twenty organisations by July 1913, 70 per cent of which were Ulster based and fronted by the Northern Committee.[24] All societies affiliated to the federation were united under a non-militant and non-party policy. But with regards to the latter it is clear that there was some flexibility. Whitehead Suffrage Society was one affiliate that closed its meetings with a rendition of the national anthem in 1914, thereby vocally identifying with the politics of unionism rather than with the federation's supposed policy of neutrality.

The public controversy that surrounded the campaign for female enfranchisement ensured that no more than a small minority of women were prepared to breach social taboos by declaring themselves suffragists. This situation was not peculiar to Ireland. Indeed, suffragists throughout Ireland were numerically analogous to those in England. By May 1912 there were approximately 3,000 members of the IWSF and IWSS, a figure that was comparable to the density of activists in England.[25] Two years later membership figures had risen to 3,500, approximately 1,000 of whom were members of the twenty Ulster suffrage societies.[26] Thus the campaign for women's suffrage was not any less popular in Ulster than throughout the rest of the country.

Yet, support for suffrage could be effectively heightened by propaganda. Boosts to the membership of existing suffrage organisations and the impetus and inspiration for establishing new associations in Ulster were provided by visiting speakers. Emmeline Pankhurst, leader of the militant organisation the Women's Social and Political Union (WSPU) and one of the most notorious English suffragettes, addressed meetings in Dundalk, Belfast, Londonderry, Cork and Dublin in October 1910, and in the following year her daughter and co-worker, Christabel, addressed an IWSS meeting in Belfast's Opera House. In January 1912 Emmeline Pethick Lawrence, another prominent member of the WSPU, lectured at several meetings organised by the IWSS in Belfast. The Northern Committee of the IWSF was able to attract speakers of an equally high calibre, hosting meetings for Charlotte Despard, founder of the Women's Freedom League, Mrs Colby, secretary of the Federal Women's Equality Association of America, and numerous representatives of the English-based National Union of Women's Suffrage Societies (NUWSS). To cite just one example of the impact of such visits, Belfast and District Women's Suffrage Week, held in April 1913 to coincide with a visit from Helen Fraser of the NUWSS, led eighty-three new members to join the IWSF and to the establishment of three new societies, situated in Holywood, Larne and Portadown.[27] Holywood Suffrage Society was notably successful, enrolling sixty members within two weeks of its establishment. However, following such initial local interest, it seems that membership figures only increased marginally. For example, Lisburn Suffrage Society was able to double its membership within a year of its establishment in 1909 and had seventy-seven members by February 1913, but during the next year only added another eight names to its membership list. There were also considerable variations in the size of individual associations. By April 1914 the Northern Committee of the IWSF represented a total of 678 suffragists in Ulster, but membership of individual societies affiliated to the federation ranged from twenty-one members in Coleraine to 110 members in Londonderry.[28]

There is little information concerning the class composition of the suffrage movement. According to one contemporary, Marie Johnson, a member of Belfast's Irish Women's Suffrage Society, the initial demand for the vote came from women of the upper middle classes:

> who considered themselves . . . important to the country, and [wanted] to share in the legislation as the men who had the vote. We ordinaries resented this, but did not refuse to support, as we were assured that our turn would come.[29]

However, in Ulster significant overtures were made to attract working-class support. The IWSF's Northern Committee was anxious to awaken 'interest on the part of Belfast working women' in December 1913,[30] and, at a meeting of this organisation held in March of the following year, the majority of the fifty women present were 'shop girls, factory hands and maids'.[31] Similar motives prompted Belfast's IWSS to preach from 'street corners' and hold dinner-hour meetings at factory and mill gates in the Belfast area to prove 'that suffragists were just ordinary women'.[32] But in Ulster, as elsewhere in Ireland and in Britain, it was educated middle-class women who formed the kernel of the suffrage movement. Female poor law guardians and local government councillors, who, due to the demands of public office, were mostly leisured and middle class, were reportedly seen as the 'mainstay of the . . . [suffrage] movement . . . their services cannot be valued too highly'.[33] Thus Charlotte Hamilton, chair of Ballymena Board of Guardians and a member and former chair of Portrush Urban District Council, also served as president of Portrush

Suffrage Society from 1913. In the following year the vice-president of this society was Mrs Robinson, a rural district councillor, whilst two poor law guardians, Frances Reid and Annie Entrican, regularly sold papers for the IWSS in Belfast.

Belfast's Irish Women's Suffrage Society became the most prolific association in the north of Ireland during the early years of the twentieth century and was accredited with effecting 'a considerable change in the public attitude toward woman suffrage in Ulster'.[34] In November 1912 Blanche Bennett, secretary of this association, recorded that the organisation had been:

> able to fill the Ulster Hall (the largest hall in Ireland) three times, and the Belfast Opera House once, and more than once almost every other available hall in the city . . . although hampered for want of funds and sufficient workers to meet the demand, nearly every large town in Ulster . . . [had] been visited, in some cases more than once. In the country we found our audiences particularly sympathetic to our cause; we got patient hearings, and cordial invitations to come again.[35]

This society pioneered the establishment of weekly open-air educational meetings. Over a twelve-month period from 1912 to 1913, forty-seven demonstrations of this kind were held and in August 1912 the society initiated an open-air campaign fund to make this work financially self-supporting. Although largely Belfast-based, with sixty per cent of its meetings being held in the city from the middle of 1912, the propaganda work conducted by this organisation in provincial areas also attracted considerable interest, because of the novelty of any suffrage presence. During a week's tour of Co. Antrim in September 1912, for instance, 500 people reportedly attended one meeting in Ballymoney.[36] Yet, in spite of the success of their provincial campaign, the IWSS remained Belfast based with ninety-three per cent of their meetings being held in the city from June 1913 to May 1914. This was possibly a consequence of their increasing sympathy with suffragette militancy which had led the association away from time-consuming provincial meetings and propaganda to focus on more combative tactics. Indeed, one palpable effect of their escalating militancy was a marked decline in the number of public meetings which were held: over a twelve-month period from 1912 to 1913, the IWSS was responsible for organising seventy-six per cent of all suffrage meetings in Ulster, but in the corresponding period of the next year only forty-six per cent of meetings were attributable to this society.[37]

By comparison, individual suffrage organisations affiliated to the Northern Committee of the IWSF worked independently in their own locality. Londonderry and Lisburn societies, for example, canvassed female municipal voters, organised speakers' classes and toured provincial districts by car to distribute suffrage literature to outlying areas, whilst the Northern Committee worked to attain pro-suffrage resolutions from Newry, Warrenpoint, Lisburn, Portrush and Belfast urban district councils. Over a twelve-month period from 1912 to 1913, the committee also organised fifteen public meetings, eighty-seven per cent of which were held outside Belfast, which was representative of the organisation's provincial base. But during the next year the IWSF and its affiliates became increasingly active, organising a total of thirty-three public meetings. This was more than double the number of meetings held in the preceding year, which highlights their escalating proselytising efforts. The IWSF did, however, retain its provincial base, holding eighty-five per cent of its meetings outside Belfast in the period 1913 to 1914.[38]

III

An articulate and definite cry for political freedom.[39]

Having established the scale of the Ulster suffrage movement, the question of motivation needs to be addressed. In 1861 John Stuart Mill argued that men 'as well as women, do not need political rights in order that they may govern, but in order that they may not be misgoverned'.[40] Suffragists agreed with Mill, setting the campaign for the vote firmly within the context of democracy. Many women, infused with a sense of urgency for this reform, claimed that the absence of any female influence in the governing institutions of the state was responsible:

> for a dearth of thoughtful attention directed to matters which concern women more intimately . . . than they can possibly concern men . . . Votes for women will everywhere train and discipline the instinct of maternal responsibility; will elicit a volume and impulse of truer thinking on all subjects connected with the most elementary needs of the people.[41]

Many educated, middle-class suffragists believed that they could make a positive contribution to the workings of the state. These arguments were further enhanced by suffragists' claims that working women, whether their labour was paid or unpaid or performed in the home or factory, remained intrinsically vulnerable without the protection of the vote:

> Politicians and statesmen can afford to disregard constituents who are unable to vote against them . . . all women are not happily placed, all women are not protected, all women have not husbands more honourable and generous than the law expects, all women have not the hearth-fire, which is their highest privilege, as well as their duty, to tend. No longer is it the province of woman alone to spin and weave, to sew and brew, to bake and preserve . . . The social conditions of to-day force women . . . to undertake the duties of citizens in addition to the duties of womanhood.[42]

In essence the vote came to symbolise women's emancipation from social drudgery, virtuous convention, economic and political subservience. This agenda was especially apparent within Belfast's Irish Women's Suffrage Society, which associated the vote with many elements of progressive social reform. Addressing an open-air meeting at Belfast's Ormeau Park in August 1913, Mrs Chambers, one of the most vocal Ulster suffragists, advanced a maternal justification for suffrage claims: 'if it were women's work to fit the children to go into the world, it was equally important to see that the world was a fit place for their children'.[43] Arguments of this type were reiterated just months later by her colleague, Dr Elizabeth Bell, who sought to counter what she deemed 'the conspiracy of silence' by publicly discussing both social and moral problems.[44] Hence, controversial issues were debated at Belfast's IWSS's weekly meetings: the desirability of extending the Bastardy Act and Criminal Law (Amendment) Act to Ireland; infant mortality; sex education; venereal disease; white slave trafficking; protective factory legislation; married women's employment and equal rights. But in striving to break social taboos by discussing these issues, Belfast's IWWS, like those working for the reform of the Contagious Diseases Acts in the late nineteenth century, ultimately failed to maximise its popular appeal by discouraging those with more conservative beliefs from joining its ranks.[45]

In addition to propaganda which aimed to make women feel responsible for their own destinies, those of their children and their sex as a whole, several influential Ulster suffragists formulated composite arguments to support the demand for the vote. To the fore was Belfast writer Mrs L.A.M. Priestley McCracken, who regularly contributed articles to the *Irish Citizen* and in June 1920 also published a series of articles in the English suffrage journal, *The Vote*.[46] Moreover, collections of her writings, *First Causes* and *Shall Suffrage Cease*, initially published in the *Citizen*, were later reprinted as a series of penny pamphlets. Like many of her counterparts, McCracken foresaw a great social awakening occurring amongst her sex as a result of enfranchisement: 'religion and morals, the home, the child, the nation, and the race, are in a perilous state so long as women's subjection and enslavement continue'.[47] At the same time she held that women had suffered sufficient disabilities and grievances to justify their demand for the vote on a democratic basis and claim the 'right of entry to the world's work under the equal laws, equal protection, and equal freedom of choice with men'.[48] Another important northern suffragist and regular contributor to the *Citizen* was Dora Mellone. She promoted the idea that women would only be able to capitalise on their earlier victories, like the attainment of equitable education and married women's property rights, by possessing the vote and implored women 'not [to] evade the responsibility; we dare not assert that we are not our sister's keeper'.[49]

With the proliferation of separate suffrage societies and the diversity of objectives associated with the vote, solidarity amongst Irish suffragists, although often lauded, was always fragile. As early as 1912 Frederick Ryan lamented the complexity of the Irish suffrage movement, which he proclaimed to be in 'such a tangle that it may seem a somewhat perilous as it is most probably a thankless task to endeavour to unravel it'.[50] Marie Johnson's recollections further highlight the diversity caused by the multi-party composition of the northern suffrage movement:

> We had Unionists like Dr Bell, Nationalists like Winifred Carney and the Misses Boylan, Liberals: Mrs McCracken; me Labour, and so was Mrs Adamson: Mrs Kavanagh was Sinn Féin. It was doubly hard for the Liberal women, for our actions were directed against the Asquith government.[51]

Johnson alluded to the difficulties that such variable political affiliations caused 'in reconciling . . . different outlooks outside the one of emancipation' amongst suffragists.[52] In addition to the divergence of political views, Ulster suffragists also had an innate understanding of their own identity. In recognition of this they formed local organisations, instead of joining southern-based associations, and, when the IWSF endeavoured to co-ordinate suffragists throughout the country, Ulster suffragists established a separate Northern Committee. Despite this, a simple north/south divide cannot be unequivocally applied, as within the Ulster suffrage movement activity was largely confined to the six north-easterly counties. Cavan and Monaghan remained largely untouched by the campaign for women's enfranchisement and, although several suffrage meetings were held in Donegal in May 1913, the *Irish Citizen* made no reference to the establishment of suffrage organisations in this county and there appears to have been no co-operation between suffragists in Donegal and the rest of Ulster. There was, however, a degree of co-operation amongst northern and southern suffragists: the treatment of suffrage prisoners was collectively repudiated from 1913 and suffragists throughout the country were united in their support for suffrage amendments to the third Home Rule Bill of 1912 to 1914. On 1 June 1912 the first mass meeting of northern and southern suffragists was held in Dublin and northern representatives included members of the IWSS from Belfast, Londonderry and Bangor and of the IWSF from Belfast, Lisburn, Armagh, Newry and Warrenpoint. This meeting was optimistically believed to represent a new spirit amongst Irish women that would overcome both political and geographical divisions. As Dora Mellone, secretary of the Northern Committee of the IWSF, opined in the *Citizen* on 15 June 1912, 'the women of Ireland are capable of united action'.

On an individual basis there were further instances of co-operation between northern and southern suffragists. Suffrage speakers regularly addressed sister organisations throughout the country. For example, Mrs Cope of Armagh Suffrage Society frequently addressed branches of the Irish Women's Reform League throughout Ireland and Dora Mellone of the IWSF undertook a suffrage tour of Sligo in August 1913. An open-air meeting of Belfast's IWSS on 30 August 1913 was addressed by Mrs Gibson of Munster Women's Freedom League, whilst Mrs Palmer of the Irish Women's Franchise League in Dublin addressed a public meeting of suffragists in Belfast's Rosemary Hall in December 1913. Hanna Sheehy Skeffington also corresponded with Mary Baker of Belfast's IWSS while imprisoned for suffragette activities in Mountjoy, which accentuates the close personal relations that existed between some Irish suffragists.[53] Further co-operation between suffrage groups was facilitated by the adoption of an anti-government campaign, a policy that was already widely used by the WSPU to oppose Liberal candidates in English constituencies. This policy was introduced to Ireland in January 1913 when the southern-based militant organisation, the Irish Women's Franchise League, and Belfast's Irish Women's Suffrage Society co-operated in organising open-air meetings and distributing suffrage literature to oppose, albeit unsuccessfully, the election of Mr Hogg, the Irish Parliamentary Party's (IPP) candidate in Londonderry. Together Margaret McCoubrey, on behalf of the IWSS, and Mrs Palmer, for the IWFL, published an electoral manifesto, *Keep the Liberal out*, in reflection of the IPP's parliamentary alliance with the Liberal government.[54] Their anti-government campaign also involved members of the local suffrage society, who distributed some 7,000 leaflets by 8 February 1913.[55] This new initiative prompted much discussion and some dissension amongst suffragists and in consequence the *Irish Citizen* invited its readers to comment. The range of views expressed clearly illustrates the diversity of opinions sheltering under the collective title of 'suffrage'. Within northern-based organisations some suffragists, like Margaret McCoubrey, welcomed the adoption of the anti-government policy and favoured abandoning all party affiliations. Mrs M.E. Cope, co-founder and honorary secretary of Armagh Suffrage Society (IWSF), shared McCoubrey's views, accentuating suffragists' sense of betrayal: 'no Party and no Government . . . [were] worthy of their support which by its actions appears to consider them unfit for the responsibility of a single vote'.[56] Others, like Mrs F. Chambers of Belfast, had serious reservations about this policy, doubting the effectiveness of advocating an anti-government campaign without first attaining women's enfranchisement, as 'the pressure of the vote is the only pressure that has any permanent value'.[57]

Within this climate suffragists struggled to maintain a public masquerade of unity. Dora Mellone, addressing an audience of 50,000 at London's Hyde Park in July 1913, alleged that Irish suffrage societies were:

> of all shades of political opinion, we have nationalists and unionists, orange and green, extremist and moderate. These women agreeing in nothing else agree on this one point . . . Now no one else has ever done this, the Irish Women's Suffrage Federation is the only political organisation which has ever held the North and South together or has ever tried to do so, is not this something to be proud of when all else seems bent on creating division and discord. Is it a small thing that we alone will have tried to repair the ancient breaches . . . [58]

Yet, by focusing solely on work of the IWSF, Mellone, somewhat ironically, provoked further disunity amongst suffragists. Members of the southern-based Irish Women's Franchise League and Belfast's IWSS both complained to the *Irish Citizen* because their associations pre-dated the establishment of the federation, accusing Mellone and the Irish Women's Suffrage Federation of reaping benefit from their earlier exertions.[59]

IV

Trembling in the valley of the shadows of the party.[60]

The trepidation with which politicians viewed the impact of female enfranchisement pre-dates the militant constituents of the suffrage movement. Suffrage bills were consistently defeated in parliament. Indeed, from 1868 to 1913 nine bills and one amendment to include women's suffrage in the 1884 Reform Bill were unsuccessfully read in Commons. No party was prepared to promote women's suffrage as part of their manifesto and any consideration of the democratic principle enshrined in women's suffrage was undercut by political expediency. In brief, the Labour Party supported adult suffrage in principle, but shared both Liberal and Irish nationalist concerns regarding the impact of increasing the number of propertied voters under the existing electoral qualifications. Members of the Irish Parliamentary Party also feared that suffrage would destroy party unanimity and impede the parliamentary progress of Home Rule. Indeed, it was IPP opposition that defeated the 1912 suffrage bill and subsequent amendments to include female enfranchisement in the third Home Rule Bill. Conservative and unionist considerations were essentially based on preserving the status quo and in December 1911 some unionists were so concerned that they publicly appealed to party members to oppose female suffrage on the basis that this reform only represented 'the thin edge of the wedge':

> and must inevitably lead to adult woman suffrage . . . [and] to the enfranchisement of a majority of female over male voters . . . consider the effects of this change . . . limited woman suffrage has become impossible . . . the choice lies between the enfranchisement of all women or of none . . . we suggest that a policy of opposition to the legislative proposals for women's suffrage . . . is a policy on which all members of the party can whole-heartedly unite.[61]

Irish suffragists experienced serious difficulties working within this politically hostile milieu. The IWSS, along with other northern suffrage societies, stated in May 1913 that it fought 'with the accepted thought that in Belfast nothing will be entertained but Home Rule struggling with Unionism'.[62] The following month Dora Mellone noted that the work of the IWSF's Northern Committee was hampered by both lack of money and support. These sentiments were reiterated by Margaret McCoubrey in a letter to Hanna Sheehy Skeffington in 1914, when she alluded to her sense of frustration at the lack of popular support for suffrage: 'I am tempted to say that the women here should be left to their doom!'[63] In spite of these difficulties, Irish suffragists continued to direct their demands towards the elected representatives of political parties. Thus, Sir Edward Carson and Joseph Devlin, Ulster's respective unionist and nationalist leaders, were frequently heckled during political meetings when suffragists 'used to arise':

> somebody would shout out, 'Mr Devlin, why haven't women got the vote', and then the stewards gathered around and bundled them out, rather mercilessly, and then some other heroine would get up in another part of the hall . . . It was a very gallant movement.[64]

In an attempt to gather support amongst those who could effect the desired legislative reform, Ulster suffrage societies asked many British and Irish politicians to receive deputations. A deputation from the Northern Committee of the IWSF, for example, secured a favourable suffrage pledge from the prospective West Belfast parliamentary candidate, Stewart Blacker Quin, on 12 April 1913. Possibly inspired by this success, the committee sent another deputation, this time to the unionist leader, Edward Carson, in March of the following year. This was one of only two suffrage deputations that he agreed to receive throughout the women's campaign.[65] Comprised of Dora Mellone, Mrs W.J. Holmes and Lilian Metge, this deputation requested that suffrage be included in any future Irish political settlement. To this Sir Edward replied in the negative: 'saying he himself was not a suffragist, and the Unionist Party were divided on the question'.[66] Other suffrage deputations were often refused a hearing. For instance, a joint militant and constitutional suffrage deputation, with representatives from the IWSF, including Dora Mellone from the Northern Committee, Margaret McCoubrey on behalf of Belfast's IWSS and delegates from the Irish Women's Franchise League, went to London on 11 June 1914 to address Asquith and Redmond, only to be turned away from the House of Commons.

Hostility towards suffragists was not confined to the political arena. According to the *Citizen*'s undeniably propagandist review of 1912, 'mob violence against suffrage meetings . . . [was] the rule'.[67] There was, however, some veracity in the *Citizen*'s claims. In June 1912 an open-air meeting of the IWSS in Belfast was forced to disperse, resulting in the arrest of several women, and in the following month Belfast Parks' Committee refused an application from the organisation to hold weekly suffrage meetings in Ormeau Park. In a more dramatic expression of hostility the *Northern Whig* suggested reintroducing the stocks and stoning suffragists.[68] These events were all indicative of an increasingly visible, though not always physical, antagonism towards suffragists. Such hostility and the lack of parliamentary progress caused widespread disillusion amongst many suffrage supporters and it seems that many women felt an increasing sense of alienation from both politicians and the political system. Mrs Cope of Armagh Suffrage Society epitomised these sentiments, expressing her mistrust of any policy which depended 'upon any political party. The history of the movement . . . showed clearly how politicians had failed – no matter what they had promised – to accomplish anything for our cause.'[69]

One of the most significant effects of suffragists' disillusionment was the arousal of vociferous hostility towards women who advocated party political considerations before the emancipation of their own sex. Beth McKillen has persuasively argued that the feud that developed between Irish nationalists and suffragists ultimately deprived the feminist movement of much popular support.[70] An assessment of suffragists' relationship with unionists suggests that this argument is also valid for the other side of the political spectrum. Suffragists scorned the political priorities of the female nationalist associations, Cumann na mBan and Inghinidhe na hÉireann. But, in Ulster this did not have the same impact in alienating support as suffragists' wholesale condemnation of 200,000 members of the Ulster Women's Unionist Council (UWUC). Such denunciation undoubtedly helped to estrange the UWUC, the largest group of politically active women in Ireland, from the suffrage cause.[71]

Suffragists and unionists had consistently viewed one another with suspicion. Many male and female unionists saw women's suffrage as a potentially dangerous political distraction from their anti-Home Rule campaign, whilst suffragists objected to politicians making 'the fullest possible use of' female support without rewarding women with the vote.[72] These divergent opinions produced considerable tension between suffragists and unionists. Hence, in June 1912 the IWSF, organising a petition to present to Liberal premier H.H. Asquith, urged suffragists to imitate the work of unionist women, not because they were revered as inspirational political activists, but to ensure that the IWSF's petition would 'not be less remarkable' than those organised by the Ulster Women's Unionist Council.[73] By October 1912, Blanche Bennett, a member of Belfast's IWSS, lamented the fact that unionist women had not marched alongside male unionists in the covenant processions to counter claims that women had no place in public life. Bennett further guaranteed female unionists' disdain by denouncing these demonstrations as 'a man's show entirely'.[74] During the next year the increasing hostility suffragists directed towards unionist women became apparent at a drawing-room meeting held by Belfast's IWSS. Here Margaret McCoubrey deplored the fact that so many women in Ulster deemed 'other questions' of more importance than the emancipation of their own sex.[75] Soon these 'other questions' were specified as party political concerns and, by August, Mary Baker, another prominent member of the IWSS in Belfast, was advising women to:

> pay more attention to the Anti-Suffrage attitude of . . . [Carson] who is being so whole-heartedly supported by his Unionist women, and who yet has the insolence to ignore the right of women to enfranchisement.[76]

The existing tension between suffragists and unionists was considerably heightened by the unionist party's decision to grant votes for women under their plans for the establishment of a provisional government in Ulster during September 1913. Suffrage was a divisive issue amongst all political parties and the unionist party was no exception. Furthermore, Edward Carson was a renowned anti-suffragist and Mary Anne, the Dowager Marchioness of Abercorn, a vice-president of the Ulster Women's Unionist Council from 1914 to 1919 and head of this association from 1919 to 1922, was also president of the Dublin branch of the Anti-Suffrage League.[77] In contrast, James Craig, the unionists' second-in-command, consistently supported women's suffrage. He was not only responsible for opening all the public galleries in the House of Commons to women, as accommodation in the Ladies' Gallery was insufficient,[78] but also addressed a suffrage meeting with Lady Betty Balfour in Lisburn. Craig's wife Cecil recorded this event in her diary in the following terms:

> J. [James] speaks very well at Lisburn . . . in favour of Women Suffrage, not then at all a popular cause! . . . J. supported them consistently from the beginning, though he did not like the ultra militant methods of the most extreme of them.[79]

The views of Edith, 7th Marchioness of Londonderry, a vice-president of the Ulster Women's Unionist Council from 1919 to 1959, further illustrate that unionism and suffrage were not diametrically opposed political objectives.[80] Edith Londonderry supported Millicent Fawcett's English association, the National Union of Women's Suffrage Societies, on the basis that women should be freed from what she depicted as 'indirect bondage':[81]

> We all agree what an astonishing, disappointing instrument [the vote] . . . is, but until there is a better one the weaker sex will continue to strive to obtain the same protection that it affords to working men. It is not 'for the noblest women in England' . . . that the vote is really desired, except for the recognition of principle, but it is chiefly wanted for her poorer sister . . . she could use it for all the factory laws and housing laws – in fact, in a hundred ways in which legislation deals directly . . . with women . . . she requires the extra protection of the vote.[82]

She also emphasised the democratic aspect of women's suffrage, an argument that had been forwarded by several of her contemporaries:

> It is conceded how much influence women possess . . . they are encouraged in their political efforts by the men, their help is sought in elections, in canvassing, and in forming various political leagues and societies . . . Surely it is a woman's right, as much as a man's, to exercise her influence, whether in her political opinions or in ordinary life, in a direct and straightforward manner.[83]

No unionist records provide any background information on the decision to grant votes for women under the plans for establishing a provisional government in Ulster in 1913. It is, therefore, impossible to proffer any definite explanation concerning unionist motivation. Was it a ruse to divide the suffrage campaign, or a miscalculated move to guarantee women's support for the unionist movement? Given James Craig's support for women's enfranchisement it seems unlikely that he would have agreed to introduce a measure that deliberately sought to undermine the suffrage movement. Indeed, it seems more probable that Craig agreed to a scheme which was presented to unionists as a logical extension of the existing close relationship between the Ulster Unionist Council and the Ulster Women's Unionist Council, which could also assist the suffrage movement. It is also possible, however, that anti-suffragists amongst the unionist party may have quietly hoped that introducing this measure would undermine the suffrage campaign by taking the impetus away from women. One known fact is that unionists never interpreted the pledge of September 1913 as a concession to suffragists, but as a reward for the Ulster Women's Unionist Council's loyalty and political work.

There was clearly confusion in suffrage echelons concerning unionists' motivation for implementing votes for women. But the unionists' pronouncement also provoked considerable rivalry amongst suffrage groups, underlining the fragile unity of the women's movement. This rivalry was especially marked in the north-east of the country, where many associations claimed to have been instrumental in winning, what they interpreted as, an important concession from the unionist party. Margaret McCoubrey of Belfast's IWSS, for example, emphasised that the essential groundwork completed by her organisation deserved recognition, whilst Lilian Metge, honorary secretary of Lisburn Suffrage Society (IWSF), claimed that the sustained campaign conducted by all northern suffragists provided the impetus for the unionists' pledge.[84] The *Irish Citizen* reacted by rejecting any suggestion that the 'servile party women' of the Ulster Women's Unionist Council had a 'share in the winning of votes for Ulsterwomen – whatever the rank and file may have felt. But they do not reject the boon which the suffrage agitation has won for them. No anti[-suffragist] ever would.'[85] The Northern Committee of the IWSF, however, believed that the UWUC was instrumental in prompting the unionists' pledge, asserting that 'no women ever earned recognition of their services better than the Ulster women have done'.[86] This association further alleged, in a letter published in the *Irish Times* on 13 September 1913, that they knew of the unionists' intention to implement female suffrage from January 1912. This caused yet more controversy amongst suffragists and gave rise to accusations of conniving with unionist politicians and of idle boasting. The Northern Committee refused to provide any explanation for withholding this information and on 22 November reiterated that the first pledge had been won from unionists solely by the efforts of their association, whilst the work of unionist party women only helped to gain the second, public concession of September 1913.[87]

What no one doubted was the significance of this move on the part of unionists, a move that Mrs L.A.M. Priestly McCracken recounted as 'epoch-making'. McCracken further alluded to her own:

> sense of pride and joy as an Ulsterwoman that to Ulster belongs the distinction of being the first to recognise the political rights of women in the British Isles . . . [in] this amazing marriage of Unionism and Woman Suffrage.[88]

But as a marriage this was both short-lived and unhappy. And even in the midst of the initial triumphalism there was some scepticism. Mrs Chambers was one of several Ulster suffragists who depicted placing credence in Carson for women's liberation as akin to following 'a will o' the wisp. The only thing they can rely on with any certainty is the known record of . . . Carson's attitude to the Suffrage movement.'[89] By October 1913 Margaret McCoubrey was also publicly expressing her distrust of both the unionist party and the entire political system:

> We know that whatever Party places a Suffrage Bill on the Statute Book, will simply do so to save its own skin . . . No doubt the Ulster Unionist Council would already gladly forget that such a statement was ever made. Sir Edward Carson seems most anxious to forget it . . .[90]

These were prophetic sentiments. The 1913 pledge was neither confirmed nor fulfilled by unionist leaders. Even following the formal constitution of the provisional government on 24 September 1913 no statement on female enfranchisement was forthcoming. Thereafter, pessimism concerning the sincerity of the unionist pledge became widespread. The *Citizen* increasingly attempted to distance itself from the pledge, alleging that suffragists never attached much practical importance to this promise and that its significance lay solely in a concession of principle. The paper's aggressive critique of unionists, and especially of members of the UWUC, also continued unabated. The development of this anti-unionist stance heightened the complexity of the suffrage movement, as some suffragists, especially in Ulster, believed the level of criticism directed towards unionists to be unjust. This was epitomised by an anonymous letter published in the *Citizen* in February 1914 which commented on the positive advances members of the Ulster Women's Unionist Council were making by invalidating:

> the cowardly desire to enjoy all the advantages of the State and leave to men all the drudgery of political life . . . The women of Ulster have

> left the Home . . . They realise that there is work in the political sphere for women as well as men . . . They have compelled their men to testify to their political ability and intelligence . . . [They] show that the interests of human beings are stronger than those of sex . . . they are a fine practical argument against Anti-feminists.[91]

Another anonymous letter from Ulster also drew attention to the potentially liberalising effect of the UWUC's work, which drew women away from domesticity 'far more than . . . the granting . . . of the Parliamentary Franchise'.[92] These differences in opinion ultimately minimised support for the women's cause in Ulster, as many women were forced to make difficult decisions concerning their political priorities. A letter from members of an unnamed Orange Lodge aptly summarised the practical effect of the *Irish Citizen*'s defamation of unionism: 'Such a display of political animus has lost the suffrage cause many friends North of the Boyne.'[93] The Ulster Women's Unionist Council refused to discuss suffrage and all moves towards conciliation between suffragists and women unionists were brusquely rebuffed. For example, in November 1913, Belfast's IWSS unsuccessfully appealed to the secretaries of local women's unionist associations to admit a suffrage speaker to their meetings:

> it ought to be the duty of these women to use all the influence they can possibly exert . . . The thought of 200,000 women all pledged to think and do as 'their men' bid them is an appalling one . . . [of] subservience.[94]

Yet the UWUC's stance was hardly surprising. The defeat of Home Rule remained their sole concern and this was unlikely to change, especially in the face of public suffragist hostility. Indeed, many suffragists continued to scorn unionists' political beliefs at every available opportunity. Thus, Mrs L.A.M. Priestley McCracken criticised all party women as 'weak-minded sisters' and remained convinced that 'intelligent, influential, moneyed and organised' unionist women had missed an exceptional opportunity by failing to demand women's suffrage as a precondition of conducting political work.[95] McCracken was a controversial writer and, although much lauded by the *Irish Citizen*, other newspapers were wary of publishing her most belligerent articles. Hence, in February 1914, the *Belfast News-Letter* refused her article on 'Ulster and women' on the basis that it was too contentious. The *Citizen* possessed no such qualms, as it fully supported the claims which McCracken, as a former unionist supporter, made. She denounced the ethical and moral distinctions which unionist women made in supporting the militancy of their own party through the arming of the Ulster Volunteer Force, whilst opposing that of suffragettes, as nothing short of 'nauseating'. Furthermore, McCracken encouraged unionist women to abandon their role as 'subservient factotum' and recognise the intrinsic ingratitude and self-expediency of unionist leaders:

> As long as woman will work and will pay, and will pass no criticism, she is a valuable and valued political asset . . . Even the fleeting phantasmagoria of citizenship for women under the Provisional Government . . . has disappeared . . . in the chilling mists of Sir Edward Carson's silence.[96]

By 1914, therefore, it was apparent that overt scepticism regarding the sincerity of the unionists' pledge was common amongst many suffragists. The subsequent appointment of only three women to the medical board of the unionists' provisional government prompted further unfavourable comment. The *Citizen* opined that this nominal representation in a 'traditional' area of female involvement served only to reinforce stereotypes. By April 1914 the paper derided both Cumann na mBan's fund-raising activities for the Irish Volunteers and the political work of the Ulster Women's Unionist Council, because of their 'Slavish attitude . . . to toady for the men . . . Women in either party camp, who display this crawling servility to the men of their party, deserve nothing but contempt.'[97]

V

Bombs exploded, buildings burst into flames, even the hospitals awaiting the use of Ulster Volunteers when the threatened Civil War should break out were set on fire.[98]

The animosity between suffragists, unionists and nationalists denied the suffrage movement of much popular support, but further support was lost through the initiation of a campaign of violence by militant suffragettes. Although the petitions and public demonstrations of constitutional suffragists should be credited with possessing considerable originality and courage, no sustained public debate was instituted by these activities. Essentially, women turned to militancy because they were frustrated by the ineffectuality of constitutional methods. Their subsequent campaign of violence demanded attention by the sheer veracity of its challenge, adopting disorderly tactics to counter the inertia of both the political system and the general public. There were serious anxieties within the suffrage movement concerning the impact of using such confrontational tactics, anxieties that both undermined the unity of the women's movement and lost it much popular support. Writing in the *Irish Review* in 1912, Frederick Ryan expressed his reservations regarding the impact of militancy:

> I condemn these recent outrages not the less emphatically because of a very vivid realisation of the injury they are inflicting on the suffrage cause itself . . . One would, indeed, suppose that they [women] would much prefer to fight on the intellectual and moral field, where they are strong, rather than on the physical field, where they are weak . . . it is indisputable that the more of persuasion and the less of fear that goes to the winning of a victory such as this, the nobler, the finer and the more fructifying will it be.[99]

The variance of sentiments expressed by suffragists concerning militancy were underlined by Hanna Sheehy Skeffington. She did not share Ryan's concerns, but instead emphasised the merits of militant action and the significance of Irish suffragists abandoning constitutional methods:

> Now that the first stone has been thrown by suffragists in Ireland, light is being admitted into more than mere Government quarters, and the cobwebs are being cleared away from more than one male intellect . . . The novelty of Irish women resorting to violence on their own behalf is . . . startling to their countrymen who have been accustomed for so long to accept their services . . . in furtherance of the cause of male liberties. There is an element of unwomanly selfishness in the idea of women fighting for themselves repellent to the average man . . . [Militancy] will be interesting material for the psychologist working out a research thesis on Female Patience in the 19th century.[100]

In spite of the differences of opinion amongst suffragists, by late 1912 militant acts were being carried out in Ulster. Indeed, one significant determinant in Ulster's militant campaign was that it predated the arrival of the English-based association, the Pankhursts' Women's Social and Political Union (WSPU) in September 1913. This counters the generalisations which have been made claiming that until 1913 all militancy was centred in Dublin and that prior to the arrival of the WSPU there had been no trace of militancy in the north of the country.[101] Belfast's IWSS was responsible for the earliest suffragette actions in the north of the country. This society defended militant tactics as early as August 1912 and just a few months later the first outbreak of militancy occurred in Ulster when windows were broken in Belfast's Donegall Square GPO.[102] This was in protest against the defeat of Snowden's suffrage amendment to the third Home Rule Bill. There was a second flurry of militancy in the province during 1913, beginning with three pillar box attacks in Belfast on 3 February. Six similar attacks occurred in the city from 21 February to 19 April 1913 and in one instance wires were cut in a Belfast telephone box. The first recorded act of militancy outside the city occurred on 23 February with an attack on a post office in Newtownhamilton in Co. Armagh, where a mourning card was found bearing the inscription of 'Votes for Women'. However, this was unusual, as suffragette activity remained largely focused on Belfast and its environs. By early 1913 the IWSS's sympathy with violent methods became increasingly apparent as the organisation debated the merits of militant action and took the decision that 'in the near future some arrangement might be made' to establish a small militant committee.[103] The next month the *Citizen* reported that, at a meeting of the Bangor branch of the IWSS, the mere mention of militancy and the Pankhursts' name produced spontaneous applause from the audience.[104] From early 1913, therefore, the majority of IWSS members played a waiting game and, as disillusionment with constitutional methods grew, further violence became a distinct possibility. Thus on 12 July 1913 more windows were broken in a suffrage protest in the north and by August of that year Belfast's IWSS pronounced government inaction as responsible for forcing women into violence. Moreover, this organisation began to issue emotive public statements in defence of militant action:

> if legalised protection of little children could be brought a week nearer by our vote, she defied the women in the crowd to say that we would not be right to burn down every public building in the land.[105]

This society's decision to become a solely militant association on 13 September 1913 coincided with the initiation of the WSPU's campaign in Ulster.[106] Indeed, it seems probable that the IWSS were encouraged to change their constitution and become a militant organisation by the establishment of an association with sister sympathies in Belfast, thus decreasing their sense of isolation.

Initially the WSPU's interest in Irish affairs was prompted by the Irish Parliamentary Party's refusal to support women's suffrage. As a result, from 1910 the Pankhursts were in contact with the more militant Irish suffrage societies and both Margaret Robinson and Dr Elizabeth Bell of Belfast's IWSS were imprisoned in Holloway in November 1911 for suffragette disturbances carried out in conjunction with the WSPU in London. In July of the following year two WSPU members also caused serious disturbances in Dublin which culminated in an arson attempt and a hatchet being thrown at the Prime Minister.[107] After this there was a respite in the WSPU's Irish activities. Nevertheless, personal contacts were quietly being cultivated. In 1912 Hanna Sheehy Skeffington met Dorothy Evans, an experienced English suffragette, in Dublin, when Evans produced letters of introduction from the WSPU's leader, Christabel Pankhurst.[108] The following year Evans became the WSPU's Ulster organiser and was quickly able to secure support for the militant association by co-operating with the most belligerent Ulster suffrage society, the IWSS.[109] This suggests that Evans was not entering an entirely unknown field of activity, either in terms of organisational structures or personnel.

From the middle of 1913 the unity of the suffrage movement became more declared than real. In addition to the rivalry induced by the unionists' suffrage pledge and the tensions provoked by the *Irish Citizen*'s anti-party critique, the arrival of the WSPU caused further apertures. In Ulster whole societies changed their name and affiliation to distance themselves from militancy. For example, Bushmills Suffrage Society, an affiliate of the IWSF, passed an anti-suffragette resolution[110] and Robina Gamble, secretary of the Londonderry branch of the IWSS, wrote to Margaret Robinson:

> the Derry Branch of the I.W.S.S. [will] be called in future the Derry Women's Suffrage Society[,] non-militant, and be affiliated to the Irish Women's Suffrage Federation . . . We regret very much that the fact that calling ourselves non-militants necessitates severing our connection with Belfast . . . it is no longer possible for Irish Societies to maintain any neutral attitude . . . Many of us . . . have very deep sympathy with the militant side, but we know we could not ask a militant speaker to come here again and the only work open to us is on the educative side. Even for a meeting of this description . . . we have a great difficulty in procuring a hall.[111]

The IWSS's identification with militancy also caused resignations from individual members, such as Mrs Heron from Cultra in

Co. Down, who left the IWSS to join her local, non-militant IWSF society.[112] Existing chasms within the suffrage movement were, therefore, augmented by the avowedly militant organisation's arrival in Belfast in September 1913. The *Irish Citizen*'s editorials intensified these divisions by criticising the work of northern suffrage societies, questioning whether Ulster suffragists had been as active 'as they should have been? If not, they can hardly be surprised if the W.S.P.U. enter on a neglected field of action.'[113] The leading article in the next edition of the paper reiterated the claim that Ulster societies had not 'done as much as they should . . . namely bringing pressure to bear on . . . Carson'.[114] Animosity of this kind was perhaps to be expected as, even preceding the establishment of the *Citizen* in 1912, individual suffragists emphasised that Irish suffrage societies should remain independent of all English organisations. This was clearly illustrated in 1910 when the English-based organisation, the Women's Freedom League, sent emissaries to Ireland. Francis Sheehy Skeffington, who was to co-found the *Irish Citizen* two years later, feared that the WFL's intention was 'to run the Suffrage movement in Ireland on purely English lines . . . they must be forestalled'.[115] The *Citizen*'s reaction to the WSPU's arrival in Ulster was analogous: accusing the militant association of interfering in Irish affairs and expressing the belief that only indigenous suffrage organisations could fully comprehend 'the psychology of their countrymen'.[116]

The split caused by the arrival of the WSPU was also apparent amongst individual suffragists who opposed the establishment of branches of an English and a militant association in Ireland. Many women, like Dora Mellone, honorary secretary of the Northern Committee of the IWSF, believed that adopting militant tactics would decrease support and that Irish suffragists should ultimately 'work out their own salvation'.[117] Furthermore, a letter from the Northern Committee of the IWSF to the Belfast press disassociated all its Ulster affiliates from militancy, emphasising:

> their disapproval of the policy of the Women's Social and Political Union in Ulster . . . In view of the alleged serious harm being done at the present time by agents of the W.S.P.U., the Northern Committee desire again to reiterate the fact that the Irishwomen's Suffrage Federation is both a non-militant and non-party organisation.[118]

This opposition did not affect the WSPU. A large number of members were not required for its activities, as a small body of dedicated workers could effectively cause widespread disruption and attract both public and press attention. Suffragettes certainly risked their personal reputations and had to endure the ridicule caused by the public perception of a suffragette 'as a mad woman who should be at home looking after her husband and children or a frustrated old maid who was taking her revenge on the male population'.[119] In spite of these considerations, some well-known northern suffragists, prompted by frustration with constitutional methods, were attracted to militancy. Although no membership figures are available for the WSPU in Ulster, one former member, Margaret Robinson, alleged that the association's notorious reputation for action 'captured many of the more ardent and active' suffrage supporters.[120] Robinson claimed that she was immediately attracted to the militancy of the WSPU and recounted that the fact that it was an English-based organisation was irrelevant: 'that did not matter to us . . . we never thought of it from that point of view'.[121] Lilian Metge was another leading Ulster suffragist who turned to militancy. Metge, the founder and former president of Lisburn Suffrage Society and honorary secretary of the Northern Committee of IWSF, quickly joined the WSPU in Belfast. Within a week of her membership she was involved in a Pankhurst deputation to the King in London, where she was arrested and held overnight.

The theme of self-sacrifice was paramount amongst suffragettes and in Ireland they were able to draw interesting vindication for militancy from the country's tradition of using violence as a political weapon. Indeed, Ireland's turbulent past was often used to justify female militancy. From July 1912 the *Irish Citizen* issued warnings about provoking women to militancy, alleging that Ireland was 'a dangerous country in which to run risks of that character. There is an abundance of revolutionary material . . . owing to its past history . . . concede, before it is too late.'[122] In a similar vein Margaret McCoubrey of Belfast's IWSS emphatically claimed that suffragettes were continuing an Irish tradition of violent protest.[123] This use of the past to extenuate the present continued and Mary Baker of Belfast's IWSS went as far to assert that the 'spirit of revolt was in Irish blood'.[124] Hanna Sheehy Skeffington agreed, asserting that 'the stone and the shillelagh need no apologia: they have an honoured place in the armoury of argument'.[125] This exoneration was not only grounded in Ireland's past, as the unionist threat of civil war and arming of the Ulster Volunteer Force during the third Home Rule crisis of 1912 to 1914 provided a contemporary parallel for suffragettes. Thus, as the suffragette campaign escalated, many comparisons were drawn between the treatment afforded to militant women and to Ulster unionists. As Christabel Pankhurst poignantly asked in the WSPU's paper, *The Suffragette,* in 1914:

> Why is the W.S.P.U. attacked, its offices raided, its paper assailed; while the militant Ulster organisation and its leaders are unmolested, its headquarters not raided, and the Unionist press, constantly inciting to militancy, not attacked?[126]

Moreover, in her account of the suffragette campaign, Christabel's sister, Sylvia, purported that 'the Irish conflict remained a perpetual incitement . . . a spur and a stimulus to feminine militancy'.[127]

The WSPU established branches in Belfast and Dublin but their campaign in Ulster developed, not only on a wider scale, but was closer in temperament to the English campaign, which focused on privately owned, rather than government property. In addition, the Ulster campaign occurred at a time when militancy in Dublin had largely ceased. The WSPU's initial aim in the province was to force Carson to fulfil his suffrage promise of September 1913 and an arson campaign was only initiated once it became apparent that this pledge was hollow in intent. The IWSS, as the most militant northern-based suffrage organisation, entered easily into close and active co-operation with the WSPU. IWSS members rallied to defend the WSPU from the serious criticisms that were published by the *Citizen*, claiming that the arrival of the militant association heightened public interest in women's suffrage as 'Ulster needed a rude awakening on the suffrage question'.[128] Initially, joint meetings were held between these two organisations, but by 20 April 1914 so many members of the IWSS had joined the ranks of Belfast's WSPU that the former society was officially disbanded.

To an English-based organisation like the WSPU, the prospect of 200,000 politically active unionist women in Ulster who were not allied to suffrage was nothing short of a temptation. The organisation, therefore, inaugurated a policy to admit unionist women into their organisation as associate members. This move to entice unionist party women into the suffrage movement led one woman to wryly question whether 'Mohamet [was] accommodating himself to the inertia of the mountain'.[129] Though this was a commendable attempt at inspired political calculation and opportunism on the part of the WSPU, too much hostility existed between suffragists and unionists to facilitate any mass exodus of female unionists into the ranks of any suffrage society. Furthermore, as the militant campaign escalated, its focus on unionist-owned property further distanced these two political interests.

The WSPU's Belfast organiser Dorothy Evans' focus was especially on the unionist leader, Edward Carson. Early in 1914 she wrote a series of letters asking him to reaffirm his suffrage pledge and, with Mary Baker and Miss Anderson, held a four-and-a-half day siege at his London home. Carson eventually received this deputation but as a result of disunity amongst his party refused to give them a guarantee:

> that he would stand out for the rights of Ulsterwomen under the Imperial Government. He said he looked upon the Provisional Government as something different, because it was only a larger extension of local government.[130]

As a result of this unsatisfactory meeting the waiting game which suffragettes played in Ulster was brusquely concluded. At a WSPU meeting in Belfast's Ulster Hall on 13 March 1914, Evans eloquently and publicly removed their truce:

> Sir Edward Carson was no friend of women unless he was prepared to stand and champion their rights as strongly as he championed the rights of men . . . he was their enemy, and he would be fought as any other politician . . . who had the power and did not use it to get their rights . . . they . . . declared war on Sir Edward Carson . . . The civil war that was absolutely certain was the one between the women and the powers that be.[131]

These caveats soon came to fruition and by April Belfast was proclaimed to be in the midst of a 'genuine revolution'.[132]

The direction of the Ulster militant campaign quickly became apparent, as Carson's betrayal of suffragists tarnished all unionists. For instance, despite her husband's public support for women's suffrage, Cecil Craig received an anonymous letter from suffragettes in June 1914 warning her to 'expect a visit from us . . . You want war in Ulster, you will get [it]'.[133] This was not an empty threat as on the following day several suffragettes, including Dorothy Evans, called to her home when Carson was present, an event Cecil Craig recorded in her diary: 'We were stupefied and then amused to see three frenzied females burst in, yelling Votes for Women. However the men soon collared them and hoofed them out pretty quick.'[134]

Initially the WSPU's Ulster campaign differed little from earlier acts of militancy. In the week following the removal of the WSPU's truce, there were twenty pillar box attacks in Belfast. However, to sustain such a high level of public attention through a policy of shock tactics and destruction alone, suffragettes became increasingly violent. Thus, in Ulster arson was soon being used as a means to maintain interest. Indeed, of seven arson attacks carried out by British suffragettes between April and May 1914, five occurred in Ulster.[135] Their arson campaign concentrated on unionist-owned property, but Newtownards Race Stand, Ballylesson Church near Lisburn and Belfast's Bowling Pavilion were also burnt. In addition, an unnamed suffragette burst into the offices of the *Belfast Evening Telegraph* and the *Belfast News-Letter* and slapped the papers' editors, in response to their inciting readers to deter militant women by taking the law into their own hands. Another indication of the extent of suffragette activity in the province can be gained from the fact that in a six-month period from March 1914, thirteen women were arrested for suffragette activities.

It has been argued that the WSPU's arson campaign damaged public perceptions of the suffrage movement, leading to alienation, decreasing funds and a loss of members.[136] In Ulster the disruption amongst suffragists caused by the arrival of the militant association was intensified by an increasingly hostile general public. This animosity was caused by the Malicious Injuries (Ireland) Act that facilitated an increase of rates to cover the cost of damage incurred to private property. Hence, as Ulster suffragettes' focused on privately-owned property, this meant that the general public paid in material terms for female militancy. Sir Hugh McCalmont and Bishop Henry received £11,000 and £20,000 respectively in compensation from the Belfast authorities for the arson attacks on their properties. In total Co. Antrim paid £92,000 in damages for property destroyed by suffragettes and a three penny levy in the pound was consequently applied to the county's rates.[137]

As acrimony amongst the general public increased, 'jeers and ridicule' gradually developed into violence.[138] There were violent scenes when suffragettes heckled Joseph Devlin, the northern nationalist leader, in Belfast in December 1913 when, even with the added protection of members of the Men's Political Union 'to save the women from rough handling', one suffragette was thrown downstairs.[139] Mrs Alexander, a member of the IWSS in Belfast, wrote in complaint to the *Belfast News-Letter* concerning the 'unnecessary violence' which was directed towards suffragettes: 'Surely two men stewards ought to be able to eject a women from a meeting without the assistance of the audience?'[140] Belfast suffragettes also claimed to have received anonymous letters threatening physical violence if their militant campaign continued, whilst Lilian Spender's account of the crowd's reaction to a suffragette disruption at a unionist demonstration further alludes to the extent of public hostility:

> Two Suffragettes interrupted while Sir Edward [Carson] was speaking, but I heard nothing but the roar of fury that went up from the crowd the moment they began. They were speedily disposed of.[141]

During 1914 physical attacks at WSPU meetings became increasingly common in Ulster. On 25 April 1914, for example, unionists were alleged to have broken up a suffragette meeting in Belfast and on 30 May a WSPU poster parade at Belfast harbour awaiting Carson's arrival led to violent protest. This involved male and, interestingly, some female unionists. The *Belfast News-Letter* consolidated the *Citizen*'s claims that suffragettes were subjected 'to physical abuse at the hands of irate mill girls' and one suffragette, Mabel Small, had her hat dragged 'from her head' by the crowd, who 'pulled her hair, and disarranged her clothing, portions of which were practically torn to tatters'.[142] In a state of collapse she was taken to hospital. This was not an isolated incident. Less than two weeks later another suffrage heckler at a meeting of East Belfast's Women's Unionist Association was attacked in a similar way: 'her hat [was] dragged off, her hair torn, she was pelted and bruised with . . . stones'.[143] British suffragettes, like Sylvia Pankhurst, also claimed that Ulster suffragettes were subjected to such violence that the WSPU's organiser, Dorothy Evans, brought a charge of assault and false imprisonment against Belfast authorities.[144] In an attempt to curtail suffragette activities in Belfast, Marie Johnson, Margaret McCoubrey and several other women were constantly 'watched [and] escorted by detectives'.[145] Indeed, the extent of public animosity was such that two Australian tourists were attacked in Ballymena on the mere suspicion of being suffragettes.[146] The response of those who experienced militant attacks further alludes to the general perception of suffragettes as unwomanly, 'wretched creatures' who were bent on violence and destruction.[147] The normally conservative *Church of Ireland Gazette*, for instance, responded to the WSPU's arson attack on Ballylesson Church on the outskirts of Lisburn by depicting those who were responsible as 'vile . . . dangerous . . . enemies of society'.[148] Militancy climaxed in Ulster with a bomb attempt on

Lisburn's Church of Ireland Cathedral on 31 July 1914, an event that Lilian Spender recorded in her dairy:

> I heard about 3 o'clock, what I thought was a big gun firing, but it proved next day to be an explosion caused by Suffragettes, who blew out the ancient east window in Lisburn Cathedral, the brutes. They were all staying with Mrs Metge, a Lisburn and a most militant lady, and today I believe nearly all the windows in her house are broken.[149]

Suffragettes arrested for this attack had to receive police protection from hostile crowds whilst being taken into custody. However, neither verbal criticism nor physical aggression effectively curtailed the suffragette campaign.

Suffragettes' disregard for authority was manifest in the trials of those arrested for militant acts in Ulster. These trials were conducted in concert with the WSPU's policy of refusing to recognise the court by frequently interrupting the proceedings. The first women arrested in Ulster for militant acts were the WSPU's organiser, Dorothy Evans, and her cohort, Madge Muir. At their trial in March 1914, the courtroom had to be cleared because of continual interruptions from the assembled suffrage supporters and as:

> The two prisoners kept up a duet which reduced the proceedings to an absolute farce . . . [T]hey would announce their intention of leaving the Court; and were only restrained from doing so by physical force.[150]

In protest, Lilian Metge, another WSPU member and trial witness, broke windows outside the court-house and was subsequently arrested. Evans consistently denied the right of the court to try her, by comparing the treatment meted out to suffragettes with that of unionists: 'Sir Edward Carson and the Craigavon party were not interfered with . . . Women to-day . . . deny the law, because they have had no voice whatever in the making of the law.'[151] Evans also tried to attack the judge and was so violent that she had to be restrained by six policemen.[152] Once imprisoned, Ulster suffragettes also used similar means to secure their release to their British compatriots: sustained hunger and thirst strikes. To try to deter women from this course of action, the Prisoners' Temporary Discharge for Ill-Health Act of March 1913, commonly known as the Cat and Mouse Act, which facilitated the temporary discharge of hunger striking suffrage prisoners until they were fit enough to be recommitted, was applied to Mabel Small, a member of Belfast's WSPU.[153]

At the very apex of suffragette violence in Ulster, amidst controversy, violence and angst, the militant campaign was abandoned. This immediate and absolute cessation of the WSPU's work throughout Britain was in direct response to the outbreak of the First World War in August 1914. The WSPU's decision was, however, reportedly 'received with displeasure and disgust by some of the keenest of its Irish members', none of whom were consulted about the cessation of their campaign.[154] The war not only caused serious disruption within militant ranks, but also marked the start of the demise of the whole suffrage movement. This was regretted by many, including one of the principal Ulster feminists, L.A.M. Priestley McCracken:

> When the first cannon-shot crashed through the peace of Europe, the world of Woman Suffrage was shaken to its depths. Its organisation, its funds, its raison d'être seemed threatened and unstable . . . Some Suffragists became war partisans, some became peace partisans.[155]

VI

Supposing England were at war with Germany, English suffragists should combine with German ones in the cause of their sex . . . [and] draw the women of both nations closer in an effort to restore peace.[156]

These were the semi-prophetic words of Mrs L.M. Coade, secretary and co-founder of Newry Suffrage Society, in 1913. The Anglo-German conflict became a reality in the following year, but the envisaged co-operation amongst suffragists across Ireland and Europe never occurred. Former suffragette Margaret Robinson remembered the impact which the outbreak of war had on the Irish suffrage movement: '[it] changed everything . . . The militants separated . . . the WSPU threw their work into the war effort'.[157] Another result of the war was 'the growing estrangement between [the] north and south' of the country as the political experiences of both areas diverged.[158] War ultimately intensified the overall complexity of the Irish suffrage movement as, in addition to the political differences caused by the Home Rule campaign and variance of opinions regarding the merits of militant or constitutional action, the *Irish Citizen* became increasingly pacifist in sentiment. This in effect meant that patriotic, pro-war Irish suffragists, who were most numerous in the north-east of the country, found themselves alienated and without a public platform.

The WSPU's withdrawal from Ulster on 22 August 1914 left a vacuum for militant action. The Irish Women's Franchise League sought to fill this gap by establishing its first northern branch, the Ulster Centre, in Belfast in September of that year. The members of the centre consistently interpreted war as a result of male misgovernment and vowed to continue with suffrage work. Operating under the motto 'No difficulty battles great zeal', the Ulster Centre was initially received with some enthusiasm, attracting former suffragettes, such as Margaret McCoubrey and Dorothy Evans, into its ranks.[159] From September to October 1914 the Ulster Centre was active: holding a suffrage meeting in Dungannon, selling suffrage papers, distributing literature and asking leading political figures like Carson, Redmond, Asquith and Bonar Law to receive deputations.[160] In an attempt to foster support, the Ulster Centre also issued pro-suffrage arguments that were reminiscent of the social feminism of the IWSS before its absorption into the WSPU. Thus the centre established a Watch the Courts Committee to publicise legal cases affecting women and children and on 9 November 1914, in a letter to Belfast's Lord Mayor, called for the introduction of a bill to provide meals for schoolchildren. In December it also sent resolutions to the Prime Minister, the Home Secretary and four Belfast MPs in protest against Regulation 40D under the Defence of the Realm Act, which had been introduced in an attempt to safeguard soldiers against venereal disease. In practice this legislation enabled any woman to be arrested and detained until a medical examination was carried out. Both the *Irish Citizen* and the IWFL's Ulster Centre believed this was a state regulation of vice which revived the infamous nineteenth-century Contagious Diseases Acts. Despite this feminist agenda, the centre remained aware that adopting a 'suffrage first' policy was seen as both unpatriotic and unacceptable during wartime. As a result, the Ulster Centre knew that its chances of mobilising sustained and popular support were limited:

> we were told in Ulster that it was folly to go on with suffrage work in the face of threatened Civil War . . . we are told that our demand for enfranchisement should be dropped . . . [during] war . . . [161]

The Ulster Centre certainly laboured under increasingly difficult conditions and, although a 'steady effort to keep the suffrage flag flying untainted and unspotted by any compromise' was made, the opportunities for suffrage propaganda decreased as the overwhelming majority of women embraced the war effort.[162] Thus, support for the association was only temporarily boosted by Sylvia Pankhurst's first visit to Belfast on 20 February 1915, when she was apparently received by a large and enthusiastic audience. In spite of this, from the middle of 1915 regular meetings of the Ulster Centre were suspended and a planned open-air propaganda campaign had to be abandoned because of insufficient support. The organisation's demise was further exacerbated in Ulster by the IWFL's increased association with the national separatist movement. For example, two members from its Ulster Centre attended Cumann na mBan's annual convention in December 1914, which appears to have alienated considerable support. And as the league petered out in Ulster the most committed feminists were left to work on an individual basis. Hence, in August 1917 Margaret McCoubrey ran a month-long peace and suffrage campaign in Belfast almost single-handedly, inspired by her belief that 'a woman looking down on a battlefield would not see dead Germans or dead Englishmen but so many mothers' sons'.[163] Despite the eloquence of McCoubrey's plea, the majority of women interpreted pacifism as unpatriotic, seeing women's enfranchisement as inconsequential in comparison to the threat being posed to Europe by the First World War.

In addition to the work of the Irish Women's Franchise League's Ulster Centre, a few suffrage societies also continued to campaign during the war. The Belfast branch of the Church League for Women's Suffrage remained active and, as a consequence of its avowedly religious basis, managed to avoid being branded as unpatriotic. This organisation made no comment regarding the outbreak of war, instead continuing with its earlier activities: holding Communion services and monthly meetings and organising a suffrage petition to the Church of Ireland synod in 1915. The Church League remained relatively small in terms of members (only twenty-nine in 1914), but its continued work provides an interesting illustration of how some constitutional suffragists remained active during the war. Another body of Ulster suffragists remained similarly active – the affiliates of the IWSF's Northern Committee. These women managed to sustain interest during the war, not by focusing on suffrage, but on patriotic war work. Thus, only limited suffrage work was undertaken by the Northern Committee after the outbreak of war: a suffrage pledge was secured from Colonel Sharman Crawford on his election to the parliamentary constituency of East Belfast and in July 1915 a similar resolution was attained from Belfast Corporation. The committee's war work was co-ordinated by an Emergency Council, organising

Red Cross and employment schemes. By changing its priorities, this association was able to maintain support: meetings continued to be held, new offices were established in Belfast's Wellington Place and local suffrage societies affiliated to the federation remained active. Indeed, representatives from suffrage societies in Belfast, Bushmills, Lisburn, Newry, Warrenpoint and Holywood attended the federation's annual meeting in January 1915 and in May of that year the Northern Committee stated that their affiliate represented over 800 members.

But it was not just the priorities of the Northern Committee that underwent change as a consequence of the war. The rhetoric of the *Irish Citizen* became not only pacifist but also increasingly sympathetic towards national separatism, supporting anti-conscription and campaigning for political status for republican prisoners. Furthermore, from 1916 it became the official organ for the Irish Women's Workers' Union.[164] As a result of its changed priorities and allegiances, the *Citizen*'s appeal to many Ulster women diminished. Moreover, this heightened discord and the demise of impetus amongst many suffragists seriously hampered the paper's publication. From February 1916 it was only published on a monthly basis and its difficulties were further exacerbated by the death of its co-founder, Francis Sheehy Skeffington, in April of that year.[165] Indeed, in 1917, for the first time since its establishment in 1912, the paper was forced to appeal for funds, with each edition being halved in size. Neither the *Irish Citizen* nor the various associations dedicated to attaining votes for women were ever able to recover their pre-war impetus.

VII

The wartime coalition government included many more suffragists than its forerunner: with Lloyd George as premier from 1916, and Balfour, Bonar Law and Lords Shelbourne and Cecil in its ranks. Women's war work and the required updating of the electoral register to include servicemen combined to secure the passage of a measure of enfranchisement in 1918. In essence suffrage was presented as a general electoral reform.[166] David Morgan has convincingly argued that by 1917 Lloyd George was able to use Tory and Liberal votes to ensure the passage of 'a bill which was neither cared for; to use a war situation to forge the bipartisan front necessary to pass the measure and enfranchise women'.[167] Fears of a regeneration of pre-war militancy may have been a government consideration, but, as the very women who had been most disruptive in the pre-war era had become dedicated pro-war campaigners, it seems unlikely that this was a major factor. And by only enfranchising the wives of local government electors, Liberal and Labour concerns surrounding a potential increase in the number of Conservative, propertied voters were removed. Moreover, only enfranchising women aged over thirty avoided a female electoral majority and politicians could, therefore, seek comfort in the likelihood of the new woman voter being 'a stable element in a changing world, one who was unlikely to seek to promote radical, feminist issues in parliament'.[168] Despite these reassurances, some anti-suffragists like Ruby Carson, wife of the unionist leader, remained unconvinced. As she recorded in her diary: 'Yesterday the house of Lords passed woman suffrage, most disgraceful.'[169]

The suffrage campaign, which was a compelling force in the decade preceding the outbreak of war, prepared both parliament and the general public for such a legislative advance. Nevertheless, in March 1918 the front page of the *Irish Citizen* issued only a muted welcome to female enfranchisement, as the age qualifier for women essentially made this an empty triumph. Although the principle of women's suffrage was conceded, the paper believed that women had only won their first move in a political game and urged suffragists to continue to work towards 'the speedy emancipation of those women still outside the pale'.[170] Yet this plea was largely ineffective. The passage of female suffrage did not lead to any sense of reconciliation amongst women. This was especially evident in the relationship between suffragists and Ulster unionists. The *Irish Citizen* became increasingly pro-nationalist in the aftermath of the 1916 rising and subsequent popularisation of republicanism.[171] Furthermore, the criticism levelled at unionists continued. In November 1918, for instance, Mrs L.A.M. Priestley McCracken denounced Theresa Londonderry, president of the Ulster Women's Unionist Council, for issuing voting instructions to unionist women, interpreting this as a self-expedient move to buttress the political fortunes of the unionists 'by capturing and creating a subservient, obedient electorate among women.'[172] In the following month the front page of the *Citizen* could express only its 'pity for Unionist women.'[173] This critique was maintained, ensuring that no reconciliation would occur between suffragists and unionists. Indeed, in one of the last editions of the *Citizen*, Edith Londonderry, a leading unionist and suffragist, was classed amongst anti-suffragists, who were emerging from 'prehistoric caves to assume public office . . . [to] reap where others sowed'.[174]

Alongside the sustained post-war hostility between suffragists and unionists, there were also significant fissures within the suffrage movement. Post war and post enfranchisement, few attempts were made to unite suffragists either in Ireland, Britain or America. All failed to recapture their former impetus. In Ireland this was reinforced by the ever-present considerations of politics. Post war the IWFL, which had already collapsed in Ulster, increasingly co-operated with Sinn Féin and Cumann na mBan, becoming involved in the 1918 election campaign for Sinn Féin's two female candidates: Winifred Carney and Constance Markievicz.[175] The *Irish Citizen* experienced serious financial problems as a result of ebbing sales and it is unclear whether many suffrage societies continued to exist following the closure of the paper in 1920 after its printing presses were destroyed by government forces. The *Citizen*'s entreaty of 1919 for women of all political parties to work towards full feminist victory with planned programmes of reform, demanding 'evolution not amelioration' had been issued in vain.[176]

From March 1914 Belfast was 'the storm-centre of the suffrage movement in Ireland', but the militant campaign, like that of the constitutional suffragists, failed to create a sufficient climate of crisis to procure government concessions.[177] It did, however, succeed in directing both press, parliamentary and public attention to women's iniquitous legislative position and the imperative need for reform. Many suffragists had serious reservations concerning the impact of suffragettes' combative tactics, some of which were realised in the inter-war period. Militancy left an identifiable and negative aftertaste in Ulster. Belfast Corporation, which in response to canvassing from the Irish Women's Suffrage Federation passed a resolution approving women's suffrage, refused to co-opt Julia McMordie as a member in 1916. This rebuff was not based on the grounds of individual merit but 'against a number of . . . the suffragettes who desire to get into the Belfast Corporation'.[178] And it is possible that many more ingrained prejudices fostered by suffragette militancy remained unspoken. But were there any more positive effects of the campaign for the vote?

Following the passage of the 1918 Representation of the People Act, many astute politicians realised that women could not be entirely ignored, as they now formed an integral part of the electorate, but the immediate impact of enfranchisement was minimal in terms of the number of women who were elected as MPs.[179] The establishment of a separate Northern Irish parliament in 1921 did little to maximise northern suffragist chances of securing electoral equality. This was characterised by the cabinet's political deliberations concerning equal suffrage in 1924, which focused not on women's democratic rights, but on following the precedent set by the imperial government.[180] Furthermore, an equal suffrage bill introduced to the Northern Ireland House of Commons by Joseph Devlin, the northern nationalist leader, in 1927 was defeated on its second reading.[181] Consequently, equal suffrage was only implemented in Northern Ireland in 1928, after it was introduced by the imperial government. This measure, just as the first instalment of votes for women which was passed a decade before, brought neither equality nor a regeneration of feminist impetus in its wake. Many suffragists envisaged that the vote would be the ultimate vehicle to sexual equality, guaranteeing 'the future welfare, spiritual, intellectual, and physical, of the human race, the progress of civilisation, and the elevation of humanity generally'.[182] But complete sexual equality could never be attained by purely legislative means. Equality was an elusive aim which continued to fox women throughout and beyond the inter-war years.

Therefore, only those with the most realistic aspirations, who believed that to have a voice in electing members of parliament was to have a fragment of political power and 'a very different thing from freedom', failed to be disappointed with the long-term impact of female enfranchisement.[183]

CHAPTER TWO

Women in Unionist Politics

The women taking such an active part went to prove that the Government were not up against a political organisation, but against a whole people . . .[1]

I

In Ireland, where nationalism and unionism dominated the political debate from the late nineteenth century, women were neither politically weightless nor inactive as a result of their continued parliamentary disenfranchisement. As Edith, 7th Marchioness of Londonderry, one of the foremost unionist campaigners, emphasised in 1909, even though women were unable to articulate their political preferences by casting a vote, they were not 'a vague indefinite force' wanting in tangible political interest.[2] This chapter seeks to assess the direction and significance of unionist women's political work, which was conducted on an individual and group basis from the 1880s. Unionism has been the focus of some historical attention: the popularisation of Ulster unionism has been recorded, as have the variances between northern and southern unionism and between Belfast and the rest of Ulster.[3] Yet to date little attention has been directed towards unearthing women's role within the unionist movement, an imbalance that this study also seeks to redress.[4]

In Ulster female participation in the unionist campaign was discernible from April 1886, when Gladstone introduced the first Home Rule Bill to the Commons, proposing to establish an Irish legislature with restricted powers. Isabella Tod, whose unionist sympathies came to override all her philanthropic and feminist concerns, reacted to the introduction of this bill by establishing a branch of the London-based Women's Liberal Federation in Belfast.[5] This initiative was prompted by Tod's 'sickening shock' at the proposed severance of the legislative union and the political turmoil that she believed would ensue:

> Knowing Ireland thoroughly, I knew that all the social work in which I had taken so prominent a part for twenty years was in danger . . . [W]hat we dread is the complete dislocation of all society, especially in regard to commercial affairs and to organised freedom of action.[6]

In April 1886 Tod, as a renowned orator and staunch unionist, was selected as the only female member of a delegation from the Ulster Liberal Unionist Association in Belfast to address meetings throughout England. This deputation travelled to England together, but it seems that members worked individually in order to maximise the scope of their campaign. Tod, therefore, addressed political meetings alone in Plymouth and Darlington in June and July of 1886.[7] This was an intrepid enterprise for any woman to undertake in the 1880s, when a female presence at a political meeting was still seen as a novelty and often aroused unfavourable comment. But if Tod experienced any hostility it did not undermine her determination to oppose Home Rule, as she dedicated the rest of her life to this purpose. In 1888, for example, she organised and addressed a unionist demonstration in Birmingham under the auspices of the Women's Liberal Unionist Association. Several years later, in 1892, at the start of the second Home Rule crisis, she also enlisted the support of Hugh de Fellenberg Montgomery, a leading member of the Irish Unionist Alliance (IUA), to arrange an anti-Home Rule meeting in Aughnacloy, Co. Tyrone. In Tod's correspondence with Montgomery she referred to the part that Belfast women were taking in organising anti-Home Rule protests in the provinces, which suggests that popular female support for unionism was gradually emerging:

> Every meeting does good, in one way or another . . . We have got about 70 ladies' names already, but no secretaries have been appointed. As soon as they are chosen, we Belfast people will retire. South Down wants our help next.[8]

The Belfast branch of the Women's Liberal Federation, which was renamed the Women's Liberal Unionist Association, was also utilised during the second Home Rule crisis. Tod, as the founder and most prominent member of this association, spearheaded a committee of sixteen women to organise a conversazione on the day preceding the unionist convention, 16 June 1892. The committee included Lady Ewart, Margaret Byers and Belfast's lady mayoress, Lady Dixon – all well-known unionists.[9] Tod briefly addressed the assembled audience of several hundred men and women at the conversazione, emphasising the very real sense of trepidation that existed amongst the unionist community:

> Seldom . . . has any social gathering met in circumstances at once so serious and so hopeful. Six years ago we were suddenly confronted by a demand to give up the national Constitution . . . for a vague and unknown Constitution, which had no roots in the past, and was to have no guidance in the future from the Imperial Parliament – the mother of free Parliaments. We were asked to throw the whole frame of civilised society into the furnace of revolution . . . We refused that monstrous demand . . . Women felt the sudden danger as acutely as men; not only for the sake of their own future, but for the sake of those women in the South . . . It is as much from a sense of duty to Ireland as for the insistence of our own right to preserve our own civil and religious liberty that Ulster raises its voice of solemn warning.[10]

Women were excluded from the convention to 'dampen any suggestion of frivolity', but hundreds attended to listen to the subsequent public addresses which were delivered from various platforms erected in Belfast's Botanic Gardens.[11]

During the second Home Rule crisis female unionists undertook increasingly public roles. In March 1893, for instance, the wife of the Church of Ireland primate was amongst several women sending anti-Home Rule letters and pamphlets to the wives of clergy in England. In Londonderry the spouses of Protestant clergy undertook a similar venture, encouraging every willing female unionist supporter to write six letters:

> to help us in trying to make some of the reasons against Home Rule more plain to our sisters, the wives of the clergy of all denominations in England, Scotland and Wales . . . It is thought that private letters thus written and sent will be more likely to be read than printed circulars.[12]

Several Ulster women, like Isabella Tod and Violet Hobhouse, also toured England speaking against Home Rule,[13] whilst across the north-east of the country female unionists met in significant numbers throughout March and April of 1893 to publicly express their resolve to oppose Home Rule. Such female support further underlines the escalating popularity of unionism: 1,000 women assembled in Strabane on 20 March to register their opposition to Home Rule; 700 and 500 women attended meetings in Omagh and Raphoe respectively during the following week[14] and in June another women's anti-Home Rule demonstration was held in Armagh.[15] A female unionist demonstration held in Coleraine on 15 April 1893 was characteristic of many other meetings. Here the assembled audience publicly declared their allegiance to Queen Victoria, claiming that living under the British constitution was nothing short of a birthright. They also predicted that Home Rule would lead to armed conflict and thus 'inflict incalculable injury on our country, and would be certain to lead to bloodshed and the other miseries of civil war'.[16] At these demonstrations signatures were often collected for various anti-Home Rule petitions, which were organised as another component of the unionist campaign. It seems that women's enthusiasm for petitioning was heightened by their inability to express their protest by the means of a parliamentary vote. Indeed, the sheer scale of female petitioning provides another indication of how unionist women were becoming politicised, which in turn constituted one part of the overall process of popularisation. An Ulster women's anti-Home Rule petition with 20,000 signatories was conveyed to London in Theresa Londonderry's own carriage to be presented to the House of Commons by Mr Ross in April 1893.[17] Later that year the Dublin-based Ladies' Committee of the Irish Unionist Alliance organised another memorial.[18] This committee aimed to have this memorial 'signed as generally as possible by all the women of Ireland over 16 years of age'.[19] In pursuit of this end, the committee approached Lady Louisa Antrim to collect signatures in Ulster. By inviting those personally acquainted to her and the spouses of local clergy to establish committees, she successfully mobilised considerable support for this initiative, collecting 11,800 female signatures within three weeks. By June 1893 this total had risen to 12,147.[20] The correspondence between Louisa Antrim and the local women who supported this venture reveals the very real enthusiasm that opposition to Home Rule aroused. As Mrs Sawyers of Lurgan wrote: 'This would be a good place for a local Centre and we shall try and work it',[21] whilst Belfast women were reportedly 'quite greedy about signing'.[22] Louisa Antrim fully utilised her own social network to rally support, but enthusiasm was not restricted to the landed aristocracy, as according to Mrs Stannus in Lisburn support was also forthcoming from:

> The lower classes [who were] . . . *most anxious* to sign . . . and if Roman Catholics refuse to sign as some have done it is because they have been *told by their clergy* they will deprive them of their religious rites.[23]

Stannus further alluded to the religious basis of unionist support, claiming that only 'Protestants and Presbyterians . . . signed, and they seemed very glad to be asked to do so. No Romanist signed. Some of them said "they dare not do it".'[24] Other women expressed both their determined allegiance to unionism and their willingness to undertake whatever action was necessary in order to effectively defeat Home Rule. As one woman informed Louisa Antrim, 'oh what is there that one would not do if one could to avert so dreadful a fate'.[25] Another of her correspondents expressed her resolve to remain in Ireland even if Home Rule was implemented:

> I have a sort of feeling that this 'Bill' never can become law – but should it – I have not the smallest intention of being driven out of my adopted country should it be possible to live in it![26]

During the second Home Rule crisis, in addition to demonstrating and petitioning, at least one woman was instrumental in establishing an organisation for male unionists. Eleanor Archdale helped an 'infant' Young Men's Association in Lisnaskea, Co. Fermanagh, which was 'struggling against many difficulties to do good in our day and generation'.[27] In subsequent years, women conducted this type of organisational work for their own sex, though in pursuit of the same objective, the ultimate defeat of Home Rule. Given the extent of female involvement in the first and second Home Rule crises, it is perhaps not surprising that women's work gradually became formalised, moving beyond individual momentum to a co-ordinated campaign of opposition. The first organisation of unionist women into an indigenous and more permanent association occurred in North Tyrone in 1907. This ancillary organisation was established with the declared aim of assisting 'the men's efforts by every means possible and suitable for women'.[28] Early in April 1907 over 400 women attended this association's inaugural meeting, which again highlights the growing popularity of unionism. Under the presidency of Mary Anne, the 2nd Duchess of Abercorn, who four years later became the first president of the Ulster Women's Unionist Council, the activities undertaken by the association in North Tyrone closely mirrored those of later protests: local meetings were held to induce women to become involved in distributing literature, fund-raising and electoral registration work. Furthermore, just as the UWUC was to seek guidance and advice from Edward Carson during the third Home Rule crisis, this earlier association approached the then unionist leader, Walter Long, to define areas where women's contribution was welcome.[29] Long advised the association to 'get in touch with individual electors and friendly associations . . . to open the Irish question in various constituencies and prepare to follow up as in '86 and '93'.[30] Obviously taking Long's advice, by the end of July 1907 twelve women speakers and twenty-five female workers from North Tyrone were preparing to work in the English constituencies of Darlington and Cornwall.[31] Two years later, unionist women in Londonderry followed North Tyrone's initiative, establishing the Women's Registration Association. Under the presidency of the Marchioness of Hamilton, this association was affiliated to the Women's Amalgamated Unionist and Tariff Reform Association in England. But after the formation of the UWUC in 1911, the Londonderry association was forced to drop tariff reform as an objective in order to affiliate with the women's unionist council, which had the maintenance of the legislative union as its sole objective.

In many ways women's involvement in the first and second Home Rule crises laid the foundation for women's involvement in later unionist politics. In spite of Isabella Tod's pioneering initiatives during the 1880s, the majority of women's work in the unionist movement was conducted on an ancillary basis. There was, for example, no apparent opposition when women were excluded from attending the unionist convention of 1886 or when Walter Long assigned women a definite auxiliary role within the unionist campaign in 1907. Women seemed content to accept this essentially conservative, but nonetheless important role: petitioning, fund-raising, canvassing and organising demonstrations for members of their own sex. Thus, by the early twentieth century a clearly defined role for women within Ulster unionism had emerged. However, in addition to women's auxiliary work, several women were well placed by virtue of their landed wealth and social position to exercise considerable influence in the political arena. Before assessing the consequence of popularising unionism amongst women of all social classes, it is important to consider the significance of this unionist élite who inspired women throughout and beyond the third and most popular phase of unionism, 1911 to 1914.

II

The involvement of members of Ulster's aristocracy, such as Lady Louisa Antrim, Mary Anne, the 2nd Duchess of Abercorn, and Lady

Edith Dixon, in unionism was apparent during the first and second Home Rule crises. Indeed, it seems that in Ulster the existence of a comparatively small, landed, Protestant, socio-political élite indirectly encouraged upper-class women's political participation from the late nineteenth century. For women with relatives or spouses who were directly involved in unionist politics, as MPs or prominent members of the Ulster Unionist Council, there was a considerable level of expectancy that they would support their family's political cause in a time of crisis. The significance of familial involvement in shaping female political consciousness was not peculiar to Ulster's landed élite. For many Irish and English women, the sphere of the family in the late nineteenth century remained 'the primary site through which their lives were ordered and contained. Frequently that meant also that the choices . . . [women] made were heavily reliant upon family obligation and opinion.'[32] From 1886 the leading families of Ulster society supported one another in pursuit of a common goal, the maintenance of the legislative union between Britain and Ireland. It seems, therefore, that female members of this unionist élite were encouraged by their families to enter the political arena in support of this objective.

There was an evident continuity in familial political involvement, as successive members of the Abercorn, Londonderry and Dufferin families predominate in both male and female unionism. Parents appear to have instilled unionist sympathies in their children. For instance, Frances Anne, the daughter of the 3rd Marquis of Londonderry, instructed her children, Blanford and Randolph Churchill, on 'the politics of Ireland'.[33] Common political sympathies were also apparent between spouses. Mary Anne, the 2nd Duchess of Abercorn, was the first president of the UWUC and her husband, James, was a unionist MP and the first president of the Ulster Unionist Association. Their son was also a unionist MP and his wife, Rosalind, became a vice-president of the UWUC in 1914, before succeeding to the presidency in 1919.[34] In addition, both Theresa and Edith Londonderry's spouses were unionist members of parliament who played an instrumental role in the anti-Home Rule campaign. Women who married into leading unionist families frequently shared, or adopted, their spouses' political affiliation. Introducing his second wife, Ruby, to a meeting of unionists in Belfast in January 1915, Edward Carson guaranteed a favourable reception from those assembled by referring to her 'as a good Ulsterman and as good a Unionist and as good a Protestant as I am'.[35] Moreover, referring to their relationship he alluded to the significance of kindred political views:

> one of the matters that had originally brought them together, from being mere friends to a more particular acquaintanceship . . . was the interest . . . she had in Ulster . . . They in Ulster had accepted her as one of themselves, and that was he knew, the greatest triumph she could have.[36]

Although Ruby Carson was English by birth, she came to regard Ulster as her second home. As she confided to her diary in 1918, she became 'more and more Ulster every time' she visited the province, empathising with the unionist populace: 'I would give anything in the world to save them from the horrors of Home Rule.'[37] Furthermore, visiting Belfast in 1923 she informed a meeting of unionists: 'I cannot claim to be an Ulster woman by birth, but I hope you will allow me to be one by adoption.'[38] Other women from English backgrounds, like Lilian Spender and Cecil Craig, also appear to have quickly accepted the political heritage of their marital families.[39] At the time of her marriage in March 1905, Cecil Craig readily admitted that she was 'innocent' of any political acumen, but by 1906 she was electioneering with her husband.[40] Like Ruby Carson, Cecil Craig came to view Ulster unionists as 'her people', and by 1935, after thirty years' residency in the province, felt that she could justly refer to herself as an Ulsterwoman.

Supporting one's family or spouse was, therefore, a determining factor in motivating upper-class women's involvement in Ulster politics. This fostered a sense of community amongst the aristocratic élite, who were all personally acquainted with one another and frequently socialised together. There were, for instance, numerous occasions when unionist wives attended debates in the House of Commons together and relations between the Carson and Craig families were so cordial that they shared a house in Belfast for the duration of the 1918 election campaign. But, even though upper-class women's political activity was conducted in support of the unionist cause and seemingly aroused little unfavourable comment, there were still strict societal guidelines controlling female conduct. Writing in February 1909, Edith Londonderry recounted her own experience of exercising political influence, working through personal acquaintance, correspondence and entertaining. Edith argued that this influence was too easily manoeuvrable and insidious:

> to obtain an object indirectly many means may be employed, some even open to deceit . . . How often do we hear that 'so and so' owes his position politically to a great extent through the agency of a clever wife; and we know that the essential feature of her cleverness consists in disguising its existence from her husband, as only by so doing can

> she obtain what she is striving for, either for him or for herself . . . We all admire an example such as this, but surely we may deplore a position where abilities are employed in such an apologetic manner, and that it should be considered so derogatory, either for the man to seek political inspiration from his wife, or for the woman to acknowledge that she has any interests at all outside the hearth and home[.][41]

This indirect influence was exercised in high society, where friends were cultivated for political means and where women were recognised as the 'semi-official leaders'.[42] Many leading unionist families divided their time between their Ulster estates and their London homes and hence participated fully in the social calendar of events commonly known as 'the season'. The Conservative Party continued to use social functions and personal association as a party tactic for longer than the Liberal Party. This provided unionist women with an opportunity to exert influence, glean information and rally support that was denied to their political counterparts. From the late nineteenth century, for example, the London home of the Londonderry family was acknowledged as 'the centre and boiling point of resistance to the Government's policy of Home Rule'.[43]

Within this social setting politics were discussed freely amongst politicians, their wives and confidantes. Moreover, the entertaining which accompanied political office gave some unionist women an opportunity to cultivate relationships with influential political figures. To cite just a few examples, in 1891 Mary Anne, the 2nd Duchess of Abercorn, invited Hugh de Fellenberg Montgomery and Arthur Balfour to attend a function at her family home of Baronscourt in Co. Tyrone after they addressed a unionist meeting in Londonderry.[44] Furthermore, Lilian Spender, lunching with the Carsons, recorded the level of trust that existed amongst the unionist élite: 'At dessert he [Carson] read out a draft of the letter he is sending to Lloyd George.'[45] Indeed, on one occasion, in answer to Ruby Carson's persistent questioning over lunch, Lloyd George was forced to affirm that Ulster would never be coerced into accepting Home Rule.[46] In addition, Cecil Craig's attendance at a party hosted by Edith Londonderry for the King and Queen at Londonderry House gave her a perfect opportunity to discuss the Irish situation with Winston Churchill. He assured her that 'Ulster would come out on top, as none of them would stand more than a rectification of boundaries'.[47] Entertaining was, therefore, an important purveyor of political information.

This social interaction also provided upper-class unionist women with the opportunity to correspond with a large number of highly influential people. Thus, in 1886 Queen Victoria wrote to Hariot, the 5th Dowager of Dufferin and Ava, in India, where her husband was serving as viceroy, in order to keep her informed of the political progress of the first Home Rule bill:

> Lord Dufferin and you will be horrified at Mr Gladstone's extraordinary and totally impracticable [Home Rule] Bills for Ireland. He has entirely broken up his own party . . . and all the best men are firmly opposed to any Home Rule.[48]

In a similar vein, Theresa Londonderry regularly corresponded with F.E. Smith, the leading Tory spokesman on unionism, and frequently discussed Ulster with Geoffrey Dawson and Colonel Repington, the editor and military correspondent of *The Times*. Theresa also corresponded with Arthur Bigge, private secretary to King George V, sending him newspaper articles on unionism and photographs of unionist demonstrations in order to convey the wholesale opposition to Home Rule amongst Ulster's Protestant populace.[49] From these social contacts an information network appears to have developed between leading male and female unionists. Hence, the editor of the *Morning Post* regularly passed information to Ruby Carson that she disseminated to her husband and political friends, who included Cecil Craig and Lilian Spender. James Craig also referred to the information that he received from three leading members of the Ulster Women's Unionist Council, whom he named 'the Wheeler, McMordie or Chichester-Clarke syndicate'.[50]

The Londonderry family was at the pinnacle of high society and, as the leading Tory political hostess of the early twentieth century, Theresa Londonderry appears to have derived great pleasure from her position of political influence. As the daughter of a Tory MP, she not only claimed that her interest in politics began at the age of ten, but that she had heard all the best political speakers by the age of fifteen.[51] A well-informed and useful ally, she could also be a harsh opponent. Theresa Londonderry was respected, admired and feared in society as 'one of the most stirring and dominating personalities of our time . . . with unrivalled experience of men and things social and political'.[52] By 1910 her political activities were widely commended, as this letter from one ardent supporter illustrates:

> It is such a delight to . . . see you more and more taking so prominent a part in affairs, for I truly think that no woman now living is to you equal in capacity for direct political energy.[53]

In such a position of influence she was taken into the confidence of many, including that of two unionist leaders, Walter Long and Edward Carson, and the Conservative leader, Andrew Bonar Law.

Theresa first became acquainted with Carson when her husband was serving as Irish lord lieutenant from 1886 to 1889. She was the only person outside Carson's family circle with whom he regularly corresponded and she remained his political confidante and one of his closest friends for over three decades. Carson obviously valued her friendship greatly, writing of their relationship: 'No one is ever more helpful than yourself and you have indeed been a kind and affectionate friend.'[54] As one of her political protégés, Theresa politically and socially groomed Carson for politics, although she was often infuriated by his lack of self-confidence. On one occasion she even compared him to 'a Derby favourite, who, when you have him saddled and bridled, and ready to lead out of the paddock, won't run'.[55] Their close friendship, however, gave rise to tensions between Carson and his first wife, Annette, who was prohibited by ill health from taking an active role in promoting her husband's career. As Carson's political reputation grew, his wife became distinctly uncomfortable with the attention that he received from other women. And, according to Carson's sister, a letter that he received from Theresa Londonderry caused 'a great row' and prompted the unionist leader to have 'all his letters sent to the Club'.[56]

The death of Andrew Bonar Law's wife in 1908 made him increasingly dependent on Theresa Londonderry for the social niceties attached to political statesmanship. Theresa, however, deliberately cultivated their friendship following Law's accession to the leadership of the Conservative Party in 1911. This was an attempt to ensure that the new Tory premier would protect unionist interests, because Theresa was concerned that Law was 'not as interested in the various principles of the Tory Party as I should have liked, such as Church, Education and Home Rule'.[57] Thereafter he was regularly invited to dine at Londonderry House and stay at the Londonderry estates in Newtownards and Durham.

Clearly, therefore, the female members of Ulster's socio-political élite were able to exert considerable influence on leading politicians through the workings of high society. The significance of this influence was markedly reinforced during the third Home Rule crisis of 1911 to 1914. During this period women from the unionist élite were expected to become fully involved in opposing Home Rule and, when a women's organisation was established in support of this objective, its leaders were drawn from the echelons of Ulster's aristocracy. This is apparent from the social composition of the UWUC's first executive committee of January 1911, when twenty-three of its fifty-nine women members were titled.[58] Upper-class women also headed local women's unionist associations which were affiliated to the Ulster Women's Unionist Council: Edith Londonderry was president of Newtownards WUA; Lady Dunleath was president of Greyabbey and Carrowdore branch and Ladies Herdman, Macnaghten and Clanmorris served as presidents of North Tyrone, North Antrim and North Down WUAs respectively.[59] Moreover, in the period 1911 to 1939, all of the presidents and all but one of the ten women who were appointed as vice-presidents of the UWUC were titled.[60] The involvement of these upper-class women was clearly of considerable importance and their political contacts, which were maintained through the workings of late nineteenth and early twentieth-century high society, were to prove most useful in the unionists' campaign of opposition to Home Rule. In addition, by adding social respectability to the movement, upper-class women's support helped to popularise female involvement in unionist politics.

Unionism attracted women's support *en masse* during the first and second anti-Home Rule campaigns as they signed petitions and attended demonstrations in their thousands. But their involvement was not sustained and after the defeat of the first and second Home Rule bills women's impetus largely declined.[61] Opposition to the third Home Rule Bill was, like its predecessors, induced by a sense of political expediency, but this was compounded by new political considerations. The abolition of the House of Lords' power of veto by the Parliament Act of 1911 effectively removed the last constitutional bulwark to Home Rule and, from a unionist perspective, ensured that any future Home Rule Bill could only be delayed, but no longer defeated outright. The resulting sense of political crisis was utilised by both male and female propagandists to encourage political activity amongst both sexes of all classes. In effect this meant that unionism was popularised, a process which encompassed the Protestant clergy, the family unit and, perhaps most importantly, women.[62] As a result of the latter, the Ulster Women's Unionist Council was formed. This association deliberately cultivated female unionism as a popular cause by adopting many of the arguments common to the rhetoric of unionism: alluding to its ruinous impact on the unity of the empire, on economic stability and the freedom of religious practice. In addition to these claims, a specifically female facet to unionism was also promoted. The UWUC successfully attracted an unprecedented number of women into the unionist movement by convincing them that what they cherished, the security of their homes and well-being of their children, were endangered by Home Rule. By appealing to women's maternal and protective sensibilities the UWUC, therefore, depicted the legislative union between Britain and Ireland as the ultimate guarantor for protecting the sanctity of the home:

> the Union meant everything to them – their civil and religious liberty, their homes and children . . . in the event of Home Rule being granted, the sanctity and happiness of home life in Ulster would be permanently destroyed.[63]

Time and again, both in the literature produced and distributed by the women's council and in addresses delivered by women at public meetings, the home was a common theme. In the rhetoric of female unionism, therefore, a strong appeal was made to convince women that opposing Home Rule was nothing short of a domestic responsibility:

> If our homes are not sacred from the priest under the existing laws, what can we expect from a priest-governed Ireland . . . let each woman in Ulster do a woman's part to stem the tide of Home Rule . . . once the Union was severed there could be no outlook in Ulster but strife and bitterness . . . Home was a woman's first consideration.[64]

The views of Jean Bates, a fervent unionist and sister of Richard Dawson Bates, the secretary of the Ulster Unionist Council, epitomised the depth of emotion prompted by the threat of Home Rule. In her interpretation it was a matter 'of life and death'[65] to resist being governed by an 'alien and anti British . . . Catholic-Celtic Ireland'.[66] The UWUC persuaded many women that they could assist in averting so dreadful a fate, thereby inculcating a sense of duty amongst its supporters. The organisation declared that women's political work was engraved 'in the blood, and . . . the heritage of generations, intensified by history and position'.[67] And this message was frequently reiterated. For example, Edith Mercier Clements' speech of 1912 was characteristic of many addresses delivered by members of the UWUC:

> Having arrived at a serious crisis in our nation's history, we believe it to be the duty of the women of Ulster to form themselves into an association . . . we will stand by our husbands, our brothers and our

> sons in whatever steps they may be forced to take in defending our liberties against the tyranny of Home Rule.[68]

The popularisation of women's unionism was alleged, with some justification, to be a 'plot [to] intensify the social pressure' of the unionist campaign, as it enabled unionist leaders to claim that the whole of Protestant Ulster, all classes and both sexes, were actively opposed to Home Rule.[69] The establishment of the UWUC, as a mass organisation, opened up a new area for political involvement for many women whose spouses and male relatives had enrolled in local unionist associations and the Orange Order. Indeed, at the inaugural meeting of the UWUC on 23 January 1911, Edith Mercier Clements, who became one of the most dynamic members of the council, announced that both the 'peeress and the peasant would be represented' within the association.[70] The leaders of women's unionism came from privileged, aristocratic backgrounds, but some of the most fervent support for unionism amongst women appears to have occurred within the working classes. According to Lilian Spender, for instance, unionist parades held in Belfast in 1914 met the greatest ardour 'in the poorest streets . . . [where] shawled women waved a baby in one arm and a Union Jack in the other'.[71] Another commentator described these working-class women as 'fanatical partisans who take religious and political differences quite as seriously as their fathers and brothers, and give them more personal applications'.[72] Ronald McNeill further supports these claims by his inference that eighty per cent of the West Belfast branch of the UWUC was composed of shop girls and mill workers and that 'No women were so vehement in their support of the Loyalist cause as the factory workers.'[73] These political passions were often verbally expressed in the workplace, and occasionally resulted in physical attacks involving both sexes:

> Their [women's] shawls are an oriflamme in the thickest of the fighting, and their high-pitched voices hurling gibes and recriminations goad their opponents . . . Anyone who has seen a mob of Belfast mill-doffers worked up to boiling point has no difficulty in understanding the devastating fury that animated the *tricoteuses* of the French Revolution.[74]

Another aspect of the popularisation of female unionism was the revival of the Association of Loyal Orangewomen of Ireland.[75] This organisation was established in Cavan in December 1887 under the presidency of Mrs Saunderson, the wife of the then unionist leader, Sir Edward Saunderson. Several branches of the association, which shared a pervasive sense of religious identification and ritual with its male counterpart, were instituted but the organisation failed to flourish and became dormant after several years. Prior to the revival of the Association of Loyal Orangewomen in December 1911 there is some evidence to suggest that women were occasionally permitted to join the usually exclusively male preserves of the Orange Order. Although information is scarce, the 1894 roll book of the Loyal Union Orange Lodge in the Ballynafeigh district of South Belfast lists at least one female member.[76] Very few references are made to the activities of the Association of Orangewomen, but by 1919 twenty-five female lodges were established, including ten in Belfast, with a collective membership of over 1,000.[77] One account also records the ardour of women's support, where their opposition to Home Rule:

> was exhibited in the enthusiasm with which they backed up the defensive operations of their male friends, but . . . was shown even more markedly in the eagerness they exhibited for the formation of a Women's Orange Association – to bring them more intimately and effectually together.[78]

Following the revival of the Association of Loyal Orangewomen, male and female lodges co-operated closely with one another, developing both a 'cordial and greatly valued' relationship.[79] Thus the Orange Grand Master of Londonderry, R. W. Kerr, paid a public tribute to the remarkable progress of the female Orange movement during the twelfth of July celebrations of 1912:

> What that meant to Protestantism no one could estimate, because they all knew that the hand that rocked the cradle ruled the world. So they said to their Orange sister:– 'Go on and God be with you in your splendid work for the truth and home and freedom.'[80]

In contrast to the ardour which political allegiance to unionism aroused amongst the working classes in Ulster, middle-class women were constrained by the mores of Victorian respectability. They were denied both the upper-class privilege of exerting political influence on the leading proponents of the unionist campaign and the freedom of political expression that was evident amongst working-class women. According to one contemporary commentator, for middle-class women to become actively involved in politics and 'thrust themselves more prominently into the limelight would have been regarded as presumptuous . . . [and] 'unladylike', though . . . a duchess or a marchioness gained prestige instead of losing caste by such performances'.[81] As a result of such constraints, the majority of middle-class women were content to attend, rather than address, unionist demonstrations and to fund-raise and canvass for unionist candidates. But, in spite of the auxiliary nature of this work, it still marked a departure from the domestic focus of middle-class women's lives. Moreover, women's widespread participation in the unionist campaign represented an advance into areas that were previously the exclusive domain of a small number of political wives.

The significance of the establishment of the UWUC and the Association of Loyal Orangewomen, therefore, lay in providing an opportunity for women from all social backgrounds to become politically active. The combination of upper-class leadership and the popularisation of unionism enabled the UWUC to attract an unprecedented number of women into the unionist campaign. Within a month of the initiation of the women's unionist council 4,000 women joined its West Belfast branch and 40,000–50,000 members had enrolled in thirty-two associations throughout Ulster by 1912. In the following year press accounts claimed that the women's council represented between 115,000 and 200,000 members and, although a level of exaggeration is to be expected, the organisation had undoubtedly become the largest female political organisation in Ireland.[82] From 1911 the political campaign conducted by the UWUC not only allowed unionist leaders to proclaim that the whole of Protestant Ulster opposed Home Rule, but also enabled their protests to reach a very wide audience. Each branch of the UWUC was linked to a women's unionist organisation in England or Scotland and their work was co-ordinated in order to maximise the effectiveness of a propaganda campaign that was conducted throughout Britain, America and the Dominions.[83]

Even though unionists campaigned on an unprecedented scale during the third Home Rule crisis, women's designated political role was not transformed. As was apparent during the first and second Home Rule crises, unionist women were content to perform auxiliary work. By September 1913, for instance, 100,000 leaflets and newspapers were sent weekly to Britain under the auspices of the women's council. Members of the UWUC were also keen to increase press coverage for their activities in an attempt to maximise publicity and, therefore, the impact of their anti-Home Rule campaign. For example, in June 1911 a female unionist demonstration was postponed because the press was preoccupied with the coronation of George V. Petitioning, which had been such a significant component of women's earlier unionist campaigns, also remained important. In January 1912 the UWUC organised a petition against the *Ne Temere* papal decree that declared mixed marriages void if not officially solemnised by the rites of the Catholic church. Within a month this petition measured a mile in length and by June had over 100,000 signatories.[84] Demonstrations remained a core component of the women's campaign and attendance figures, although likely to be subject to some aggrandisement in sympathetic press accounts, do suggest that mass enthusiasm was inspired amongst female unionist supporters who 'were being brought very close to each other because . . . the peril which threatened them and their children was drawing nearer'.[85] To cite one example, 25,000 unionist women congregated in West Belfast to welcome Carson on his first visit to the area in 1913. This was believed to be the largest assemblage of women that had ever occurred in Ireland.[86] Furthermore, the fact that 218,206 men expressed their opposition to Home Rule by signing the solemn league and covenant in 1912, compared to 234,046 female signatories on the women's declaration, effectively highlights the comparative strength of women's unionism.[87]

Determination amongst women to assist in bringing about the defeat of Home Rule had been apparent in 1886 and 1893, but during the third and most severe crisis of 1911 to 1914, women's political participation reached new heights. By September 1913 a permanent staff of twenty-six female unionist 'missionaries' from Ulster was resident in England, addressing meetings, electioneering and occasionally using ingenious means to attract audiences. Mrs Sinclair, for example, used lantern slides and was accompanied by a conjuror to entice support from Maidstone's working classes in 1911. Three years later, at the height of the Home Rule crisis, H.V. Wilkins, a unionist electoral agent in London, reported on the work of Ulster women in the Buckinghamshire, Bethnal Green and Poplar by-elections. Male canvassers were allocated 'the rougher parts of the Division', but Wilkins wholeheartedly commended women's work:

> I cannot speak too highly of the work of these ladies . . . It was found necessary to send out an extra person . . . Miss Kingsborough, the Ulster Lady Dispatch Rider, volunteered . . . and although on many occasions the weather was simply deplorable she insisted upon

> carrying out her duties . . . It was suggested that a distribution of literature should be made to those electors who left . . . by early trains . . . Miss Leatham, Mrs ffrench Beytagh and Miss Kingsborough readily undertook this work although it necessitated their getting up at 4.30 a.m.[88]

During the third Home Rule crisis the social contacts of the female unionist élite were effectively used to foster support in England. A considerable number of upper-class English women joined the Duchess of Abercorn's 'Help the Ulster Women Committee', which drafted evacuation schemes to provide shelter for women and children in the event of civil war breaking out in the province. Furthermore, the Duchess of Newcastle, Lady Duncombe and Viscountess Chilston all offered Theresa, Marchioness of Londonderry, financial and practical assistance for the unionist cause. Indeed, it was largely due to Theresa Londonderry's influence:

> amongst leaders of the Unionist Party in England, and her unceasing efforts[,] that the [Ulster Women's Unionist] Council was able to obtain so many openings in Great Britain for its workers during the third Home Rule crisis.[89]

In addition to this support, the strength of women's unionist convictions during the third Home Rule crisis also led many former friends in opposite political camps to dissociate themselves from one another. Cecil Craig claimed that Theresa Londonderry showed these 'feelings very openly' and that she ousted Lady Pirrie of Belfast from her social circle because of her husband's conversion to nationalism:

> One day on the Terrace of the House of Commons, Lady Pirrie, whose husband had ratted to the other side, rushed up to her and after greeting her said what very changeable weather we are having. Lady [Londonderry] sniffed loudly and replied I dislike change of any sort, and turned her back on her.[90]

Margot Asquith, wife of the Liberal Prime Minister, was also excluded from all the social functions hosted by Theresa Londonderry because of political differences over Home Rule.

The impact of the widespread politicisation of unionist women was of considerable consequence, as one Ulster woman wrote in 1914: 'One cannot go anywhere in Protestant Ulster without finding women whose whole time is occupied in preparing [UVF] hospitals, collecting money, holding meetings, and organising deputations.'[91] However, for some women, membership of the UWUC led them into strictly unconventional activities. In the mobilisation of the Ulster Volunteer Force (UVF), Lady Dufferin was instrumental in requesting that a central authority be established in order to co-ordinate the training and recruitment of nursing and first-aid personnel.[92] As a result of her initiative three representatives of the UWUC were appointed onto the UVF Medical Board to draft this scheme: Lady Hermione Blackwood, Mrs G.H. Wheeler and Mrs Robert Campbell. A total of approximately 3,000 women enlisted in the UVF from 1913 to 1914, working in the ladies' signalling section which was established in November 1913 and as ambulance and dispatch riders, postal workers, typists and intelligence workers who deciphered police messages. At least three women were also actively involved in ferrying arms to safe houses during the Larne gun-running of 24 April 1914[93] and another so-called 'worthy old dame' stood at the entrance of Larne harbour blacking out car registration numbers with tar.[94] Another woman helping to unload arms at Belfast tied revolvers and bullets around her waist and successfully defied troops to search her whilst 'pregnant'.[95] Although there is a folklorish infamy in these accounts, some indication of women's resourcefulness and dedication to the unionist cause can be gleaned from them. These activities were, however, exceptional and the overriding majority of UWUC members continued to execute ancillary work of an intrinsically gendered nature.

Asquith introduced the third Home Rule Bill to the Commons in April 1912 and, although it was fervently opposed by both unionists and Conservatives, it passed its final reading in January 1913. Its subsequent defeat in the House of Lords only deferred its implementation for two years, a political development that aroused serious anxieties within the unionist community. Lilian Spender recorded her fears, which were shared by many, concerning a political compromise:

> Why should Unionists dally with the idea at all, when the Government is obviously so helpless to coerce Ulster, I can't imagine. If the *whole party* would unite to oppose Home Rule, I am *certain* we would win. It is so hard to sit here and realise how little England, as a whole, understands the situation.[96]

The leaders of the Ulster Women's Unionist Council struggled to maintain unity amongst their rank and file as disillusionment and frustration concerning the effectiveness of their constitutional campaign emerged by the middle of 1914. With this apparent unrest, in February the organisation was prompted to publish an appeal to female factory and mill workers to maintain peace: 'Unionist sisters . . . be patient under all provocations . . . strive earnestly to preserve . . . order.'[97] In spite of this appeal, by June some UWUC members were convinced that force was the only effective way to oppose Home Rule. This faction wanted the financial resources of the unionist campaign to be directed solely towards the Ulster Volunteer Force and refused to continue constituency work and 'be made the fool of the English Conservative Party . . . who have no regard for Ulster except as a lever for securing their own return to power'.[98] This threatened to split the women's council, as many female unionists remained convinced of the effectiveness of working solely by constitutional means in English and Scottish constituencies. The resulting dissension was so severe that the UWUC president, Theresa Londonderry, sought Edward Carson's assistance.[99] The organisation, advised by both its president and the unionist leader, subsequently decided to continue its constituency campaign, but amidst this dissension the whole political situation was dramatically altered by the outbreak of the First World War in August 1914.

III

The unionist campaign was officially suspended for the duration of the war when the oft-proclaimed loyalty of Ulster unionists to Britain and the empire was put to practical use. Throughout 1914 to 1918 the women's council fund-raised and undertook extensive war work: financing UVF hospitals, making military dressings, sending comforts to men in active service and recruiting for both Voluntary Aid Detachments and the forces. Work of this nature not only assisted the war effort but also allowed the social interaction between unionist women to continue. This was not without political implications, as a communications network was maintained by the wives of prominent unionists, who passed information amongst themselves and on to their male spouses, many of whom left Ulster to undertake active military service. Like many war wives, Lilian Spender wrote daily to her husband whilst he was at the front. She kept him informed of any political developments that affected the unionist position and he sent letters for her to forward to Edward Carson.

Other UWUC members were in daily contact with each other, working together and pouring 'out political gossip . . . by the hour' at unionist headquarters in Belfast for the Ulster Gift Fund and in London for Ruby Carson's Comforts for the Ulster Division Fund.[100]

The third Home Rule Bill passed into law on 18 September 1914 only to be immediately suspended as a result of an agreement which had been reached between unionists and the Irish Parliamentary Party. In spite of this suspension, many unionists, including Lilian Spender, were appalled. She wrote of her anger at the government's 'base treachery. It's the meanest thing this Government has ever done . . . we must just wait until the War is over. Then we'll fight!'[101] Indeed, the level of female opposition was such that Richard Dawson Bates advised the UWUC's president, Theresa Londonderry, not to call a meeting of the women's council for fear of arousing further disunity in September 1914. The uncertainty of Ulster's political future ensured that the UWUC embarked upon some political work during the war: individual members continued to articulate the unionist message and electoral registers were maintained. In addition to this work, several women in positions of social privilege also promoted the political interests of unionism throughout the war. Perhaps most importantly, Edith Londonderry founded 'The Ark', a weekly political club which met at Londonderry House from 1915. Many of the social events that had been seriously curtailed by the war became encapsulated into this weekly gathering. And, with all the leading political figures as members, 'The Ark' provided a setting for women to continue to exert indirect political influence. War work also provided some opportunities for social interaction between leading female unionists and those in positions of power. In 1917, for instance, Ruby Carson met the Queen when visiting a hospital for wounded soldiers and their conversation veered dangerously near the political at Ruby's initiative when she referred to the lack of nationalist enlistment in the Ulster Division.[102] Ruby also met the Prime Minister socially the following year, shortly after her husband had left his cabinet post in the admiralty, and in her diary she recorded her feisty response to the premier's statement that he wanted her husband back in the cabinet: 'Then you must give Ulster all she wants.'[103]

During the war, therefore, it is clear that the political fortunes of Ulster remained a source of serious concern. In response to the passage and suspension of the third Home Rule Act, unionism became increasingly 'Ulster' focused and partition began to be considered as a solution to the Irish question. Considerable opposition was aroused amongst unionists as the geographical definition of Ulster was narrowed to encompass only its six north-easterly counties. Indeed, from the middle of 1914 the UWUC's advisory committee articulated their reticence to partition Ulster, asking Theresa Londonderry to consult with Carson on this matter. He responded by appealing to 'the ladies to keep quiet', reassuring them that Ulster would be fully consulted in any forthcoming political settlement.[104] Theresa Londonderry reiterated this advice, requesting that no political work be undertaken: 'the great thing at the moment is to keep absolutely quiet; not have a meeting, write a letter or anything'.[105]

Despite these appeals, partition continued to cause considerable disarray amongst both male and female unionists. In 1916 Edith Wheeler consulted Theresa Londonderry on the viability of the UWUC adopting a scheme to assist female emigration from the three excluded counties of Cavan, Monaghan and Donegal to Ulster. This suggestion gives some indication of the sense of community that existed between unionist women, who felt bound to one another by their shared political beliefs: 'We all feel that unless we do something like this we will be unable to look old friends and fellow Covenanteers straightly in the face.'[106] Two weeks later Edith Mercier Clements reinforced these sentiments in another letter to Theresa, outlining the impact partition would have on UWUC members in the three excluded counties:

> many of them at present are too sad to even want to attend our committees and we must show them that they are more to us now than ever before because of their inestimable and incomparable self-sacrifice . . . You can hardly form any idea of how many women are irreconcilable and never would have consented to anything which meant the breaking of the Covenant.[107]

Just days later Edith Wheeler, perhaps in an attempt to prompt a reconsideration of partition, alerted Theresa Londonderry to the great upsurge in republican sympathy in the aftermath of the Easter Rising which had occurred throughout the proposed excluded counties of Ulster:

> I have been all through Cavan, Monaghan and Donegal – (the Nationalist parts) and I find things are very bad. Where there used to be one Sinn Feiner there are ten and where hundreds, thousands. It is now the *strong* party in Ireland . . . The Nationalists are working hard, distributing leaflets, . . . sending speakers to the colonies – collecting money in U.S.A. and here for the rebels.[108]

Attempting to maintain unity and prevent public dissension led some unionists to try to reconcile women to the idea of partition. Hugh de Fellenberg Montgomery, for example, tried to persuade Mrs M. Sinclair, the honorary secretary of North Tyrone WUA, that the women's declaration and men's covenant of 1912 were not undermined by accepting six-county exclusion, but that this was the only alternative to an Irish legislature:

> If I enter into a solemn covenant to give you a certain house . . . and that house . . . is swallowed up by an earthquake I obviously have to reconsider my position, . . . our duty [is] to oppose Home Rule in any way we can, and, if we cannot prevent its being introduced in some part of Ireland, to prevent its being introduced in as large a part of Ireland as we can . . . the six counties is the most we can absolutely secure.[109]

The deliberations that occurred over partition highlight the essentially conservative nature of the UWUC. In spite of the serious opposition to partition which continued to vex the association throughout the war, the UWUC's position was epitomised by Cecil Craig's statement of April 1919: 'they would rather remain under the Union, but if that was not possible they had to do the best they could'.[110] And ultimately the UWUC sanctioned the Government of Ireland Act of 1920 that superseded the 1914 Home Rule Act and established a six-county state with limited legislative powers in Ulster.

IV

The passage of two measures of women's suffrage, in 1918 and 1928, were of considerable consequence for female unionism. The political considerations of the unionist party concerning their electoral fortunes led them to reconsider the importance of women's support, which could now be expressed through a parliamentary vote. In 1913 the Unionist Clubs of Ireland removed their exclusionary ban on women members by deleting the word 'male' from their constitution.[111] In practical terms this was only of limited import, because the majority of female unionists had already joined local women's associations affiliated to the UWUC. But, as a symbolic gesture of solidarity, this was of some significance, as women, who were still unable to exercise the parliamentary franchise, were admitted to a recognised and mainstream facet of unionism. However, the policy-making and most powerful body of unionism, the Ulster Unionist Council, did not follow this initiative. In 1911 it admitted representatives from both the Apprentice Boys of Derry and the Unionist Clubs to its ranks, a move which prompted the UUC to be described as 'the most democratic and representative forum that Ulster unionism had ever inspired'.[112] But, in terms of gender, and in terms of granting official recognition to the female organisations that were also working for the unionist cause, the UUC was neither truly representative nor democratic. The UUC's constitution did not emphatically exclude female membership, but women were prohibited in practical terms because nominated district representatives had to be registered as voters. This effectively excluded the membership of women until the passage of the Representation of the People Act in 1918. So, from 1911 the UWUC was the only mass organisation excluded from the auspices of the Ulster Unionist Council. This exclusion gradually aroused considerable hostility amongst women. The UWUC publicly expressed this for the first time in 1916, passing a resolution requesting direct representation on the UUC. At the same time, Rosalind, Duchess of Abercorn, utilised her social contacts within the unionist leadership to encourage Edward Carson to investigate 'opening the way for the extension of the Constitution of the Ulster Unionist Council'.[113] Neither of these attempts met with any success.

From early 1918 female unionists increased their efforts to gain admittance to the UUC. In January of that year, Theresa Londonderry raised the issue of female representation with Carson, and several months later Hariot, Marchioness of Dufferin and Ava, interviewed Richard Dawson Bates, the UUC's secretary, on behalf of the UWUC.[114] She emphasised that many members of the women's council felt alienated by this lack of official recognition: 'we have been ignored . . . [we] do not want a separate party here with a separate policy but . . . a distinct recognition'.[115] Edith Wheeler estimated that democratic representation of women on the UUC should amount to forty per cent, but felt that even ten to twelve per cent would allow women to 'bring up the questions on which we are . . . just as well able to judge as men'.[116] Women's dissidence was reinforced by the manner in which the UWUC had been overlooked throughout the war. The council highlighted that it had not been consulted during the political deliberations over partition or the proposed federal scheme. In June 1918, just three months after women were enfranchised, the UWUC fully expressed its sense of indignation in a written statement to the UUC. This emphasised the women's council's belief that its reputation had been seriously undermined:

> During the last four years of war, our opinion on any one political matter has never been asked. We ourselves have been mute, under what we consider has been a slow and insidious disintegration of our power . . . [and we] realise many anxieties, difficulties and dangers that have to be faced by the Men with regard to the Vote for Women, and its possibility of future elections. But . . . we have not been treated as comrades . . . We must have more power for immediate action . . . let us stand out now for the rights and liberties of the Ulster Women's Unionist Council.[117]

This uncharacteristic call for a recognition of women's rights from the normally circumspect UWUC, coupled with women's enfranchisement, prompted a change of attitude amongst unionist leaders. Carson, although a publicly renowned anti-suffragist, appears in private correspondence to have been sympathetic towards the UWUC's appeal for representation on the UUC.[118] He had not, however, attempted to modify the UUC's constitution to facilitate women's entry. But, under changed circumstances in 1918, Carson agreed to receive a deputation from the UWUC to discuss this issue. Further evidence of his support can be found in a letter to Theresa Londonderry written in 1918 in which he encouraged her to continue the work he initiated whilst visiting Ulster earlier that year:

> I hope you will bear in mind how necessary it is that the women should have their full share in the organisation in Ulster. I did my best when I was over to lay the foundation of this policy.[119]

The fact that the unionist leader actively promoted women's admission to the UUC underlines the significance of the passage of the first measure of women's suffrage in March 1918. This legislation undoubtedly had a positive impact in securing women's admission to the Ulster Unionist Council. Unionist leaders, prompted by concerns for their own political fortunes, could no longer discount women, who now formed an important component of the electorate, which would be insensate for any astute politician to ignore. Therefore, to consider the number of women elected to parliament as the only tangible outcome of female enfranchisement overlooks the reconsideration of women's political potential that occurred. But, even with these new considerations, support for women's admittance to the UUC was not universal. Richard Dawson Bates, secretary of the UUC, was still very reluctant to endorse female representation, privately referring to the UWUC as 'a more or less effete organisation'.[120]

However, self-interest meant that his foremost concern was for party unity and he conceded that in order 'to prevent any friction it would be as well to give them [women] a small direct representation'.[121] In spite of this, Bates inferred that Edith Wheeler's determination to secure female representation on the UUC was not based on a demand for equal or democratic treatment, but was spurred on by the influence of Miss Roe, a cohort of the former suffragette leader, Emmeline Pankhurst. Bates alleged that Roe, who was in Ireland at this time, had put 'mischief into Mrs Wheeler's head' by encouraging the UWUC to act as an independent body in an attempt to gain 'control of the Ulster women, ostensibly for the object of the maintenance of the Union, but really for their own political ends'.[122] Lack of any further information prevents an assessment of this charge. The Pankhursts' suffragette campaign had been defunct since the outbreak of the war and suffrage momentum largely diffused, but it is possible that personal influence was being privately exercised. More generally, however, the implementation of suffrage legislation ultimately prompted Carson to recommend establishing a committee of eight men and women to discuss the future of the UWUC. In October 1918 a compromise was reached and the women's council was granted twelve representatives on the UUC. This representation, although of numerical equality to that of the Unionist Clubs, was still nominal at under three per cent and far below the twelve per cent that the UWUC previously fielded as a conservative proposal.[123] The passage of women's suffrage was undeniably the instigator of this change and even the UUC's annual report of 1919 noted that women had been admitted to its echelons as a direct result of the extension of the parliamentary franchise.[124]

Electoral considerations were also to the fore in discussions concerning the amalgamation of the male and female unionist organisations which coincided with the measures of suffrage passed in 1918 and 1928. Unionist commentator Ronald McNeill openly acknowledged this in a letter to Theresa Londonderry: 'Now that women are enfranchised it is important that they should be definitely organised everywhere in our political associations'.[125] Unionist deliberations were based on the best means of guaranteeing female electoral support, but amalgamation did not occur, as the majority of UWUC members were unenthusiastic. Cecil Craig, for instance, addressing a special meeting of the women's council in the aftermath of the 1928 Representation of the People Act, rejected the proposed amalgamation outright. This was on the grounds that amalgamation would result in the women's council forfeiting its individual identity and hence curtail the effectiveness of its campaign. Perhaps more interesting is the fact that Craig also claimed that 'women worked better when acting on Committees by themselves'.[126]

Following the first instalment of women's enfranchisement in 1918, both male and female unionist leaders were clearly anxious to encourage women to utilise their votes to further the unionist cause. Richard Dawson Bates endeavoured to bolster women's loyalty to unionism through the Association of Loyal Orangewomen. In June 1918 he tried to enlist the support of the UWUC's president, Theresa Londonderry, for what he referred to as this 'first rate' organisation. Bates encouraged Theresa Londonderry to join the association, as he believed that her patronage would attract 'a great many of the working women and others into the local [Orange] associations, and getting them to take an interest in parliamentary matters'.[127] Female unionist leaders shared Bates' concerns, but they tried to rally women's electoral support by organisational means and by interpreting the vote as a way for women to protect all that they had fought for during the third Home Rule crisis and the First World War. This was clearly apparent in an address delivered by the Duchess of Abercorn to women unionists in Belfast during the election campaign for the first parliament of Northern Ireland in 1921:

> They had never clamoured for the vote, but now it had been given to them she was confident they intended to use it to the safety, honour, and welfare of their Church, their country, their homes, and their children by helping to put a strong local Government in power.[128]

The UWUC not only sought to align female voters to the unionist cause by rhetorical means, but they also provided practical instruction to ensure that women did not waste their votes by spoiling ballot papers. As a result, the UWUC worked in conjunction with the Irish Women's Civic Federation (IWCF) to instruct women on their voting rights under the Representation of the People Act of 1918. The UWUC undertook this work for the six north-eastern counties of Ulster, with the IWCF taking responsibility for Cavan, Monaghan and Donegal. The UWUC continued to perform this sort of work throughout the inter-war period. During the 1925 electoral campaign, for example, women were very proactive – canvassing, providing assistance in tally rooms and escorting electors to the polls. Indeed, women, encouraged by the UWUC, reportedly queued in their hundreds to gain admission to polling stations 'long before the doors were opened' and 'made the fight all their own, and threw all their energies into the endeavour to secure a decisive triumph for the loyalist cause'.[129] Enthusiasm of this sort can partly be explained as a real commitment to the unionist cause, but it also seems that many women regarded casting their vote as something of a privilege. As Winifred Campbell recalled of her mother living in the Shankill area of Belfast:

> Mother never went [to vote] until the late afternoon, holding onto her little bit of power as long as possible. When at last she decided to go and although the polling station was only two streets away, she travelled in the largest, grandest car the Unionist Party could provide, to record her vote.[130]

In organising female voters the UWUC never sought to advance any feminist cause, as maintaining support for unionism remained a priority. One of the most poignant reminders of the women's council's essential conservatism came in 1921 when the organisation ignored an appeal from the Women's Advisory Council to promote female candidates in the forthcoming Northern Irish elections.[131] Throughout the inter-war years the UWUC never promoted women's parliamentary candidature, affirming that male unionists were best suited to these positions. This conservatism was reinforced by the attitude of unionist leaders, who were clearly wary of the unknown phenomenon of female parliamentary candidates. Hence in 1921 Edward Carson publicly advised women when selecting candidates 'to choose the man who they thought would best represent their views'.[132] These convictions were reiterated by James Craig, who urged that 'before any woman put herself forward for Parliament she should fully consider the matter. Patience . . . should be the watchword of the moment.'[133] In spite of the evident lack of encouragement from either the UWUC or unionist leaders, three women, Dehra Parker, Julia McMordie and Margaret Waring, were elected as unionist members of the Northern Ireland parliament in the period 1921 to 1940.[134] And, in the less powerful realm of municipal politics, unionists were less reticent to support female representation. Women were gradually admitted to poor law and municipal administration from the late nineteenth century and thereafter the impact of both female candidature and the municipal franchise was known. Indeed, the UWUC supported female unionist candidates in urban district and county councils from March 1919 and in poor law elections from 1920.[135] This was presented as an attempt to further unionist hegemony over municipal administration, but it is also possible that the underlying motive was to encourage women's electoral support by defining an acceptable public role for unionist women.[136]

Due to the continued efficiency of the UWUC and the significance of the women's vote in helping to maintain unionist support after 1920, female unionists gradually became involved in many aspects of unionist politics. In April 1920, for example, unionists in Tyrone issued a memorial calling for a reconsideration of Ulster's six-county exclusion. This was signed by one woman, Mrs Greer, whose name appeared alongside unionist notaries such as Lords Bangor, Rodner and Clanwilliam.[137] In several instances, male and female unionists also electioneered and fund-raised together and in 1926 jointly administered the Belfast and Bangor branches of the Junior Imperial League.[138] Further evidence of the increasing occurrences of co-operation between male and female unionists is provided by Mid Armagh's Men's and Women's Unionist Associations which held joint meetings from the late 1920s for the purpose of selecting UUC delegates and candidates for parliamentary elections.[139]

Perhaps as a result of the UWUC's improved status within the unionist movement, some women were sufficiently confident to publicly express their support for universal suffrage in the months preceding the passage of the Representation of the People Act of 1928. This had been impossible during the entangled and politically fraught pre-war suffrage campaign. But by 1928 Mrs Ainsworth Barr, honorary treasurer of the UWUC, used rhetoric which would have been inconceivable during the third Home Rule crisis in order to record her support for equal suffrage: 'Girls of twenty-one had just as much common-sense as men of twenty-one, and perhaps a great deal more.'[140] The leaders of women's unionism were also much more forthright in welcoming electoral reform in 1928 than in 1918. Following the first instalment of women's suffrage, the UWUC had emphasised that as an organisation it 'had never clamoured for the vote'.[141] A decade later the response was very different. Cecil Craig, the UWUC's president, addressing a meeting of women unionists in North Belfast, unconditionally welcomed what she referred to as the 'flapper vote'.[142] UWUC vice-president Edith Londonderry was similarly enthusiastic: 'Few things have given me more satisfaction [than] when the Women's Franchise Bill was passed in the House of Commons, giving the same political status to women as men.'[143]

Following the passage of the Representation of the People Act in 1928, a female electoral majority was created in Ulster, as 500,000 women (representing fifty-two per cent of the total electorate) were now enfranchised. Of these women, twenty-nine per cent were new voters and this situation prompted widespread concern regarding the political fortunes of unionism. Unionist leaders reacted by publicly courting female support. The clearest example of this came on 10 May 1929 when James and Cecil Craig organised and addressed a rally for newly enfranchised women in Belfast. This was an attempt to ward off the electoral threat posed by independent unionists and local optionist candidates by securing women's support for the unionist party. James Craig attempted to woo the support of the assembled audience of over 1,000 women by emphasising both the allure of political work and the inherent nature of unionist sympathies amongst women: 'Once they were enmeshed in the web of politics they would find them interesting and absorbing . . . The spirit of loyalty was born into the women of Ulster.'[144] Craig went on to call upon the 'flappers' of Ulster to save the province: 'Be modest in all things, but don't be too shy to come out and vote, . . . get right into the middle of the scrum, vote Loyalist'.[145] Four days later Cecil Craig published a manifesto specifically for female voters in the *Belfast News-Letter* and *The Times*, suggesting that women's support for unionism was of 'especial importance . . . owing to the recent extension of the franchise'.[146] After 1928 unionists continued to court female support in an attempt to maintain the party's appeal. And this, coupled with Craig's populist style of leadership, may also explain why he made regular financial donations to the UWUC.[147]

The introduction of universal suffrage in 1928 furthered another reconsideration of women's political stature. Essentially this continued the process that had begun in the aftermath of the first instalment of women's suffrage in 1918. Thus, at James Craig's suggestion, three representatives from the UWUC were invited to attend the UUC's annual lunch in 1929. Prior to this date, although the wives of leading members attended this function, women unionists never constituted a formal delegation. In 1929 women were also invited to an Ulster Reform Club reception for the first time and two years later UWUC was offered membership of the Central Committee of Representatives from Unionist Associations in London.[148] An analysis of the number of female delegates appointed to the UUC further underlines the inroads which women gradually made into unionism. In addition to the twelve UWUC representatives, women's enfranchisement meant that from 1918 women who were registered as voters could also be appointed as delegates of local unionist associations to the UUC. Moreover, after 1918 the wives of several unionist MPs and senators were also selected as *ex officio* members of the UUC. To take 1923 as an example, 133 women were appointed to the UUC, representing twenty-seven per cent of its total delegation.[149] Although the level of female representation on the UUC was subject to some fluctuation, it remained at between a quarter and a fifth of the UUC's composite membership throughout the inter-war period.[150]

The maintenance of female interest in unionism via the UWUC and the Association of Loyal Orangewomen ultimately helped to maintain unionist hegemony in the newly established Northern Irish state. Women's support was continually cultivated and sustained attempts were made to make unionism, as a political creed, appear relevant to Ulster's inter-war position. Thus, the organisation expanded its objectives to encompass opposition to socialism and Sinn Féin, to support the purchase of empire-produced goods and the introduction of stricter licensing legislation. This effectively encouraged women to join the UWUC and the Association of Orangewomen. Over an eight-month period from April to November 1929, for example, thirty-three new associations of the women's council were established; in 1931 another two new women's unionist associations and a further eight new branches were formed; UWUC speakers addressed 168 meetings, made 1,150 house visits and sent 4,192 circulars. Several new women's Orange lodges were also established: St Patrick's lodge was installed with twenty-six female members in May 1921 and another was formed in the Knockbreda area of South Belfast in 1926. The common loyalties between the Association of Loyal Orangewomen and the UWUC were recognised in 1920 when the council bestowed official representation to this organisation.[151] The connection between these two associations was compounded by an overlap in personnel: Miss Leah Garratt, the Grand Secretary and later Grand Mistress of the Association of Orangewomen, was a member of the Holywood branch of North Down Women's Unionist Association and Mrs Dixon, a vice-chairman of the UWUC, proudly referred to herself as an Orangewoman, 'because she believed that their Order was the most loyal in the land . . . and its traditions the highest and best'.[152] Furthermore, Mrs Woodside of St Anne's Women's Unionist Association, volunteered to distribute copies of the UWUC magazine, *Ulsterwoman*, to members of her local women's Orange lodge[153] and in February 1932 Miss Currie urged female unionists in South Tyrone to become Orangewomen.[154]

The UWUC remained the largest women's political organisation in Ireland, but its intrinsic conservatism ensured that no attempts were made to redefine women's social or legislative position or secure female parliamentary representation. The UWUC always maintained that their first priority was to protect the unionist cause. As a result, the division of political work along gender lines continued within unionism. Female unionists electioneered, disseminated propaganda, educated women voters and accepted responsibility for the incubation of political sympathies amongst the next generation of unionist supporters. In essence, just as a good mother would teach her children the difference between right and wrong, many leading unionists believed that a sound political education was equally important. In 1925, Edith Londonderry alluded to this maternal aspect of politics, emphasising the need for women to:

> acquire a wider political outlook in order to train and influence the coming generations . . . to become sound politicians, in the same way as it was in the hands of mothers to bring up their children as useful citizens.[155]

Another prominent unionist, Hugh Pollock, the Northern Ireland Minister for Finance, also referred to the importance of women's didactic work, discharging the duties of 'school teachers' amongst the young.[156] In order to fulfil this role in the inter-war period, members of the UWUC became actively involved in attracting future voters to unionism by running organisations which aimed to inculcate unionist sympathies amongst children: Pioneer Clubs, the Junior Imperial League and junior units of both the UWUC and the Association of Loyal Orangewomen.

The political relevance of domesticity and the home in the rhetoric of female unionism also remained important. This was reinforced by widespread pro-natalist and eugenic interests concerning the size and health of the nation that emerged in the aftermath of the First World War. As a direct consequence, women were revered as wives and mothers. The impact of this ideological climate is discernible within women's unionism. The title of a journal produced by the UWUC from 1925 to 1927, *Northern Ireland, home and politics, a journal for women*, reveals a fusion of domestic and political interests.[157] In this journal, articles concerning politics were published alongside those which promoted housewifery as a near science, with numerous domestic management, laundry and gardening hints.[158] Moreover, the UWUC claimed that there were social and domestic aspects to unionism 'which none but women can fully understand'.[159] Female unionists, therefore, continued to be largely interested 'in matters concerning herself, her family and her social circles, the things she knew most about, in the order of housing, education and social services'.[160] With these considerations it was not surprising that in 1932 Cecil Craig recommended that addresses should be given at women's unionist meetings on dressmaking, hygiene and any other matters which would be helpful to women in the home. Only a few individual female unionists felt constrained by this domestic focus. Thus the dissatisfaction which Helen McLean, the UWUC's organising secretary, expressed in 1937 was unique and her claim that women could 'use their brains for the welfare of the country . . . as well as in the important but rather restricted area of the home' had little impact on the UWUC's work.[161]

V

Let them be on their guard, and see to it that Protestantism, good government . . . and the Union Jack still prevailed . . . [162]

Just as women's designated political role within the unionist movement changed little over time, individual members of Ulster's aristocracy continued to exert considerable political influence. The establishment of the parliament of Northern Ireland in 1921 strengthened the unionist political élite by creating a local power base. Moreover, the serious levels of sectarian strife that occurred during the 1920s drew the unionist community even closer together. Lilian Spender alluded to this in 1921, comparing life in such a close-knit community which was unified by common political affiliations as akin to:

> living . . . on the edge of an extremely active volcano, [and] tends to make people seek each other's society, and try to drown anxieties in friendly intercourse . . . One meets the same little group of friends at each other's houses . . . [163]

Members of the Northern Ireland cabinet socialised together and supported one another through the turbulent and violent years of the newly established state. For women this was reinforced by a network of social and charitable clubs in Belfast that attracted prominent unionists as members and patrons. For instance, the Countess of Clanwilliam, the president of North Down's Women's Unionist

Association, also headed the Alpha Club, the women's equivalent of the Rotary Club. The Belfast branch of the Women's League of Health and Beauty was also popular, having several leading female unionists amongst its members, including Lady Dixon, Cecil Craig and the Duchess of Abercorn. From this élite two outstanding female unionist leaders emerged during the inter-war period: Cecil Craig, president of the UWUC from 1923 to 1942 and wife of the first Prime Minister of Northern Ireland, and Edith Londonderry, who replaced Theresa Londonderry as the foremost political hostess and confidante to several important political figures.

Cecil Craig often played down her political talents, asserting that 'she was not gifted with the ability to take her husband's place and make a political speech'.[164] In spite of her modesty, numerous press tributes were paid to the prominent political role that she undertook. By 1926, for example, the *Daily Herald* believed that she was 'a valuable political asset . . . A trained and polished speaker, with a graceful presence, a facile gift of language, and an effective delivery'.[165] Her appointment to the presidency of the UWUC in 1923 was also of considerable significance. She instituted a successful scheme of re-organisation in 1924 that strengthened contacts between the central body of the women's council and its affiliates throughout Ulster. She was also the driving force behind the establishment of classes to train women unionists in the so-called 'arts of discussion and of conducting meetings'.[166] These initiatives allowed the UWUC to sustain both members and interest throughout the inter-war period. Cecil frequently addressed meetings of female unionists, claiming that the aims of the Irish Free State were totally at variance with those of Ulster unionists. These speeches also helped female unionists to maintain a sense of purpose. She repeatedly accentuated the need for women unionists to continue their political campaign, warning members of the UWUC that relaxing their vigilance was 'dangerous[,] futile, . . . insane . . . if in the future Ulster's liberties should be attacked they could carry on and carry through to victory as they did in the past'.[167]

Cecil Craig's political role was significantly augmented as a result of the failing health of her husband from the mid-1930s. Although Cecil denied that she was able to effectively deputise for her husband, she was increasingly called upon to do just that. During the election campaign of November 1933 she was forced to stand in for him at numerous meetings and election rallies, on one occasion addressing three political meetings in four consecutive days.[168] James Craig's health gradually deteriorated, with the result that Cecil also undertook a leading role during the next election of 1938. This provoked a considerable amount of press comment and led the *Daily Mail* to remark: 'Seldom has the first shot in a campaign been more effectively fired by a woman.'[169] Cecil Craig's heightened political profile also caused some speculation that she would stand for election after her husband's death on 24 November 1940. But, although approached, she refused to stand, explaining that she was 'too shattered by J's loss to take part in any public affairs'.[170] At the same time Cecil also stated that she intended to sever all political connections, in response to the lack of support which her husband received during the last months of his life. Some unionists had levelled serious criticisms at the government's languid and ineffective response to the outbreak of the Second World War in 1939 and Edmund Warnock, parliamentary secretary to the Northern Ireland Ministry for Home Affairs, even resigned over this issue.[171] Cecil recorded her bitter disappointment in her diary, levelling blame at those who had criticised her sick and ageing spouse:

> I felt sore at the way a comparatively small number of peevers were allowed to harass and pinprick my own dear P.M. without his own solid backbenchers in the House having had the guts to stand up and attack them. These had undoubtedly hastened his end, so I had no wish to have anything further to do with politics.[172]

Cecil's desire to disengage herself from all political ties after her husband's death also led her to tender her resignation from the presidency of the UWUC. But the council refused to accept and Cecil consequently retained this position until 1942, when she left Ulster to live in England, although she remained a vice-president of the association until her death in 1960.

The other principal political figure in women's unionism during the inter-war period was Edith Londonderry. She not only inherited the title of Marchioness of Londonderry after Theresa's death in 1919, but a position of social prestige as the leading Tory hostess. Edith shared not only her late mother-in-law's political enthusiasm but also her ambition to shape events, direct careers and adopt the role of political confidante. In pursuit of these ends she corresponded with many leading political and influential figures, including Queen Mary, Stanley Baldwin, Bonar Law, Neville Chamberlain and Harold Macmillan.[173] Indeed, such was Edith's political empathy that her advice was actively sought. As Samuel Hoare, the British Home Secretary, emphasised in one of his many letters to her:

> You must let me talk over these . . . other political questions with you . . . Your mind is so fresh and vigorous that it does me a great deal of good to discuss politics with you.[174]

Edith's consuming political interest, coupled with her position of social privilege, enabled her to effectively negotiate between leading political figures. In 1922, for example, she was actively involved in trying to establish a die-hard Conservative Party as a consequence of growing disillusionment and unrest with the coalition government. In pursuit of this end she co-operated with Salisbury, Carson and Roland McNeill and her efforts in this direction were highly commended by the Duke of Northumberland:

> I am so glad you are taking the lead in getting all those who think like us to me. It is not at all pushing and there is nobody else who could do it as well as you.[175]

It was, however, Edith's relationship with the premier of the first Labour government, Ramsay MacDonald, which captured the attention of politicians, the public and the press and realised the potential of her influence. Widowed in 1911, MacDonald came to rely on Edith as his closest friend and confidante. The Boundary Commission was established in 1924, in accordance with Article 12 of the Anglo-Irish Treaty, in order to consider the geographical definition of Ulster. The Commission seriously unnerved unionists, raising doubts about the future of the province. The UWUC responded by reiterating that unionists' loyalty to Britain and the empire was unrelenting, issuing a statement which was reminiscent of those dating from earlier political crises:

> The firmness of our leaders and the steadfast loyalty of the people, by God's help, brought us through the crisis, and we go forward to face whatever further dangers may await us with a firm and united front.[176]

Edith Londonderry shared the UWUC's concerns and her association with MacDonald enabled her to exert considerable influence to ensure that unionist interests were protected in the Commission's report. When the Northern Ireland government refused to appoint a delegate to the Commission, the significance of her influence was heightened. During 1924 Ulster's boundary became a common topic in both letters and conversations between Edith and MacDonald. She outlined unionists' sense of unease, the importance of maintaining

Ulster's territory and the need for compromise and trust between the London and Belfast administrations:

> You ask me to do my poor best to help towards peace and get my friends to meet you reasonably. But to enable us to do this, you must be reasonable too and keep the faith with Ulster.[177]

MacDonald's replies often underlined the impact of Edith's influence within the clannish workings of the decision-making process:

> This new Irish trouble is most worrying. I am rigidly opposed to hasty legislation and I must make it clear that the Government intends to keep faith, I know that you will do your best to get your friends to meet us reasonably . . . Do not let us revive these evil passions of hate and strife. This is a thing to settle between friends.[178]

Edith frequently reiterated that unionists accepted the 1920 Government of Ireland Act only on the understanding that the territorial definition of the province was 'absolutely final' and she, therefore, asked MacDonald to:

> extend to us the . . . hand of fellowship and maintenance and throw to us the olive branch? This is my request to you . . . You may rely on my helping you all I can to keep the peace, only you must help us too.[179]

When the Commission finally reported in 1925, Ulster territorial boundaries were unaltered. It is difficult to ascertain the exact impact of Edith Londonderry's influence in securing these ends, but her persuasive arguments and tempered reasoning with MacDonald seem, at least, to have helped to maintain a unionist perspective in the Commission's deliberations. The close relationship between Edith and MacDonald continued throughout the 1920s, but it became increasingly controversial. This became very apparent following MacDonald's appointment as Prime Minister to the national government in 1931, especially after he appointed Lord Londonderry as Secretary of State for Air. This provoked rumours in high society and in the press concerning Edith's 'petticoat influence' as the '*via media* of the Cabinet'.[180]

In addition to Edith continuing the family tradition of political hostess, she also worked by more direct means as an active vice-president of the UWUC for forty years and as president of the

Newtownards Women's Unionist Association. She took more than a nominal interest in these appointments. For example, she successfully accentuated the need for 'fresh blood' and effective organisation to rejuvenate the Newtownards branch in the inter-war period.[181] Furthermore, in 1922 the Northern Ireland cabinet asked Edith to organise the Ulster Women's Volunteer Association to enlist and train a body of 'loyal' women who would be prepared to help the government 'in case of extreme emergency, and to replace men called out for active service'.[182] Edith Londonderry was perhaps an obvious choice for this position, not only because she was a dedicated and influential unionist, but also because she pioneered the establishment of the Women's Legion during the First World War. The Ulster Women's Volunteer Scheme was avowedly non-political in nature, but, as the enrolment of women was undertaken through the organisational machinery of the UWUC, the identification of loyalty with unionism is clear. Edith appointed paid county organisers to administer this scheme and formulated detailed plans to prepare for an emergency situation, 'arising either of a serious military nature due to Sinn Féin or an internal nature due to strikes on a large scale'.[183] It was envisaged that this association would ensure that 'the essentials of life to the community . . . that is, the supply of food, water, fuel and light' were maintained and female personnel were recruited to staff government departments, the police, St John's Ambulance and the Red Cross Association.[184] It is unclear how long this association remained in operation, but it provides an interesting example of unionists' continued sense of unease under escalating sectarian strife. However, the establishment of the Ulster Women's Volunteer Scheme also exemplified women's continued ancillary role in the unionist movement, a role which had been consistently assigned to women during the earlier Home Rule crises and the First World War.

The careers of Edith Londonderry and Cecil Craig illustrate that the political influence exercised by the female members of Ulster's aristocratic élite also changed little over time. Their entrance to the kernel of unionist politics was guaranteed by their marriage to leading unionists. But both women's influence, like that of their predecessors, was only consummated by the depth of their own political convictions and resolute determination to defend the unionist cause. Ultimately their work not only helped the UWUC to sustain members and interest, but also ensured that Ulster's boundaries remained intact.

VI

The popularisation of unionism amongst 'women from shabby streets, whose husbands are on the "dole" and amongst . . . [those] from the smart suburbs whose husbands earn thousands a year', allowed unionist leaders to justify their claims that the whole of Protestant Ulster was united in opposition to Home Rule.[185] Women's political work enabled unionist electoral and propaganda campaigns to be waged on a much wider scale, both geographically and in terms of the amount of information which was disseminated. In addition to the work of the UWUC, several women also utilised their position of social privilege to wield considerable political influence in support of unionism. Theresa Londonderry, for example, ensured that Ulster remained to the fore of the Conservative Party's political considerations, whilst her daughter-in-law Edith worked to secure Ulster's position, both territorially and constitutionally.

Whether conducted on an individual or group basis, however, women's work in the unionist movement was significantly shaped by gender. From the late nineteenth century women were assigned a subordinate role by male unionists and this role changed little over time. A reconsideration of women's political significance was forthcoming following the passage of women's suffrage in 1918 and universal suffrage a decade later. From 1918 female unionists were courted as voters with considerable success, but the impact of women's enfranchisement was limited. So, in spite of James Craig's declaration that nothing was 'more remarkable . . . than the extraordinary growth of the influence of women in the sphere of politics . . . Woman has come into her place, as a co-partner in political life and thought', women were never encouraged to come forward as parliamentary candidates.[186] Given these considerations, it is perhaps unsurprising that only three women were elected as unionist members of the parliament of Northern Ireland in the period under analysis. Furthermore, although women's political work was important in helping to maintain unionist hegemony by instructing women and the next generation of voters in unionist principles, this was ancillary work. Therefore, the women's 'place' in the unionist movement that James Craig referred to continued to be fundamentally shaped by gender.

CHAPTER THREE

Women in Nationalist Politics

I

Be a woman, on to duty,
Raise the world from all that's low,
Place high in the social heaven,
Virtue's fair and radiant bow . . .[1]

The level of female participation in nationalist politics remained lower in Ulster than elsewhere in Ireland. This was partially a result of the innate religious composition of the province, with Catholics constituting 42.7 per cent of Ulster's nine-county populace and only 34 per cent in the post-partition six-county state of Northern Ireland.[2] In addition to this there were also specific determinants influencing the development of both male and female nationalism in the north-east of the country. The small number of educated, middle-class Catholics in Ulster resulted in nationalist lay leadership remaining comparatively weak. To counteract this, the Catholic Church undertook an important political role. Class also appears to have affected the direction of political activity, as nationalists had few opportunities for influencing policy or cultivating political benefactors through the workings of high society. In addition, by comparison with the rest of the country, northern nationalism not only lacked co-ordinated organisational structures and indigenous initiatives, but was beset by disunity.[3] This chapter seeks to consider the cumulative effect of these factors on the direction and development of women's involvement in nationalist politics in Ulster from the late nineteenth century.

There are source problems involved in a study of this nature. Firstly, there are very few private papers relating to nationalist women, which is indicative of the existing class distinctions between nationalists and unionists in Ulster. The overwhelming majority of nationalists were not drawn from the province's landed, social élite and hence did not possess the leisure time to correspond widely or document the day's events or political gossip in a diary. Furthermore, few of the principal nationalist activists left large collections of papers. Indeed, nearly all the papers of Joseph Devlin, the leader of northern nationalism for the greater part of the period under analysis, were destroyed on his instruction following his death in 1934. The surviving correspondence of Devlin, and of his colleagues, makes no reference to women's influence or political participation.[4] In addition, there are no records that relate specifically to female nationalist associations in Ulster. This problem is exacerbated by the dearth of press comment regarding women's political work, which makes it very difficult, for example, to determine the extent of female electioneering.[5]

Despite these problems, it is clear that several pioneering and influential women with nationalist sympathies were active in Ulster from the 1890s and that they effected important work in the campaign for Irish independence. In addition, Ulster women took part in a variety of cultural, constitutional and republican nationalist organisations: the Nationalist Association of Irishwomen, the Irish Women's Centenary Union, the Gaelic League, the United Irish League, the Ancient Order of Hibernians, Inghinidhe na hÉireann and Cumann na mBan. And it is the diversity, extent and impact of these individual and collective activities that this chapter seeks to assess.

II

Yes Ireland shall be free
From the centre to the sea
And hurrah for liberty
Says the Shan Van Vocht[6]

It is widely recognised that Irish nationalism stagnated in the years following Parnell's death, as 'hopes seemed shattered, and all patriotic work for Ireland was completely arrested'.[7] In this atmosphere the establishment of a journal, *Shan Van Vocht*, which aimed to revive Irish nationalism, was likened by one contemporary observer as akin to 'a candle in the darkness'.[8] *Shan Van Vocht* was first published in Belfast in January 1896 by the two most prominent female nationalists in Ulster, Alice Milligan and Anna Johnston. Given the demise of nationalism, the paper's declared intent of gathering 'the scattered and disheartened few, . . . the faithful in exile, and the half hopeless at home . . . who in the wilderness, still had not entirely lost faith in Ireland's cause', was of considerable importance.[9] *Shan Van Vocht* was the first publication to air advanced nationalist views in Ireland.

Ultimately it succeeded in regenerating interest in the campaign for Irish independence: inspiring many people throughout Ireland to join the Gaelic League and participate in celebrations which were held to commemorate the centenary of the United Irishmen's rising of 1798.

Shan Van Vocht was not Milligan and Johnston's first literary venture. In 1895 they edited the first three editions of the *Northern Patriot*, a paper which was established by Belfast's Henry Joy McCracken Literary Society as an organ of expression for northern nationalism:

> to remind their brethren in the other provinces, that here in the darkest part of the land, surrounded by an overwhelming majority of opponents, few in number, but strong in faith, they are still fighting their corner and keeping the green flag flying.[10]

Under Milligan and Johnston's editorship, the *Northern Patriot* mirrored sentiments which were later reiterated by *Shan Van Vocht*: that factionalism amongst Irish nationalists was detrimental to the cause of independence and that united, popular action was necessary to counter political inertia. The paper claimed 'there is not one of us but can achieve something for the cause of Ireland in the humblest as in the highest sphere'.[11] In essence the *Patriot* aimed to create a common platform for nationalists who shared the objective of Irish independence, but disagreed on the methodology to be deployed in the fulfilment of this aim.

Milligan and Johnston's involvement with the *Patriot*, and later with *Shan Van Vocht*, represented a progression of their extensive nationalist interests. Alice Milligan, as one of the most active members of Belfast's Henry Joy McCracken Literary Society, was elected as its vice-president in August 1895. She was also a member of the Irish Literary Society and the Gaelic League and regularly lectured to a variety of nationalist associations in the city. Similarly, Anna Johnston was active in a variety of literary and political organisations, such as the Gaelic League, the Charles J. Kickham Literary Society and the Amnesty Association, of which her father was president.

For both women, as was the case for many female unionists, familial influence was an important instigator of political activity. Milligan and Johnston both came from backgrounds where enthusiasm for Irish culture and nationalism was prevalent. Alice Milligan's father was a renowned antiquarian and fellow of the Royal Irish Academy, and it appears that he instilled his enthusiasm for Irish culture in some his children. Of the Milligan siblings, Charlotte established the Irish Folk Song Society and Ernest was a member of the Gaelic League and founder of the Belfast branch of the Socialist Republican Society.[12] The experiences of the Milligan family also, however, accentuate the difficulties involved in overemphasising the impact of familial influences on the development of political sympathies, as one daughter, Edith, became a staunch unionist. Although the three Milligan sisters collaborated to produce an Irish song book, Alice described Edith as a 'rabid imperialist'.[13] And Edith's membership of the Ulster Women's Unionist Council and marriage to George Wheeler, a well-known unionist solicitor, aroused considerable tensions within the family circle. As a result, it appears that Edith regularly excluded Alice from family invitations and when the former Fenian leader, John O'Leary, was invited to stay at the Milligan's family home in order to address the '98 celebrations in Belfast, Edith aired her indignation: 'Imagine having *that* man in the house!'[14] Anna Johnston's familial background was more republican in sympathy than the cultural nationalism of the Milligan household. As the daughter of Robert Johnston, a Fenian veteran and Ulster's representative on the supreme council of the Irish Republican Brotherhood, it was claimed that Anna inherited not only nationalist sympathies, but 'a gift for politics'.[15]

In addition to the significance of familial support in nurturing nationalist sympathies, there was also an important social network that linked those with common political objectives in the city of Belfast. Alice Milligan and Anna Johnston lived in close proximity to one another on Belfast's Antrim Road and their neighbours included several prominent nationalists, including Bulmer Hobson, the secretary of the Irish Republican Brotherhood and later a vice-president of Sinn Féin, and Francis Joseph Bigger, a renowned historian and antiquarian. Bigger's home became the focus for the Gaelic literary and language revival in the city and nationalists often gathered at his house to debate and socialise. Milligan and Johnston were also acquainted with many prominent literary figures who became active in the Gaelic revival, including W.B. Yeats, Standish O'Grady and George Russell (AE). This social network, although not comparable to the workings of high society in unionist circles, nevertheless helped to counter isolation amongst northern nationalists.

Perhaps as a result of their somewhat sudden departure from the *Northern Patriot*, Milligan and Johnston ensured that they had complete control over their next literary venture. Editing *Shan Van Vocht* was a full-time concern. Indeed, Alice Milligan was described as 'drudging like a charwoman in the offices of the paper'[16] and in practical terms both women:

> managed it, edited it, paid for it, wrote a great part of it . . . It must have meant a great deal of devotion, of putting aside the gaieties and softness of life, of hard work, of courage under discouragement . . . These two girls did everything short of printing the paper, even addressing the copies sent out.[17]

Shan Van Vocht's content and rhetoric differed only slightly from the *Patriot*. Its articles were largely historical, literary and antiquarian, reflecting the stirrings of the Gaelic revival. The paper frequently interpreted Ireland's past allegorically, in an attempt to induce interest in contemporary politics, a trait that was a common characteristic of European literary renaissances.[18] Milligan and Johnston, both as accomplished poets and respected members of the revival movement, utilised their social contacts to persuade many prominent figures and writers, including a considerable number of women, to contribute to the paper: Alice and Mary Furlong, Barry Delaney, James Connolly, Kathleen Tynan, James Clarence Mangan, Edith Dickson, W.B. Yeats, and Douglas Hyde. Indeed, by 1899 the paper purported, with some justification, 'to have attracted the support of nearly all the best poets'.[19]

The editorials of *Shan Van Vocht* resolutely expressed the belief that Irish freedom could only be attained by popular and unified protest. The paper was, therefore, openly used as a platform to foster enthusiasm for Irish nationalism and counter the apathy and disunity that had characterised the independence movement for several years. The establishment of home reading circles, for example, was promoted to overcome the lack of library facilities, with Alice Milligan proffering advice on suitable reading material. The paper also publicised the activities of the amnesty movement and the Gaelic League, fully supporting the revival of the Irish language and the 'patriotic policy of de-Anglicising the Irish nation'.[20]

Celebrating the centenary of the United Irishmen's rising of 1798 was anticipated by many nationalists as an excellent opportunity to unite their movement and nurture 'a spirit of resolute patriotism by Irishmen who have hitherto stood apart, divided from each other by the supposed impassable lines of political differences'.[21] *Shan Van Vocht*, as a non-partisan journal and the leading publication of advanced nationalist beliefs, played an important role in rallying support for the centenary. But undertaking this role effected a definite shift in the paper's impetus. Prior to September 1896 *Shan Van Vocht* avoided commenting on current events, but thereafter there was heightened interest in the paper concerning Ireland's contemporary situation.[22] Indeed, through the pages of *Shan* Milligan and Johnston promoted a pro-active, constitutional campaign in order to procure Irish independence:

> Ireland's cause is high and holy . . . Stern and terrible deeds are often done and may justly be done in such a strife as ours, but this method of bombthrowing and blowing up buildings without aim or reason other than mere desire of vengeance is imbecile and wrong . . . Ireland has not yet fallen so low that anyone need take upon himself the *role* of avenger of a martyred land.[23]

Publicising the centenary and the need to establish a common nationalist platform became recurrent themes in the paper. And this stance became increasingly significant as factionalism emerged amongst the disparate components of Irish nationalism commemorating the 1798 rising. Milligan and Johnston heralded the centenary as an unprecedented opportunity for united action that, if not capitalised upon, would have dire repercussions for the future:

> If the Centenary of '98 is to glory and the men of Ireland are still found sulking apart, or still worse, closing in deadly fratricidal struggles, . . . our country's doom is sealed: she will be a slave, and deservedly a slave forever.[24]

With Milligan and Johnston's evident nationalist enthusiasm expressed via *Shan Van Vocht* and their participation in a proliferation of local nationalist associations, it was unsurprising that they were at the fore of organising Ulster's centennial celebrations. Both women attended meetings of the '98 Centenary Committee in Belfast from its inauguration in March 1897. At the first meeting of this body Alice Milligan, consistent with the pleas for unity published in *Shan*, forwarded two resolutions in an attempt to reconcile nationalist differences. Thus, she successfully pledged the committee to abstain from official communication with any political party and to oppose the election of MPs as office-bearers on its executive.[25] Milligan was subsequently appointed secretary of the Ulster executive of the '98 movement, which was perhaps indicative of her contemporary standing amongst northern nationalists.[26] Both women also took a prominent public role in the '98 celebrations, joining a small group, which included William Rooney and Maud Gonne, on a 'Gaelic crusade' around Ireland to lecture on the United Irishmen.[27]

The '98 centenary provided a specific focus for nationalists, especially in the aftermath of the popular unionist celebrations which were held to commemorate Queen Victoria's diamond jubilee in 1897. *Shan* highlighted many nationalists' belief that Victoria's sixty-year reign was responsible for exacerbating Ireland's economic deterioration: 'Millions have emigrated, millions have been evicted, millions have been starved to death.'[28] However, despite the existence of many shared nationalist grievances, the organisational structure of the centennial movement was complex. Faction fighting quickly emerged amongst male nationalists aligned to one particular party: Dillonite, anti-Parnellite, Healyite, or Redmondite.[29] This effectively hindered the development of the envisaged reunification of nationalist forces. Even though a compromise was reached with the establishment of an amalgamated organisation, the United Irish Centennial Association, the movement failed to overcome the personal rivalries that continued to mar the commemorations.

As partisanship escalated within the centennial movement, *Shan*'s appeal for unity was increasingly directed towards female nationalists. As both Alice Milligan and Anna Johnston were in positions of significant influence within nationalism they were able to inspire and organise other women to become politically active. From 1894, Milligan and Johnston, as the foremost female nationalists in the province, played a pivotal role in establishing branches of a formative women's organisation, the Nationalist Association of Irishwomen. Alice Milligan was appointed as first president of the Belfast branch and the association's work was publicised through *Shan*. Although no overall membership figures are available, some women in Ulster clearly shared Milligan and Johnston's zeal for Irish independence.[30] Members of the association included Margaret Pender, who regularly addressed meetings of the Young Ireland Society in Belfast. As the author of several popular nationalist novels, Pender was alleged to have stimulated 'the patriotic ardour of many who possibly would have grown weary of the struggle for Ireland's freedom', with her name being 'sufficient to bring a large audience together'.[31] Other women who joined the organisation were similarly committed to nationalist principles. Miss M. Craig, for instance, helped to establish a branch of the Gaelic League in Larne, Co. Antrim, and was described as 'a highly gifted and patriotic young northern lady, . . . who takes a deep interest in all matters affecting the progress of the patriotic cause'.[32]

There was a didactic element to the work of the Nationalist Association of Irishwomen that bore many similarities to the activities of the Gaelic League. In its central Belfast branch the study of Irish history, literature, music, art and language were all encouraged in order to foster nationalist sympathies:

> to create a taste for literary developments, and thereby sustain the prestige of Belfast in the national and literary efforts of the future . . . spreading some national ideas among the women of Ireland.[33]

Social events, such as musical and literary evenings, dances and conversaziones, were also held in an attempt to publicise the women's work and encourage membership. In addition, the Nationalist Association decorated nationalist graves in an attempt to nourish female patriotism:

> in the home . . . [to] make the names of our holy dead familiar to the women, the girls, the little children of Ireland, who could share in the beautiful and pious custom, the observing of which is now in the less capable hands of men.[34]

From 1896 *Shan Van Vocht* appealed for a national day for the decoration of patriot graves in Ulster to be initiated and an amalgamated committee of the Nationalist Association of Irishwomen, the Amnesty Association and the Charles J. Kickham Literary Society was formed to raise funds for wreaths, which were subsequently made in *Shan*'s Belfast office. Partially as a result of this impetus, the practice of patriot grave decoration became increasingly popular during the '98 centennial celebrations.[35]

The Nationalist Association of Irishwomen seems to have been renamed the Irish Women's Centenary Union in an attempt to promote harmonious celebrations amongst women commemorating the '98 rising. In Ulster, female nationalists laboured to re-create a sense of solidarity amongst disparate nationalist factions, though they were determined to unite 'the memory of the dead with faith in the living, our pride in the past, with hope for the future'.[36] It appears that women embraced the wider objectives of the nationalist movement concerning independence and the Irish-Ireland revival, but as a result of continued female disenfranchisement were less aligned to any specific nationalist faction. Indeed, it was claimed that women could avoid factionalism, as they were 'not called upon to have any opinion whatsoever as to who has the right to speak for Ireland in the British parliament'.[37] As Milligan and Johnston poignantly asked in the pages of their paper: 'Is it not a fortunate thing that the better half (numerically, of course . . .) of the population of Ireland is not involved in the difference of the polling booths?'[38]

In an attempt to publicise the aims of the Irish Women's Centenary Union, a circular from nine women was issued in November 1897. This emphasised that, in honouring the martyrs of '98, the organisation's intention was not to intrude on the sphere of existing centennial committees, but to initiate new work that was intrinsically suited to women. Members of the Nationalist Association of Irishwomen had already performed some of the work highlighted by the circular, such as decorating patriot graves, but reference was also made to several new areas for female involvement:

> the collecting of memorials of '98, and the publication of records, and doubtless it will be found possible to arrange in Belfast an exhibition of '98 relics and portraits, combined with a sale of home industries, and concerts of Irish music.[39]

The establishment of the Irish Women's Centenary Union provided a secure and neutral ground for the execution of these tasks, which Milligan and Johnston believed was indicative of what could be attained by rising above partisanship: 'it is surely a hopeful and healing sign to see a number of Irish women working together on a high and patriotic platform above the strife and turmoil'.[40]

Encouraged by *Shan Van Vocht* and the Irish Women's Centenary Union, two female '98 commemoration clubs were established in Belfast: the Mary Ann McCracken Decoration Club and Maids of Erin Centenary Club. It is unclear whether any more female centenary associations were formed, but the pivotal role of Alice Milligan and Anna Johnston in defining a role for women in the nationalist movement and fostering united action at least amongst some Ulster women should be recognised.[41] The pervasive influence of these two women was also apparent in the objectives of the Irish Women's Centenary Union. This organisation echoed sentiments previously expressed in *Shan Van Vocht*: that women were not only responsible for 'moulding the minds of the growing generations of the Irish race' but should also endeavour to heal the rifts between male nationalists and to 'give them safe guidance out of the hurly-burly of the political faction fight'.[42] In Ulster, Milligan and Johnston defended the establishment of the Irish Women's Centenary Union as the most effective way to encourage female participation in the '98 commemorations. But this was also interpreted as a pragmatic measure, as *Shan* claimed that women were less likely to be scrutinised, and thus prohibited, by the authorities. Some nationalists amongst Belfast's commercial class also subscribed to this view, choosing to be represented at the centennial celebrations by female family members because they feared that identification with the movement could alienate Protestant custom.[43] The comparative success of the women's centenary celebrations in Ulster was a direct consequence of their determination to overcome factionalism, but maintaining *Shan Van Vocht*'s non-party stance became increasingly difficult. Indeed, as no financial support for the paper was forthcoming from any particular nationalist grouping, the paper was obliged to close in April 1899. *Shan Van Vocht* was subsequently usurped by Arthur Griffith's paper, the *United Irishman*, although this seems to have occurred without animosity, as Milligan and Johnston sent a list of their subscribers to Griffith in Dublin.

In *Shan Van Vocht* Milligan and Johnston succeeded in establishing a popular journal with a non-party bias to connect various literary, cultural and nationalist associations such as the Gaelic League, Sinn Féin and the Gaelic Athletic Association. But the paper's import also extended beyond Ireland. It had an American agent, correspondence was published from readers in America, Canada, South Africa and Quebec and it was mailed 'all over the world, wherever the kindly Irish were to be found'.[44] *Shan Van Vocht* was, therefore, highly influential in popularising the Gaelic revival movement throughout and beyond Ireland, bringing 'many a soul . . . to the charms of the old ways'.[45] The work of Milligan and Johnston, and that of their contributors, reached a very wide audience, fundamentally preparing the ground for the 'Gaelic harvest' that soon followed.[46] As one contemporary, Bulmer Hobson, acknowledged, the paper's espousal of advanced nationalist thought brought him 'for the first time in touch with the new forces that were beginning to stir in Ireland'.[47] Indeed, throughout nationalist realms the paper was widely accredited with reviving an interest in nationalism which had been dormant since Parnell's death. As Maud Gonne wrote: 'we were full of almost envious admiration of some members of the *Shan Van Voght* [sic], the daring little paper'.[48] *An Phoblacht* also recognised the paper's significance in reawakening latent nationalist demands for Irish independence:

> The unperishable spirit of freedom which lay dormant owing to centuries of oppression and the despondency caused by the Fenian failure of 1867 was once more revived . . . [This was] largely due to the publication of a stirring and fearless little organ known by the appropriate name of An Sean Bhean Bhocht (Shan Van Vocht) . . . This little paper voiced the gospel of nationality fearlessly and unmistakably.[49]

In addition to *Shan*'s influence, Milligan and Johnston also defined a role for women within the nationalist movement that was of considerable consequence. The establishment of the Nationalist Association of Irishwomen and the Irish Women's Centenary Union designated specific social and educational activities as suitable for women's involvement, activities which were later adopted by several other nationalist associations.

By April 1899, when *Shan Van Vocht* ceased publication, the Irish-Ireland revival and the Gaelic League were in full working order. The latter was established in 1893 by Eoin MacNeill and Douglas Hyde to facilitate the revival of Gaelic language and culture as living entities that would constitute the foundation of Irish life. The league, unlike its antiquarian predecessors the Celtic Literary Society and the National Literary Society, was the first organisation of its type to admit women as members. Indeed, female involvement was perceived as fundamental to its progress, as the league asserted that the Irish language belonged to all, regardless of age, class or sex.[50] Its progressive attitude to female membership did, however, produce some criticism from the Catholic Church and local clerics frequently refused permission for branches of the league to meet in their church halls if mixed sex classes were held.[51]

In Belfast there had been some interest in reviving the Irish language before the formal establishment of the Gaelic League in 1893. The success of P.J. O'Shea's Irish language classes, held in conjunction with Nationalist Field Clubs, from 1890 provided the motivation for establishing a branch of the league in the city in 1895. The league's membership in Ulster, as elsewhere in Ireland, was urban based and drawn largely from the upper-middle classes. By the early years of the twentieth century there were an estimated 500 Gaelic Leaguers in the north-east of the country.[52] Given these figures, the association could not be referred to as popular. This is reinforced by an analysis of the number of Irish speakers in the province recorded in the 1911 census: 2.3 per cent of Ulster's population, representing 29,423 individuals.[53] In Ulster, therefore, it is clear that the league never maximised its potential support base. This was not peculiar to the province, as throughout the country it was apparent that Irish interests only enthused a minority, 'attracting idealistic young men and women who were regarded as eccentrics by the general population'.[54] In spite of this, A.E. Cleary claimed that women, 'though more shy at coming' to meetings, often became 'the most earnest and useful members'.[55] The league's journal, *Claidheamh Soluis* (Sword of Light), also emphasised that its female members represented 'the more eager and serious-minded women of the town' and alluded to the importance of social events in inducing female participation by claiming that 'a few [women] who like dancing or eager-minded men' enrolled their support.[56]

Helen Macnaghten, the co-founder of Bushmills Suffrage Society, was also an active member of the league. Writing in 1910, she revealed not only her personal enthusiasm for the organisation but also the emotive allure of participating in a movement of national importance: 'no one who cares for Ireland could keep outside the League . . . there are now 500,000 Gaelic Leaguers in Ireland so we are growing powerful'.[57] Macnaghten's private correspondence also illuminates how she utilised her own social network in order to generate support for the league. She regularly sent literature relating to the work of the league to her friend, Anne Richardson, the vice-principal of Westfield College in London. Indeed, the correspondence between these two women reveals that Macnaghten compelled her friend to join the league and give financial assistance to fund both its activities and continued expansion:

> It is thee I want to join us before I die . . . will thee not think a little of thine own country now, I am sure it is that thee will be asked about on the day of judgement and it will trouble me indeed if thee has nothing to say.[58]

Lack of any more correspondence relating to the Ulster activities of the league prevents an analysis of how commonplace Macnaghten's appeal was, but, given Milligan and Johnston's use of social contacts to encourage contributions to *Shan* from the leading figures of the revival movement, it may be that this was fairly commonplace.

In addition to Macnaghten's proselytising work for the Gaelic League, many other female members executed important educational and organisational work. The nature of women's work in the league was very similar to that performed by the Nationalist Association of Irishwomen and the Irish Women's Centenary Union. Alice Milligan, for example, freed from the commitment of editing *Shan Van Vocht*, worked as a travelling lecturer for the league in Cork, Londonderry, Antrim and Donegal between 1904 and 1906 and was nominated to *Coiste Gnotha*, the organisation's highest ruling committee.[59] She was also appointed as a delegate of the league's Belfast branch to ask the Society for the Extension of University Teaching to establish a course of lectures on Irish literature and language.[60] Although the success of this request is unknown, Milligan's nomination suggests that women were given considerable responsibility within the Gaelic League. Further evidence for this is provided by Margaret Dobbs' appointment to the organising committee of the Glenariff *feis* in 1904. Dobbs, a playwright, Irish scholar and dedicated member of the league, was closely associated with establishing and administering Irish language schools on Rathlin Island, Co. Antrim, and in Gortahork, Co. Donegal. She, like many members of the league, believed that Ireland without the Irish language was 'quite meaningless'.[61] In more general terms, the female members of the league were given responsibility for organising the league's social activities, which suggests that there was a division of tasks on gender lines. Indeed Jenny Wyse Power claimed that this aspect of the league's work was almost wholly in the hands of its female members:

> who by absorbing the Irish traditions, and themselves giving expression to Gaelic ideas and culture, influenced in no small degree the growing effort to wean the people from an Anglicisation which had gone all too far.[62]

Although the league was inherently non-political in nature, this became increasingly difficult to maintain. In 1910 Helen Macnaghten, for example, alluded to the difficulties of separating the work of the league from wider demands for Irish independence. Even though Macnaghten was personally 'convinced' that the league was working on non-political lines, she highlighted the difficulties of maintaining this position, claiming that a number of branches had been suppressed for discussing politics.[63] Furthermore, local league branches in Ulster were described by the pro-unionist press as:

> hotbeds of political and religious agitation. Their meetings are usually held after mass, or on a Sunday . . . and generally the local curate is in the chair . . . bristling with hatred of England . . . with exhortations to his hearers to hold fast to the religion and language of their fathers.[64]

Although the bias of this report is clear, the non-political stance of the league was coming under increasing pressure and from 1913 enthusiasm for the association decreased throughout Ireland. This occurred largely as a result of internal discord between the league's president, Douglas Hyde, and an extremist faction that had succeeded in displacing the organisation's non-political stance by 1915. Thereafter the league could only be described as representing the cultural annex of the national independence movement.[65]

The Gaelic League's admittance of women into its ranks on an equitable basis to men was undoubtedly progressive and female members of the league appear to have conducted work of a similar nature to its male members. However, women were also given responsibility for organising the social programme of the league and this work bore a striking resemblance to that of the formative women's cultural nationalist organisations in Ulster: the Nationalist Association of Irishwomen and the Irish Women's Centenary Union. By the end of the nineteenth century, therefore, in both unionist and cultural nationalist circles, a gendered aspect to women's political role was emerging. Was a similar trend appearing within the constitutional facets of Irish nationalism?

III

In comparison with the cultural aspects of Irish nationalism, only limited opportunities were available for women to become involved in constitutional nationalism at the turn of the century. It seems that nationalist politicians, such as John Redmond, were slower to recognise the potential of women's political work than their unionist counterparts. This, coupled with the religious composition of Ulster, meant that women's involvement in constitutional nationalism was never numerically comparable to that of unionists. Nevertheless, in Ulster women joined several constitutional nationalist associations. Moreover, there are many similarities both in the type of work which women performed and in the impact which female enfranchisement had on the political considerations of both nationalist and unionist leaders.

The United Irish League (UIL), established by William O'Brien in 1898 to agitate for land reform, was subsumed into the reunited Irish Parliamentary Party in June 1900.[66] In Ulster the UIL succeeded in reconciling the diverse strands of constitutional nationalism and by December 1917 had an estimated 5,955 members.[67] Women were not permitted to join this organisation, but in Belfast there were two ladies' branches which were active from the early years of the twentieth century.[68] There is little information concerning the purpose or activities of these two groups and the absence of any organisational or private records makes assessment difficult. The *Irish News* was the only paper to make any reference to the existence of these female associations, but provides no indication as to their inauguration or size.[69] In 1905, however, the northern nationalist leader Joseph

Devlin commended the support which had been forthcoming from women over the past 'trying nine years . . . All through that time the ladies had given assistance and encouragement, both material and moral.'[70] This dates women's auxiliary support, whether performed in an individual or group capacity, to the mid 1890s. It is possible that the establishment of the United Irish League at the very time when the Irish Women's Centenary Union was winding down its activities provided the stimulus for this group to reorganise as a female ancillary of the UIL. Certainly the ladies' branches of the United Irish League undertook many of the social functions which the Centenary Union and its predecessor, the Nationalist Association of Irishwomen, performed. This is apparent in the *Irish News*' account of the Belfast Ladies' Branch of the UIL during 1905, where it noted that women had 'always been singularly successful in the organisation and carrying out of the various social functions held under its auspices'.[71]

In addition to this work, women also became involved in fund-raising activities, organising a week-long sale of goods to secure funds for nationalist registration work in June 1905. This event was opened by John Dillon, nationalist MP and later leader of the Irish Parliamentary Party. Dillon was accompanied by his wife and she briefly addressed the assembled audience, commending women's work and emphasising the positive example that it set to women in the rest of the country:

> Ladies, we in the other parts of Ireland cannot do better than to follow the example you have shown us of how women can be courageous and true to the highest principles of Irish Nationalism and fearless in living up to those ideas.[72]

This sale, and the numerous female names included in the lists of collectors and subscribers that were published periodically in the *Irish News*, illustrate that some Ulster women were certainly willing to contribute financially to the nationalist cause. Although there is little information concerning the specifics of the female branches of the UIL, their very existence necessitates a refinement of the view that all constitutional nationalist associations were exclusively male and bereft of female support.

Women's participation in constitutional nationalism, however, always lacked a province-wide organisational structure similar to that developed by the Ulster Women's Unionist Council. This lack of organisation was so apparent that it aroused some press comment in the early twentieth century. An article in the *Irish News*, published in March 1905, alluded to 'the want of organisation prevent[ing] Irish women from associating themselves with the public aspirations of their country'.[73] The gradual, but deliberate, cultivation of unionism as a popular movement led Carson to advise and abet the Ulster Women's Unionist Council from its initiation in 1911. Nationalists, however, did not have the same political motivation to encourage women's political participation. The 1910 election left the Irish Parliamentary Party (IPP) relatively secure in its political alliance with the minority Liberal government. They were, therefore, confident that a third Home Rule Bill would be introduced to the Commons, with the removal of the House of Lords' power of veto in the following year further boosting their optimism. With assured parliamentary support for their political agenda, the IPP did not need to cultivate female support. The party leader, John Redmond, for example, only addressed his first meeting of nationalist women in October 1914. He even confessed to being somewhat overwhelmed by the exclusively female audience assembled at the Clonard Picture House on Belfast's Falls Road: 'I have never addressed a meeting of women before. (Cheers and laughter.) The effect upon me is somewhat awe-inspiring, but I feel I should get used to it in time.'[74] Redmond, accompanied by the northern nationalist leader Joseph Devlin, was warmly received by the women at the meeting, with his arrival allegedly marking 'the signal for a great outburst of cheering, the audience rising and waving handkerchiefs . . . Not a seat of the spacious building was vacant; and a great number were perforce refused admission.'[75] The absence of any female nationalist leaders was, however, underlined by the fact that Thomas Maguire, a Belfast solicitor, presided at this meeting. Norah McCloskey, secretary of the committee responsible for organising this event, did deliver a short address but this was only to esteem Mrs Redmond's supportive role in helping her husband carry 'the weighty burthen' of political office and made no reference to politics.[76]

In concert with the effect of nationalists' political considerations, women's somewhat muted role in constitutional nationalism may also be related to the opposition of the Catholic Church to women's participation in public affairs. Clerical involvement in Irish nationalism was not a new phenomenon. Throughout the nineteenth century the clergy were very politically active: registering nationalist voters, presiding at political meetings, canvassing voters and selecting candidates. In short, clerical influence was an accepted feature of nationalist politics. The existence of a relatively small, educated,

Catholic middle class in Ulster led to a dearth of nationalist lay leadership and this appears to have reinforced the significance of clerical leadership in the province. Thus it has been claimed, with some justification, that the clergy 'had almost taken control' of northern nationalism by the 1890s.[77] The Catholic Church may have undertaken the role of defender of the religious minority in Ulster, but this also guaranteed conservatism with regard to women's social intercourse.[78] One female constitutional nationalist association was established, however, which not only enshrined this conservatism, but also assigned a specific political role for women: the Ladies' Auxiliary of the Ancient Order of Hibernians (AOH).

In Ulster the northern nationalist leader Joseph Devlin recognised the political potential of the hibernians as a popular, grassroots nationalist organisation in the late nineteenth century. Devlin became president of the AOH and succeeded in harnessing this organisation to the United Irish League to provide nationalism with the support it had previously lacked in Ulster.[79] Established in 1910, the Ladies' Auxiliary represented one component of a hibernian revival that was orchestrated by Devlin in an attempt to establish 'a sort of Hibernian family circle'.[80] With the declared objective of defending Catholic interests, the male and female branches of the AOH were less avowedly political than either the UUC or UWUC. Hibernians, however, justified their political activities in the following way: 'from time to time public questions on which it may be our bounden duty to take part in politics [arose], when grave issues for the nation's future are at stake'.[81] As a result of this somewhat ambiguous position, the hibernians electioneered and prescribed definite political duties for its female members to perform – many of which were similar to the work executed by members of the UWUC.

Hibernianism was a comparatively popular movement. By the time Redmond addressed his first women's meeting in Belfast in 1914 there were reportedly several hundred branches of the Ladies' Auxiliary throughout Ireland, which claimed to represent all social classes from 'the lady of means to the domestic worker'.[82] Female hibernianism, like its male counterpart, was strongest in Ulster, where the order superseded the United Irish League as the primary nationalist association. But after the 1916 rising the diffusion of northern nationalist support between the republicanism of Sinn Féin and the constitutional nationalism of Devlin, the UIL and the AOH was significant. In Ulster the hibernian association survived the challenge posed by republicanism and, as northern constitutional nationalists lacked any alternative organisation, it experienced something of a revival during the early 1920s. In essence the order represented 'the only organisation the Catholics had and that its membership was, on that account, rapidly increasing'.[83] This was reflected in the number of women's branches established in the province. References to overall membership figures of the Ladies' Auxiliary are scarce, but the figures (see Table 1) published in the *Hibernian Journal* in 1923 represent the first available statistical analysis of the association.

Table 1: Branches of the Ladies' Auxiliary of the Ancient Order of Hibernians in Ulster, 1923[84]

COUNTY	TOTAL BRANCHES	LADIES' AUXILIARY
Antrim	31	4
Belfast	31	10
Londonderry	47	4
Armagh	51	10
Down	47	10
Fermanagh	33	2
Tyrone	56	2
Total	296	42

In 1923 14 per cent of the Ulster branches of the AOH were female and by 1925 there were reportedly over four times as many branches of the Ladies' Auxiliary in the province than elsewhere in the country.[85] In more general terms it appears that familial connections were as important in encouraging women's support for hibernianism as with unionism: mothers, wives, daughters and sisters of male hibernians were alleged to have joined the Ladies' Auxiliary. The *Hibernian Journal* further highlighted the significance of family ties by claiming that 'no one has supported the Order with more determination than the widows of deceased members who encourage their sons to follow the example of their fathers'.[86]

From Table 1 it is apparent that there were pockets of popular female support for hibernianism in Belfast, Armagh and Down. This does not totally equate with the provincial strength of male hibernianism. However, lack of information concerning the leaders or membership of individual branches of the Ladies' Auxiliary makes it difficult to explain the geographical distribution of female support. Only in Belfast can the comparative strength of female hibernianism be effectively explained. This was a result of working-class allegiance to Joseph Devlin, the constitutional nationalist leader and president of the hibernian movement. This support was especially marked in Devlin's West Belfast constituency, where he was regarded by both sexes as a champion of working-class rights. From his election to parliament in 1906 Devlin supported various measures of reform which alleviated the lot of the working classes, such as the extension of the National Health Insurance Acts to Ireland which provided sickness, unemployment, maternity, disability and sanatorium benefits. He also favoured improved working conditions, the introduction of an eight-hour working day, paid holiday provision and equal wages for women workers.[87] Press coverage of one of Devlin's election meetings records the level of female enthusiasm: the balcony of St Mary's Hall in West Belfast was 'crammed with women, many of whom waved flags'.[88] Devlin also received numerous presents from female mill workers in his constituency and the inscription attached to one gift epitomised the level of trust which women placed in the northern nationalist leader: 'the working women and children who never forsake a friend . . . doffers, spinners, weavers, humble workers, say we will never desert you'.[89] With this level of female support it was perhaps unsurprising that a social held by hibernian women on Belfast's Falls Road was allegedly 'taxed to its utmost capacity, so great was the attendance'.[90]

The Ancient Order of Hibernians claimed that its attitude towards women was progressive and that it was the first Irish national association 'to break with the tradition that the less women interfered with public life the better'.[91] But the AOH essentially undertook the role of protector of Catholic interests and thus epitomised the Church's view of women's allotted social role, a role that did not extend to elective public office. Hence women were not encouraged to stand as electoral candidates either in municipal or national assemblies and the auxiliary's relationship with male hibernians remained one of mutual assistance and co-operation. Each female member was encouraged to aspire to education in order to facilitate 'enlightenment, and uplifting by every means in her power those whose ignorance and misery drag their country down'.[92] From this statement it is clear that women were assigned a specific role within the hibernian movement. It was in the realm of exercising 'true Christian charity' that women were initially deemed useful: visiting the sick, caring for 'distressed brethren and alleviating the lot of [their] . . . poorer sisters'.[93] But, from these philanthropic beginnings, the scope of the Ladies' Auxiliary gradually increased. By 1915, for example, the organisation was believed to possess a 'latent power' in distributing propaganda and combating the sale of undesirable literature.[94] In addition, the charitable interests of the women's auxiliary extended to campaigning against intemperance, securing employment for young Catholic girls and moral rescue work. The organisation also purported to offer benefits to its own female members, with the declared object of promoting their spiritual and temporal welfare and providing for their social and intellectual intercourse. This prescribed role within the hibernian movement was, however, significantly changed by the passage of the Representation of the People Act in 1918.

The AOH's response to women's enfranchisement bore a striking similarity to that of unionists. Like unionists, hibernians had, 'without exception, put the cause of Home Rule – which means the welfare of Irish women as well as men – before the 'Votes for Women' campaign'.[95] But once female enfranchisement was attained, members of the Ladies' Auxiliary were depicted as representing 'what is best and strongest in the Catholic womanhood of the nation [possessing] a power they never had before in determining by constitutional means the course of legislation'.[96] After 1918 the *Hibernian Journal* refuted the idea that women had no place in public life, emphasising the importance of the female role in protecting the family: 'woman is man's helpmate; . . . everything that concerns his life and the life of the family is her concern'.[97] Furthermore, during 1918 to 1919 a rash of articles defining women's role in the organisation appeared in the journal as the AOH attempted to foster female allegiance to constitutional nationalism. In addition to woman's duty to protect her co-religionists and her family and care for the weaker elements of society, the *Hibernian Journal* also alluded to the educational benefits of joining the ladies' association. Attending meetings, for example, was claimed to 'break the monotony of pursuing household duties . . . and for the business girl will give an idea of how business concerns are conducted'.[98] By September 1919 the progress and continued expansion of the auxiliary was estimated to be of great importance in the development of the organisation:

> Women are now admitted into practically all the professions; they have a voice in the country, too long denied them; their administrative ability, as well as their aptitude to learn, were amply demonstrated during the war. There is no reason why their power for good in the Hibernian movement should not be availed of to the utmost.[99]

In essence, the vote prompted a serious reconsideration of the role of women within constitutional nationalism. Thus, after 1918 female hibernians were seen as capable of protecting Catholicism:

> the protection of our race and the achievement of the freedom of our beloved land are not the special prerogative of any sex or section . . . The social companionship and friendship acquired by membership of the A.O.H., and the facilities for social enjoyment and mental improvement provided . . . should not be the monopoly of the male members.[100]

Like the Ulster Unionist Council, the AOH was also aware of the need to make internal changes in its hierarchical structure in order to fully maximise female membership and ensure that women's votes were cast in the right direction. As a result, moves were made to recognise 'a member of the Ladies' Auxiliary in every sense as a Hibernian, and entitled to [the] . . . fullest confidence and every sympathy'.[101] The rules of the AOH were subsequently amended in 1919 to sanction the attendance of representatives from local branches of the Ladies' Auxiliary at county board meetings. In that year further changes were implemented when women became entitled to share the full financial benefits which membership of the organisation afforded to its male members in terms of loans, holiday funds and endowment assurance.

The escalating division amongst northern nationalists also encouraged a reconsideration of women's role within hibernianism. The Representation of the People Act was implemented at the very time when both the United Irish League and the Ancient Order of Hibernians were experiencing serious political competition from Sinn Féin. Joseph Devlin was forced to admit that it was a struggle to maintain support for constitutional nationalism: 'The whole job is an exceedingly difficult one. The want of machinery, the lack of funds, and the difficulty of raising enthusiasm are making our position an extremely hard one.'[102] With these internal problems it was perhaps doubly important for Devlin to use the Ladies' Auxiliary as a means of securing the support of newly enfranchised women for constitutional nationalism. In spite of these difficulties, the changes that occurred within nationalism, as within unionism, were successful in rallying women's support. Hence the Ladies' Auxiliary remained the most popular women's nationalist association in Ulster throughout the inter-war years.

Also, in concert with unionists, throughout the 1920s there were increasing occurrences of co-operation between male and female hibernians. In July 1925, for instance, a mixed sex committee organised the biennial conference of the AOH in Belfast and on occasion members of the Ladies' Auxiliary donned 'handsome regalia' to parade alongside their male counterparts.[103] Women also became increasingly active in the AOH's social programme: joining Belfast's Hibernian Drama, Literary and Debating Societies, regularly attending dances and outings, whilst classes specifically designed to appeal to women became very popular.[104] It was therefore as a direct consequence of women's enfranchisement and competition from Sinn Féin that women's role within hibernianism changed. After 1918 women were depicted as 'a powerful asset', recognised as an important source of political labour to help counter Sinn Féin by conducting canvassing work for constitutional nationalist candidates and preparing electoral lists. This type of work, coupled with the hibernians' reaction to the establishment of a female electoral majority in Ulster in 1928, bore many similarities to the UWUC and the UUC respectively. Hibernians claimed that the 'fair sex is now a mighty power in the body politic' and attempted to secure newly enfranchised female voters' support for constitutional nationalism by endorsing a scheme to reorganise and increase membership of the Ladies' Auxiliary in 1928.[105] Throughout the following year several new ladies' branches were established in Armagh and Down and the AOH's efforts to enlist women's support continued into the 1930s. In 1936, for example, every male division of the organisation was urged to form a ladies' association in recognition that women had an intrinsic place within the hibernian movement:

> Every Irish Catholic woman has a special interest in advancing the Faith, in safeguarding the religious birthright of children who are in danger of falling into the hands of the proselytiser, in helping to look after the widows and the orphans . . . [and] female discarded prisoners: the instruction of young mothers in humble homes in the care of newly born children . . . The extension of the franchise makes women now as potent a force in the State as the other sex.[106]

Joseph Devlin initially cultivated women's support for hibernianism as part of a campaign to popularise nationalism throughout the province. The very term 'auxiliary' epitomised the part that 'sister Hibernians' were called upon to perform, with their work being interpreted as an extension of high religious ideals and familial duty.[107] However, the AOH redefined women's role as a direct consequence of female enfranchisement and competition from republicanism. The *Hibernian Journal* may have continued to promote the domestic sphere as the realm where women exercised a refining influence by 'moulding the character of each new generation', but women's status within the movement was undeniably enhanced.[108] Thus, after 1918 the Ladies' Auxiliary was treated as an essential component of hibernianism with specific philanthropic, didactic, electoral and organisational duties to perform.

IV

Woman rushes in where man fears to tread, and makes him foolish . . . I am weary living in a world ruled by men with mouse-hearts and monkey brains and I want a change.[109]

The diversity of nationalist organisations is further underlined by women's involvement in republican nationalism. To counter the somewhat *ad hoc* nature of women's involvement in constitutional nationalism at the turn of the century, Maud Gonne initiated a separate female nationalist association, Inghinidhe na hÉireann (Daughters of Erin), in 1900. Alice Milligan and Anna Johnston continued their work to involve Ulster women in the nationalist movement in the early twentieth century by helping Gonne to establish this society. Johnston, for example, attended Inghinidhe's inaugural meeting in Dublin on 12 October 1900 and was subsequently elected as one of its vice-presidents. This appointment was perhaps to be expected, as she had previously served as one of four vice-presidents of the Patriotic Treat Committee, an informal women's association which provided the impetus for the establishment of Inghinidhe na hÉireann.[110] Although nationalist women, in Belfast at least, had previously been organised into the Nationalist Association of Irishwomen, the Irish Women's Centenary Union and ladies' branches of the UIL, Inghinidhe na hÉireann was established in response to women's continued exclusion on the basis of gender from nationalist organisations such as the Celtic Literary Society and the National League, the successor to the Land League and predecessor of Sinn Féin. According to Gonne, Inghinidhe was 'a meeting of all the girls who, like myself resented being excluded, as women from National Organisations. Our object was to work for the complete independence of Ireland.'[111]

Inghinidhe na hÉireann sought to popularise nationalism by co-operating with men who shared their aspirations and thereby refute claims that women's interests and capabilities were 'bounded by frying pans and fashion plates'.[112] Inghinidhe also aimed to promote Irish as a living language, developing a combined cultural and political agenda that was more radical in intent than that of the Gaelic League. Its members, for instance, had to be Irish by birth or descent and take a pledge to work towards Irish independence. However, as with its political opposite, the Ulster Women's Unionist Council, Inghinidhe na hÉireann also considered women's emancipation to be of less importance than its national political objectives. One initiative, however, which separated Inghinidhe from both its predecessors and contemporaries was the publication of *Bean na hÉireann*. This monthly journal was established in 1908 and was the first Irish nationalist publication aimed specifically at women. It was through the pages of *Bean na hÉireann* that the organisation expressed its support for the use of physical force to procure Irish independence.

Little information exists concerning the size, geographical distribution or specific activities of individual branches of Inghinidhe na hÉireann. It is therefore difficult to assess the size and activities of the Ulster branches of this organisation. What is discernible is that the extreme nationalism advocated by Inghinidhe na hÉireann was too nonconformist to attract popular support. For instance, a branch of Inghinidhe established in Belfast in 1903 by Miss O'Farrell developed into one of the most belligerent associations in Ireland, holding regular rifle practice to add a practical dimension to Inghinidhe's revolutionary message. But such activities were too radical for many women and it appears that only a minority participated in these lessons, although all members of the Belfast branch received instruction on the cleaning and loading of weapons.[113] Inghinidhe was well aware of the limited appeal of its aggressive nationalism, but remained optimistic that:

> the time will come when every woman in Ireland will believe . . . that National and Separate Independence is our heritage, and it is to be won, by the courage of our hearts and the strength of our aims. Indirectly we have benefited our own sex . . . the expression of militant nationalism must do much to command the respect of men, and compel them to readjust their views on women as a possible force in the fight against foreign dominion.[114]

Despite this confidence, and even though the association sought to counter apathy by fostering a spirit of female comradeship, encouraging its members to meet in each other's homes, Inghinidhe did not develop into a popular organisation. It remained a collection of interested individuals, rather than a united association working towards a singular objective. Nevertheless, the organisation did motivate some women to embark upon further political activity in the aftermath of the '98 centenary and was responsible for an increased level of female participation in the ranks of the emergent Sinn Féin party, which was developing within the Gaelic League. In Ulster, however, this development was of less consequence than elsewhere in the country. Until 1916 Sinn Féin remained comparatively unpopular in the province, as the majority of northern nationalists remained aligned to the Irish Parliamentary Party. But by that date there had been further reorganisation within the ranks of female nationalism and Inghinidhe na hÉireann had become a branch of Cumann na mBan (Irishwomen's Council).[115]

The Irish Republican Brotherhood reacted to the escalating militarism of Ulster unionism and attempted to undermine the political credibility of the Irish Parliamentary Party by establishing the Irish Volunteers in November 1913. Under the presidency of Eoin MacNeill, the volunteers' manifesto declared that there would be tasks for women to perform. The new women's ancillary association formed to execute this work was Cumann na mBan.[116] The allotted roles for women in the Irish Volunteers and Ulster Volunteer Force had much in common. Women in both Cumann na mBan and the UVF possessed ancillary status, providing first aid, home nursing, drill and signalling instruction to their members and fund-raising extensively to equip the volunteers. However, women had no control over how these funds were disseminated. Like the female members of the UVF, it was to the members of Cumann na mBan that responsibility was assigned for 'taking care of the details of house-keeping such as running messages, sewing uniforms and wrapping bandages so that the men could be about the greater business of fermenting an Irish nation'.[117] There were also many similarities in the rhetoric used by Cumann na mBan and the UWUC to maximise support for their respective campaigns. Both associations focused on the security of their homes and protecting their children. Thus Cumann na mBan proclaimed that:

> the liberty of the enslavement of the nation affects every home and every individual man and woman and child in the country . . . Is not the liberty of the children of Ireland, the life-blood of the nation, at stake? . . . [Women] . . . only want to be organised. Wherever the men of Ireland are fighting for liberty they will not hesitate to help them.

> From the very nature of things the role of women will be different from that of the men, and rightly so. It is not ours to undertake physically and directly the defence of the nation . . . They [women] are here because they fear for the liberty of the home, and . . . the blow aimed at the freedom of the men of Ireland strikes the women and children as well.[118]

The domestic milieu of Cumann na mBan was also apparent in their fund-raising efforts to arm the Irish Volunteers:

> Each rifle we put in their hands will represent to us a bolt fastened behind the door of some Irish home to keep out the hostile stranger. Each cartridge will be a watchdog to fight for the sanctity of the hearth.[119]

Each branch of Cumann was affiliated to a local battalion of Irish Volunteers and, although the organisation remained theoretically independent, military orders from volunteer captains were adhered to and branches were instructed to identify with the volunteers' work in every possible way.[120] The ancillary status of Cumann na mBan, enshrined since its inception in 1913, changed little over time. This became particularly apparent in June 1914, when, after John Redmond successfully demanded twenty-five representatives from the Irish Parliamentary Party to be admitted onto the executive of the Irish Volunteers, Cumann na mBan made no attempt to appeal for a similar representation.[121]

In Belfast Nora Connolly, daughter of the socialist republican leader James Connolly, was responsible for establishing a branch of Cumann na mBan.[122] As was apparent for many nationalist and unionist women, siblings frequently shared kindred political views. Nora Connolly's sister, Ina, served as president of Belfast's Cumann and both women admitted to having been significantly influenced by their father's political beliefs. Indeed, James Connolly actively encouraged his daughters' political interests by taking them as children to meetings and discussing political issues at home, when:

> he never just gave answers, but helped her [Nora] puzzle her way out; and showed his disappointment if she ever accepted a statement without a torrent of 'whys' and 'buts' and 'ifs'.[123]

As a direct consequence of Nora and Ina Connolly's familial connections, they were at the very core of nationalist politics. Both women were involved in a proliferation of nationalist associations in

Belfast, including the first branch of the Young Republican Party and the Besty Gray *sluagh* of the Fianna, the nationalist scout association that was established by Constance Markievicz. The Belfast *sluagh* was the only female branch of the Fianna in Ireland and the Connolly sisters had shown considerable determination in securing women's admission to this organisation: in 1912, they succeeded, by a majority of one, in passing a resolution which facilitated female membership.

Other members of Belfast's Cumann included several women who worked closely with James Connolly and were well acquainted with his family: James Connolly's secretary, Winifred Carney, attended the first meeting of Cumann na mBan in 1914 and became one of its most active members.[124] Nelly Gordon, an organiser for Connolly's Irish Textile Workers' Union, and Marie Johnson, a suffragist and former ITWU secretary, also enlisted their support for the Belfast branch. Other female members of nationalist families were prompted to join Cumann na mBan, as their male relations joined Sinn Fein and the Irish Volunteers, as 'Mothers, wives, sisters, sweet-hearts – were all dragged into that cauldron of self-sacrifice . . . to prove that sex was no deterrent in the National fight.'[125] For some women, however, membership of Cumann na mBan represented a progression from their interests in cultural nationalism. Margaret Dobbs, for instance, was a Gaelic League enthusiast who became an active member of Cumann in Belfast and was appointed to the association's executive committee in Dublin in April 1914.[126]

In Belfast it seems that Inghinidhe na hÉireann became fully absorbed into Cumann na mBan. There was also an interesting overlap in the activities of the Belfast branches of these two associations, as both became renowned for their weekly rifle practices which were held to instruct women 'to fight for an Irish Republic' in the most pragmatic way.[127] Like Inghinidhe na hÉireann, the Belfast branch of Cumann na mBan became one of the most militarily aggressive in Ireland and its members were sufficiently confident to challenge local volunteers to a shooting competition in 1914. The explanation for the militaristic pursuits of Belfast's Cumann may be a result of James Connolly's espousal of militant republicanism. Nora Connolly, for example, opined that the Belfast members were well trained in military matters because 'We used to go and listen to my father's military lectures.'[128] James Connolly, however, wryly alluded to Cumann na mBan's somewhat paradoxical interests of shooting and nursing: 'You're learning to puncture and then to mend the puncture.'[129]

The discord amongst northern nationalists is clearly apparent in Nora Connolly's account of the opposition that was directed towards Cumann na mBan in Ulster. The organisation faced animosity not only from unionist adversaries, but also from constitutional nationalists such as the United Irish League and the Ancient Order of Hibernians. These associations did not perceive Cumann na mBan as an ally in the campaign for Irish independence and as a consequence were 'antagonistic and . . . ready to jump' on its members:

> We [Belfast's Cumann na mBan] must keep to our own district, and even then meet hostility . . . we know the exact number of our workers, and have no expectation of sympathy. It is dogged, determined work, in an atmosphere of hostility we are never allowed to forget for a moment.[130]

In the aftermath of the 1916 rising Cumann na mBan benefited from the upsurge in republican support. This was not only apparent in the influx of female members but also in the number of Cumann's branches: increasing from 100 in December 1917 to approximately 750 by September 1921, 93 (12 per cent) of which were located in Ulster.[131] Although none of the membership figures for the organisation are entirely reliable, Cumann na mBan undeniably experienced remarkable growth in terms of interest and support. In Ulster, however, the organisation remained comparatively weak in relation to the rest of the country. Alice Cashel, Cumann na mBan's general secretary, for instance, attempted to mobilise support in north-east Tyrone from February 1918, and in October of that year Louise Gavan Duffy was sent from Dublin to try to establish branches in Armagh and Down. This campaign formed part of a co-ordinated republican effort to bolster support throughout Ulster, as a Cumann report of 1918 underlined:

> it was the Province in which we were weakest, and . . . we were requested by Eamon de Valera to join with the Irish Volunteers and Sinn Féin in a simultaneous effort to range the Ulster counties on the side of an Irish Republic.[132]

But the success of this venture was limited. By January 1919, Cumann na mBan had a total of 4,425 members and although individual branch membership figures were not collated the association clearly remained less active throughout the north of the country.[133] Indeed republicanism remained a divisive issue in Ulster and a significant section of northern nationalists remained loyal to Joseph Devlin and the Irish Parliamentary Party.

In spite of this division, some branches of Cumann na mBan managed to survive in the province. Delegates from branches in Belfast, Armagh, Coalisland, Clogher, Dundalk, Londonderry, Newry and Enniskillen attended Cumann's annual convention in 1918 and two Ulster representatives, Winifred Carney and Mrs McCullough, were appointed to Cumann na mBan's executive. At this convention representatives from Belfast successfully proposed the initiation of study circles as a means of politically educating women and encouraging debate on 'social subjects':

> such as matters from an Irish Ireland point of view, and Parliamentary and Local Government, and thus aid in developing the character and initiative of our women, so as to enable them to participate intelligently in the Government of the Country under an Irish Republic.[134]

Such an approach was in stark contrast to their belligerent stance of the pre-war period, but this change in the northern branches' activities was most probably one consequence of residing in an atmosphere of considerable sectarian hostility.

As was evident amongst unionists and constitutional nationalists, the passage of women's suffrage also prompted a reconsideration of republicans' electoral strategies. Following the passage of the Representation of the People Act in 1918, members of Cumann na mBan helped to revise electoral registers and undertook an important role in encouraging women to vote for Sinn Féin. In that year Cumann na mBan also issued a pamphlet, *The present duty of Irishwomen*, which claimed that failing to cast a vote for Sinn Féin was analogous to nothing short of treason. Sinn Féin was similarly anxious to align newly enfranchised women to republicanism, issuing a manifesto entitled *An appeal to the women of Ireland*. This alleged that Irish women's influence was such that they could not only select the government, but could secure 'the ancient ideal of our people'.[135] Prompted by these considerations, Sinn Féin also ran two female candidates in the 1918 election – Constance Markievicz and Winifred Carney. Markievicz was successfully elected as the first female member of the House of Commons, though she declined to take her seat. Carney, a former secretary of James Connolly and an active member of Belfast's Cumann na mBan, lacked both the independent means and high public profile of Markievicz. She was, therefore, much more reliant on party support to enable her to conduct an effective electoral campaign in the Victoria constituency of Belfast. Little support for her workers' republican programme was forthcoming, either in this constituency or from Belfast's pro-nationalist press. Indeed, only two of her election meetings were reported by the *Irish News*. But Carney attributed her defeat, not to her nonconformist manifesto or lack of publicity, but to insufficient support from her own party:

> I had neither personation agents, committee rooms, canvassers or vehicles, and as these are the chief agents in an election, it was amazing to me to find that 395 people went to the ballot on their own initiative, without any persuasion. The organisation in Belfast could have been much, much better.[136]

Carney's allegations are reinforced by an assessment of the individuals who addressed her election meetings. Here the lack of support from any official Sinn Féin representatives is remarkable. At a meeting held in Belfast's St Mary's Hall in December 1918, for instance, Carney relied solely on other female nationalists for support, such as Alice Milligan, Alice Cashel, who was Cumann na mBan's general secretary, and Countess Grace Plunkett, the wife of the nationalist MP for North Roscommon.[137] Another of Carney's meetings was addressed by her friend and fellow Cumann na mBan activist, Marie Johnson.[138] Given these considerations, it is difficult to avoid the conclusion that there was a tokenist element to Sinn Féin's female candidature.

The strength of Cumann na mBan in Ulster was further undermined in the years following the Government of Ireland Act of 1920. This was characteristic of the disillusion, apathy and discord experienced within northern nationalism throughout the inter-war period. Miss Brady, who was one of forty-six Ulster delegates attending Cumann na mBan's 1921 convention, requested that a full-time, trained organiser be sent to Ulster immediately, which indicates that the state of the association in the province was far from satisfactory.[139] In more general terms, Cumann's escalating extremism and increased co-operation with the Irish Republican Army (IRA), a force which was re-formed from the Irish Volunteers during the war of independence, may have alienated more moderate nationalist support throughout the country. Cumann na mBan also experienced some internal dissension as a result of its anti-Treaty predilection and a number of members left the organisation in order to establish Cumann na Saoirse (Society of Freedom).[140]

By February 1925 support for Cumann na mBan was limited to areas which had been most affected by the war of independence, 'where the fight was keenest and the opposition of the enemy strongest':[141]

> Where there are only three or four girls in a town, or even in a county, they should not be discouraged, but should keep in touch with one another and seize every opportunity for getting their branches going again.[142]

As a consequence of declining republican impetus, Cumann na mBan's membership was reduced to several hundred members during the early 1930s when republicanism reached 'its lowest ebb, its ideals a bankrupt travesty of a previous age'.[143] The association's convention reports make very little reference to the work of its Ulster branches and it seems that its Belfast branch was only sporadically active during the early 1930s: its members protested against imperialism during the outdoor relief riots of October 1932, and Mary Donnelly and Sarah Grimley received two- and three-month prison sentences respectively for posting up republican literature in Belfast in opposition to the Prince of Wales' visit to the city in 1933.[144] Cumann na mBan was further diminished by internal discord. In 1933 an extensive campaign in the north was planned, but this never came to fruition due to problems caused by a breakaway group, Mna na Poblachta (Women of the Republic).[145] By the early 1940s the whole organisational structure of Cumann na mBan had collapsed and the few women possessing radical nationalist sympathies in Ulster, as in the rest of Ireland, were left bereft of direction and support.

Although Cumann na mBan was never a truly popular organisation, its significance lay in assigning women an ancillary role which was, it seems, common to many women who became politically active in not only the cultural, constitutional and republican facets of nationalism, but also in unionism. And perhaps what is more interesting is that the overwhelming majority of these women were content to accept this role and the associated gendered division of politics.

V

The disunity amongst nationalist factions which marred the '98 centenary celebrations affected nationalism throughout the early twentieth century. Northern nationalist women continued to participate in a variety of nationalist associations, but their enthusiasm was seriously undermined in the inter-war period. The Anglo-Irish Treaty of 1921, which sanctioned the exclusion of the six north-eastern counties and established dominion status for the remainder of the country, came as a bitter disappointment to northern nationalists. Their chagrin was reinforced, firstly by the failure of the Boundary Commission to adjust Ulster's borders in 1925 and secondly by the removal of the proportional representation voting system in 1929.[146] As John Nugent, national secretary of the Ancient Order of Hibernians, emphasised, synthesis amongst nationalist factions represented the first step in ameliorating the political situation: 'If our northern people are to be rescued we must first have unity.'[147] Yet, little pragmatic work was done to realise this aim and no strategy appropriate to northern nationalists' predicament as a permanent minority was formulated.[148] Partial political reconciliation between constitutional nationalism and Sinn Féin was only forthcoming with the establishment of the National League, under Joseph Devlin's presidency, in May 1928. But this association failed to mobilise widespread support and the pro-Treaty Sinn Féin section of northern nationalists remained outside its jurisdiction. Disunity was further reinforced by Devlin's death in 1934 and, as Patrick O'Neill, MP for Mourne, highlighted in 1937: 'we never had a leader since Devlin died, and until we get one I am afraid things will not be remedied'.[149] After 1934 nationalists remained distrustful of the legitimacy of the Northern Irish state and, when their elected representatives did enter the parliamentary arena, their opposition was rarely effective in the face of unionist hegemony.

Nationalist reluctance to stand for elective office and the steps which the unionist government took to dominate state administration, combined with women's ancillary role in the nationalist movement, meant that women were not encouraged to stand as either parliamentary or municipal candidates.[150] No female parliamentary candidates were forwarded by nationalist parties in Ulster from 1921 to 1940 and unionists continued to dominate municipal politics. The impact of female enfranchisement was, therefore, limited to encouraging a reconsideration of women's political significance as voters. This was apparent not only within the Ancient Order of Hibernians and Cumann na mBan, but also in November 1927 when Joseph Devlin introduced an equal suffrage bill to the Northern Ireland parliament. Given the absence of documentation, it is difficult to offer any firm conclusions on Devlin's reasons for introducing this measure, but it seems most likely that this was an attempt to bolster nationalists' electoral support. Introducing this measure to the

Commons, Devlin emphasised that women needed the vote to improve their working conditions: 'female employment constitutes to a large extent the most powerful part of our industrial life in our mills and factories . . . They [women] are the least vocal of all those who suffer wrong.'[151] Even though this bill was defeated on its second reading by twenty-five votes to fourteen, it reinforces the change that occurred in women's political stature from 1918. Thereafter, women were seen as a fundamental component of the political process.

Women in Ulster became involved in all strands of nationalist politics. In cultural nationalism this occurred through the pioneering initiatives of Alice Milligan and Anna Johnston in establishing *Shan Van Vocht*, the Nationalist Association of Irishwomen and the Irish Women's Centenary Union, and through the work of the Gaelic League. Women also enlisted their support for constitutional nationalism through the United Irish League and the Ladies' Auxiliary of the Ancient Order of Hibernians, and for republicanism through Inghinidhe na hÉireann and Cumann na mBan. In spite of the variance of aims and levels of support which existed amongst these groups of politically active women, much of the work which they performed was gendered and ancillary: mobilising female support, decorating nationalist graves, organising social events, assisting the Irish Volunteers, canvassing female voters and updating electoral registers. This, coupled with the similar work that was conducted by unionist women, suggests that many women in Ulster, regardless of their political affiliation, were content to perform political work of this nature because they believed that theirs was an equal, but different, role.

CHAPTER FOUR

Women Poor Law Guardians

How could you know what mothers want, or tell what daughters need . . . The state is but a larger house . . . [1]

I

Irish women were prohibited from participating in poor law administration until the passage of the Poor Law Guardian (Ireland) (Women) Act on 31 March 1896.[2] The poor law was an integral part of municipal government and was the first area of public administration open to women. This analysis focuses on four boards of poor law guardians situated in Ulster: Ballymoney, Belfast, Lisburn and Londonderry. These boards were selected not because of their geographical location, but because of the high level of female representation. Indeed seventy-one women, representing forty-five per cent of the total number of female guardians in Ulster, served on these four boards in the period 1896–1940.[3]

The perimeters of poor law administration gradually increased as the demands placed upon the system changed. By the middle of the nineteenth century boards of guardians were not only providing indoor relief for the destitute poor, but were also managing fever hospitals and infirmaries, administering a dispensary system which provided localised medical care for the sick poor, assisting emigration schemes and boarding out orphans and deserted children in the community. Although a considerable proportion of poor law administration was uniform in terms of managing the daily running of the workhouse and its attached institutions, there were several important distinctions between the four boards under analysis. Belfast was the largest union in Ulster, providing indoor relief for 1,000 paupers; Londonderry was the biggest union outside Belfast, with accommodation for 800, whilst Ballymoney and Lisburn were both sizeable market towns and their unions provided beds for 700 and 800 paupers respectively.

In 1903 a Vice Regal Commission recommended the abolition of the whole workhouse system, suggesting that it should be replaced by a network of district hospitals and specialised institutions. No action was forthcoming to implement these proposals and in Northern Ireland the poor law system remained intact until 1948 when it was replaced by eight health and welfare authorities. There was, however, a significant reduction in the number of recipients of indoor relief during the inter-war period. The need for relief was reduced by a series of legislative measures which introduced old age pensions and sanctioned the establishment of institutions to care exclusively for the sick and mentally and physically disabled. This resulted in the amalgamation of several workhouses in Ulster and their infirmaries were transformed into district hospitals to care for the health of the local community, instead of the destitute. Amalgamation occurred in two of the unions under analysis. Both Ballymoney and Lisburn transferred their workhouse inmates to Coleraine and Lurgan in 1918 and 1919 respectively, leaving the guardians with responsibility for administering boarding out schemes, infirmaries, fever hospitals and dispensary systems. Thus their administrative burdens were seriously reduced and throughout the inter-war period both boards met twice per month, instead of weekly. Several other boards also scaled down their operations and by 1948 only a few workhouses were still operative in Ulster, collectively providing accommodation for 654 inmates, representing a ninety-three per cent reduction in the provision of indoor relief in the province.

The Poor Law Guardian (Ireland) (Women) Act of 1896 was introduced to parliament by the Belfast MP, William Johnston. This bill passed through all of its parliamentary stages comparatively easily. One provincial newspaper in Ulster described the speed of its enactment as 'almost phenomenal'.[4] The fact that Ireland was being brought into line with existing legislative provisions in England and Scotland, where women had been admitted to this area of local government from 1869 and 1882 respectively, explains the absence of any serious opposition to the legislation. Despite the inevitability of the legislation being introduced to Ireland, both the Belfast and Dublin branches of the Irish Women's Suffrage and Local Government Association actively campaigned for the implementation of this reform.[5]

Isabella Tod, the foremost women's rights activist in Ulster, was the leading member of Belfast's IWSLGA.[6] Writing in the July 1887 edition of the *Englishwoman's Review*, Tod claimed that women in Ireland deserved to be admitted to this realm of municipal administration on the following grounds. Firstly, it was unjust for Irishwomen to be 'left long behind' their British and Scottish counterparts.

Secondly, women, as ratepayers, had a legitimate and democratic right to participate in local government administration.[7] And finally, Tod refuted the idea that women could effectively implement reform through philanthropic means alone:

> Only those ladies who know that they have the support of the ratepayers who elected them will venture to criticise effectively, to insist on troublesome work being done, to go where the officials may not wish them, and where often it would be quite unsuitable for men to go, and to urge new plans which they see to be wanted.[8]

In addition to Tod's tempered reasoning, the IWSLGA's campaign for poor law reform was undoubtedly strengthened by the ability to cite positive examples of the 'wise administrators' of English and Scottish female guardians.[9] From the very inception of their campaign specific areas of poor law administration were identified as being especially suited to women's experience and capabilities. These arguments were utilised in an attempt to convince legislators that women possessed the necessary experience to make a positive contribution to this public office. Similar rhetoric was used in both the English and Irish campaigns, with municipal government being interpreted as nothing short of domestic politics.[10] The duties and responsibilities of guardians were compared to household management, an area where all women had direct and, it was argued, relevant experience:

> The economy of a workhouse is the economy of a house . . . but dealing with larger sums and quantities. The management of officials needs the same kind of wisdom as the management of servants.[11]

Moreover, reformers contended that women's preordained nurturing qualities were essential to effective poor law management:

> The idea that men, however exemplary in the performance of their duties, can adequately supervise the dietary, the clothing, the nursing, and the children's departments . . . without the aid of competent, experienced women, is too preposterous to be entertained by any intelligent person who understands the workings of the system.[12]

But claims of this sort were not restricted to female reformers, as the Marquis of Londonderry, supporting the introduction of the 1896 bill to parliament, also alluded to the special qualities which women could bring to poor law administration and to 'the strong feeling in Ireland, especially in Ulster':

> that there was a certain sphere of work in which the services of women on boards of guardians would be of great value . . . they could look after pauper women and children, the training of girls for service, and the food and sanitary arrangements far better than men.[13]

Under the regulations of the 1896 act, women as occupiers or householders, rated occupiers, lodgers of premises worth £10 per annum, non-resident leaseholders for a term of sixty years with profit rent of £10 and as non-resident freeholders with £20 yearly profit were enfranchised and entitled to stand as candidates in poor law elections. An estimated 100,000 Irish women were hence admitted to the municipal franchise.[14] Even though one of the IWSLGA's main objectives was attained through the passage of this legislation, it continued to work on the practical issues. By October 1896 the association had 'been in communication with ladies in various parts of Ireland . . . with a view to having candidates ready' for the forthcoming poor law elections and had organised several visits to workhouses in Dublin.[15] Furthermore, in Belfast Isabella Tod held a meeting at her home on 23 September 1896 in order to make preparations for a public meeting to discuss women's poor law work.[16] However, in Belfast another association, the Society to Brighten Workhouse Life, supplemented both Tod's work and that of the IWSLGA. In 1899 this voluntary organisation, which provided treats and entertainments for the inmates of Belfast's workhouse, expanded its philanthropic work in order to support all the city's female poor law candidates. This was with the exception of Mary Galway, the official candidate of the Belfast United Trades and Labour Council.[17] After this date the society remained active, combining charitable work with diligent electoral support for female poor law candidates. For instance, during the next poor law election of 1902, the *Belfast Evening Telegraph* commented that the 'nominees of the Society to Brighten Workhouse Life had no reason to complain of the organisation on their behalf'.[18]

It has been claimed that English female guardians 'always comprised the lion's share of elected women – [representing] over three-quarters in 1923'.[19] In Ulster the distribution of women throughout the realms of municipal government was similarly weighted towards poor law administration: a total of 173 individual women were elected as poor law guardians, representing 67 per cent of women's total municipal representation in the period 1896 to 1940.[20] However, the numerical increase of women poor law guardians was gradual. Indeed, 19 per cent of all the unions situated in Ulster had no female members throughout the period under analysis (see Table 2).

Table 2. Women poor law guardians in Ulster, 1899–1940[24]

	1899	1902	1905	1908	1911	1914	1920	1924	1927	1930	1933	1936	1939	Total per union
Antrim	–	–	–	–	–	Ø	Ø	–	–	–	–	–	–	0
Armagh	–	–	–	–	–	–	2	4	2	4	2	2	3	19
Ballycastle	–	–	–	–	–	–	–	–	–	–	–	–	–	0
Ballymena	1	1	1	2	2	2	–	3	Ø	Ø	Ø	3	Ø	15
Ballymoney	3	2	3	4	4	5	6	6	7	4	4	2	3	53
Banbridge	1	–	1	1	1	2	2	1	2	1	1	3	3	19
Belfast	5	4	3	6	6	7	10	8	10	8	8	9	7	91
Castlederg	–	–	–	–	–	–	–	–	2	–	–	–	–	2
Clogher	–	–	–	–	–	–	–	–	–	1	–	–	–	1
Coleraine	5	5	5	5	5	5	3	3	3	3	3	3	3	51
Cookstown	–	–	–	–	–	–	–	–	–	–	–	–	1	1
Downpatrick	–	–	–	–	–	–	–	–	–	–	–	–	–	0
Dungannon	–	–	–	–	–	–	–	–	2	1	1	1	1	6
Enniskillen	–	–	–	–	–	–	–	–	–	–	–	–	–	0
Irvinestown	–	–	–	–	–	–	–	–	–	1	1	1	2	5
Kilkeel	1	–	–	–	–	–	–	1	1	–	–	–	–	3
Larne	–	–	–	–	–	–	–	–	–	–	–	–	–	0
Limavady	2	2	1	1	2	3	1	2	1	–	1	1	1	18
Lisburn	2	1	1	2	3	2	3	2	2	3	2	2	2	27
Lisnaskea	1	–	–	–	–	–	–	–	–	–	–	–	–	1
Londonderry	5	3	3	3	3	3	3	4	5	8	8	8	7	63
Lurgan	4	2	–	–	–	–	–	1	2	1	1	–	–	11
Magherafelt	–	–	–	–	–	–	2	3	1	1	3	4	3	17
Newry	–	1	1	2	2	2	1	–	–	–	–	–	–	9
Newtownards	–	–	–	1	1	–	–	3	2	3	3	4	4	21
Omagh	–	–	–	–	–	–	–	5	3	–	–	2	2	12
Strabane	–	–	–	–	–	–	–	6	7	7	6	6	6	38
Total per annum	30	21	19	27	29	31	33	52	52	46	44	51	48	483

The first Irish woman guardian was Miss E. Martin, co-opted onto Lisnaskea's board of guardians for the district of Lisbellaw in September 1896. As Martin was unopposed in this appointment, the local press depicted her co-option as 'a walk over', although conceding that she possessed 'excellent business habits':

> we have no doubt that her presence at the Board will do much to soften the asperities that sometimes arise from differences of opinion, and will have a beneficial effect and healthy influence on the general proceedings.[21]

By 1899 thirty women were serving as poor law guardians in Ulster, but an increase in the number of women holding this position only occurred sporadically over the next fifty years. This is clearly illustrated by a comparative analysis of female representation in 1899, just three years after women were admitted to poor law administration to the end of the period under analysis, 1940. In 1899 women represented 3.1 per cent of the total number of poor law guardians in Ulster and by 1940 this had only increased marginally to 5.4 per cent.[22] Throughout the period 1896 to 1940, women represented an average of just 4.2 per cent of the total number of guardians in the province. From Table 2 it is also apparent that in several instances the election of a woman guardian did not set any precedent for further female representation. Miss Martin was appointed as the first Irish female guardian in Lisnaskea in 1896, but no other women were elected in this district. Similarly, the first, and last, women guardians were elected to Castlederg in 1927 and in Cookstown the first female guardian was not elected until 1939, forty-three years after women were admitted to poor law administration.

Drawing any firm conclusion concerning the geographical distribution of female guardians throughout the province is difficult. Certainly the areas with the highest level of female representation were large urban centres: Ballymoney, Belfast, Coleraine, Lisburn, Londonderry and Strabane (see Table 2). This fits the urban determinant that has been identified by Patricia Hollis in her work on English women guardians.[23] In Ulster, however, this trend was not absolute, as boards in small provincial centres such as Irvinestown, Kilkeel and Magherafelt had several women members, whilst sizeable towns like Antrim, Larne and Enniskillen lacked any female representation (see Table 2). The inconclusive nature of the geographical distribution of female guardians throughout the north-east of the country suggests that the small number of women who held these positions were exceptional, either by virtue of personal ability, ambition or circumstance.

In addition to those elected, a significant number of women were co-opted and a policy developed of replacing deceased female guardians, or those who resigned their seats, with other women. On the four boards of guardians under analysis here, a total of nineteen women, representing 27 per cent of the female guardians serving in these districts, were co-opted. Of these, seventeen (89 per cent) replaced other women and only two female guardians were co-opted in lieu of male guardians. The success of replacing male with female guardians was mixed and on the boards under analysis there are three examples of women being unsuccessfully proposed as successors to male guardians.[25]

Reacting to their minority status on boards, women guardians occasionally called for an increase in female representation. When tendering her resignation from Lisburn board in 1912, Anna Barbour openly appealed for more women to come forward and stand as poor law candidates:

> The reason that it makes it especially hard for me to give up the work of a Guardian is that I have realised more and more . . . that it is essentially a woman's work and it has been a cause of great regret and amazement to me . . . that the public do not realize this – and that out of some 40 . . . Guardians, whose work it is to care for the sick and aged – the mothers, – children and orphans of the poor – only three are women.[26]

But it seems that women met resistance on the rare occasions when they took practical steps to increase female representation. Hence in 1928, and again in the following year, the female members of Lisburn board failed to have Dr May Quin co-opted as a hospital governor. This was despite the emphasis which they laid not only on her personal qualifications for the position, but also on the fact that she was 'in touch with the Lisburn people' and there was a need for increased female representation: 'we have so few ladies on our Board you should give them a chance'.[27]

Yet in spite of the comparatively small number of women serving on boards of guardians, it appears that their appointment as office bearers was not directly linked to their numerical representation. To cite 1914 as an example: Lily Ann Barr, the only woman guardian in Ballymena, was appointed as chairman of the board and Lady Gertrude Keightley, one of only two women guardians in Lisburn, was also selected as chairman. Moreover, some female guardians were quickly elected to office. By 1909 two of the three office bearing positions on Ballymoney's board were held by women and Lady Frances Macnaghten was elected as the deputy vice-chairman of this board in June 1915, only three months after her co-option.[28] The majority (82 per cent) of female office bearers in the period under analysis were, however, appointed to the less important positions of vice and deputy vice-chairman (see Table 3). The chairmen of boards of guardians were responsible for sanctioning all decisions, presiding over weekly meetings and serving as a member of all the board's committees. Vice-chairmen, by comparison, were

Table 3. Women office bearers on boards of guardians in Ulster, 1896–1940[29]

OFFICE	NO. OF WOMEN ELECTED	PER CENT OF TOTAL FEMALE OFFICE BEARERS	PER CENT OF TOTAL RESPECTIVE OFFICE
Chair	32	18	3
Vice-chair	55	31	5
Deputy vice-chair	91	51	8

also appointed to every committee, but, as they only chaired weekly meetings when the head of the board was absent, their responsibilities were comparatively less arduous.

As with the fluctuating number of women elected as poor law guardians in Ulster, there were also considerable variations in the number of women who were elected to office. The number of women officeholders peaked in 1928 with the appointment of ten women. But, five years later, in 1933, this number had fallen to two – the lowest figure recorded in twenty-seven years. Regardless of this fluctuation, women's appointment to office clearly outnumbered their numerical representation. Of the total number of women elected to boards of guardians in Ulster in the period 1896 to 1940, 37 per cent held office. Despite this, some women were reluctant to accept the heightened responsibilities attached to office. In 1908, for example, Florence Clark refused to stand for the position of vice-chairman of Belfast's guardians as 'she did not feel capable of the position'.[30] In 1918 she again refused to stand, this time as chairman, although 'she acknowledged that her nomination represented a compliment to the female members of the board'.[31] On Ballymoney's board, Mrs E.F. Montgomery also declined to stand for the position of chairman in 1934, although, unlike Clark, she later agreed to accept this position and the increased responsibility that accompanied it.[32]

But to focus solely on the numerical representation of women guardians belies the work of many individuals who made a long-term commitment to poor law administration. The average term of service amongst the female members of Ballymoney, Belfast, Lisburn and Londonderry guardians in the period 1896 to 1940 was eleven years, but some female guardians completed exceptional terms of service. Josephine O'Neill was a member of Londonderry's board of guardians for twenty-seven years, retaining the position of deputy vice-chairman for twenty-three years;[33] Florence Clark was a guardian on Belfast's board for twenty-two years, and held the position of deputy vice-chairman for six years and that of vice-chairman for four years.[34] Decades of service were not only limited to those who were elected to office, as Margaret Gilliland served as a guardian on Londonderry's board for a remarkable thirty-nine years[35] and Sarah Andrews was a member of Belfast's guardians for twenty-two years.[36] Another indication of women's commitment to poor law work can be gained from an analysis of attendance figures. To take Lisburn board of guardians as an example: in 1916 Louisa Stannus and Lady Gertrude Keightley, the only women on its sixty-six member board, both attended 96 per cent of meetings held over a twelve-month period, a record which was only equalled by one male guardian.[37] In 1930, the female members of this board were its most regular attendees.[38] On an individual basis some women's attendance record was exemplary. A letter to the *Irish News* on 26 May 1902, for instance, accredited Jane Payne of Belfast's board with attending an average of four committee meetings per week. During the next year Payne and her colleagues, William O'Hare and Susanna Munce, were the three most regular attendees on Belfast's board and, several years later, in 1927 Belfast guardians noted that no member had a better attendance record than Lily Coleman.[39]

Standing for any elective position demanded a certain amount of confidence and it has been claimed that for a woman to forward herself as a local government candidate 'required a thick skin and a great sense of duty'.[40] In a similar vein, an anonymous article in the *Westminster Review* in 1885 defined the reasons for women's reluctance to stand as poor law guardians in the following terms:

> The novelty of employment, the publicity of the election, the real wearisomeness of the work, and the exaggerated unpleasantness have all caused women to shrink from offering themselves as candidates.[41]

This reputation was partially deserved. Poor law work was often difficult and unpleasant: caring for the sick, mentally and physically disabled, elderly and destitute in often insanitary and overcrowded conditions.

An abundance of leisure was a prerequisite for any philanthropic endeavour and the work of a guardian was more time consuming than most. Weekly board meetings were often of several hours' duration. Moreover, as poor law work was delegated to various committees, attendance at five or six meetings per week was not uncommon. Giving evidence to a local government inquiry into the administration of Belfast union, Lily Coleman, who in 1929 became the first female chairman of this board, gave an indication of the commitment involved in poor law work:

> We are the great unpaid, I give three quarters of the working day to the public . . . We stand . . . between the Government and the public as a kind of safety valve to see that the legislation is properly carried out to the flesh and blood of the community who pay the rates.[42]

Though the majority of female guardians appear to have been dedicated to poor law work, some women were unable, or unwilling, to make such a commitment. Mrs M. Donagh, Miss Florence Stevenson and Miss Leinster were all disqualified from Londonderry's board for non-attendance and Dupre Fennell resigned from Belfast's board in 1902 as she was unable to devote sufficient time to her work. Kate Megahy gave up the chair of Belfast's guardian's boarding-out committee in 1903 for similar reasons and Agnes Shaw, elected to Belfast board in June 1908, resigned just six months later due to lack of time. The level of time and commitment entailed also meant that many working women would have found it very difficult to participate in poor law administration. Hence the majority of female guardians appear to have been middle class and not involved in any paid employment. Lily Coleman was one of the few working-class guardians, running her own drapery shop and workroom on Belfast's Donegall Road in order to financially support her family while her husband was ill and unable to work.[43] Coleman's class background was, however, exceptional, as on Belfast board the majority of women guardians were middle class. Catherine McCann, for example, was a daughter of the manager of Belfast's Opera House; Adela Thompson was married to a customs official and Mrs E.M. Montgomery was married to a chartered surveyor.[44] It also appears that several women guardians were of a higher social status than their male counterparts. Although the husbands of both the Countess of Kilmorey (elected to Kilkeel in 1898) and Lady Macnaghten (co-opted to Ballymoney in 1914) also served as poor law guardians, a number of other titled women also became involved in poor law administration: Lady Brooke was elected to Lisnaskea in 1898, Lady Keightley was elected to Lisburn in the following year and Lady Anderson was elected to Londonderry in 1924.

II

The admission of women to poor law administration presented a new opportunity to become involved in their immediate locality, helping society's most vulnerable members. Essentially, the appointment of women guardians represented a formalisation of female philanthropy, which had become increasingly popular from the middle of the nineteenth century. Women's motivation for philanthropy can partly be explained by a combination of wealth, leisure and compassion. But it also seems that philanthropy was used as a family substitute amongst widows and spinsters and as a means of countering boredom amongst middle-class English housewives.[45] In Ulster, references to personal motivation for either male or female poor law guardians are rare, making it difficult to generalise on the impetus behind an individual's decision to become involved in unpaid public work. Miss Louisa Stannus of Lisburn guardians provides the only example where public volunteerism may have been used as a relief for solitude. In 1912, following the death of her brother, she remarked that her 'world was very lonely . . . he was all I had'.[46] Lily Coleman of Belfast's board gave a fuller explanation of her reasons for becoming a guardian in 1938, recounting that it was her sense of horror at the state of Belfast's workhouse, following her son's admission to its infirmary, which prompted her to stand for election. Her concern was to ensure that 'such a condition of affairs would never exist again'.[47]

From Coleman's evidence it is clear that philanthropy was an important motivating factor in prompting her poor law candidature. Undoubtedly philanthropy was seen as a socially acceptable pursuit for the upper and middle classes and by the middle of the nineteenth century the significance of women's charitable work was being acknowledged. Reverend Charles Kingsley was one of several commentators who romanticised over the special qualities that women could bring to philanthropy:

> Human friendship, trust, affection . . . the smile of the lip, the light of the eye, the tenderness of the voice . . . The magic sweetness, grace and courtesy may shed a hallowing and humanizing [sic] light over the meanest work.[48]

The 1899 International Congress of Women also claimed, in more realistic terms, that social welfare work demanded: 'Trained intelligence . . . [and] a knowledge tested by experience'.[49] In Ulster during the nineteenth century upper and middle-class women actively supported many charities. Some charities separated male and female work by establishing ladies' auxiliaries, such as the Ladies' Society of St Vincent de Paul and the women's committees of Belfast Charitable Society and Workshops for the Blind. Other charities were run by and for women: female penitentiaries, Belfast Prison Gate Mission, Belfast Ladies' Relief Association and the Ladies' National Association.[50] In addition, some branches of nineteenth-century philanthropy brought women directly into contact with the poorer elements of society and with poor law administration.[51] Indeed, in the urban centres of Ulster there was a tradition of visiting the poor.[52] This was noted by Reverend McIntyre during his visits to working-class areas of Belfast in 1854 when he recorded that the city's Ladies' Visiting Committee ministered care, advice and material assistance to those in need.[53]

Other charities were active within the workhouse. In Belfast, a ladies' committee was initiated on the recommendation of the English reformer Elizabeth Fry following her three-month tour of Ireland in 1827. This committee supervised the female department of the workhouse, securing situations for female inmates, assisting children's education, improving standards of cleanliness and care and visiting the institution at least four times per annum.[54] Later in the nineteenth century other women joined the Society to Brighten Workhouse Life and the Brabazon Society, which organised employment schemes for the sick, aged and bedridden recipients of indoor relief. Women involved in work of this nature witnessed the failings of the poor law system at first hand: the overcrowded and insanitary conditions and the lack of specialised care for children, the sick, elderly and insane who were maintained in the workhouse. And it was through this charitable and auxiliary tradition that women gained invaluable experience for poor law administration.[55] Several women in Ulster were renowned within their locality for administering care to those in need or distress before standing for poor law election or being co-opted onto a poor law board. Annie Entrican and Elizabeth Willis, for example, both became known to Belfast's board of guardians through their work as secretaries to the Society to Brighten Workhouse Life and they were subsequently co-opted as guardians in 1910 and 1911 respectively. Several other female philanthropists in Belfast also became poor law guardians: Annie Knight ran the Girls' Friendly Society of Ballymacarret Church in East Belfast;[56] Arabella Fennell was an educational reformer;[57] Caroline Pim was president of Cliftonville Home for the Blind and Mary Ryan's 'philanthropic and social work in the city' was highly commended following her appointment to Belfast's board of guardians in 1929.[58] In addition, another two Belfast guardians, Ethel Macnaghten and Anastasia McCready, established the Belfast Union of Girls' Clubs in the early twentieth century. This organisation encouraged self-help and education for working-class women by providing practical instruction in cookery, writing and needlework in forty clubs located throughout the city. However, other female guardians became involved with poor law administration in a more informal capacity. This was evident in the appointment of Louisa Stannus to Lisburn board, as from 1900 she donated gifts to the workhouse and from 1908 annually invited the workhouse children to her home. The following year she again became involved with Lisburn guardians through her attempts to adopt an illegitimate orphan.[59]

An additional motivating factor for some female guardians appears to have been familial support for their work. Of the seventy-one women who served as guardians on Ballymoney, Belfast, Lisburn and Londonderry boards, there are two examples of women being co-opted to replace their spouses: on Lisburn board Mrs George Clarke and Mrs Anna Barbour were co-opted in lieu of their husbands in 1901 and 1907 respectively. There are also several examples of husbands and wives serving together on the same board. In Londonderry Margaret Morris successfully nominated the co-option of her husband as a poor law guardian and in Kilkeel the Count and Countess of Kilmorey held the respective positions of chair and vice-chair in 1898. In some instances the familial networks amongst guardians were more intricate. This was apparent when Lady Frances Macnaghten followed her husband onto Ballymoney's board in 1915, whilst their daughter Ethel was co-opted as a poor law guardian in Belfast in February 1908. In addition, the relatives of several female guardians had previously served on poor law boards: Louisa Stannus' father was a former member of Lisburn's board of guardians and on Londonderry board three daughters of a former male guardian were appointed.[60] Also, in Londonderry, Margaret Gilliland's sister-in-law was elected to the board in 1924. It is unlikely that the involvement of a family member in poor law work would have automatically guaranteed support for any woman anxious to follow a similar path of public volunteerism, but it is possible that some women may have been encouraged to stand for election. Moreover, the involvement of a family member in poor law work would certainly have enabled women to gain a realistic impression of the arduous duties of a poor law guardian and, more importantly, of the time and commitment entailed in their execution.

It seems that the majority of female guardians identified the office as an end in itself and not as an apprenticeship to a wider political career. In Ulster only a handful of female guardians possessed feminist sympathies and became involved in local government through a desire to further the women's movement: Ethel Macnaghten, co-opted onto Belfast's board in 1908, was also the co-founder of Bushmills Suffrage Society and both Frances Reid and Annie Entrican were poor law guardians in Belfast and prominent members of the Irish Women's Suffrage Society.[61] In spite of this, none of these women ever attempted to procure any support for suffrage from the boards of guardians that they represented. In practical terms there were strict limitations on what female guardians could achieve in forwarding these interests, as only business relating directly to the poor law could be discussed and any motions with political overtones were hastily ruled out of order at board meetings. Lisburn guardians went so far as to prohibit its workhouse officials from attending or taking part in any political meetings from 1900.[62] So, although female guardians illustrated women's ability to exercise their powers of citizenship in an elective position, they had little opportunity, and in many cases an apparent lack of desire, to promote women's suffrage.

Contemporary comments relating to women's poor law work are scarce. This was most probably one consequence of the public apathy concerning poor law administration. Voting levels remained consistently low, with poor law elections producing little local excitement or enthusiasm.[63] According to the *Belfast Evening Telegraph* there was 'absolutely no interest' in the 1899 poor law election and in the St Anne's electoral division of Belfast there was reportedly 'very little for the clerks to do', with under 100 votes being polled in the Clifton ward of the city.[64] This was not an isolated occurrence, as all candidates struggled to counter the apathy of a largely disinterested electorate. Hence in Belfast during the poor law election of 1902, Jane Payne was at the polling station before 8 a.m., whilst Kate Megahy had vehicles and workers at her disposal.[65] As a result of the limited press coverage which poor law elections received it is difficult to generalise on the extent of female electoral support for women candidates. The only press comment relating to the existence of tangible female support for women guardians in Ulster came in June 1902, when the *Belfast Evening Telegraph* commented that female voters 'loyally supported the members of their sex' during the recent poor law election.[66]

In concert with general public apathy, political parties also remained largely indifferent to poor law elections. This can be explained by several factors: unions did not tally with parliamentary constituencies, workhouse inmates were disenfranchised and the execution of poor law work was largely non-political in nature. Moreover, it is difficult to assess the specific political affiliation of individual guardians, as press coverage of poor law electoral campaigns and results was sporadic, whilst the records of individual boards do not list the party affiliation of their members. Nevertheless, using the surnames of individual guardians as a guide, albeit not an entirely satisfactory indicator, it does appear that the majority of women, like their male colleagues, were Protestant. The Ulster Women's Unionist Council was the only political organisation in the province to actively encourage its members to stand as poor law guardians, presenting this as a means to further unionist hegemony over state administration. This organisation provided financial and electoral assistance to aspiring female guardians from March 1920, designating poor law work as 'women's work'.[67] Even though the records of the UWUC provide few figures on the number of women who stood as poor law candidates under its auspices, its support was in sharp contrast to the widespread reluctance amongst northern nationalists to become involved in state administration following partition and the Government of Ireland Act of 1920.[68]

III

It has been suggested that the somewhat cliquish nature of boards of guardians meant that the most active members could control the administration.[69] This analysis can effectively be applied to female guardians in the areas of the poor law that they dominated: areas where it was perceived that women had both a naturally ordained interest and direct experience as mothers and as philanthropists. Male guardians seemingly possessed few reservations concerning the delegation of responsibility for the more intimate aspects of poor law administration to women. Following women's appointment to poor law boards there was an immediate division of poor law work amongst guardians on gender lines and a specific women's role was quickly discernible. Nineteenth-century feminist campaigners for poor law reform had envisaged that such a separation of duties between male and female guardians would occur. In 1881, for example, the always astute Isabella Tod acknowledged the existence of areas of poor law administration that she believed were specifically female in interest:

> The care of the poor generally and especially of women – the care of the children, towards whom pity is in no way mixed with censure: the prevention no less than the cure of sickness – these are the principal objects for which boards of guardians exist, and they are all women's duties.[70]

Two decades later the IWSLGA was still drawing attention to the urgent need for 'the more considerate treatment of the poor; and for this it is the influence of the tender-hearted motherly element upon our Boards that is more especially indispensable'.[71] The rhetoric of the reform campaign was realised in the work of women who were appointed as guardians. Initially, the separation of labour on the basis of gender may have been a consequence of female guardians' eagerness to prove that they were worthy of the position, with the necessary aptitude, experience and determination to make a valuable contribution to poor law work. Thus, once women were elected, matters pertaining to domestic economy, the diet and clothing of inmates, the appointment of female staff, illegitimacy, orphans, education and workhouse visiting all became female preserves. It has been recognised that English women guardians made significant changes to the areas of poor law administration that they dominated, changes that were 'to a degree unequalled by most of their male colleagues'.[72] And from women's poor law work in Ballymoney, Belfast, Lisburn and Londonderry it seems that a similar conclusion can be drawn.

The composition of committees to administer poor law work in Ulster clearly illustrates the gender division of duties. In the four unions under analysis, male guardians focused on building maintenance, internal finances, letting contracts and tenders, ordering supplies and employing male staff. Only a few women were appointed to finance and work committees and none to farm committees in the period 1896 to 1940. Belfast's first female guardian, Kate Megahy, was appointed to the workhouse visiting committee and a committee to report on the standard of nursing in the fever hospital in 1897.[73] During the next year she successfully proposed that substantial improvements be implemented in the workhouse infirmary and that female staff be provided with uniforms.[74] A similar pattern soon emerged in Londonderry and Lisburn. From 1899, Londonderry women guardians joined their male colleagues on the house committee that was responsible for weekly inspections of the institution and Gertrude Keightley, the only female member of Lisburn's board, was also appointed to the house committee.[75] By 1902 Keightley was serving on all the committees with responsibility for clothing, schools, visiting and selecting uniforms for nursing staff.[76] This trend was equally apparent in Ballymoney from the late nineteenth century, as the female members of the board were appointed to the house committee and frequently visited the workhouse alone, or in the company of another female guardian. Ballymoney was, however, peculiar in the permanent appointment of all female guardians to its visiting committee from 1901, with male guardians only being placed on a monthly rota visiting system.[77] This practice was not implemented in Londonderry until 1924, when two female members of the board, Margaret Gilliland and Josephine O'Neill, were made permanent house committee members.[78]

Possibly as a result of this high level of personal contact with inmates and staff, women guardians became very involved in managing the internal discipline of the workhouse. Thus, in Londonderry, Josephine O'Neill, Minnie McCutcheon and Margaret Elliot were appointed to interview and admonish troublesome inmates in 1934.[79] Women also endeavoured to improve the welfare of workhouse inmates. For instance, in Ballymoney female guardians put forward motions to improve provisions for the care of sane epileptics in the workhouse, and in Londonderry Margaret Morris tried to move that three hours be the maximum length of confinement in refractory wards for disobedience.[80] In addition, from 1906 female guardians in Belfast were anxious to remove inmates with special needs to external institutions and in Lisburn Minnie Beattie campaigned for six years to induce the Northern Irish government to establish a home for mentally defective children.[81]

Women also became very involved in appointing and managing female staff, especially domestics and nurses. In 1899, only a month after her co-option to Lisburn board, Gertrude Keightley was selected as a member of a committee which persuaded a wardswoman to retain her position[82] and two years later, on Londonderry's board, Margaret Morris was delegated by the guardians to interview an infirmary nurse in order to induce her to withdraw her resignation.[83] Female members of the four boards under analysis also strove to increase the number of qualified nursing staff employed in workhouse infirmaries. In 1897, for example, Kate Megahy, the only female member of Belfast's guardians at the time, unsuccessfully proposed that an additional five nurses be appointed in order to improve the standard of care in the workhouse infirmary.[84] Margaret Morris had similar aspirations in Londonderry and was instrumental in the appointment of a qualified nurse to the workhouse infirmary in 1900, although she had to propose this motion three times before it was finally sanctioned in January 1901.[85]

From the late nineteenth century female guardians were also appointed to single-sex committees. This was apparent in Ballymoney, where female guardians were made solely responsible for compiling a new diet for the workhouse inmates in 1900 and again in 1902. Similarly Belfast's women guardians were formed into a committee to conduct an investigation into the standards of cleanliness amongst children maintained in the workhouse. Indeed, by 1904–5 women on all the boards under analysis were procuring clothing for workhouse inmates and were given responsibility for examining inmates' bedding and clothing. Furthermore, some matters were immediately passed over for the consideration of female guardians. For instance, in 1912 the Countess of Aberdeen, president of the Women's National Health Association, sent a circular to boards of guardians outlining the importance of midwifery care. In both Ballymoney and Londonderry unions this memorandum was automatically passed over to the female members of the board for consideration.[86]

In other aspects of poor law administration, such as providing out-relief, women worked alongside their male colleagues to decide who was eligible for assistance. This was one of the most difficult areas of guardians' work, but even here the impact of women's influence is tangible, as on occasion they endeavoured to implement reform.[87] Just two months after her election to Lisburn guardians, Louisa Stannus visited a couple who had applied for out-relief. She subsequently reported on the discrepancies of the out-relief system between the sexes: 'If the case were reversed and the woman in receipt of the pension . . . the man would get the relief – this seems very unfair from a woman's point of view.'[88] In spite of this protest, the Local Government Board refused to make any exceptions to the ruling that men in receipt of a pension could not be granted relief. In 1918 Stannus unsuccessfully attempted to introduce another amendment to out-relief provisions to allow widows with one child to apply for assistance.[89] The economic depression of the late 1920s placed immense pressure on the already inadequate system of out-relief and, in Belfast union, meetings held twice a week to assess applications for out-relief regularly lasted between seven and eight hours.[90] From 1931 to 1934 Belfast guardians dealt with 219,297 applications for out-relief, at a weekly cost of between £400 and £460, and Londonderry's board of guardians assessed 850 weekly applications for out-relief during 1933 to 1935.[91] The administrative burden of this work was only removed when the Northern Ireland Ministry for Labour established a new department to implement a means-tested scheme for unemployment benefit in 1935.[92]

In addition to the practical day-to-day considerations of workhouse administration, women guardians also sought to care for children and free them from the stigma of pauperism. This involved a multiplicity of areas: illegitimacy, education, emigration and boarding out. Illegitimacy remained primarily the concern of female guardians. Boards of guardians generally interpreted escalating illegitimacy rates as a social problem which was inextricably linked to the hereditary nature of pauperism and consequently believed this to be one realm where female guardians could influence the less upstanding members of their own sex.[93] It is clear that women guardians undertook considerable responsibility for caring for unmarried mothers maintained in the workhouse. The master of Belfast workhouse, Robert Wilson, for example, favoured the appointment of a ladies' committee to 'quietly and unostentatiously' find suitable employment for unmarried mothers[94] and, when a woman inmate became pregnant in Londonderry workhouse, a committee of female guardians consented 'to look after her welfare'.[95]

All the boards under analysis were also concerned about the cost of maintaining unmarried mothers and illegitimate children in the workhouse and female guardians were appointed to committees which tried to persuade women to name putative fathers to allow the union to reclaim maintenance costs. In 1901 a committee of women guardians in Londonderry interviewed unmarried pregnant women for this purpose and a female member of the board, Margaret Morris, unsuccessfully proposed the prosecution of all the putative fathers of illegitimate children who were maintained in the workhouse.[96] Women quickly came to dominate this area of poor law administration. Indeed, from 1912 female guardians in Londonderry were appointed as a permanent committee to 'interrogate' female inmates in what was deemed to be 'a certain condition'.[97] Lisburn guardians adopted a similar approach, leading the Local Government Board to inform them that they could not compel unmarried women to make affidavits regarding the paternity of their children.[98] By 1911 all the female members of Ballymoney guardians were appointed to a committee to consider an illegitimacy bill and female guardians in Belfast were also actively involved in tracing the fathers of illegitimate children maintained in the workhouse. In a few instances boards of guardians were able to institute legal proceedings to reclaim maintenance costs after an affidavit had been signed by the child's mother, but, despite the desire to lessen illegitimacy rates and reduce the cost of maintaining the illegitimate, change in this area could only be implemented at a legislative level.

From the end of the nineteenth century the ideology that the workhouse was an unsuitable environment in which children could mature as responsible citizens free from the stigma of pauperism became increasingly popular. An integral part of this conviction involved the education of workhouse children in the non-institutionalised environment of national schools. Many female guardians were appointed to committees to report on the plausibility of implementing this practice. In 1899 Belfast became one of the first Irish unions to consider such a scheme and one of its female guardians, Emily Callwell, thus communicated 'with the best authorities in England for the purpose of obtaining information' on their educational practices.[99] In 1910 Lisburn guardians followed suit, establishing a children's committee for this purpose and authorising Annie Barbour to interview the managers of local schools and select suitable clothing for the workhouse schoolchildren.[100] On Ballymoney and Londonderry boards of guardians, female members also provided the impetus for introducing these improvements in April and January 1900 respectively.[101] In addition, women on Belfast's board were involved in pressing for improvements in educational provisions for children maintained in the workhouse infirmary. This issue was first raised by Jane Payne in 1904 and three years later her colleague, Sarah Thomas, succeeded in securing the appointment of a teacher for child epileptics and convalescents in the workhouse. As a direct consequence of their initiatives a school for convalescent children was established in Belfast's workhouse infirmary by 1910.[102]

Nowhere was female influence more apparent than in the administration of boarding out schemes. From the turn of the century the practice of boarding out, or fostering, children from the workhouse in the local community became increasingly common in Ulster, as elsewhere in Ireland.[103] This was identified solely as women's work and women played a fundamental role in developing the ideology that the workhouse was an unsuitable environment for children. Boarding out was first suggested in 1861 by Mrs Archer in her pamphlet *Prolonged protection for pauper girls* and in 1874 Mrs Nassau Senior, the first woman appointed to the English Poor Law Inspectorate, reported that:

> The enormous buildings that are erected for the reception of pauper children, seem to point to a belief that we are to have an ever-increasing race of paupers throughout the centuries to come. Against such a belief boarding-out is a protest.[104]

In 1862 legislation was passed to facilitate boarding out children under the age of five in Irish unions, and in 1869 this age limit was extended to ten years. As further legislative measures were passed in 1876 and 1898 the perception grew that boarding out afforded the only opportunity for breaking the hereditary cycle of poverty.[105] It was even asserted that children brought up in the workhouse would 'return later in life as surely as the homing pigeon will return to its loft . . . We have frequently found . . . an illegitimate baby, its mother, and its grandmother in the Workhouse.'[106]

Responsibility for administering the boarding out system was delegated to women at the suggestion of the Local Government Board in 1899 and ladies' boarding out committees subsequently became the only permanent all-female bodies in the boards of guardians' administrative structure.[107] Following the regulations of the Local Government Board's Boarding Out Order of April 1899, Londonderry and Belfast formed their first ladies' committees for this purpose in June 1899 and January 1900 respectively. Ballymoney also established a ladies' committee in 1900 to care for its seven boarded-out children. The establishment of these committees depended on the extent of boarding out in specific unions. In Lisburn, for example, only one child was boarded out in 1900 and Gertrude Keightley, as the only female guardian, consented to visit and report on this child's progress. But there was a steady increase in the extent of boarding out schemes from the early twentieth century. Belfast, as the biggest union in Ulster, had the largest scheme, involving 132 children by 1911. Thirty-six children were boarded out in Londonderry union in 1926 and by 1939 this number had increased to 122. Women appointed to these committees considered the suitability of foster homes and delivered 'advice, encouragement, or warning . . . seeing also that the wants of the heart and the soul are supplied'.[108] This involved an assessment of practicalities, such as sleeping arrangements and matching the religious affiliation of the child to its prospective foster parent. The moral training of boarded-out children was also considered, as foster parents were meant to encourage habits of industry, cleanliness and thrift.

For lone female guardians the expansion of boarding out schemes entailed considerable labour. In 1900 only one child was boarded out in Lisburn but by 1906 this number increased to four. Gertrude Keightley, as the only female guardian on Lisburn's board, undertook full responsibility for visiting, clothing and supervising these children and felt under such pressure that she tendered her resignation from boarding out work, stating: 'No committee requires so much time and attention, the constant supervision of the homes, and the regular inspection of the children.'[109] Keightley refused to withdraw her resignation, even though her colleagues claimed that her work was 'almost indispensable'.[110] Thereafter all poor law guardians in Lisburn were delegated to visit boarded-out children in their respective electoral divisions. However, it seems that this arrangement was short-lived, as by 1907 Marie Dickie, the Local Government Board's inspector, reported that the high standard of foster homes throughout Lisburn union was:

> largely due to the efforts of the Lady Guardian . . . who has devoted much time and trouble to the selection of homes and clothing, as well as teaching the foster parents the best method of managing and caring.[111]

Dickie defined this as 'special work' and the loss of Keightley as 'Incalculable . . . the Guardians would find it difficult to deal properly with what is so essentially a woman's work'.[112]

Boarding out was seen as such an essentially female task that women were appointed from outside the ranks of the guardians to serve on these committees in an auxiliary capacity. This supplementary practice was most probably initiated because the number of female guardians was insufficient to cope with the work involved and in some cases women were appointed to boarding out committees of boards which had no female members in order to assist the work of male guardians. Membership of a boarding out committee involved a certain amount of personal expense, such as the cost of travelling to foster homes.[113] This would undoubtedly have deterred working-class women from becoming involved and it appears that the auxiliary members of boarding out committees, like the majority of guardians, were mainly drawn from the upper middle classes.[114] Again, familial connections were important in the selection of these women. For example, Miss McElderry, the daughter of the chairman of Ballymoney guardians, served on its boarding out committee in an ancillary capacity from 1909 and four women on Clogher's committee were wives of guardians in 1930.[115] For some women, administering boarding out schemes acted as an informal apprenticeship for poor law work. In 1908, for instance, both Sarah Blackwood and Sarah Finlay became guardians on Belfast board after working on its boarding out committee for several years.[116]

Many female guardians appear to have possessed a deep-seated sense of duty towards the children in their care, a duty which they occasionally defined as acting 'as parents would regarding their own children'.[117] On a more regular basis than male guardians, women proposed that orphaned and deserted children be adopted by the board under section 1 (1) of the 1899 Poor Law Act, whereby guardians assumed all the powers of parents until the child reached the age of eighteen. Moreover, some female guardians were evidently concerned about freeing children from their guidance and care. In May 1930 Lisburn board adopted Louisa Stannus' resolution that boarded-out children leaving the guardians' care 'should be brought before the Board and given some useful advice as to their future behaviour and conduct in life'.[118] With this sense of responsibility and the close contact which female guardians maintained with inmates, it is perhaps not surprising that on occasion they personally fostered workhouse children. To cite just a couple of examples: Margaret Morris of Londonderry board fostered a workhouse child in 1909 and Louisa Stannus fostered a child in 1921 and three years later took an illegitimate infant into her home after its mother's arrest in Lisburn. On occasion women guardians also employed workhouse inmates. Again, to cite just a few examples, Charlotte Hamilton of Ballymoney guardians took a girl into her home to train as a servant in 1900 and Kate Megahy of Belfast board employed a workhouse boy in 1905.[119] Ladies' boarding out committees also helped to find suitable employment for inmates and in some cases individual members personally financed the training of workhouse girls in domestic service and boys in technical instruction, occasionally supplementing the wages of former inmates to enable them to remain in employment and prevent readmission to the institution. A similar desire to remove children from the institutionalised environment of the workhouse also prompted boarding out committees to promote emigration schemes. From 1904, members of Belfast's committee were working in conjunction with Dr Barnardo's and the Birmingham Diocesan Society to organise child emigration schemes to Canada. The full extent of women's support for emigration can be ascertained from the fact that members of both Belfast's and Lisburn's boarding out committees frequently paying for the costs of passage.[120] On occasion, individual women also lent money to children to enable them to emigrate and give them 'a fresh start in life' free from the slur of pauperism.[121]

These committees also actively campaigned to have the legislative restrictions controlling their work removed. In 1910, 1913 and again in 1914, Belfast's ladies' boarding out committee requested that the Local Government Board take steps to extend the legislative restrictions controlling boarding out to children whose parents were physically or morally unfit to provide proper care. Furthermore, in 1911 Gertrude Keightley successfully persuaded Lisburn's board to appeal to the chief secretary, as the president and parliamentary representative of the Local Government Board, to extend section 1 of the 1902 Pauper Children Act to Ireland. Without this provision boarding out remained restricted to deserted and orphaned children, a legislative framework which Keightley believed placed at a 'cruel disadvantage':

> just the class of children that most urgently need the influence of a good working home to counteract the well known hereditary tendencies, which, despite every care in teaching in workhouse schools, almost invariably brings them back to the Workhouse, either as unmarried mothers or as . . . hopeless wasters.[122]

It appears that demanding an extension of boarding out regulations to include those whose parents were deemed unfit was an abiding concern for female guardians. Florence Clark of Belfast guardians regularly corresponded with the Local Government Board from 1901 to try and instigate legislative change in this area, emphasising that the ladies' committee felt constrained and wanted the means to 'rescue' children:

> from the evil contamination inseparable from unrestricted control by their parents and we hold it is the duty and privilege of the Guardians . . . to save the little ones. Why the children should perforce remain inmates of the Workhouse we fail to understand. A careful study of the relative Acts of Parliament convinces us that this result was never intended by the legislation.[123]

Although the Local Government Board agreed to submit this resolution to the government, no action was forthcoming to introduce legislative change and Belfast's ladies' committee was forced to continue its campaign to have these constraints removed into the 1930s.[124]

In recognition of their interest in child welfare, boarding out committees were delegated sole responsibility for considering the provisions of the 1908 Children's Act, which made it compulsory to register and inspect children being nursed for financial reward. In the next year the members of Ballymoney's boarding out committee temporarily acted as infant life protection visitors in order to carry out the provisions of this act. Their findings were far from satisfactory, further convincing them of the necessity for appointing a full-time and paid official to carry out inspection work.[125] Women guardians on Lisburn's board also recommended that this legislation should be fully implemented and were so convinced of the need for regular inspection to effectively care for children that they offered their own services as protection visitors.[126] Female guardians were also concerned that both boarded- and hired-out children should be inspected by women and from 1901 Belfast's boarding out committee campaigned to have a female children's inspector employed by the Local Government Board. This was a common practice in England, where it proved 'highly beneficial in the checking of irregularities and in ensuring better care and treatment'.[127] In May 1902 Marie Dickie was appointed as the first female inspector for boarded-out children in Ireland and the women guardians of Belfast congratulated themselves on having influenced this appointment. This committee also suggested that children maintained in external institutions by guardians should be visited by female inspectors and as a direct result of their proposals this practice was implemented in Belfast union from 1904.[128]

There was a tendency for many Irish girls to leave the workhouse and take up situations, especially in domestic service, only to be re-admitted to the institution unmarried and pregnant.[129] With this trend it is not surprising that female guardians sought to protect those in their care. In 1905 Belfast's boarding out committee protested against the practice of relieving officers inspecting girls hired out from the workhouse, on the basis that this was 'unnecessary and even prejudicial . . . [keeping] up the connection with the workhouse, and harms the girls in the opinion of those around her'.[130] As a result, from 1905 these women undertook sole responsibility for this work, which they believed they could execute in a more discreet manner. From subsequent reports compiled by this committee it does seem they conducted this type of visiting sympathetically, endeavouring not to act in any official capacity but to cultivate a relationship with former workhouse girls in domestic employ. In addition to this work, in an attempt to ensure that foster children were well cared for, boarding out committees frequently recommended that maintenance payments to foster parents be increased. Deputations from Belfast's committee met with the board's finance committee to successfully secure an increase in foster-parenting allowances in 1908 and on Lisburn's board Gertrude Keightley made enquiries regarding maintenance costs paid by other unions and successfully recommended an increase to 6*s*/0*d* per week in 1918.[131] But other motions to increase allowances were not so successful. In 1908 Margaret Gilliland unsuccessfully tried to introduce two motions to increase these payments in Londonderry union, but these were not approved until January 1910.[132]

The humanising aspect of the work of women guardians was most apparent in their boarding out work. At the turn of the century Belfast's boarding out committee believed that the cut and material of the clothes supplied to boarded-out children was too distinctive and changes were subsequently made to make those fostered in the community unidentifiable as paupers.[133] Two years later this committee took the decision to stop stamping children's clothes with a distinguishable mark and refused to submit its reports to the press in order to protect the identities of boarded-out children. Similarly, on Londonderry's board, Margaret Morris was anxious to reduce boarded-out children's association with the workhouse and in 1903 successfully persuaded the board to inspect children in their foster homes instead of bringing them to the institution. These committees also advertised in the press for the parents of deserted children in an attempt to reunite families and this practice provided the impetus for the introduction of a history sheet system which recorded background information on individual inmates in Belfast union. The ladies' committee attempted to persuade the board to implement this system from 1907, but was only successful two years later. This scheme aimed to minimise the number of permanent workhouse inmates by tracing the parents of deserted children, the putative fathers of illegitimate children and the spouses of abandoned wives in order to persuade them to remove their children and partners from the institution or pay maintenance costs. Women became largely responsible for administering this system, which by 1911 was identified as a crucial aspect of poor law work:

> the Lady Guardians have taken a very great interest, and they have spent a vast amount of time visiting the homes of the children and

> their relatives, with a view to having the children removed, and their efforts have been very successful . . . [in the] connecting of families together.[134]

This scheme was a major success. As a result of these investigations 267 children and 102 parents were discharged from Belfast's workhouse during 1912 to 1913, saving individuals from the stigma of pauperism and the union £649 in costs. Indeed, this scheme was so successful that it was later extended to consumptive and able-bodied inmates and, in 1935, to gynaecological patients maintained in the workhouse infirmary.

Nineteenth-century reformers like Isabella Tod attempted to carve a niche for women in municipal politics by claiming that certain aspects of poor law administration were especially suited to women. This was successful and it is clear that a definite women's role subsequently developed. Female guardians focused on the more intimate tasks of the day-to-day running of the workhouse and caring for women and children, whilst their male colleagues concentrated on areas such as finance and building maintenance. More importantly, women were able to instigate important reforms in the areas of work that they dominated. This had the effect of improving lax administrative practices and the standard of care for recipients of indoor relief and protecting the welfare of those maintained outside the institutionalised environment of the workhouse. Yet, in the work of a guardian there was a fine dividing line between conscientiousness and over-zealousness.

The 1909 Royal Commission on the Poor Law, attending an unnamed meeting of Irish guardians, was appalled by the lack of business transacted:

> owing to the obstructive methods of one lady member. This is an illustration of the fact, that, whilst Lady Guardians can, if well disposed, do much to improve Poor-Law administration, if on the other hand they are obstructive and quarrelsome, they can defy procedure and rules, which men would be compelled to obey.[135]

This description is possibly of Londonderry, as from 1900 Margaret Morris frequently overrode this board's authority and disrupted meetings in an attempt to counter inefficient administration. Morris regularly complained directly to the Local Government Board, a stance that was neither appreciated by the guardians nor the board. In addition, she visited Londonderry's workhouse and infirmary several times a week and her overt criticisms aroused serious discontent amongst staff. As a result of her somewhat persecutory approach, the chairman of Londonderry's board was compelled to remind her that guardians 'could not interfere with the patients, or give directions, or dictate to the officials'.[136] Although some of Morris' complaints were upheld, her approach undoubtedly fostered serious tensions, forcing her to defend her work:

> I bear no malice . . . my sole object [is] that proper care and attention be given to the sick poor, and I trust I have only to appeal to this Board or to the Local Government Board to have that end accomplished.[137]

Her faith was, however, ill-founded, as her colleagues became increasingly reluctant to support her and repeatedly ruled her motions out of order. But Morris continued unabated, even forcing her way into the maternity ward of the union infirmary with her husband in July 1900. This compelled the board to regulate visiting hours and pass a resolution that all visitors had to be accompanied by a workhouse official. But this had little effect, as Morris declared that she would defy these regulations. She was subsequently expelled from the guardian's weekly meeting, causing such disorder that the whole meeting was forced to adjourn.[138] These problems escalated. Morris' regular disruption of meetings led to the establishment of a committee to consider proper conduct for guardians in January 1901 and by July of that year her interference was deemed to be seriously detrimental to the whole institution. The following month, with workhouse staff threatening to institute legal proceedings against her for slander, Morris was threatened with suspension from the board for alleging that the relieving officer of the union had fathered an illegitimate child who was maintained in the workhouse. By December 1904, as a result of her complaints, a sworn inquiry was held by the Local Government Board, but the only recommendation made which upheld her allegations was that stricter supervision be enforced for inmates employed in the workhouse.[139] Three years later Morris was prohibited from visiting the infirmary, but, undeterred, she climbed through a window, forcing the board to institute legal proceedings. But the board lost the case and was thus compelled to remove the embargo on Morris' visiting.[140]

This provides an extreme example of one woman's disregard for regulations and procedures. Although the majority of women on the four boards under analysis, individually and as a group, seem to have worked tirelessly, their duties were often far from easy. In 1939, giving evidence to the Ministry for Home Affairs inquiry into the administration of Belfast union, Lily Coleman outlined some of the difficulties which she encountered as a poor law guardian, highlighting the paucity of information and guidance available: 'not once was a regulation laid before me to mark, learn and inwardly digest, and act upon . . . there is not one single item to suggest where your duties begin and where they end'.[141] She also claimed that there was a 'stone wall of regulations' inhibiting the work of the female members of Belfast's board:

> Some of us women . . . had a little talk just before the Board rose . . . we decided . . . [to] have a general inspection of certain wards . . . we did not want to rant and roar . . . We . . . began to make a report and we were closured. We were told we had no right to go round inspecting the Institution and the wrangling became so great that the next morning we were faced in the local press with half-inch type 'Lady Guardians' Snubbed. Called Nosey' . . . not very complimentary to women who thought they were doing their duty to the Institution.[142]

With the absence of any guidelines, some newly elected female guardians evidently struggled to define what was acceptable behaviour. This problem was apparent in 1897 when an inmate of Belfast's workhouse alleged that Kate Megahy, the only female member of the board at this time, had unduly tried to influence her religious opinion.[143] In June 1900 the Catholic chaplain of Belfast's workhouse made a similar complaint against another female guardian, Lizzie Carson, for preaching to an inmate and making insulting references to Catholic worship. In both cases the board took no action.[144] Only months later Carson experienced further difficulties and was forced to tender her resignation after making a false charge against the workhouse master.

A result of women remaining such a conspicuous minority within the board room environment was that the performance of individual woman guardians tended to reflect on the other female members of the board. The appointment of women to office was not only portrayed as a compliment for all the female members of the board, but when women like Margaret Morris or Lizzie Carson disregarded regulations it was perceived to be detrimental to the reputations of other female guardians. This was illustrated by James Oswald who, in 1900, called for Carson's resignation from Belfast guardians on the basis that her unsubstantiated allegations 'seriously reflected on every Member of this Board . . . especially in the interests of the Lady Members'.[145]

IV

Service not Self[146]

Despite the problems caused by the lack of guidance that was available for poor law guardians, it seems that women experienced little hostility from their male colleagues. Indeed the gender division of poor law work certainly appears to have countered any animosity between male and female guardians. Throughout the period under analysis male guardians continued to take responsibility for workhouse finance and maintenance. There were therefore areas concerning women and children and the more intimate aspects of poor law administration that men were content to delegate to their female colleagues. In 1924 Robert Andrews, the chairman of Belfast guardians, openly supported this gender division of duties, referring 'to the excellent work which the ladies carry on as Guardians, some [of which] . . . could not be done by other members of the Board'.[147] Further acclamation was forthcoming in 1926 when Thomas Gibb, chairman of Belfast guardians, praised the women members 'who had attended regularly from the morning till late in the evening until the business was transacted, a support which he valued very much'.[148] Individual boards also regularly paid tribute to the special nature of women's work. Belfast's board of guardians, for example, commended Lulu Dickie's work in the context of helping those members of society who could no longer help themselves, caring for children and improving accommodation for the imbeciles and epileptics who were maintained in the workhouse.[149] Another indication of the support which female guardians received is the fact that some women who attempted to resign their duties were persuaded to continue as guardians. Both Gertrude Keightley and Charlotte Hamilton attempted to resign from Lisburn and Ballymoney boards, in 1905 and 1928 respectively, but were persuaded by their colleagues to reconsider. The reappointment of female guardians following their resignation also suggests that their work was valued. For instance, in 1927 Belfast guardians co-opted Esther McDonnell, an ex-guardian, back onto the board because of her 'very important work amongst the women and children . . . [she] showed practical kindness in a quiet manner . . . the poor will be benefited by her co-option'.[150]

Like their male colleagues, women were content to accept the gendered division of poor law work. It seems that female guardians were more than happy to assist the destitute and vulnerable, striving to improve standards of care and maintain closer contact with the workhouse inmates, than many of their male colleagues. The most enduring testimony of the satisfaction which women derived from poor law administration can be found in the tributes following their death or retirement. Sir Samuel Keightley, husband of the late Lady Gertrude Keightley, who served as chairman of Lisburn guardians for seven years, informed the board that many of his wife's 'happiest and most useful days were spent in . . . [poor law] work'.[151] These tributes also reinforce the idea that the gender division of poor law work was widely supported. Mrs Pim wrote of the sense of fulfilment which the late Louisa Stannus derived from her membership of Lisburn's board of guardians, especially in caring for children:

> her greatest happiness was found in working for the welfare of the children, and she greatly valued the opportunities which her Membership of the Board gave her . . . the duties of her office [were] a labour of love.[152]

Furthermore, women's focus on specific areas of poor law administration seems to have fostered a sense of camaraderie and solidarity amongst female guardians. In 1934 Lily Coleman claimed that the female members of Belfast's board not only worked together in areas which were earmarked as intrinsically suited to women's capabilities and experience, but that they had 'much to be thankful for as there was no feeling of jealousy. They worked hand in hand for the benefit of the community.'[153]

The admission of women to the public office of poor law guardian may not have modified the conservative views of what constituted women's work, but their role in poor law administration was of considerable significance. Many female guardians, drawn to this work by philanthropic and altruistic considerations, were instrumental in initiating important reforms that helped to reshape poor law administration. Indeed, some women were so determined to initiate reform that they were even prepared to resign from office: Louisa Stannus resigned from Lisburn's boarding out committee in February 1925 in opposition to the Local Government Board's refusal to sanction the payment of transport costs incurred by women visiting boarded-out children[154] and in 1929 all seven women appointed to Belfast's history sheet and child welfare committee temporarily resigned, in protest against the Local Government Board's appointment of a male inspector under the Children's Act, believing that this position was best suited to a trained female nurse.[155]

Many of the areas of administration which were dominated by women also became increasingly important as the societal demands on the poor law altered in the early twentieth century. In 1918 Lady Gertrude Keightley, as chairman of Lisburn's board, clearly identified the extent of these changes:

> workhouses are no longer a necessity . . . [The] famine days are now gone, should misfortune again assail our people in the form of poverty it is questionable if we would again be disposed to huddle the respectable poor in the workhouse . . . the present tendency . . . of the very poor is to shun the workhouse if the means of existence can be obtained outside.[156]

This heightened the importance of women's role in poor law administration: removing children and those with special needs from the institutionalised surroundings of the workhouse, improving standards of inspection, encouraging emigration schemes, campaigning for legislative change and attempting to combat the cycle of pauperism. It has been alleged that workhouse officials 'dreaded the prying of inquisitive and interfering ladies practised in the art of detecting domestic lapses',[157] but such an approach had a significant impact in addressing lax administration and implementing many overdue reforms. In essence, female poor law guardians were as active and dedicated as their male colleagues. Thus women's influence outweighed their comparatively small numerical representation and, although they remained a minority on boards of guardians, working largely within 'traditional' areas of female involvement, these were areas that were indispensable to the effective and benevolent administration of the poor law.

CHAPTER FIVE

Women Local Government Councillors

The woman who takes up any form of public service literally gives herself, her time, her powers and sympathies to help uplift the nation.[1]

I

From the late nineteenth century successive legislative reforms gradually admitted Irish women as voters and candidates to the arena of local government. Indeed, a pattern in the admission of women to the realms of government can be traced in relation to the jurisdiction of specific bodies. Initially women were admitted to the less powerful areas of poor law and district council administration, and only later to county and borough councils and to parliament. The Local Government (Ireland) Act of 1898, which established a municipal franchise on the same terms as the poor law legislation of 1896, certainly bestowed on women 'a privilege which was eagerly availed of'.[2] However, before the passage of this act, Irish women's exclusion from municipal administration was not absolute. In Belfast women had already been admitted to the local government franchise by the Municipal Corporations (Ireland) Act of 1887, which allowed every householder and ratepayer, regardless of sex, to elect members of the city's corporation. This act was introduced to parliament by three Belfast MPs: William Ewart, James Corry and William Johnston, who collectively sought to establish an adult household franchise in order to curtail the corporation's expenditure.[3] Though this provided the impetus for the introduction of this legislation, the North of Ireland Women's Suffrage Society, led by Isabella Tod, campaigned to secure recognition for female municipal rights within this act.[4] Tod initiated several personal meetings with the bill's sponsors and succeeded in persuading Lord Erne to introduce an amendment in order to clarify women's legislative position by substituting the term 'person' for that of 'man'. Thus, by 1890, 4,756 women were registered as voters in Belfast and by 1895 this number had increased to 6,200, representing 16 per cent of the city's total municipal electorate.[5] Tod believed, with some justification, that this act guaranteed further legislative reform for Irish women. Writing in the July 1887 edition of *The Englishwoman's Review* she emphasised that the admission of women to Belfast's municipal electorate established a precedent for the whole country: 'The satisfaction with which we view the passing of this Bill is much increased by the fact that it will practically secure the same right for women in all Irish towns.'[6] And there were moves towards realising this goal. From February 1892 the government pledged to introduce an extensive reform of Irish local government, and a bill, which included female householders in the municipal franchise, reached a second reading in that year.[7]

But the North of Ireland Women's Suffrage Society's ongoing campaign for local government reform was thrown into considerable disarray by the death of Isabella Tod in 1896. For over twenty years Tod had been the 'foremost champion in the educational, political, industrial, and moral struggles' conducted by women in Ulster and she had dedicated much of her 'bright and rapid intellect, . . . ready pen, and . . . admirable gift of speech . . . [to] the service of women'.[8] For several years the suffrage and local government reform campaign in Ulster, and especially in Belfast, reportedly laboured 'under much discouragement in consequence of the lamented death of their indomitable leader'.[9] It seems that, as a direct result of Tod's death and the lack of any successor to co-ordinate suffragists and local government reformers in Ulster, many women turned to the Dublin-based IWSLGA for both inspiration and direction. This explains why, in 1896, the North of Ireland Women's Suffrage Society became a branch of the IWSLGA. The links between these two organisations had always been close: the IWSLGA was formerly known as the Dublin Women's Suffrage Society, an association that developed from a committee which was formed after Tod organised a suffrage meeting in Dublin as part of her pioneering Irish tour in 1872.[10] The northern society was ultimately rescued from collapse by its incorporation into the organisational structure of the IWSLGA. By 1898 the association's annual report recounted that the northern campaign was fully reconstituted 'on an efficient basis, and may once more be expected to take its fitting place in the van of Irish progress'.[11] Indeed, by that year three committees campaigning for local government reform and promoting the interests of women, 'irrespective of creed or politics', were established in Coleraine, Dungannon and Portadown.[12]

From the late 1890s the IWSLGA's campaign was reminiscent of Isabella Tod's earlier work, as the association attempted to initiate municipal reform by co-operating with sympathetic MPs. Foremost amongst these men was staunch unionist and Orangeman, William Johnston, who also earned himself a reputation as an 'indefatigable friend of women's interests' by introducing both the Municipal Corporations (Ireland) Act of 1887 and the Poor Law (Ireland) (Women) Act of 1896 to parliament.[13] The IWSLGA's annual report of 1902 further enhanced Johnston's standing by attesting that he knew 'no politics where the interests of his fellow-country-women were concerned'.[14] In addition to maintaining good personal relations with those who could introduce the necessary reform to facilitate women's entry into the more powerful echelons of municipal politics, the IWSLGA also forwarded hundreds of letters to MPs, female poor law guardians and other interested societies and individuals. The association claimed that their campaign, specifically a written appeal to the Irish chief secretary, successfully secured support for local government reform and the establishment of two member constituencies for district councils. This move was prompted by concerns that women would not be elected as rural and urban district councillors in single-member constituencies because voters 'would desire to elect a man to represent them in religion and politics, and only after that would they elect a woman to see to the sick poor'.[15] Yet, in spite of these claims, it is difficult to gauge the specific impact of the IWSLGA's campaign, as Irish municipal reform, like the poor law reform which preceded it, was implemented largely to bring the country into line with English and Scottish legislation.

In addition to admitting women as voters and candidates in district council elections, the Local Government (Ireland) Act of 1898 also simplified the whole system of Irish municipal administration. This legislation, mirroring the provisions of the English Local Government Act of 1888, established a comprehensive system of democratic control over local affairs. Under the provisions of the 1898 act, six county councils, thirty-two urban district councils, thirty-two rural district councils and two county boroughs, in Belfast and Londonderry, were established in Ulster.[16] By superseding the fiscal duties of the grand jury system, the newly established county councils became the most powerful component of Irish local government. Furthermore, the power of boards of guardians to raise, levy and collect the poor rate was transferred to county council jurisdiction. Initially county councils had no public health functions, but following the precedent set by local government administration in England and Wales their spheres of duty were increased. Hence, by the early 1920s county councils had full responsibility for a diverse spectrum of tasks: implementing education and library schemes, maintaining roads and public works, providing care for the blind and mentally ill, inspecting schoolchildren, providing medical treatment for consumptives, and administering county infirmaries, fever hospitals and maternity and child welfare schemes.

Two subordinate channels of municipal administration were also created by the 1898 act: urban and rural district councils. The urban sanitary authorities, instituted under the Public Health Act of 1874, were transferred to the newly established urban district councils. As the sole rating authority in urban areas, these councils were marginally more powerful than their rural counterparts. In addition to sanitation, urban district councils had responsibility for working-class housing, water, gas, electricity, street-lighting and cleaning, road maintenance, the notification and prevention of infectious diseases, hospital services and the management of burial grounds. By comparison, rural district councils replaced the administrative functions of the baronial presentment sessions. As these rural councils were unable to levy taxes, they were not financially autonomous. They were, therefore, obliged to present their expenditure to county councils in order to finance and administer public health regulations, sanitary provisions, provide labourers' cottages and maintain roads and burial grounds in their localities.[17]

Irish suffragists hailed the passage of the Local Government (Ireland) Act as a 'political revolution' that would bring in its wake a major change in the government's attitude towards women's civic capabilities.[18] In spite of this, the reform initiated in 1898 was incomplete. Both the electorate and personnel of the two most powerful municipal bodies, county and county borough councils, remained exclusively male. In England, Wales and Scotland women were disqualified from this area of municipal politics until 1907, but in Ireland this position was not amended until 1911. In practice, this exclusion meant that women remained partially disenfranchised, electorally classified alongside the clergy, criminals, paupers, aliens and bankrupts. Interestingly, even amongst those who campaigned for women's admission to other areas of local government administration, this disqualification aroused little concern. Anna Haslam, one of the most dedicated members of the IWSLGA, remained convinced that few women would have stood as county and county borough council candidates, as its functions were not:

> so well calculated to enlist their [women's] sympathies, or draw out their special gifts. And on the whole it is certainly better that Ireland should not precede Great Britain in the extension of these franchises.[19]

However, the exclusion of Ireland from this reform in 1907 stimulated a renewed interest amongst members of the IWSLGA. During the association's campaign to initiate local government reform in the late nineteenth century, many of their appeals were based on demands for equitable Irish and English legislative provisions. Therefore, following English, Scottish and Welsh women's admittance to county and county borough administration, it was not surprising that the IWSLGA reiterated its appeals on the grounds of democracy. This issue was raised at the association's annual meeting of 1910, when Florence Clark, a member of Belfast's board of guardians, successfully proposed that a memorial be forwarded to the Prime Minister, leading members of the cabinet and MPs. This requested the extension of the 1907 act to Ireland to counter the 'derogatory inequality' caused by the continued denial of Irish women's 'constitutional rights'.[20] Irish women were admitted as voters and candidates to county and borough councils in the next year, but again it is difficult to determine the specific role of the IWSLGA's campaign in achieving this legislative change. Like both the Poor Law Guardian (Ireland) (Women) Act of 1896 and the Local Government (Ireland) Act of 1898, reform was introduced in 1911 in order to remove the existing legislative anomalies between England and Ireland. Nevertheless, the IWSLGA wholeheartedly welcomed the removal of 'the stigma under which our fellow-countrywomen have laboured since the passage of the corresponding English and Scottish acts in 1907'.[21]

II

By 1911 women were admitted to all areas of Irish municipal administration. Although suffragists claimed that poor law and local government reform cumulatively produced a 'remarkable development of public spirit amongst women in Ireland . . . [and] opened up a boundless field of useful public work for philanthropic Irishwomen', the level of female representation remained very low.[22] In the period 1896 to 1940, a total of 260 women served as poor law guardians and local government councillors in Ulster: 173 women (representing 67 per cent of the total number of women in local government in Ulster in the period under analysis) served as poor law guardians, forty-four (17 per cent) as rural district councillors and eighteen (7 per cent) as urban district councillors. Within the most powerful components of municipal government the levels of female representation were even lower: only ten women (representing 4 per cent of the total number of women in local government in the province from 1896 to 1940) served as county borough councillors, nine (3 per cent) as county councillors and six (2 per cent) as borough councillors.[23] These figures suggest that the power of specific local government bodies not only affected women's admission to municipal administration but also the level of female representation. This is clearly illustrated by the fact that almost four times as many women in Ulster held the least powerful local government position of poor law guardian as were elected as rural district councillors (see Table 4).[24]

Moreover, both the small number of women involved in local government work and the relationship between the power of specific municipal bodies and female representation can be discerned from analysing the average female representation on the various bodies of local government in Ulster from 1896 to 1940: female poor law guardians averaged 4.2 per cent,[25] whereas female borough councillors averaged 1.8 per cent, female county borough councillors 1.6 per cent and female county councillors 1.4 per cent.[26]

As with female poor law guardians, an increase in the number of women councillors only occurred gradually. This is clearly illustrated by a comparative analysis of female representation in 1899, a year after women were admitted to district council administration, to the end of the period under analysis in 1940. In 1899 there were five female rural district councillors, representing 0.7 per cent of the total. By 1940 this number increased to nineteen, representing 2.7 per cent (see Table 4). The figures for other local government bodies were similarly low. In 1899 there were three female urban district councillors in Ulster, representing 0.86 per cent of the total. By 1940 this figure had only increased to four, representing 1.1 per cent. Furthermore, in the immediate aftermath of women's admission to county and borough county administration in 1911, no female candidates stood for election. Indeed, female representation on these, the most powerful municipal bodies, occurred comparatively late, as it took a decade for women to come forward as candidates. By the outbreak of the Second World War there were just five female county

Table 4. Women rural district councillors in Ulster, 1899–1940[27]

	1899	1902	1905	1908	1911	1914	1920	1924	1927	1930	1933	1936	1939	Total per council
Antrim	–	Ø	–	–	–	–	–	–	–	–	–	–	Ø	0
Armagh	–	–	–	–	–	–	–	–	–	–	–	–	–	0
Ballycastle	–	–	–	–	–	–	–	–	–	–	–	–	–	0
Ballymena	–	–	–	1	1	–	1	1	1	1	1	1	1	9
Ballymoney	1	1	1	1	–	–	–	1	1	1	1	1	1	10
Banbridge	1	–	–	–	–	–	–	–	–	–	–	–	–	1
Belfast	–	–	–	–	–	–	–	–	–	–	–	–	–	0
Castlederg	–	–	–	–	–	–	–	–	2	–	–	–	–	2
Castlereagh	–	–	–	–	–	–	Ø	–	–	–	–	–	–	0
Clogher	–	–	–	–	–	–	–	–	–	1	–	–	–	1
Coleraine	1	1	1	1	1	1	1	1	–	–	–	–	–	8
Cookstown	–	–	–	–	–	–	–	–	–	–	–	–	–	0
Downpatrick	–	–	–	–	–	–	–	–	–	–	–	–	–	0
Dungannon	–	–	–	–	–	–	–	–	–	–	1	1	1	3
Enniskillen	/	/	/	/	–	/	/	–	–	–	–	–	–	0
Hillsborough	–	–	–	–	–	–	–	–	–	1	1	1	1	4
Irvinestown	–	–	–	–	–	Ø	–	–	–	1	1	1	2	5
Kilkeel	Ø	–	Ø	–	–	–	–	1	–	1	–	–	–	2
Larne	–	–	–	–	–	–	–	–	–	–	–	–	–	0
Limavady	1	2	1	1	2	3	1	2	1	–	1	1	1	17
Lisburn	Ø	–	–	Ø	1	Ø	1	1	1	1	1	1	1	8
Lisnaskea	–	–	–	–	–	–	–	–	–	–	–	–	–	0
Londonderry	–	–	–	–	Ø	Ø	Ø	Ø	Ø	Ø	Ø	Ø	Ø	0
Lurgan	1	–	–	–	–	–	–	–	–	–	–	–	–	1
Magherafelt	–	–	–	–	–	–	2	3	1	1	1	3	3	14
Moira	–	–	–	–	–	–	–	–	–	–	–	–	–	0
Newry no. 1	–	–	–	–	–	–	–	–	–	–	–	–	–	0
Newry no. 2	–	–	–	–	–	–	–	–	–	–	–	–	–	0
Newtownards	–	–	–	–	–	–	–	1	–	1	2		3	11
Omagh	–	–	–	–	–	–	–	1	1	–	–	–	–	2
Strabane	–	–	–	–	Ø	–	–	5	Ø	5	5	5	5	25
Tandragee	–	–	–	–	–	–	–	–	–	–	–	–	–	0
Total per annum	5	4	3	4	5	4	6	17	8	14	15	19	19	123

councillors and two county borough councillors, representing 2.8 per cent and 2 per cent of the respective Ulster totals.

The distribution of women throughout the various strands of local government further underlines the correlation between the level of female participation and the jurisdiction of specific municipal bodies. Two of Ulster's six-county councils were without any female representation in the period up to 1940.[28] Furthermore, of the thirty-two rural district councils, seventeen (53 per cent) had no female representatives, whilst twenty-three (72 per cent) of the more powerful urban district councils lacked any women members in the corresponding period.[29] On boards of guardians, the least powerful municipal body, the comparative figure was 19 per cent. As a result of the very small number of women serving on boards of guardians and local councils in Ulster it is very difficult to draw any firm conclusions concerning their geographical distribution. In spite of this, the available evidence does suggest that women elected to all of these municipal positions were exceptional in terms of personal ambition, circumstance or qualification.

A smaller number of women were appointed to office on local councils than on boards of guardians. This was not only a result of the lower level of female participation but also of reduced opportunity, as there was no position of deputy vice-chairman on local councils. A cumulative total of only nine women held office on borough, rural and urban district councils in Ulster from 1898 to 1940: seven in the position of vice-chairman and two in the position of chairman – Charlotte Hamilton on Portrush Urban District Council and Minnie Beattie on Lisburn Rural District Council. No women were appointed to office on county or borough county councils and this can be explained by the level of female representation and women's comparatively late admission to this arena of county administration. However, as was apparent for female poor law guardians in Ulster, the election of a woman to office was not always linked to a high level of female representation: Minnie Beattie, the only female member of Lisburn Rural District Council, was appointed as its vice-chairman in 1927, and a decade later Annie Martin, the only female member of Hillsborough Rural District Council, was also elected to this position. On occasion, however, women were reluctant to accept office. To cite one example, at Jessie Kydd's request a motion was withdrawn to appoint her as vice-chairman of Coleraine Urban District Council in January 1920.[30] Other women were unsuccessfully nominated for office: Charlotte Hamilton, the first woman elected to Portrush Urban District Council in January 1906, was proposed but not appointed to the position of vice-chairman in 1907.[31] Three years later, however, she was successfully appointed to this position and became council chairman in the following year.

Although the *Irish Citizen* believed that female local government councillors would have an opportunity to enlighten the general public on issues especially affecting women, such as suffrage and the necessity of rooting out the 'social evil' of venereal disease, it seems that few women undertook such roles.[32] Like the majority of female poor law guardians in Ulster, feminism was not the driving force behind women's involvement in municipal politics. Rather it was a genuine desire to improve the immediate locality.[33] Charlotte Hamilton's proposal of a suffrage resolution to support an extension of 'the parliamentary vote to woman householders' to Portrush Urban District Council in October 1911 can only be described as exceptional.[34] In spite of the apparent lack of feminist impetus amongst female councillors, it does seem that, for some women at least, experience on a less powerful public body did form a kind of apprenticeship for further civic participation. A third of women serving as urban district councillors, county councillors and county borough councillors in Ulster from the late nineteenth century also served as poor law guardians: Florence Clark, a former vice-chairman and member of Belfast's board of guardians for over twenty years, was elected to the city's corporation in 1923; her colleague Lily Coleman, the first female chairman of Belfast's board of guardians, was elected unopposed to Belfast Corporation in 1930 and both Lilly Ann Barr and Miss J.V. Douglas were elected as urban district councillors and poor law guardians in Ballymena and Banbridge respectively.[35] Moreover, for some women participation in municipal politics led to a parliamentary career. As far as it is possible to generalise on the three women who were elected to the parliament of Northern Ireland in the period 1921 to 1940, all had been involved in local government in some capacity.[36]

III

The above analysis reveals not only how small women's representation on local government bodies was, collectively averaging just 1.4 per cent of the total council positions available in Ulster from 1898 to 1940, but also that there was a definite correlation between the level of female representation and the jurisdiction of specific local government bodies. It is impossible to provide just one explanation to account for the very small number of women serving as local government councillors, but an anonymous letter to the *Irish Citizen* alleged that the difficulties of women's municipal candidature were 'manifold' and that female voters were at the mercy of unscrupulous registration agents who frequently struck names from the electoral register on the slightest of pretexts.[37] Qualification was deemed by the *Citizen* to be especially difficult for married women, who were 'practically ineligible under existing registration-law. No registration agency takes any real interest in women-voters because they do not possess the Parliamentary vote.'[38] Although the propagandist element to these claims is apparent, there were concerns regarding the efficiency of the registration system outside suffragist echelons. Indeed preceding the passage of the Representation of the People Act of 1918, women's political associations, such as the Ulster Women's Unionist Council and the Ladies' Auxiliary of the Ancient Order of Hibernians, regularly attempted to update electoral lists in order to promote their respective political interests.[39]

Irish suffragists were clearly concerned that women's continued parliamentary disenfranchisement would impede their participation in municipal administration. But what changed after the passage of the Representation of the People Act in 1918? This legislation created female electoral majorities in four of the six counties of north-east Ulster, prompting political parties to reconsider their electoral strategies to mobilise female electoral support.[40] As a direct consequence all parties, with the exception of Labour, ran female candidates in the next Irish municipal election of 1920.[41] Yet, in spite of this, women's parliamentary enfranchisement had little tangible impact on the number of female local government councillors and after 1918 there was no immediate or sustained increase in women's representation and numbers continued to fluctuate throughout the inter-war period. As a result legislative reform was increasingly identified as an insufficient guarantor of female municipal representation. The *Irish Citizen* called for the initiation of a sustained campaign to encourage women to stand as local government candidates:

> Ireland had but a few woman councillors . . . Women must wake up, and women's societies throughout Ireland must insist at the coming elections . . . that a good proportion (we should say half) of the newly elected bodies be women. Now, not the eve of the election is the time to begin to choose women candidates.[42]

But the suffrage movement never fully recovered from the decline in support caused by the outbreak of the First World War and this disunity was exacerbated by the passage of the Representation of the People Bill of 1918, which removed the only unifying factor in the suffrage campaign. This seriously curtailed the possibilities for launching any initiative on the lines envisaged by the *Citizen* and few attempts appear to have been made from feminist echelons or elsewhere to actively encourage women to stand as local government candidates. The Ulster Women's Unionist Council was the only political organisation to publicly advocate women's involvement in municipal affairs, encouraging its members to stand not only as poor law guardians, but also as county and urban district councillors, in order to further the unionist cause.[43] As there is no record of the number of women who availed themselves of this support, or of their record of electoral success, it is impossible to ascertain whether the support of a political organisation coupled with financial backing significantly affected the number of female candidates. However, the UWUC's call of 1932 'that it would be helpful to the Unionist cause if more women would come forward for Local Government and Town Council work' indicates that there was still some way to go before unionists, at least, were satisfied with women's municipal representation.[44]

In addition to party support, a certain type of woman was also deemed 'suitable' for executing the duties of public office. The personal qualifications that contemporary commentators believed prospective female councillors should possess were very similar to those demanded of female poor law guardians:

> [She] must be guarded in word and deed, for she is subject to public criticism; humble . . . and dignified because she represents womanhood; judicial, because there are two sides to every question . . . [and] kind, for it is woman's task to help the desolate and oppressed.[45]

Such high expectations were, however, tempered by the realisation that most women were:

> the modest violet type that shrinks (even when thoroughly qualified) from taking up public work . . . There are times when modesty ceases to be a virtue and becomes poltroonery . . . Women with leisure (they often have more of the commodity than men), with gifts of education, with broad sympathy, should regard it as a positive duty to come forward and take up the burdens of public office. We are told that Dante had a separate and sufficiently excruciating kind of hell for souls who sinned, not by committing crimes but by omitting active virtues.[46]

Even though the duties of municipal administration were less socially orientated than those of guardians, for both positions women were required to have gained relevant experience in social welfare by working in a philanthropic capacity. In addition, some women also managed to obtain experience by working informally on local government bodies.[47] Bessie Quin, a member of Armagh County Council, had formerly been appointed as a representative on the council's regional education committee;[48] Anna Barbour, the first woman elected to Antrim County Council, was a former member of the council's tuberculosis committee[49] and Dorothy Robertson was elected as a rural district councillor in Limavady after serving as a member of the council's regional education committee for several years.[50] However, the demands placed on prospective candidates must have limited the number of women who believed that they were suitably qualified both in terms of personal attributes and experience. A 1911 article on women's work within the realms of local government went as far to recommend that prospective female candidates:

> For about a year . . . ought to attend every open meeting to the authority to which she desires election . . . At the same time she should do her best to become personally known to the electors and acquainted with their special needs, but always taking care to make no promises as to what she will do if elected, and confining herself to such remarks as 'the matter shall have my consideration'.[51]

Such a time-consuming approach would have dissuaded all but the most determined women from participating in municipal politics. But time was not the only consideration for prospective municipal candidates.

Even though standing for local government was less expensive than parliamentary candidature, with the cost being estimated at a minimum of £50, it was claimed that several female independent municipal candidates laboured to finance their own electoral campaigns.[52] Thus, as was apparent for female poor law guardians, the cost of an electoral campaign, coupled with practical considerations concerning the hours of unpaid labour involved in public office, precluded working-class involvement. The demands of economics and time may also have affected the marital status of female councillors. Any unmarried woman participating in local government administration had to be supported through private means, as it was practically impossible to combine public office with a working day in paid employment. Participation in municipal politics was certainly easier for married women with sympathetic and supportive spouses. This appears to have been the experience of the majority of female councillors in Ulster from the late nineteenth century: 59 per cent and 73 per cent of the total number of female urban and rural district councillors respectively, and all female county councillors, were married.

As in many other areas of women's political activity in Ulster, familial association and support was an important factor in motivating female local government candidature. In 1933 the chairman of Armagh County Council congratulated the council on the personnel of its members, which secured 'the purity of public life':

> Many of the oldest families in the County are represented. I hope they will continue to give good service, as their ancestors did in the past. It is also a subject of thankfulness that those who have 'a stake in the country' are with us in large numbers.[53]

Within this cliquish boardroom environment there were some striking examples of familial association. Sisters-in-law Lady and Mrs Herdman served with their husbands on Strabane Rural District Council from 1924; Anna Barbour joined her husband on Lisburn Rural District Council in 1911 and in 1924 both she and her husband became members of Antrim County Council. Moreover, when women were co-opted onto local councils, it was usually to replace a retired or late husband. Bessie Quin and Mrs Sinclair were unanimously co-opted onto Armagh County Council and Strabane Rural District Council in lieu of their late husbands in 1925 and 1930 respectively,[54] whilst Mrs Calvert's husband 'retired in her favour' from Armagh County Council in 1936.[55] It is possible that women without familial influence, either as members of well-known local families, or as relations of serving or former councillors, may have been discouraged from standing as candidates in municipal elections. Furthermore, non-familial based co-options onto municipal bodies occurred only infrequently. This, coupled with the lower level of female representation on local councils in Ulster, as compared to boards of guardians, meant that the tendency for female members to be replaced by other women did not develop. Tandragee, Ballycastle, Banbridge, Downpatrick and Larne rural district councils consistently co-opted three men onto their ranks. Opportunities for co-opting women were further diminished on Castlereagh Rural District Council, as it regularly deemed the co-option of additional councillors unnecessary. It is also apparent that the co-option or election of a woman to a local council, as to a board of guardians, did not establish any precedent for further female representation. In 1899 Mrs J. Walker and Mrs Greer became the first, and last, female rural district councillors in Banbridge and Lurgan respectively and in 1929 Mrs J.W. Johnston was co-opted as the first and only woman on Clogher Rural District Council until the outbreak of the Second

World War. A similar situation is apparent amongst female urban councillors. Although Jane Ritter became one of the first female urban district councillors in Ireland with her election in Limavady in 1899, no other women served on this council up to 1940. Furthermore, Agnes Clarke, Mary McCammon and Mrs E.S. Perfect were the only female members of Dromore, Portadown and Warrenpoint Urban District Councils respectively. Occasionally, women, even those with considerable local government experience, were unsuccessfully nominated for co-option. Gertrude Keightley provides the most striking example of such an occurrence. Even though she was one of the most active members of Lisburn's board of guardians from 1899 and chairman of this body from 1913, she was unsuccessfully nominated as a rural district councillor for Hillsborough in 1920.[56]

In addition to the practical considerations of standing for elective office, there is some evidence to suggest that female candidates occasionally experienced serious difficulties in mobilising electoral support. The press coverage given to municipal elections was sporadic, but at least one woman experienced a crushing electoral defeat before standing successfully at the next election. Alice Mary Young was the sole female candidate standing for election to Ballymena Rural District Council in 1914, but she came last in the poll with only thirteen votes.[57] Young was, however, determined and her perseverance was duly rewarded at the next municipal election of 1920 when she was successfully returned as a rural district councillor. Other women were less resilient and seem to have lost both confidence and the desire to become involved in municipal politics after an electoral defeat. In 1932, for example, two women, Martha Patton and Mary McCutcheon, stood unsuccessfully as candidates for Ballymena Rural District Council and they did not forward themselves as candidates in the next or subsequent elections. It is possible that electoral defeat, like that experienced by Patton and McCutcheon, may have deterred other women from coming forward as candidates. Some women also experienced difficulties being re-elected as councillors. Despite Lilly Ann Barr's competence and exemplary attendance record as the first female urban district councillor in Ballymena from 1899, she was defeated in the next election of 1902.[58] She was, however, re-elected at the next election in 1905 and subsequently served as councillor for the next twenty-five years. Dorothy Robertson, a member of Limavady Rural District Council, experienced a similar fluctuation in her electoral fortunes. In 1924 she was successfully elected, but failed to be returned at the next triennial election of 1927. The council co-opted her back onto its ranks as an additional member and she served until 1930, when she was again defeated at the polls. In that year a motion to co-opt her was defeated, but, undeterred, she stood as a candidate in 1933 and was successfully elected.[59]

Another factor contributing to the level of female candidature was indifference to municipal politics. This was a consistent feature in Ulster. The *Irish News*' coverage of the 1902 local elections highlights the widespread apathy: 'the polling was slack everywhere, and in some of the constituencies not half of the voters went to the poll'.[60] In 1920 Richard Dawson Bates also alluded to the 'general public apathy on the part of the public in regard to the Elections, which is frequently the case in Municipal matters'.[61] The indifference to municipal politics is further accentuated by the fact that the average electoral turnout for Belfast's municipal elections in the period 1899 to 1939 was 45 per cent.[62] This situation was not peculiar to Ulster. Lord Snell claimed in 1935 that English local government work was 'taken for granted by the general public, and when the periodical elections take place only a comparatively small proportion of the electors trouble to record their votes'.[63] But, in spite of these similarities, there were also important distinctions. Ulster was something of an anomaly in comparison with the rest of the country and with England. Following partition, the level of public disinterest was markedly reinforced by widespread disillusion amongst northern nationalists with all facets of Northern Ireland's state apparatus. The local government elections of 1920 left twenty-five local councils in Ulster controlled by nationalists, many of whom publicly declared allegiance to Dáil Éireann. This caused considerable embarrassment to the Northern Irish government. The control of local government in the six north-eastern counties of the country was transferred from Dublin to Belfast on 21 December 1921 and to facilitate this the Local Government (Emergency Powers) Act was passed. This legislation gave the Northern Ireland Ministry for Home Affairs permission to dissolve local authorities and appoint commissioners if councils refused to recognise the authority of the newly established state. In 1922 another local government bill was introduced to abolish the proportional representation voting system in municipal elections and establish an obligatory declaration of allegiance to the crown and government for all councillors.[64] The cumulative effect of these controversial legislative measures was significant. Apathy, which had been a consistent feature of municipal politics, increased, with many nationalists boycotting municipal elections. After 1924 nationalists controlled only two local councils in Ulster and no council with a unionist majority in 1924 was recaptured by nationalists.[65] In addition to this, on the rare occasion when a proposal was made to co-opt nationalist councillors onto municipal bodies, it was rejected outright. For instance, a suggestion that Downpatrick Rural District Council should co-opt three nationalist councillors in the mid-1920s was defeated, with several members 'taking exception . . . intimating that the Nationalists had refused to carry on under the old system and also deliberately refrained from getting nominated'.[66]

These legislative measures, coupled with the existing widespread disillusion amongst the northern nationalist community, caused considerable stagnancy in municipal politics. As early as 1923 Lilian Spender remarked on the high level of uncontested municipal seats: 'We aren't much excited over our local elections. Most of them . . . are unopposed, so once more I am defrauded of exercising my vote.'[67] Furthermore, the number of uncontested municipal seats increased throughout the inter-war period. In Ballymena no polls were taken in any of the wards in 1926 and in Belfast only two seats were contested in the corporation elections of 1931. By 1939 there was only one contested seat on the city's corporation. It has been estimated that the average number of uncontested seats in Ulster in the period 1923 to 1955 was as high as 96 per cent for rural district councils, 94 per cent for county councils and 60 per cent for urban district and borough councils.[68] There were also numerous vacancies on local councils that again points to the widespread disinterest in municipal politics: there were three vacancies in Newcastle, one in Warrenpoint and five in Londonderry in the early 1920s. The existence of such a high level of apathy, uncontested seats and consistently low electoral turnouts suggests that municipal politics were not popular and continued to be monopolised by the unionist party machine throughout the inter-war period. It seems likely that in addition to the practical prerequisites of leisure and financial security, which excluded many women from participating in local government, few were prepared to stand for a largely unpopular position or be seen to question unionist hegemony.

No single explanation can adequately account for the low level of women's representation in local government. The number of suitably qualified women was limited by the practical considerations of possessing sufficient economic means and free time and having the personal motivation to stand for such an onerous and unpaid public position. Of the small number of women who stood as candidates, some experienced serious difficulties in mobilising, and in some instances maintaining, electoral support and it is possible that this deterred other women from coming forward as candidates. Moreover, the general public apathy that characterised Ulster local government was significantly exacerbated by legislation heightening northern nationalists' reluctance to participate in the workings of the Northern Irish state after 1920. But what was the experience of women who, regardless of these considerations, served as local government councillors?

IV

Just as nineteenth-century campaigners made claims concerning the unique contribution that women would make to poor law administration, they also foresaw that female local government councillors would contribute to the public good by virtue of their intrinsic feminine qualities. On 23 July 1887 Isabella Tod wrote to the *Northern Whig* not only to record her personal satisfaction at the passage of the Municipal Corporations (Ireland) Act, but her aspirations for women councillors. She opined that a division of duties on the basis of gender would occur in municipal administration and that female councillors would concentrate on solving 'the great social and moral questions':

> which ought to be the end for which party politics are only the means . . . [Women] can influence efficiently all matters concerning the peace and good order of the streets, and progress of sanitary reform, the cause of temperance, and other questions in which they have a vital interest.[69]

Tod's predictions were shared by the IWSLGA, whose annual report of 1898 emphasised that female district councillors would 'devote themselves to the sanitation, [and] the better housing of the poor'.[70] Three years later the IWSLGA expanded these ideas, presumably in an attempt to encourage women to come forward as local government candidates in the wake of legislative reform:

> There are certain departments within the jurisdiction of these Boards in which the help of experienced women councillors is an absolute necessity. It is not too much to affirm that the thorough sanitation of

> the respective Districts, more especially in the case of common lodging-houses, [and] . . . the provision of healthy Labourers' Cottages . . . will never be adequately carried out until it is largely entrusted to the control of such women, assisted by keen-eyed and well-trained Female Inspectors.[71]

This delegation of specific areas of local government administration on the basis of gender was pervasive. In 1927 Dehra Parker, a member of Magherafelt Rural District Council and the only female member of the Northern Irish parliament at the time, also drew attention to the essentially feminine aspects of municipal work.[72] Parker claimed, on the basis of her own experience, that local council work fully embraced 'the root and fibre of . . . home life' and did not entail any departure from domestic responsibilities, alleging that it was possible for a female councillor to:

> combine her public with her private duties . . . and bring their training as housewives to bear upon the running of any institutions under their control . . . woman's influence [was] . . . far-reaching and essential . . . every Board would be improved by the presence of one or two suitable members.[73]

The envisaged separation of municipal duties on the basis of gender was realised. This division was not as manifest as on boards of guardians because the low level of female representation precluded women from dominating specific areas of local government administration and because local government jurisdiction was less socially orientated than that of the poor law. It is important to note, however, that the information collated in the minute books of local councils is less detailed than that for the boards of guardians. Furthermore, councils often made decisions on a collective basis and there is little information concerning the appointment of committees. Yet, even with these limitations, it is possible to discern that there was a domestic and fundamentally gendered aspect to the work of women municipal councillors in Ulster from the late nineteenth century onwards.

In her electoral manifesto of 1926 Julia McMordie, the first woman appointed to Belfast Corporation in 1918, and an alderman on this body from 1920, summarised her own municipal interests, which revealed the gendered basis of her work:

> I have tried to do all I could for the best interests of the Ratepayers. When I first joined the Corporation I chose Committees where I

> thought I could be of service, such as The Public Health, The Maternity and Child Welfare, The Children's Act, The Tuberculosis (of which Committee I have been Chairman for six years.) I am also a Member of the Belfast Education Committee, and Chairman of the School Medical Services Sub-Committee . . . I am very much interested in the Health and well being of the Citizens, more especially of the children . . . I love the work, [and] . . . I will do my best for the good of all sections of the Community.[74]

The majority of women councillors in Ulster appear to have shared McMordie's interests, serving on committees with responsibility for administering the educational, public health and housing provisions of their own localities.[75] By comparison, male councillors tended to deal with the classification and maintenance of roads and serve on agriculture, stocktaking, allotment, water or building planning and maintenance committees.[76]

With regards to education, women were frequently appointed to education, school attendance and technical instruction committees, with some also introducing motions to improve schooling and resist legislation that would curtail municipal control over education. On Armagh County Council, Bessie Quin successfully increased the educational provisions of her district by proposing that two acres of land be purchased as the site of a new public elementary school at Tandragee in 1928.[77] Over the next two years she was instrumental in opposing the Education Amendment Bill, which attempted to limit the jurisdiction of county councils, depriving them 'of practically all powers to manage transferred schools, even . . . schools built out of public funds'.[78] On Quin's suggestion the council withheld all expenditure until the bill was in a 'fixed and final form: [and] that for the present no other building operations in connection with which loans are required will be sanctioned, and the transfer of no further school accepted'.[79] Several years later, similar motives prompted Minnie Beattie to successfully move that a resolution be adopted by Lisburn Rural District Council in opposition to the introduction of an education levy. Beattie interpreted this as an 'autocratic' means of raising revenue that contravened 'the constitutional method of carrying out Local Government Administration':

> we are convinced that the taxable capacity of the majority of people in Northern Ireland is unable to bear at present such a huge new burden [with] . . . declining incomes . . . continued depression, increasing taxation and unemployment in trade and agriculture . . . necessitates

immediately the strictest economy on behalf of the Government and all rating authorities.[80]

Female councillors also became involved in administering public health provisions. Several women successfully introduced resolutions to increase the standards of staff in council employ, the effective implementation of existing legislation and the initiation of new policies. In 1914, Charlotte Hamilton and Amelia Whyte of Portrush Urban District Council were appointed to a committee to implement the suggestions of the National Health Commission by working in conjunction with the principals of local schools to enrol children in dental clinics.[81] In addition, in 1917 Lilly Ann Barr, the vice-chairman of Ballymena Urban District Council, successfully moved that a female health visitor be sent on a hygiene course run by the Royal College of Science in Dublin.[82] But the separation of local council work on the basis of gender was most apparent in areas relating to child and maternal health. In 1926, on the motion of Bessie Quin, Armagh County Council agreed that similar legislation to the Midwives and Maternity Homes Act of 1926 passed by the imperial government should be introduced to Northern Ireland.[83] Moreover, several female councillors were appointed as council delegates to establish local maternity and child welfare committees. On Portrush Urban District Council, for instance, the female members were delegated to work in conjunction with the local district nursing association in order to establish a maternity and child welfare scheme from 1916.[84] Women councillors also regularly proposed that council grants be awarded in order to finance these schemes, which were established in many areas of Ulster during the 1920s.

Sanitary provision was another important component of municipal administration and a significant proportion of female councillors worked to improve standards within their own localities. In 1907 Charlotte Hamilton drew Portrush Urban District Council's attention to 'the advisability of making a charge of 4/- per annum for domestic sewerage . . . and of removing refuge at regular intervals from poorer parts of [the] District'.[85] Jessie Kydd, a member of Coleraine Urban District Council, was similarly concerned for the public health of her district. She quickly responded to an outbreak of typhoid in 1922 by successfully proposing that the local water supply should be analysed.[86] Several women also recommended that investigations to assess local sanitary conditions be instigated: Mrs Herdman, a member of Strabane Urban District Council, suggested in March

1937 that the council's medical officer for health report on sanitary provisions[87] and Minnie Beattie of Lisburn Rural District Council also proposed that sanitary inspections be made of the locality. Indeed, Beattie was to respond promptly to a complaint made by the residents of Dunmurry in 1925 regarding the 'vast amount of serious sickness' in their district, which they believed 'beyond a shadow of a doubt' was a consequence of inadequate sanitation: 'the root of the evil lies at the door of the insanitary conditions'.[88] At the next council meeting Beattie suggested that sewerage connections be made to a number of houses in this area, successfully proposing that the council's solicitor institute legal proceedings against a local landlord for his failure to comply with a sanitary notice regarding the condition of his tenant houses.[89] Three years later, in March 1928, Beattie, who was now vice-chairman of the council, was appointed to a committee to report on the failings of local sanitary provisions:

> it was felt that owing to the great increase in population . . . in the district due to the number of new houses . . . that a regular system of house cleansing should be adopted, together with a more effective measure of sanitary inspection. We believe that if this is carried out, much of the sickness and discomfort in the district would be diminished.[90]

Responding to this report, Beattie successfully proposed that an additional sanitary officer be appointed and that the council apply for a £10,000 loan in order to implement sewerage improvements throughout Lisburn. Her concern for public health continued. The following year Beattie was responsible for proposing that the council adopt parts I and III of the 1890 Public Health (Amendment) Act which related to sanitary provision and, with three male councillors, she again investigated the sanitary condition of houses, this time in the Derriaghy district of the town.[91]

Other women were similarly active in striving to counter inefficient public health administration. Alice Young, one of only two women who served on Ballymena Rural District Council up to 1940, drew attention to several deaths from tuberculosis which had not been reported by the council's medical officer for health[92] and Charlotte Hamilton, a member of Portrush Urban District Council, was also anxious to increase public awareness of this disease. In 1907 Hamilton was appointed as the council's delegate to attend the tuberculosis exhibition held under the auspices of the Women's National Health Association in Dublin.[93] In December of that year she also organised a local public meeting to discuss both the treatment of tuberculosis and preventative steps which could be taken against the disease.[94] Two years later she made further moves in this direction, by successfully proposing that the council adopt the sections of the Tuberculosis Prevention (Ireland) Act of 1908 which were applicable to municipal administration.[95]

With public health remaining a core concern for women councillors, it is not surprising that housing standards and provisions also attracted their attention. In May 1908 Charlotte Hamilton alluded to the 'grave need' for workmen's houses in the Portrush area,[96] whilst in Lisburn Minnie Beattie was again to the fore, successfully proposing that demolition orders be applied to several council-owned properties in a poor state of repair. Beattie also suggested that an application for a loan be made to the Ministry of Home Affairs to increase the availability of working-class housing by building more labourers' cottages in 1930.[97] Presumably as a result of these initiatives, she was nominated as a member of a committee to appoint tenants to labourers' cottages, and in 1938 accompanied the council's chairman on a deputation to the Ministry of Home Affairs to appeal for a rent reduction for newly built properties at Dunmurry.[98] She also drew the council's attention to the importance of ensuring that houses which were unfit for human habitation were not re-let and successfully proposed that a recreation ground be established in Lisburn.[99] Several other female councillors in Ulster shared Beattie's concerns: Mrs Merrick, a member of Strabane Rural District Council, persuaded the council to rescind their decision to increase rents on labourers' cottages, whilst her colleague Lady Herdman succeeded in doubling the number of labourers' cottages which the council were building.[100] All the female members of this council were formed into a committee with sole responsibility for administering an inspection scheme to encourage tenants to maintain council-owned properties. Moreover, Coralie Hermon, a rural district councillor in Irvinestown, initiated an improvement scheme to take 'lands compulsorily [for] . . . the provision of house accommodation' in 1939.[101]

The issue of gender was also evident in the appointment of non-council members to local government committees. This gave some women an opportunity to become involved, albeit in an informal capacity, in municipal affairs. As with the work of female councillors, women were mainly appointed to committees relating to health and education, thus reinforcing the identification and designation of specific areas as suitable for women. Hence, seven women were appointed to Antrim's school attendance committees in the mid-1920s and three women, including Mrs Christie, the wife of Coleraine's mayor and council chairman, were appointed to its district child and nursing committee in 1927. There was also a tendency for councils without any female members to appoint women to child and maternal welfare committees. Mrs Todd and Miss McConnell were appointed to Ballyclare's welfare committee, as the wife and daughter of two rural district councillors, and Belfast's Rural District Council regularly appointed at least three women to its welfare committee from the early 1920s, which was chaired by Mrs McClean, the wife of a rural district councillor.

On occasion the appointment of these women to local government committees did arouse adverse criticism. Such opposition clearly suggests that the perception of municipal administration as a male preserve continued. In 1924 Armagh County Council was forced to defend its appointment of the wife of a council member and the wife of the council's secretary to its thirty-three-member regional education committee. Responding to criticism from Portadown's Chamber of Commerce regarding the composition of this committee, the council not only emphasised the women's familial links with the council, but also the necessity for female representatives:

> It is only right that women should have direct representation on the Committee, I do not see that any of the District Councils have, so far, nominated anything but men . . . the members suggested are, so far as possible representative of all classes of the community; and every part of the County.[102]

Two weeks later the council reiterated that appointing women to this committee was only democratic:

> the necessity for the direct representation of women, who number more than half the adult population in the County, can hardly be called into question. They form, too, a large proportion of the electorate. Two, therefore, out of thirty-three is not excessive representation.[103]

Once appointed to council, either in an elective or co-optive capacity, the demands of public office in terms of time and responsibility were considerable. In 1920 the *Irish Citizen* claimed, in a somewhat alarmist manner, that there was 'every possibility of [female councillors] . . . being overworked'.[104] Women's attendance records were, however, on a par with their male colleagues and, amongst female councillors in Ulster in the period up to 1940, only one woman openly admitted that the demands of office were too great. Bessie Quin was forced to tender her resignation from Armagh County Council's infirmary committee as:

> the meetings . . . are held on Monday mornings. She said this was a very busy morning with her, and as she was also a member of the Mental Hospital committee, which, too, meets on Monday morning, she could not devote two Mondays in the month to public duties.[105]

Quin's heavy voluntary workload epitomises the public spirit needed to execute the duties of municipal government. Even though municipal politics lacked the prestige attached to the parliamentary assembly, it was here that the immediate needs of the neighbourhood were met, where 'ladies of means and leisure' could make an 'individual contribution to the stock of experience and practical insight upon which the welfare of their town depends'.[106] Female councillors' longevity of service certainly suggests that some women found municipal administration personally fulfilling: Minnie Beattie was a member of Lisburn Rural District Council for twenty years[107] and Mrs Macausland and Mrs Montgomery served similar terms of service as rural district councillors in Coleraine and Ballymoney respectively.[108] Another indication of the satisfaction which women derived from participating in local government administration can be gained from the instances where women served as both poor law guardians and local government councillors and continued their association with municipal administration after retirement. Anna Barbour was still a member of Lisburn's Regional Education Committee in the 1930s even after she retired from Antrim County Council in 1927.

The majority of female local councillors in Ulster appear to have been competent, conscientious and esteemed by their colleagues. For instance, Minnie Beattie thanked Lisburn Rural District Council for their 'consideration and kindness' during her four years as chairman in June 1934.[109] Moreover, councillors regularly paid tribute to the work of deceased or retired female members: Armagh County Council praised the late Frances Calvert as a 'popular and painstaking Councillor',[110] whilst Portrush Urban District Council esteemed the late Amelia Whyte's 'splendid qualities of heart and mind, and her interest in the welfare of the district'.[111] But in spite of these tributes the predictions of local government reformers like Isabella Tod and members of the IWSLGA concerning women's role in municipal politics were only partially fulfilled. As was apparent for women poor law guardians, female councillors were content to become involved in the most socially orientated aspects of local government administration – education, housing and public health. A specific woman's role is, therefore, discernible.[112] However, many nineteenth-century reformers also envisaged that at least one woman would serve on every local government body. These expectations remained unfulfilled. The level of female representation remained very low, collectively averaging only 1.4 per cent of the total council positions available in Ulster from 1898 to 1940. Nevertheless, although women did not come forward in any significant numbers to stand as local government councillors as a result of practical considerations concerning the demands of public office and widespread public apathy towards municipal politics, women's admission to this area of government did represent an increase in their civic responsibilities from the late nineteenth century. Writing in 1938, Edith, 7th Marchioness of Londonderry, was one contemporary observer who recognised the portent of this change:

> The great and increasing share that women are taking in public life . . . is very remarkable when we consider the comparatively short time it is since public opinion recognized the fact that the inclusion of women in responsible positions was of material benefit to the State.[113]

CHAPTER SIX

Women Members of the Parliament of Northern Ireland

Women MPs would be all-round politicians, and helpful on all subjects, not alone those which affected women and children. Women would represent men's interests as well as a man.[1]

The legislative demands of the suffrage movement were at least partially satisfied in 1918 by the passage of the Representation of the People Act and the Parliament (Qualification of Women) Act, which cumulatively enabled women who were aged over thirty to vote and stand as parliamentary candidates. But what was the effect of this legislation, both in terms of the level of female parliamentary candidature and the careers of the women who were successfully elected as members of the Northern Ireland parliament from its establishment in 1921 until the outbreak of the Second World War? As the study of female poor law guardians and local government councillors has revealed, there was a correlation between the power of government bodies and the level of female representation. This pattern is corroborated by the fact that only three women in the period under analysis (representing 2.28 per cent of the total parliamentary force) were elected to the apex of public administration in the province: the parliament of Northern Ireland.[2] This level of parliamentary representation was similar to Britain, where women represented 1.2 per cent of the total number of MPs from 1921 to 1939.[3]

It is clear that no precedent was set for female candidature by the election of two women, Dehra Parker and Julia McMordie, to the first parliament of Northern Ireland in 1921.[4] The explanation for this is undoubtedly linked to the small number of women who stood as electoral candidates: from 1921 to 1940 only five women stood, representing 2.06 per cent of the total candidature.[5] Based on these low figures, 60 per cent of the total number of female candidates were successfully elected. The two unsuccessful women candidates were Mrs E.M. Clow, a local optionist candidate in the St Anne's constituency of North Belfast in 1929, and Mrs P.B. Moody, a progressive unionist candidate in the Bloomfield constituency of East Belfast in 1938.[6] Clow, receiving 2,209 votes (15.6 per cent), was resolutely defeated by two unionist candidates, Major J.H. McCormick and Colonel P.J. Woods, who received 47.2 per cent and 37.2 per cent of the vote respectively.[7] Although Mrs Moody fared somewhat better in 1938, receiving 3,988 votes (29.7 per cent), she was also defeated by a unionist candidate, Captain Herbert Dixon.[8] It seems that in parliamentary, as in municipal, elections women were disheartened by defeat, as neither Clow nor Moody stood as candidates in subsequent electoral contests.[9] As was similarly apparent in the study of women in local government, no single answer can effectively explain women's reluctance to come forward as candidates for public office. However, many of the factors that help to explain the low level of female municipal candidature also seem to be applicable to women in parliament. Practical considerations of time, economics and sufficient personal motivation accumulated to limit the number of potential female candidates.[10] But the fact that the parliamentary apparatus was newly established seems not to have affected the number of female candidates in Northern Ireland. The traditions of procedure may have been less entrenched than those of the imperial parliament, which was described by Labour MP Edith Summerskill as 'a boys' school that had decided to take a few girls', but it still seems that only a few exceptional women felt qualified to stand as parliamentary candidates in Northern Ireland.[11] This situation was intensified by the fact that no political party actively encouraged women to come forward as parliamentary candidates, either in the immediate aftermath of women's partial enfranchisement in 1918 or throughout the inter-war period. Furthermore, widespread disillusion amongst the northern nationalist community following the Government of Ireland Act of 1920 resulted in no nationalist women being forwarded as candidates.[12]

It is difficult to draw any firm conclusions from a sample of only three women, but it seems that in Northern Ireland, as in Britain, involvement in local government did provide some women with the necessary 'self-confidence and motivation to contemplate trying to take a greater role in public life'.[13] The three female members of the parliament of Northern Ireland all served as JPs and both Julia McMordie and Dehra Parker were local government councillors. In

1918 McMordie became the first woman on Belfast Corporation and in 1929 she was appointed as the city's first female high sheriff,[14] whilst in Magherafelt Dehra Parker served both as a rural district councillor and chairman of the local board of guardians.[15] It has been claimed that some women standing for parliamentary election in Britain were already well known for their voluntary work as party speakers and organisers.[16] This is also valid in an Ulster context. The three female members of the Northern Ireland parliament were all active members of the Ulster Women's Unionist Council, with Parker and McMordie holding senior office in this organisation: both were appointed vice-chairman of the council and in 1919 McMordie was selected as a vice-president, a position which she held for over two decades.[17] The absence of any private papers belonging to Parker, McMordie or Waring makes it very difficult to assess their motivation for standing as parliamentary candidates. Yet, in spite of the absence of documentary evidence, their earlier activities display both public spirit and loyalty to the unionist cause, which appear to have formed the basis of their political careers.

In parallel with the hopes which local government reformers had for women councillors and poor law guardians in the late nineteenth century, an editorial in the September 1918 edition of the *Irish Citizen* anticipated the impact of women's admission to parliament. The *Citizen* opined that female MPs could effectively transform parliament from an 'exclusive male club [to] human assemblies where both sexes were represented'.[18] The paper also expressed the misgivings of some Irish feminists concerning women MPs becoming 'party' propagandists, lacking any feminist agenda.[19] Essentially, these anxieties represented a continuation of their earlier criticisms of party women for consistently placing political considerations before the enfranchisement of their own sex during the suffrage campaign. In a later edition of the *Citizen*, published in November 1918, the feminist writer and active suffragist, Mrs L.A.M. Priestley McCracken, further accentuated the need for independent female candidates, untainted by party politics and 'untrammelled by . . . selfish aims, [and] ignorant of the shibboleths of parties':

> unless we want the Lady Londonderrys, and the Sir Edward Carsons, and the Mr Dillons, to carry them off as tame pussy cats to purr in contented acquiescence to male guidance within the House . . . meek, docile, but useful in assisting men's plans.[20]

In spite of the eloquence of her plea, McCracken, like many suffragists, was to be disappointed. Parliament was not transformed by women's admission. Not only did very few women stand for election, but none came forward as independent candidates. Furthermore, none of the three female MPs ever referred to themselves as feminists. Parker, McMordie and Waring were all elected as representatives of the Unionist Party and worked in a political climate where forwarding any feminist agenda would have mitigated against the dictates of their own party. Moreover, by the time Dehra Parker and Julia McMordie were elected in 1921, the feminist impetus of the pre-war suffrage campaign had decreased to such an extent that it was negligible. So, what were the political priorities of these three undoubtedly exceptional women and did they make a tangible difference to the parliament of Northern Ireland in the first two decades of its existence?

II

Julia McMordie's political interests were more 'women' focused than those of both her male and female colleagues. McMordie's support for women's issues was clearly apparent from her maiden speech to the Commons on 5 April 1922, when she resolutely defended the appointment of female police officers. With only two women officers in a 3,000-strong force in the city of Belfast, she called for a numerical increase, proposing that their representation should at least be doubled:

> I think everybody who has ever been in the Belfast Police Court . . . would see the very great need there is for policewomen . . . the influence . . . cannot be over-estimated . . . I am not at all depreciating the work of the men . . . They do their level best, but I really must say that there are some cases where a woman's influence is superior to that of a man. (Hon. Members: Hear, hear) . . . there are many cases affecting women and children who can tell their story with much greater ease to a woman than to a man.[21]

Although McMordie did not support equal pay, an issue that some British feminists were promoting at this time, she drew the Commons' attention to the necessity of providing equal allowances and pensions for female officers:

> I do not see why women should serve without any hope of a pension any more than men should[,] I have never been one who thought that

> a woman who did the same work as a man should get the same pay – I am very modest in that respect – but I do think the women should be eligible for any emoluments or pensions that men are entitled to.[22]

Julia McMordie reiterated her support for female police officers by opposing the Constabulary Bill in May 1922 on the grounds that it did not contain a clause dealing with women officers.[23] This was an important and ultimately successful stand. McMordie was undoubtedly a staunch unionist, but her party loyalties did not make her a sycophant, nor did they guarantee her support for any bill simply on the basis that it was backed by the unionist government. By threatening to vote against both party and government, McMordie, backed by Donald Thompson, MP for East Belfast, and William Grant, MP for North Belfast, successfully managed to insert a clause which defined the term 'constable' as inclusive of both sexes to this bill.[24]

As was apparent in poor law and local government administration, women in parliament also focused on welfare issues. This appears to have been common not only to Northern Ireland but also to Britain, where the majority of female MPs only addressed the House on welfare issues. During McMordie's four-year parliamentary career she raised several similar issues for debate in the Northern Ireland House of Commons.[25] The first of these occurred in May 1922, when Dr Morrison, MP for Queen's University, alleged that government funding was having little tangible effect on improving the treatment and prevention of tuberculosis. McMordie responded by highlighting the importance of maintaining this funding, emphasising that it enabled local authorities to provide sanatoriums and open-air schools for tubercular children:

> where we can treat the children who have been in contact with some elder members of their families who are affected by tuberculosis . . . people who are quite incurable . . . must have some place to go. We cannot leave them in their very small homes, which are generally overcrowded at the best of times.[26]

McMordie was also anxious to improve educational facilities, accentuating the need for employing specially trained teachers for disabled children[27] and questioning whether funding was available for female school inspectors.[28] Unemployment was the only other issue that McMordie commented on during her parliamentary term. This was a constant source of concern for the Northern Ireland government, with unemployment levels averaging between 13.2 per cent and 23.9 per cent of all insured workers per annum throughout the 1920s.[29] In April 1924, although McMordie could proffer no solution to this escalating problem, she did express her disillusion at the continually high levels of unemployment:

> Anything that can be done to help the working men I am absolutely convinced has been . . . done . . . with regard to the number of unemployed at present . . . a great many of them to my mind are unemployable. We regret to see so many disabled soldiers . . . but a great many of these men are in receipt of a pension for the disability under which they labour . . . posts . . . available for such men are mostly filled by firms who have their own disabled men to provide for. So I do not believe we shall ever get over unemployment in Belfast.[30]

Julia McMordie did not stand for re-election in 1925.[31] On the occasions when she addressed the House, she proved a capable orator, but during her four-year parliamentary term she failed to make a sustained contribution to the Commons. Indeed, she did not deliver her maiden speech until April 1922, ten months after the first parliament had convened, and, apart from the instances referred to above, rarely contributed to debates or posed questions during the Commons' weekly oral answer sessions.

Margaret Waring's parliamentary career bore many similarities to that of McMordie. Waring delivered her maiden speech during the Ministry for Education's estimates in June 1929, when she highlighted the lack of institutional care that was available for mentally handicapped children in Northern Ireland:

> At the present time there is no home or institute in our Six Counties to which these children can be sent . . . it is very important that these children should learn something rather than that they should grow up useless, or worse than useless, members of the community.[32]

William Grant, MP for the Duncairn area of North Belfast, congratulated her for raising 'a question which . . . meets with the sympathy of all sections of the House'.[33] Despite the warm reception which this speech received from the Commons, Waring's parliamentary debate was minimal. Indeed, from March to November 1930 she made no contributions to the House at all. But though lacking in parliamentary experience Margaret Waring was selected to second the motion of Mr Young, MP for Bann Side, during the debate on the King's address at the opening of the 1931 parliamentary session. As Waring had only addressed the House on three earlier occasions she was understandably apprehensive about executing this task, informing the House:

> I wish this important duty had fallen into more capable and experienced hands than mine. At the same time I count it as a great honour not for myself, but for my constituency, that I should have this duty entrusted to me, and I will endeavour so far as I am able to follow the high standard of debate.[34]

In the course of a competent and lengthy speech, Waring outlined her views on forthcoming legislative developments and on the economic situation in the province:

> Unfortunately there is still grave depression in our industries and in agriculture, with a corresponding lack of employment for our people. It is, therefore, more than ever necessary to economise our resources whenever and wherever possible.[35]

She continued by commenting on the forthcoming Town Planning and Housing Bill, which advocated slum clearance and improved housing, emphasising the importance of ensuring that this measure was approached in a non-partisan manner:

> no matter what our views may be on other subjects surely every hon. Member desires to see a healthier and therefore a happier Ulster . . . it is useless to talk of demolishing old houses until dwelling-houses are available for our working people at a rent that the ordinary working man can afford to pay. At the present time I think such accommodation is not available, in the country at any rate . . . the real object of this Bill is to make Ulster a model Province so far as housing conditions are concerned.[36]

Waring further alluded to the government's proposal to reduce housing subsidies and although she recognised that 'it may be necessary to agree to the reduced amount, on the principle that half a subsidy is better than none at all', this could affect the housing provision in rural areas which had only started to take advantage of this subsidy and possibly exacerbate unemployment in the building industry.[37] Waring also used this as an opportunity to reiterate her own concerns for providing adequate care and accommodation for mentally handicapped children:

> our first care should be for those unfortunate people who are incapable of caring for themselves . . . I hope that the Bill will also deal with the care of mentally deficient children, because there is urgent need for legislation in that direction.[38]

Throughout this speech Waring illustrated that she was a capable orator, causing one member of the House to remark: 'We would like to hear more of the hon. Member for Iveagh than we have in the past.'[39] Despite this encouragement, Waring did not develop into a dynamic backbencher. After seconding Young's motion in 1931, she only made one further parliamentary contribution, raising by now a familiar topic of setting up a home for mentally handicapped children.[40] She did not stand for re-election in 1933.

With parliamentary debates as the only available source, it is difficult to fully explain why McMordie and Waring made only a minimal contribution to the Commons. Neither woman seems to have encountered any identifiable hostility from their male colleagues that could have dissuaded them from addressing the House. On the occasions when they did comment on legislation or raise issues for debate, both women were well received. It may be that McMordie and Waring only felt confident to comment on areas relating to women, where they had direct experience and knowledge: children's welfare, health or McMordie's somewhat more progressive support for female police officers. What is significant is that both women's parliamentary contributions were different from that of male members of the House and that gender was central to defining areas of debate where they felt that they could make a positive contribution.

III

Of the three women elected to parliament, Dehra Parker was outstanding, not only in the longevity of her thirty-five year career, but also because she was the only woman who was ever appointed to cabinet during the existence of the Northern Ireland parliament, 1921 to 1972. She served as the parliamentary secretary to the Ministry for Education from 1937 to 1944 and as Minister for Health and Local Government from 1949 to 1957.[41] Parker's maiden speech was received with cheers from the Commons on 1 December 1921. Her address made specific reference to the payment of government ministers and emphasised the need for providing sufficient remuneration in order to allow 'any man or any woman in the future to hold office even if his or her private means were a negligible quantity'.[42] In a proficient address she displayed considerable oratory skills and a wry wit that came to characterise much of her parliamentary debate: 'As a woman I know that there is a general feeling that we are popularly supposed not to be very well up in questions of rigid economy . . . as far . . . as matters connected with our wardrobe are concerned.'[43] Thomas Donald, MP for East Belfast, was one of several members who congratulated Parker on her performance: 'I am sure I am voicing the opinion of every member present when I say that she has done credit to herself[,] . . . to her sex and to hon. Members of this House.'[44] Similarly, Captain Herbert Dixon, another MP for East Belfast, remarked: 'I do not think that I, or anyone else in this House, ever heard a more eloquent maiden speech than that made by the member of Derry.'[45]

Despite this sterling presentation, it appears that Parker initially found it difficult to cope with the demands of parliamentary procedure. In 1923 she requested that additional time should be allocated in order to allow MPs to fully consider draft legislation and alluded to the problems that she was experiencing:

> [there is] legal phraseology which I find rather hard to understand at first sight. They make reference to Acts, copies of which I often find impossible to obtain . . . in Belfast. There is no time to consult or get advice . . . The result is that we cannot put forward small amendments.[46]

However, it seems that Parker managed to overcome these difficulties, as she quickly gained a reputation in the Commons as a stalwart unionist. She consistently defended the unionist government, often reaffirming her trust in James Craig's premiership: 'the Prime Minister has a great ability to lead us . . . we are as safe in his hands as we ever have been'.[47] Her standing as a steadfast unionist was such that by 1924 she was selected as the first woman in Britain to present the annual address on behalf of the House following the King's speech at the opening of the parliamentary session.[48] Parker interpreted this not only as a personal honour and a compliment to her constituents, but also as a tribute to women:

> I believe that I am correct in saying that I am the first woman, at any rate in the British Empire, who has had this privilege . . . and I take it as a recognition of the altered position of our sex in the Councils of the Empire and (Hon. Members: Hear, hear.) – and also in coming nearer home, as a recognition, perhaps of the work that has been

> accomplished by the women of Northern Ireland. (Hon. Members: Hear, hear.) . . . I value it most highly.[49]

Parker was a voluble orator, effectively defending both herself and her party from the criticism that passed freely from one side of the Commons to the other. She frequently contested the opposition members' charges of unionist gerrymandering by criticising nationalists' lack of foresight and recurrent sectarian focus which provoked feelings 'which it would, perhaps, be better to leave unroused' and awakened 'memories which . . . for the sake of unity and peace in this Province should not be revived'.[50] In 1925 she used similar rhetoric to defend the government from the opposition's claims that they had done little to remedy the high levels of unemployment. Parker appealed to the opposition members to make constructive suggestions that would help alleviate the situation, instead of merely criticising the government:

> They want us to believe that they have a monopoly of the milk of human kindness in their breasts . . . they know perfectly well that the Government have done everything in their power . . . unemployment benefit is . . . on the same basis as in Great Britain . . . it has been a terrible drain . . . Hon. Members opposite would wish the country to believe that for the past four years the Government has sat here . . . doing nothing, wasting public money, mutually admiring each other, never stretching out a hand to alleviate the distress and misery . . . only stretching out our hands . . . to grasp our salaries . . . we are suffering in this question from a curse left to us by the war.[51]

Parker was again one of the first members of the House to rise to the government's defence in 1927. Opposing a vote of censure that alleged that the unionist administration failed to represent all sections of the community, she ridiculed the nationalists' former policy of abstaining from taking their seats in the House of Commons in the following terms:

> If they thought this Government was not acting in the interests of . . . people, why did they not come in sooner and give us some of their wisdom, and help the Government to put matters right? . . . in this small State we have conferred benefits upon those people in the same degree as benefits have been conferred upon them in Great Britain . . . we carved out a new State in the midst of anarchy. They [the Government] have had to deal . . . with the aftermath of war and the industrial depression arising from that aftermath, and with strikes . . . to deal with internal trouble . . . The Government have dealt with crime and chaos. They have formed order out of disorder.[52]

Parker also rejected the opposition's frequent allegations of government partiality and in 1929 cited her own constituency work as an example of the equitable treatment which she believed was afforded to both religious communities:

> It is quite absurd to try to say that because I do my best to represent the Unionists who sent me here I do not also do my best to represent those of another faith and another party.
>
> I have only to-day had several letters from members of the party opposite . . . with regard to old-age pensions and questions relating to unemployment. I always deal with those questions just as well, and just as faithfully for my Nationalist voters as I do for my Unionist voters.[53]

This was a claim that Parker often reiterated. Thus in 1934 she claimed: 'Every man is entitled to his own opinions and to his own faith . . . we on this side of the House work just as much for the Roman Catholic electors, who do not send us here, as we work for the Protestant electors who do send us here.'[54] But later in the same debate she contradicted these liberal sentiments, clearly revealing both her own, and her party's, political priorities by highlighting that their primary objective was to resist any attempts to undermine the legislative union:

> We intend to stand for fair play for all classes and all creeds and to do justice to them, but we are determined, by every means in our power, not to allow those within our borders to endeavour to sever or to divide our inheritance.[55]

As one of the most resolute unionists in the House, Dehra Parker supported some of the most contentious government legislation introduced in an attempt to restore law and order in the increasingly turbulent province and reinstate unionist control of municipal administration. The Special Powers Bill was introduced in 1922 with the specific aim of curtailing sectarian violence. Contributing to the debates on this bill, Parker denied charges of religious bias, attesting that this legislation would be applied with equal vigour in both the nationalist and unionist communities:

> representing thousands of women in the Six Counties . . . I feel I can say that I have been shocked . . . by the terrible outrages, bloodshed, and violence . . . the strongest measures are absolutely needed now . . . [to] strike the necessary fear into the hearts of the criminals . . . once this Bill is passed the law will be ruthlessly and impartially

> administered and that criminals will be brought to justice, no matter what side they belong to and no matter what their political convictions or religious denomination may be.[56]

The following year she supported further controversial legislation: the introduction of promissory oaths for those in government employ. Parker justified this measure on the basis that loyalty was imperative to the stability of the Northern Irish state: 'it seems a matter of common sense that we do not want rebellion in any of our Government departments and we certainly do not want to have rebels entrusted with the education of Ulster'.[57] Parker reiterated these now familiar sentiments in 1926 when she paid tribute to the 'ungrudging sacrifices' of the special constabulary and denied that the religious composition of this force was deliberately weighted in Protestant favour. As one third of this force was designated for Catholics, she felt that it was unfair to blame the government for failing to fill this quota:

> I do not as a rule intervene in matters which I feel are not my particular province . . . [but] it is entirely the fault of the members of . . . [this] persuasion if they are not now members – respected members – of that force . . . there are members of . . . [this] persuasion in that force, and just as efficient members as those of any other persuasion.[58]

The Northern Ireland government inherited a relatively strong system of local government, a situation that was exacerbated by proportional representation in municipal administration having the unforeseen effect of working to Sinn Féin's advantage. By 1921 to 1922 this party controlled a significant number of local councils who refused to recognise the authority of the Northern Irish state. In an attempt to regain a foothold in municipal affairs the unionist government introduced legislation to abolish PR in municipal elections and by April 1922 twenty-one local authorities which refused to recognise the authority of the Northern Irish state had been dissolved.[59] This provoked much resentment and ill feeling, prompting Parker to address the House at some length. As a member of Magherafelt Rural District Council, which had formerly been controlled by nationalists, Parker used the most non-conciliatory rhetoric when she urged the government to adopt a reactionary approach in its consideration of reinstating these councils:

> Is gross disloyalty to receive no punishment . . . is treason to be so lightly overlooked, and so lightly pardoned? . . . Let us not forget the

> . . . insults we had to endure in the past . . . I come from an area where . . . 247 labourers' cottages were built, and of these only 47 were given to Unionists . . . We have had to sit there and listen to our King being insulted, to our Government being derided. We have been told that killing is not murder unless committed by the foreign invader . . . [and] that rather than recognise the Northern Government the hillsides would be running red with blood.[60]

In defence of the government and aroused by opposition members' references to past sectarian outrages, Parker issued a clear statement of detriment towards the nationalist community. She thus fell prey to the sectarian references that she regularly derided the opposition members for using in the Commons by claiming that such exacting legislation was required because of 'the mentality of the minority'.[61]

Another indication that Dehra Parker's foremost political priority was to support the unionist government came in November 1927 when she opposed Joseph Devlin's Representation of the People Bill. Devlin's motivation for introducing this measure was presumably to increase the nationalist vote by enfranchising women aged over twenty-one.[62] As the only female member of the House it seems that Parker felt some compunction to contribute to this debate, though it is apparent that she found it difficult to reconcile her party's interests with those of gender. Parker rose to address the Commons after the Prime Minister had outlined his opposition to this bill and, like the premier, she clearly accepted the democratic principle of one person one vote by stating that women:

> were eminently fitted to take the responsibility of the equal franchise . . . Those who are fitted to be the mothers of a great race are surely equally fitted to select those who are going to frame the laws to govern that race.[63]

She went on to affirm that unionists' opposition to this bill was essentially pragmatic, based on the practicalities and cost of introducing electoral reform ahead of the imperial parliament, as subsequent amendments would have to be made to ensure parity with Westminster. Parker also questioned Devlin's motivation for introducing this measure, depicting the northern nationalist leader as:

> The Pied Piper of Hamelin . . . with the servant girls of Derry and Tyrone flocking behind him on the primrose path . . . he might see himself in the role of the great benefactor, crowned with laurels, by the youth and beauty of the Six Counties . . . [64]

In the ensuing debate other members of the House levelled serious criticism against Dehra Parker, which illustrates her difficult position as the only female parliamentary representative. Thomas Henderson, Independent Unionist MP for Shankill and long-time adversary of Parker, went as far to claim that she was a discredit to her sex for not introducing this measure herself.[65] The government introduced a Representation of the People Bill in October of the following year,[66] when the issue of equal suffrage aroused only minimal debate as parliamentary attention converged on nationalists' opposition to the residency and company clauses contained in this legislation.[67] Such opposition prompted Parker to reiterate her mistrust of Devlin's motivation for introducing his equal suffrage bill during the preceding year, alleging that political expediency had been his only objective:

> they were going to gain by the admission of this other portion of womanhood of Northern Ireland to the franchise. Now that they think that under these two Clauses something is going to be done to counteract that advantage they are prepared to throw the women of Northern Ireland between the ages of 21 and 30 overboard. This has been a revelation.[68]

As this was a government-backed measure, Parker did not hesitate to expand her previous arguments in defence of the principle of equal suffrage, predicting that a new era of progress would now commence:

> I believe that . . . [women] will rise up and shoulder their burden; I believe they will educate themselves in the political problems of the day, and that they will exercise the franchise just as well as their brothers . . . I think it means the bridging of almost the last gulf of the differentiation between the sexes . . . I think it was won by woman for herself – through the attitude of patriotism she displayed during the war, and the work she carried on . . . she will make use of her new power wisely. I believe it is a step on the onward march of civilisation, a step which leads us further and further from those dark days when woman was simply a slave and a chattel in the home. I believe this step is one which this country and which the nation will never regret.[69]

Yet, to fulfil this vision, Dehra Parker designated no place for feminism. Addressing the Woodvale and Falls Branch of the Women's Unionist Association in Belfast in 1927 she revealed her own political convictions by referring to any 'woman who put . . . her sex before her party principles' as 'misguided'.[70] It seems that Parker based her political career on this maxim. Her foremost concern remained the defence of unionist hegemony and in 1935 she informed the

Commons that she had not found it necessary to raise issues for debate which affected women's rights because of the unionist government's progressive standpoint:

> Since I have been a Member of this House I have never taken up the attitude that I was here to defend, or pretend to defend the work of women who put forward the claim that they should be given equal rights on every occasion. I never put that claim forward . . . I am not an advocate . . . that women in every case should have equal duties and equal rights with men. I know that the Prime Minister, and in fact all the members of the Cabinet have always shown the greatest sympathy in that direction. I know the Prime Minister has always been prepared to give every opportunity to women to put forward their view and to take their part in public life wherever possible. Therefore, it has not been necessary that I should say anything on that subject.[71]

But, in spite of her claims to the contrary, Dehra Parker did comment on the majority of legislation affecting women which was passed by the Northern Ireland parliament in the first two decades of its existence. When supporting legislation of this sort, she did, however, attempt to avoid being labelled as a 'woman's' MP by making only passing reference to her sex, instead concentrating on the need for reform or the intricacies of the bill. In 1923 Parker first raised an issue which related specifically to women when she called, albeit unsuccessfully, for the introduction of a quota of female representatives on the Education Advisory Council.[72] Later that year she made a much fuller statement to the Commons on the need for decisive action to bring Ireland into line with existing English legislative provisions with regard to unmarried mothers. Carefully defining her own position as non-feminist, she proffered her full support for Dr Morrison's motion on this question, drawing attention to the fact that in England both the unmarried mother and illegitimate child were protected under the provisions of the Bastardy Acts of 1872 and 1873. Similar legislation had never been introduced in Ireland, a situation that Parker likened to 'the dark ages':

> the present condition of affairs here cries aloud for a remedy. I am not making an appeal . . . on behalf of the women . . . I am one of those who believe that what we sow we must reap. It is the mother who reaps in shame, sorrow, anguish and suffering, and it is the nature of things for the father to pass on. But surely we can expect, we can demand, that the financial responsibility is to a certain extent borne by the man. We cannot allow him to escape . . . It is the innocent child who suffers in these cases.[73]

An Illegitimate Children Bill was introduced to the Commons in April 1924 with the purpose of repealing the Bastardy (Ireland) Act of 1863 and making fathers liable for financially supporting their children. Given her earlier stand on this issue, it was unsurprising that Parker wholeheartedly welcomed this reform, informing the Commons that an injustice endured by 'weak, unfortunate women in Northern Ireland' had finally been corrected:

> They have sinned, but they have had to bear the burden of their sins alone and unaided, in pain, and shame, and sorrow . . . helpless children . . . may now in the future be properly cared for, properly clothed, properly educated . . . outside the workhouse.[74]

Parker's express interest in this issue was apparent as she successfully introduced an important amendment to ensure that once a child's maintenance payments were awarded they would be properly administered in order to provide appropriate care and education.[75]

Despite her declared reluctance, on occasion it seems that Parker felt compelled to address the Commons as a woman MP. Supporting the Widows' Pensions Bill in 1925 she admitted that she occupied 'a rather singular position in this House, because I am the only woman in it, and I felt that I had to speak for the women and children who are so much affected by this Bill'.[76] Similarly, during the debates on the Criminal Law Amendment Bill she spoke again 'on behalf of the women of this Province', emphasising the need for legislation to protect 'the potential mothers of the next generation and who represent the future of Ulster'.[77] Moreover, at the committee stage of this bill she strongly opposed a proposal to increase the age of consent, a sensitive issue which the Conservative MP Nancy Astor referred to as 'a most uncomfortable debate for any woman'.[78] Parker's opposition was based on the fact that girls aged between sixteen and eighteen could not be considered as children. Perhaps more interestingly, she also dwelt on the possibility of unscrupulous women blackmailing men by accusing them of assault. This, combined with the way in which Parker carefully defined her own position during this debate, reinforces the idea that she wanted to avoid being categorised as a champion of women's rights:

> I feel that in taking up the position I am adopting I will in no way act other than . . . hon. Members should wish that their womanhood should act . . . we are not here merely to legislate for the protection of our girls and young woman.[79]

Using this approach she was, therefore, able to make important contributions to legislation affecting women and introduce an essentially female perspective to the House, without becoming categorised, marginalised or alienating party support.

Dehra Parker certainly made several impassioned appeals to the Commons in defence of women's interests. One of the most forthright occurred in 1934 during debates on the Summary Jurisdiction Bill, when she referred to the need for female magistrates. Other members of the House had not raised this facet of the bill and Parker justified submitting her views, not only on the basis that she was a JP with direct and personal experience in this area, but also 'on behalf of the women and . . . children':[80]

> I may be permitted as a very humble Back Bencher . . . to say that I am sorry to see his [Dawson Bates] courage and his determination so misapplied . . . I do think that it would be a very grave disaster if [women magistrates] were to be done away with.[81]

When this bill reached the committee stage she again reiterated the importance of women magistrates, conveying to the Commons the fundamental need for women's representation in this area of jurisdiction to take depositions in criminal assault cases and reside in children's courts:

> There is the necessity for woman's outlook, the woman's point of view, especially in dealing with children. She naturally understands the child better than any man can, because her first and most important task in life is the child . . . a child's life can be absolutely ruined by one mistake in the handling of its first offence . . . [The Bill] eliminated the possibility of women magistrates sitting in cases in which their presence . . . is very necessary. The cases . . . have hitherto been dealt with by the magistrates as a whole. Now they are to be decided by one man. . . . Some of the work to which I have alluded may be unpleasant, but as long as women take their part in public life they can give help here that is absolutely essential.[82]

Parker did not vote against the government by opposing this bill, as it seems that her anxieties were soothed by the Minister for Home Affairs' proposal to establish a commission to examine the legal implications of the Children's Acts.

In addition to defending the unionist government and commenting on the majority of legislation which was introduced to the Commons which affected women, Dehra Parker also believed that one of the fundamental duties of an MP was to voice constituents' grievances. Thus, as the representative of a largely rural constituency, Parker supported legislation which protected the fishing and farming industries.[83] In 1925 she also moved an unsuccessful amendment to the Widows' Pensions Bill that would have provided relief for agricultural labourers and farmers, whom she believed were 'in a far worse condition financially than the countless numbers of unemployed in the cities'.[84] In addition, she applauded the government's decision to reinstate rural housing subsidies in 1937, noting with some justification, that she was partially responsible for this measure: 'I feel I am one of those who brought this matter very forcibly to the attention of the Ministry.'[85] Although improvement was forthcoming in this area, Parker continued to appeal for an increase in the allotted housing subsidy, stressing the importance of providing affordable housing for labourers. It was also in striving to respond to her constituents' needs that she developed an intricate knowledge of the drainage problem of the River Bann and in 1925 she appealed, somewhat tentatively, to the government to initiate reform in this area[86]:

> I tremble lest I should be unable to deal adequately with it and to convince the Government of the necessity for immediate action . . . it is a matter that should be faced and dealt with by the State . . . We really want more than word and more than sympathy. We want action . . . We have a Parliament of our own sitting in our midst to redress our wrongs, to right our grievances, to protect our own flesh and blood.[87]

Parker's grasp of the technicalities of this situation surprised some of her colleagues. In response to her motion, Thomas Henderson, the Independent Unionist who later became involved in some of the most heated verbal exchanges with Parker, made an interesting reference to male preconceptions regarding women's parliamentary interests:

> When I came to this House I said to myself – I am the father of a small family – if there is any question affecting motherhood I will appeal to the Member for Derry to give me the information I require. From the admirable speech she has made to-day she has shown that she knows more than is required by the ordinary mother. She has delivered a great technical speech . . . I believe the hon. Member is made of the right stuff.[88]

The northern nationalist leader, Joseph Devlin, also congratulated Parker, though he advised her not to entrust all her confidence in the government: 'fight them day and night . . . Worrying in politics is like fighting in war, and surely when her constituents sent her to Parliament she is eminently capable of discharging that Parliamentary function.'[89] As a result of her initiative the government introduced a Drainage Bill to the Commons in October 1925, but Parker continued to emphasise the exigency for further measures to fully ameliorate this problem: 'This Bill will help a few now. It will help hundreds I believe shortly, but I also believe that it will ruin thousands eventually unless it is followed by that larger measure of relief.'[90] Although the government agreed to implement a comprehensive drainage scheme for the Bann, Parker continued to raise this issue during members' question time. She felt so strongly on the subject that she informed the Commons in 1925 of her intention 'to press it and mention it on every possible occasion'.[91] True to her word, she badgered the government to confirm that this scheme would be implemented. Thus, for example, during the budgetary debates in 1928, she stated:

> I am very sorry indeed that there is no provision made for this purpose in the Budget . . . and that consequently another year will be lost, another year of suffering to the farmers who are so deeply affected by this terrible evil.[92]

Her persistence brought results and eventually led to significant improvement when the schemes that she called for came to fruition during the late 1930s.

In addition to representing the interests of her rural constituents, Dehra Parker was also a pragmatist. Throughout her career she remained acutely aware of the reforms which the government could afford to introduce, as she stated in 1925: 'it is quite useless to come here and make fine speeches when it is obvious we have not got the money necessary to carry those speeches into effect'.[93] Parker urged that it was expedient for the state only to provide services that were economically viable and, to use her own phrase, 'to cut our suit according to our cloth'.[94] As a result she advised that educational and housing improvements should be scaled down, in view of Northern Ireland's languishing inter-war economy.[95]

Although she was one of the strongest government supporters, Dehra Parker, like her former colleague Julia McMordie, occasionally criticised the government. In May 1927, she asked the Ministry for Education to reconsider abolishing grants that enabled local education authorities to provide instruction in domestic economy. She levelled further criticism against the government and specifically at Richard Dawson Bates, the Minister for Home Affairs, during debates on the Summary Jurisdiction Bill in 1934. This legislation curtailed the powers of justices of the peace by distinguishing between their jurisdiction and that of resident magistrates. Parker emphasised that this reform should only be initiated cautiously, in order to prevent alienating public opinion, and, as a JP, she also questioned the rationality of Northern Ireland pioneering this amendment.[96] Also in that year, her reaction to the Local Government Bill could only be described as one of disillusion.[97] Parker had been a member of the local government commission, which took three years to report, from 1924 to 1927. There was then a decade of delay before the government even considered the commission's proposals. Although Parker acknowledged that the aims of the commission were, in hindsight, unattainably high and that significant economic changes had occurred, she was disappointed that their suggestions to introduce uniformity in tuberculosis prevention schemes, abolish the indoor relief system and establish county health authorities were not sanctioned by the government. This led J.W. Nixon, the Independent Unionist MP for the Woodvale area of Belfast, to wryly proclaim: 'A great miracle has been enacted . . . The member for South Derry (Mrs Parker) has actually criticised the Government.'[98] Parker's opposition was sufficient to prompt her to introduce a successful amendment against the 'viscous' plebiscite clause contained in this bill.[99] She justified this on the grounds that it would 'be practically impossible for any local authorities to get any benefits conferred . . . because the majority of the ratepayers might object to the expense of the benefits'.[100] Her objections were not based on the idea of government accessibility, indeed this was a principle that she fully supported, but she believed that public inquiries provided adequate opportunities for ratepayers to expound their views. She further emphasised that the far-reaching consequences of introducing this at a municipal level could reverberate to parliament, undermining the role of MPs as the elected representatives of the people and thus harming the very principle of democratic government.[101]

On occasion Parker was also frustrated by the government's policy of following the legislative impetus of Westminster. During the Commons debates on the Illegitimate Children Bill in April 1924, for example, she suggested that illegitimacy cases should be heard *in camera* and, although she did not introduce an amendment on this issue, she aired her frustration at the government's lack of initiative: 'Are we to be hidebound by tradition all the time? Can we not strike out for ourselves? Must we always copy other legislation? Must we always copy what has been done across the water?'[102] Similar motives led her to criticise the government in 1934 after she raised the question of procuring pensions for embroidery outworkers who were excluded from the provisions of the Blind Pensions Act. Parker emphasised the need for this reform because of the prevalence of women employed in this sort of work throughout the province: 'I know we have to walk step by step with Great Britain, and we are proud to do so, but I do suggest that here is something which probably concerns us more than any part of the United Kingdom.'[103]

Yet, both Dehra Parker's criticisms of the government and her disillusion at their lack of initiative were only intermittent. Essentially she remained one of the most vocal government supporters and her loyalty was duly rewarded in December 1937 when she was appointed as parliamentary secretary to the Ministry for Education.[104] Parker had already shown a keen interest in education in the Commons, as a member of the Lynn committee in the early 1920s and chairman of Magherafelt's Regional Education Committee. With this appointment she became the first woman to hold government office in Northern Ireland, prompting Professor Reverend Robert Corkey, an MP for Queen's University, to claim that in this instance 'a woman would be the best man for the job'.[105] As a result of Parker's innate belief in the value of education she showed both enthusiasm and flair for her departmental brief. She commented in 1939:

> it is difficult to see in what direction the nation's money could be spent to better advantage than in preparing and equipping its future citizens to take up and carry on the work when this generation lays it down.[106]

In concert with her views concerning MPs' responsibility to their constituents, she also believed that it was crucial for the Ministry for Education to be accessible, an approach which differed from that of her predecessors:

> we are in very close touch with the teachers, and they are able to come and see us frequently . . . and advise us from their practical experience of the actual effect of the rules and regulations we make . . . we receive similar valuable assistance from the elementary and technical teacher . . . This spirit of helpfulness and co-operation is one of the strongest features in our educational life here, and I hope that it may never grow feeble.[107]

One of a parliamentary secretary's principal duties was to answer questions from the House and Parker consistently represented the ministry in a factual and concise manner. She was also responsible for introducing several education bills to the Commons: the Physical Education Act of 1938; the Queen's University Act of 1938, which was a non-controversial measure to enable the university's treasurer and secretary of the academic council to become members of university senate; the Teachers' Salaries and Superannuation (War Service) Act of 1939; the Education (Evacuated Children) Bill and Education (Emergency Provisions) Act of 1940. But the most important legislation that she introduced during her seven-year term as parliamentary secretary was the Education Act of 1938. This legislation fundamentally reformed Northern Ireland's education system by introducing uniformity with English provisions and inaugurating the principle of compulsory schooling until the age of fifteen, establishing nursery schools and technical classes and embracing the ideal that every child, regardless of class or religion, had a right to education. This was a contentious measure, as local authorities were expected to finance the cost of the increased educational provisions. Yet Parker managed, with government support, to defend the passage of this bill through parliament by presenting it as a step towards improving educational facilities and emphasising that it was 'a crime to stop a child's education at 14'.[108]

Parker was as competent and self-assured in the position of parliamentary secretary as she had been throughout her earlier parliamentary career. J.A. Oliver, a civil servant who worked for Parker during the 1950s, described her as 'capricious, an adroit politician and a most formidable operator'.[109] The sheer length of her career was certainly unprecedented for any female member of the Commons. Parker sat as an MP for thirty-five years, whilst the average term of service for the other women who sat in the house from 1921 to 1972, was eight and a half years. Moreover, as the only woman ever appointed to the Northern Ireland cabinet, her achievements were undoubtedly considerable. As the *Belfast News-Letter* remarked, she was 'most attentive to her duties; even an all night sitting has no terrors for her'.[110]

Yet Parker's political career was not without fault. She was occasionally inconsistent, failing to meet her own exacting standards for avoiding sectarian references in the house. Nor was she was universally popular with her fellow MPs. Her return to the House after a three-year absence in March 1933 was largely welcomed, but, as one of her colleagues, J.C. Duggan, the principle assistant secretary to the Ministry for Finance, commented: 'With some members – and not always those in opposition – she has not been popular, because she is at times, inclined to put them right: in fact, she commits the unforgivable sin of knowing too much.'[111] Furthermore, the criticism that she levelled against nationalist, labour and, occasionally, independent unionist members of the House was often caustic in tone and personal in content. One of the few occasions when the issue of her gender was raised in the Commons occurred in October 1925, when Joseph Devlin retaliated against Parker's accusation of 'seeking cheap popularity outside his own constituency' by alleging that she used her minority position in the house to her own advantage: 'Because the hon. Member is a lady does she think that she is entitled to insult hon. Members of this House? . . . She should not take advantage of her sex.'[112] Perhaps she was not beyond pushing the parameters of parliamentary acceptability, but old age was catching up with her. As Parker herself remarked, 'I've been in the thick of things for years'.[113] After such a long period of public service it was perhaps not surprising that, aged seventy-five and with failing health, she decided to retire as Minister for Health and Local Government and as MP for Londonderry in 1957. She was, however, content with her own achievements, declaring: 'I have accomplished some things which can be chalked up to my credit, and I have a very clear conscience about anything I have done in the interests of my country. I feel more inclined to live what is left of my life for MYSELF and NOT for the Public.'[114]

IV

The contention that British women MPs encouraged 'the widely held idea (explicit or implicit) that men and women should occupy separate metaphysical space – that is, concern themselves with different areas of policy' – cannot be applied to Northern Ireland.[115] Within the limits of analysing the careers of the three women who were elected to the Northern Ireland parliament from its establishment in 1921 until 1940, despite the similarities between the level of female candidature and representation, the interests and performance of female MPs differed. During both Julia McMordie and Margaret Waring's brief parliamentary careers they chose to contribute primarily to women's issues and it seems that gender was a crucial factor in defining areas of their debate. Moreover, the three women who were elected to the Commons in the period under analysis did introduce an essentially female perspective to the house. However,

Dehra Parker's career invalidates any sweeping assessment of female MPs' political considerations as essentially gender based. Parker contributed to all the main areas of debate: constitutional, welfare and economic. Undeterred by controversy or criticism from opposition members of the House, she quickly established a reputation as not only an excellent orator, but also one of the staunchest unionists in the Commons. As J.C. Duggan remarked: 'It was she – and often she alone of her own party's back-benchers – who, when Lord Craigavon was the target of personal attacks . . . rushed into the fray in his defence.'[116] Indeed, such was her reputation that she was once described as 'an expert white-washer of the government'.[117] White-washer or not, throughout Parker's career her primary focus remained the defence of unionist hegemony, as her opposition to Joseph Devlin's Representation of the People Bill in 1927 proved beyond doubt.

In spite of these priorities, Dehra Parker also made a valuable contribution to the majority of debates on women's issues and initiated important amendments to several legislative reforms, including the Illegitimate Children Act and Summary Jurisdiction Act. However, she consistently refrained from contributing any feminist agenda to the house. This stance is perhaps unsurprising, given the wholesale demise of feminist impetus after the first instalment of women's suffrage in 1918 and Parker's unquestionable loyalty to her party. It seems likely that Parker successfully deployed this as a deliberate tactic to avoid being categorised, and as a consequence marginalised, as solely a 'woman's' MP. As her unionist colleague Captain Herbert Dixon remarked, she 'made a lasting impression on the House, but great as she was a Parliamentarian, she had shown that she was equally a woman'.[118] This balancing act enabled Parker to make a valuable and distinct contribution to the Commons. However, even though her career was outstanding in terms of both achievement and longevity, all women who were elected to the parliament of Northern Ireland were exceptional. This claim is not based on their parliamentary contributions or because they successfully countered electoral bias, but that they came forward as candidates to the most powerful, and overwhelmingly male, elective assembly in the province.

Conclusion

Ray Strachey wryly depicted the average woman in 1901 as politically outcast, economically deprived, under-educated and over-flattered.[1] By 1940 many changes had occurred and a cluster of legislative reforms had been implemented to facilitate women's full participation in all aspects of social, economic and political life. Women could vote and stand as MPs and local government councillors, whilst the Sex Disqualification (Removal) Act of 1919 opened the jury service, the legal profession and the upper echelons of the civil service to women. The regulations controlling divorce, child legitimacy and guardianship were also effectively transformed and numerous national insurance and pension acts, the Employment of Women and Young Persons Act of 1935 and the Factories Act of 1938 cumulatively improved the working environment.

Of all these legislative measures, women's suffrage was expected to instigate the most dramatic change. But suffrage did not emancipate women or prompt an influx of women into the parliamentary arena. After the passage of the Representation of the People Act in 1918 it quickly became apparent that women would not vote as a bloc and, as Vera Brittain eloquently affirmed, 'the old bogey of a great feminine phalanx uniting to defeat men on every major issue now appeared as the hallucination which it always had been'.[2] It is, therefore, perhaps understandable that the idea of suffrage having little effect on women has been 'almost axiomatic'.[3] There were obvious limits to the impact of suffrage, but after 1918 one tangible effect of female enfranchisement was that women, who now represented an important component of the electorate, could no longer be disregarded or overlooked in the political calculations of any party. In Ulster the change which occurred as a result of this democratisation of politics was clearly apparent. Women were courted by both nationalist and unionist politicians and were consequently given representation on both the county board committees of the Ancient Order of Hibernians and the Ulster Unionist Council. Thus, suffragist Lucy Kingston's prediction of the impact which woman's suffrage would have was remarkably accurate:

> The effect of the enfranchisement of Irishwomen upon the political parties in Ireland may be measured by the effect which this reform is likely to have on the fortunes of the parties themselves . . . 'the woman-element in politics' will be inextricably bound up with party feeling.[4]

In essence, suffrage accelerated the notion that women were civically competent. Hariot, the 1st Marchioness of Dufferin and Ava and a vice-president of the UWUC, alluded to this change that occurred in attitudes towards women. Writing in the inter-war period she emphasised that women were now expected to participate in public life, as it was 'so much more the fashion for women to be actively engaged in some useful work' in comparison to the recent past, when:

> it was very difficult for young women to break through the unwritten laws of custom which . . . discouraged all initiative on their part; but now it is impossible for any girl or woman to claim exemption from the duty of working for others on the grounds that she is not sufficiently old, or sufficiently independent to undertake it.[5]

Women, Hariot concluded, whether involved in philanthropy or politics now met 'with no opposition where their predecessors had to enter by force'.[6]

The imperial government's organisation of a women's conference in 1943 proffers further evidence of the attitudinal changes referred to by Hariot Dufferin and of the perception of women as an intrinsic constituent of the political process. A delegation of one hundred and fifty women representing charities, industries, trade unions, the professions and women's organisations from Northern Ireland attended this conference in London with the aim of bringing women 'into direct contact with those of His Majesty's Ministers who are responsible for aspects of national policy which particularly affect women'.[7] This conference openly acknowledged the 'double share' which women assumed in the work of the nation and sought to give them an opportunity to shape future legislative developments:

> They are employed in every industry and service which supports the fighting men, they have to maintain . . . their homes under the exacting conditions of war economy. After four years of war we are able to look beyond the darkness . . . to a season of better prospects but of enduring problems, in the solution of which the full experience of women will be required.[8]

Even though women's political stature was enhanced by suffrage, the gendered nature of women's political work was not altered. From the late nineteenth century, gender was crucial in defining an acceptable political role for women. This was apparent not only in female political organisations, but also in the elective positions of poor law guardian, local government councillor and, following women's suffrage, members of parliament. Women were, for instance, assigned an auxiliary role within the unionist movement and many of the facets of cultural, constitutional and republican nationalism. In spite of the variance of aims and levels of support that existed between these groups of politically active women, the division of work on gender lines gave rise to many similarities in the methods deployed by women for political ends. Members of female ancillary associations, such as the Ladies' Auxiliary of the Ancient Order of Hibernians, the Ulster Women's Unionist Council and Cumann na mBan, all conducted important didactic, electoral and propagandist work: mobilising female support, updating electoral registers, canvassing, distributing propaganda, organising social events and politically educating future voters and members of their own sex. Women's political organisations thereby made a significant contribution to both the nationalist and unionist campaigns.

It is, however, too simplistic to assess women's role in Ulster politics as solely male defined. Women's political associations also developed specific stratagems to foster support amongst members of their own sex by cultivating a female aspect to both unionist and nationalist ideologies. Members of Cumann na mBan and the UWUC both emphasised that the sanctity of their homes and children were endangered by political developments concerning Ireland's independence. Women consequently defined a domestic milieu to the political agenda. Furthermore, nineteenth-century municipal reformers attempted to carve a female niche in the public sphere by pinpointing specific areas where women, by virtue of their philanthropic and maternal experience, could made a distinct contribution to local government administration. In so doing, women such as Isabella Tod celebrated the difference between the sexes, in an attempt to convince both legislators and the general public that there was ample room for both men and women in local government. The envisaged separation of municipal duties on the basis of gender was also realised. Both female poor law guardians and local government councillors became involved in the most domestic and welfare-orientated aspects of municipal administration. Women, therefore, identified their own areas of interest, which were distinct from those of men who were elected to the same position. The importance of gender was also apparent in defining areas of debate for the female members of the Northern Ireland parliament, and even Dehra Parker, one of the most vehement supporters of the unionist government in the Commons, made a significant contribution to legislation which affected women. Ultimately, then, there were important differences between the work which was undertaken by women and by men for political purposes.

Gender not only shaped the type of political work executed by women, it also affected the level of female representation on elective bodies. In Ulster, poor law boards, which were the least powerful and most socially orientated area of municipal administration, attracted the highest level of female representation. Indeed, 67 per cent of women who were elected to local government in Ulster in the period 1896 to 1940 stood as poor law guardians, whereas no women stood as candidates for Westminster and only three women were elected to the Northern Ireland parliament, the most powerful and overwhelmingly male elective assembly in the province. A statistical analysis cannot, however, adequately uncover the diversity of political activities undertaken by women. Furthermore, the relationship between numerical representation and possessing political influence is not absolute. Some exceptional women were able to exercise considerable influence because, like Theresa and Edith Londonderry or Cecil Craig, they held positions of social privilege, or because, like Anna Johnston and Alice Milligan, they were unusually committed to political ideals. The fallacy of focusing solely on the numerical aspect of women's political participation is also underlined, perhaps most notably in the administration of the poor law. Female guardians, though constituting only a tiny minority (4.2 per cent) of the elective total, had a significant impact on administering and, in many respects, humanising the poor law.

The popularisation and democratisation of politics brought an unprecedented number of women into the political arena from the 1890s onwards. The work undertaken by women may have remained ancillary, circumspect and different from the political gesticulations of men, exciting little comment from contemporary observers, but it formed a fundamental component of both popular politics and state administration. The majority of women were, however, only able to spare a little time to help update an electoral register or perform administrative duties. It should not, therefore, be taken as read that women's ancillary work implied a lack of political commitment or competence. Instead this should be linked to the practicalities of day-to-day living, which for many women entailed not only domestic and childcare duties but also paid employ. The difficulties which women faced when embarking on any political activity were accurately assessed by Dehra Parker in April 1927:

> Women's activity, as far as politics are concerned, is restricted by her home ties, and therefore the number of women who are suited for political careers is lessened accordingly to the extent of these ties.[9]

Thus an increase in the number of women who were returned to both municipal and national assemblies in Ulster only occurred very gradually, because the basic considerations associated with executing unpaid and time-consuming work in any elective position remained unchanged.

Only a few suffragettes and members of Cumann na mBan deviated from taking an auxiliary role as a result of frustration with constitutional methods and male dominance of the political *modus operandi*. But such extremism was not widespread. The majority of women in Ulster, regardless of their political affiliation, appear to have acquiesced in the role which was assigned to them and which they sometimes assigned for themselves. The division of political work on gender lines consequently aroused little adverse comment from women, because they believed their role to be equal but different. The majority of women neither perceived the separation of political work on gender lines as marginalisation, nor did they want to stand as parliamentary candidates. Thus the disillusion expressed by Nora Connolly, the former head of the Belfast branch of Cumann na mBan, was exceptional:

> Progressive and revolutionary women have no voice in the council of the revolutionary movement . . . showing . . . 'damnable patience' and are content to be the drudges of the movement . . . [We] must insist that men and women in Ireland have equal rights and duties and a surrender of any one of these rights and duties is treason to Ireland.[10]

Even though the limitations of generalising on women's personal motivation for becoming politically active have been apparent throughout this study, with the exception of the suffrage movement, gender was not a primary motivating factor. For women in Ulster, religion, altruism and public spirit were all more important as instigators of political activity. The heady impact of familial influence was also often apparent, as '[o]ne's family of origin shaped one's potential for living and working: one's whole . . . life, whether one married or not, was coloured by notions of family'.[11] But gender did significantly affect women's political role: shaping the type of work performed by women, the elective positions they were attracted to and their status within political associations. In addition, any notion of political disinterest amongst women is dispelled by a consideration of the contribution women made to Ulster politics by both individual and group activity. Of equal importance was the uniqueness of their contribution, which, in the final analysis, suggests that gender allowed a shared historical experience to develop amongst many politically active women in Ulster from the late nineteenth to the early twentieth centuries.

Appendix A

ULSTER SUFFRAGE SOCIETIES, WITH THEIR DATE OF ESTABLISHMENT[1]

1873	North of Ireland Women's Suffrage Society established.
1896	North of Ireland Women's Suffrage Society became the Belfast branch of the Irish Women's Suffrage and Local Government Association (IWSLGA).
1908	Bangor branch of the Women's Freedom League (WFL) established.
1909	Belfast branch of IWSLGA reorganised as Irish Women's Suffrage Society (IWSS) and established branches in Londonderry and Whitehead. The Bangor branch of the WFL changed its affiliation to join the IWSS.
1909	Lisburn Suffrage Society established.
1911	Northern Committee of the Irish Women's Suffrage Federation (IWSF) established with the following affiliates: Armagh, Belfast, Ballymoney, Bushmills, Coleraine, Holywood, Larne, Lisburn, Londonderry, Portadown, Portrush, Warrenpoint and Rostrevor, Whitehead.
1913	Belfast branch of the Church League for Women's Suffrage established. Belfast branch of Women's Social and Political Union established.
1914	In April the IWSS was disbanded. Its members joined the Belfast branch of the WSPU. The Belfast branch of Men's Political Union for Women's Enfranchisement and the Irish Women's Franchise League Ulster Centre were also established during 1914.

Appendix B

DETAILS OF THE WSPU'S MILITANT CAMPAIGN IN ULSTER, 1914[2]

24 Jan. Joseph Devlin heckled at a nationalist women's meeting in Belfast. Three WSPU members, including the Ulster organiser Dorothy Evans, were arrested.

27 Mar. Arson attack on Abbeylands House in Whiteabbey, Co. Antrim, causing damages of £20,000. This property belonged to Sir Hugh McCalmont, the late brother of Colonel McCalmont, a former unionist MP and uncle of Major McCalmont, a unionist MP for East Antrim. The grounds of Abbeylands had been used to drill UVF corps.

31 Mar. Dorothy Evans and Madge Muir arrested after police found explosive substances and a revolver in their flat at 113 University Street, Belfast. At the hearing of this case Lilian Metge, a WSPU member, was arrested for breaking windows outside Belfast's Court House in protest against women being denied access to the courtroom.

8 Apr. Trial of Evans and Muir. Continued court disruptions led to the adjournment of the case. Both women were remanded until 14 April and refused bail. Sea View House in Belfast was damaged in an arson attack.

9 Apr. Arson attack on Bishop Henry's Orlands Mansion in Kilroot, Co. Antrim. Suffrage literature left at the scene proclaimed that the attack was in response to Carson's betrayal of Irishwomen. Mabel Small was arrested for stoning the Old Town Hall in Belfast. She was sentenced to two months' hard labour. Hunger striking secured Small's temporary release under the Cat and Mouse Act. She was later unconditionally released.

11 Apr. Evans and Muir refused an offer of bail. They were released without bail the following day.

14 Apr. Arson attack on Bangor station in Co. Down.

15 Apr. House burnt in Londonderry with damages estimated at £325.

16 Apr.	Carson heckled by suffragettes during a week-long visit to Ulster. The WSPU picketed UVF displays.
18 Apr.	Teahouse in Belfast destroyed, with damages estimated at several thousand pounds.
20 Apr.	Scheduled retrial of Evans and Muir, but both women failed to appear in court. They were subsequently re-arrested and the trial adjourned.
21 Apr.	Evans and Muir rearrested without warrants. Violence in court led to separate trials. The trials were adjourned and Evans and Muir refused offers of bail.
22 Apr.	Arson attack on Annadale House in Belfast caused damages of £500. A suffragette meeting in Belfast broken up by unionists. Trial of Evans and Muir resumed, but again adjourned because of court disturbances. Both women refused to accept offers of bail.
25 Apr.	Evans and Muir released from Crumlin Road Jail as a result of sustained hunger and thirst strikes.
30 Apr.	Evans and Muir rearrested.
31 Apr.	Arson attack on Wallace Castle in Lisburn, Co. Antrim.
2 May	Windows broken at unionist headquarters in Belfast in sympathy for the WSPU prisoner, Mabel Small.
3 May	Belfast Bowling and Lawn Tennis Pavilion burnt, causing damages of £889.
4 May	Unconditional release of Evans and Muir.
26 May	Damages of £20 caused to greens at Knock Golf Club in East Belfast.
30 May	WSPU poster parade in Belfast.
1 June	Four suffragettes attacked by unionists at Belfast docks.
2 June	Evans and two other suffragettes broke into James and Cecil Craig's house while Sir Edward Carson was present.
3 June	Arson attack on Ardmillan House in Fortwilliam Park in Belfast. Two WSPU members, Madge Muir and Mary Larmour, were arrested for this attack. They were released from Crumlin Road Jail after a six-day hunger and thirst strike. Muir was wanted on explosives and arms charges but the authorities were unable to trace her after her release. An unnamed suffragette burst into the offices of the *Belfast Evening Telegraph* and the *Belfast News-Letter* and slapped the papers' editors in protest at their incitement of readers to take the law into their own hands to counter suffragette activity.

4 June	Dorothy Evans and Maud Wickham interfered in UVF display at Baronscourt, Co. Tyrone.
6 June	Suffragettes disrupted a unionist demonstration being held at Balmoral, Belfast.
16 June	Motor garage destroyed in Belfast.
24 June	Minimal damage caused in arson attack on Ballylesson Parish Church near Lisburn, Co. Antrim.
3 July	Arson attack at Ballymenoch House in Belfast caused damages of £20,000.
12 July	Slight damage caused by an arson attack on a UVF hospital.
21 July	Dorothy Evans arrested at the home of Belfast's Lord Mayor whilst seeking asylum. She was arrested, but secured her release four days later by hunger and thirst striking.
22 July	Evans brought to assize court, but she interrupted the trial so frequently that Mr Justice Dodd refused to continue. She was remanded to the next assizes in six months' duration. This was of questionable legality.
29 July	Race stand burnt in Newtownards, Co. Down, causing damages of £750.
31 July	Explosion at Church of Ireland Cathedral in Lisburn, Co. Antrim. Four WSPU members were arrested: Lilian Metge, Dorothy Evans, Maud Wickham and Miss Carson. Each woman was released on £100 bail.
8 Aug.	Trial of Metge, Evans, Wickham and Carson. They refused to recognise the authority of the court and were subsequently remanded in custody.
12 Aug.	The four women listed above were released from prison as a result of sustained hunger striking. After their release Carson and Wickham immediately broke windows in Donegall Square post office in Belfast. They were rearrested and sentenced to a month's imprisonment but further hunger striking secured their release on the following day. Their trials were postponed until the next assizes.
15 Aug.	Suffragettes attacked by police and guards at Belfast station.
22 Aug.	WSPU offices in Belfast closed due to the outbreak of the First World War.
Dec.	*Nolle Prosequi* ensured that the pending cases against suffragettes were dropped.

Notes

INTRODUCTION

1 Mary R. Beard, *Women as a force in history: A study of traditions and realities* (New York, 1946), p 247.
2 C.J. Hamilton, *Notable Irishwomen* (Dublin, n.d.), preface.
3 Diary of Cecil Craig, 21 Jan. 1927 (Public Record Office of Northern Ireland [hereafter PRONI], D. 1415/B/38/163–277).
4 Lil Conlon, *Cumann na mBan and the women of Ireland, 1913–25* (Kilkenny, 1969), cited p 239.
5 Throughout this work, the term 'Ulster' is used to refer to the six north-eastern counties which became known as Northern Ireland as a result of partition and the Government of Ireland Act of 1920. The term 'gender' is used to refer to the cultural constructions of masculine and feminine whilst the term 'sex' is used to refer to biological difference.
6 The focus of this study is on mainstream politics. As a result, though deserving of a separate study, smaller political movements, such as labour and communism, have not been included. Some mention is made of women in the labour movement in J.F. Harbinson, 'A history of the Northern Ireland Labour Party, 1891–1949' (unpub. MSc. dissertation, The Queen's University of Belfast, 1966). See also Hazel Morrissey, 'Betty Sinclair: A woman's fight for socialism', *Saothar*, 9 (1983), pp 121–32. For a study of women's involvement in trade unionism see Jonathan Hamill, 'Women in the Belfast textile operatives, 1890–1939' (unpub. PhD diss., The Queen's University of Belfast, 1999). See also Austen Morgan, *Labour and partition: The Belfast working class, 1905–1923* (London, 1991); David Bleakley, *Saidie Patterson: Irish peacemaker* (Belfast, 1980); Fred Heatley, 'The York Street Co-operative Women's Guild, 1913–1921', *North Belfast History Magazine*, ii (1986), pp 21–4, and John Gray, *City in revolt: James Larkin and the Belfast dock strike of 1907* (Belfast, 1985).
7 On the Irish suffrage movement see Rosemary Cullen Owens, *Smashing times: A history of the Irish women's suffrage movement, 1899–1922* (Dublin, 1984), and Cliona Murphy, *The women's suffrage movement and Irish society in the early twentieth century* (Hemel Hempstead, 1989). On female nationalism see Margaret Ward, *Unmanageable revolutionaries: Women and Irish nationalism* (Dingle, 1983), and *In their own voice: Women and Irish nationalism* (Dublin, 1995).
8 This is with the exception of the official history of the Ulster Women's Unionist Council by Nancy Kinghan, *United we stood: The story of the Ulster Women's Unionist Council, 1911–74* (Belfast, 1975). Kinghan was the UWUC's organising secretary from 1938 to 1971. See also Diane Urquhart, 'The Ulster Women's Unionist Council, 1911–40' (unpub. MA diss., The Queen's University of Belfast, 1992), and '"The female of the species is more deadlier than the male"? The Ulster Women's Unionist Council, 1911–40' in Janice Holmes and Diane Urquhart (eds), *Coming into the light: The work, politics and religion of women in Ulster, 1840–1940* (Belfast, 1994), pp 93–123.
9 Robert Wuthrow, *Cultural analysis* (London, 1984), p 136.
10 Maria Luddy and Cliona Murphy (eds), *Women surviving* (Dublin, 1989), p 3.
11 See Joan Wallach Scott's persuasive argument in *Gender and the politics of history* (New York, 1988); S. Jay Kleinberg (ed), *Retrieving women's history: Changing perceptions of the role of women in politics and society* (Oxford, 1988), and Gerda Lerner, *The majority finds its past: Placing women in history* (Oxford, 1979).

12 Universal male suffrage was established under the Representation of the People Act of 1918. This act also enfranchised women aged over thirty.

13 For a discussion of this in a British context see Pat Jalland, *Women, marriage and politics, 1860–1914* (Oxford, 1986).

14 The Primrose League admitted men and women into its ranks and had half a million members by 1887 (figure from Martin Pugh, *The Tories and the people, 1880–1935* [Oxford, 1985], p 25). The Women's Liberal Federation had 80,000 members by the mid 1890s (figure from Patricia Hollis, *Ladies elect: Women in English local government, 1865–1914* [Oxford, 1987], p 58). The Women's Labour League had seventy branches by 1910, but no overall membership figures are available (Hollis, ibid., p 62).

15 Thirty-five branches of the Primrose League were established in Ireland, with a collective membership of 1,500 by 1912. Eight of these branches were situated in Ulster. Some members of leading unionist families were involved. For example, Theresa, 6th Marchioness of Londonderry, was a member of the league's executive committee in 1887. Her husband led the Belfast branch and the Duke of Abercorn became chancellor of the league in 1893 (Pugh, *The Tories and the people*, pp 89, 168, 215). See chapter II for analyses of the Belfast branch of the Women's Liberal Federation and Theresa Londonderry's political career.

16 David Rubinstein, *Before the suffragettes: Women's emancipation in the 1890s* (Brighton, 1986), cited p 163.

17 Lilian Lewis Shiman, *Women and leadership in nineteenth-century England* (London and Hampshire, 1992), cited p 205.

18 Ibid., p 127.

19 I use the term 'suffragette' to distinguish supporters of militant action from constitutional suffragists. This is in accordance with its contemporary meaning. The *Daily Mail* coined the phrase 'suffragette' in 1906 (Lisa Tickner, *The spectacle of women: Imagery of the suffrage campaign, 1907–14* [London, 1989], p 8).

20 Jane Rendall (ed), *Equal or different: Women's politics, 1800–1914* (Oxford, 1987), p 4.

21 In the nine counties of Ulster, Protestants constituted 57.3 per cent of the population. Following the partition of the six north-eastern counties in 1920, Protestants constituted 66 per cent (Jonathan Bardon, *A history of Ulster* [Belfast, 1992], pp 443, 496).

22 Diary extract from Theresa Londonderry, 5 Dec. 1918 (PRONI, D. 3084/C/B/1/14).

CHAPTER ONE

1 Extract from a poem by Walt Whitman, *Irish Citizen* [hereafter *IC*], 18 Oct. 1913.

2 On the Irish suffrage movement, see Rosemary Cullen Owens, *Smashing times: A history of the Irish women's suffrage movement, 1899–1922* (Dublin, 1984); Cliona Murphy, *The women's suffrage movement and Irish society in the early twentieth century* (Hemel Hempstead, 1989), and Margaret Ward, '"Suffrage first – above all else!" An account of the Irish suffrage movement', *Feminist Review*, 10 (Feb. 1982), pp 21–36.

3 Renate Bridenthal and Claudia Koonz (eds), *Becoming visible: Women in European history* (Boston, 1977), p 2.

4 Marilyn J. Boxer and Jean H. Quataert (eds), *Connecting spheres: Women in the western world, 1500 to present* (New York and Oxford, 1987), p 197.

5 Isabella Tod (1836–96). Tod was also an education reformer, unionist and temperance activist. For a biographical study see Maria Luddy, 'Isabella M.S. Tod', in Mary Cullen and Maria Luddy (eds), *Women, power and consciousness in nineteenth-century Ireland* (Dublin, 1995), pp 197–230. See chapters III, IV and V for Tod's involvement in unionist politics and the campaigns to admit Irish women to poor law and local government administration.

6 Lilian Lewis Shiman, *Women and leadership in nineteenth-century England* (London and Hampshire, 1992), cited p 148.

7 See Lee Holcombe, *Wives and property: Reform of the married women's property law in nineteenth-century England* (Toronto and Buffalo, 1983).
8 Maria Luddy, 'Irish women and the Contagious Diseases Acts, 1864-86', *History Ireland*, 1, no. 1 (Spring, 1993), pp 32–4. Tod served on both the executive of the Ladies' National Association in London and on the general council for the Repeal of the Contagious Diseases Acts.
9 Figure from Luddy, 'Irish women and the Contagious Diseases Acts', p 33. The Contagious Diseases Acts were repealed in 1886.
10 Helen Blackburn, *Women's suffrage: A record of the women's suffrage movement in the British Isles* (reprint, New York, 1971, of orig. ed., London, 1902), p 127. In September 1880 Tod organised further suffrage meetings in Belfast and Londonderry, which were addressed by Helen Taylor, John Stuart Mill's stepdaughter.
11 See Marie O'Neill, 'The Dublin Women's Suffrage Society and its successors', *Dublin Historical Record*, 38, no. 4 (1984–5), pp 126–40. This organisation was later renamed the Irish Women's Suffrage and Local Government Association (IWSLGA).
12 Blackburn, *Women's suffrage*, p 209.
13 Isabella Tod, 'Women and the new franchise bill: A letter to an Ulster member of parliament', in Jane Lewis (ed), *Before the vote was won: Arguments for and against women's suffrage* (London and New York, 1987), pp 396–403.
14 Ibid., p 397.
15 Blackburn, *Women's suffrage*, p 209.
16 *IC*, 20 Feb. 1915.
17 Figures from Louise Ryan, 'The *Irish Citizen*, 1912–20', *Saothar*, 17 (1992), p 107.
18 See appendix A for a list of Ulster suffrage societies.
19 *IC*, 25 May 1912, categorically states that Belfast's Irish Women's Suffrage Society was a successor of the Belfast branch of the IWSLGA.
20 Margaret Mulvihill, *Charlotte Despard: A biography* (London, 1989), p 94. The *IC* makes no reference to the Irish branches of the WFL.
21 Based at 1 Dunluce Avenue, Belfast, the men's society was affiliated to the London headquarters of this organisation, established in 1910 by Victor Duval. Until 1913 this association was an auxiliary of the WSPU. The honorary secretaries of the Belfast branch were Mr G.A. Wedgwood and Mr E. Dempster. Its honorary treasurer was Mr J.T. McCoubrey, husband of Margaret McCoubrey, a prominent suffragist and later suffragette.
22 Walkington was a pioneer of equal educational rights in Ireland and she was the first Irish woman to take an LLD degree. She was amongst the founders of the Belfast Suffrage Society that was affiliated to the Irish Women's Suffrage Federation and was a vice-president of the federation. Following her death in 1918, the *Irish Citizen* stated: 'Feminism in Ireland had sustained a heavy loss' (*IC*, Oct. 1918).
23 In 1909 Metge established Lisburn Suffrage Society, serving as its secretary and from 1914 as its president. She also became an honorary secretary of the Northern Committee of the IWSF. In May 1913 she severed her connections with these organisations as a result of 'differences in administrative work' (*Lisburn Standard*, 1 May 1914). She later joined the militant campaign of the WSPU in Belfast.
24 The following suffrage societies were affiliated to the Northern Committee of the IWSF: Belfast, Warrenpoint and Rostrevor, Newry, Armagh, Lisburn, Portrush, Bushmills, Londonderry, Holywood, Larne, Ballymoney, Coleraine, Portadown, Whitehead.
25 *IC*, 25 May 1912. The *Citizen* presented these figures as a conservative estimate. The IWSF figure was for all-Ireland; that of the IWSS relates to its Belfast, Whitehead, Londonderry and Bangor branches.
26 Ibid., 30 May 1914.
27 Ibid., 3 May 1913.
28 Ibid., 18 Apr. 1914. The following is a list of societies which were affiliated to the Northern Committee, with percentages of the committee's total membership given in brackets: Belfast 84 (12 per cent), Ballymoney 24 (4 per cent), Bushmills 45 (7 per cent), Coleraine 21 (3 per cent), Londonderry 110 (16 per cent), Holywood 55 (8 per cent), Larne 47 (7 per cent), Lisburn 80 (12 per cent), Newry 48 (7 per cent), Portrush 62 (9 per cent), Warrenpoint 62 (9 per cent), Whitehead 40 (6 per cent). Membership figures were not given for the Armagh and Portadown societies.

29 Owens, *Smashing times*, p 85. Marie Johnson (1890–1974) helped James Connolly establish the Irish Workers' Textile Union in Belfast. She was a member of the IWSS in the city and of the Irish Women's Franchise League's Ulster Centre from 1914. She was elected to Rathmines Urban District Council in 1925, becoming the first female labour councillor in the Irish Free State. She married Tom Johnson, later leader of the Irish Labour Party.
30 *IC*, 13 Dec. 1913.
31 Ibid., 14 Mar. 1914.
32 Ibid., 16 Aug. 1913.
33 Ibid., 14 June 1913. See chapters IV and V for an analysis of women in local government in Ulster.
34 Ibid., 25 May 1912.
35 Ibid., 30 Nov. 1912. In this edition of the paper a list of public meetings held throughout the country included twenty-seven in Ulster: Armagh, Ballycastle, Ballymena, Ballymoney, Bangor, Belfast, Bushmills, Carrickfergus, Coleraine, Donaghadee, Dungannon, Enniskillen, Greenisland, Holywood, Islandmagee, Lisburn, Larne, Londonderry, Lurgan, Newcastle, Newry, Portadown, Portrush, Rostrevor, Strabane, Warrenpoint, Whitehead.
36 Ibid., 7 Sept. 1912.
37 The Northern Committee of the IWSF was responsible for the remaining suffrage meetings. In the period 1912 to 1913 sixty-two suffrage meetings were held in Ulster. In the corresponding period 1913 to 1914 a total of sixty-one meetings were held. Figures calculated from meetings reported in the *IC*, May 1912–May 1914.
38 Figures calculated from meetings reported in the *IC*, May 1913–May 1914.
39 Ibid., 17 Jan. 1914.
40 David Morgan, *Suffragists and liberals: The politics of woman suffrage in England* (Oxford, 1975), p 8.
41 *IC*, 23 Nov. 1912.
42 L.M. McCraith, 'Irishwomen and their vote', *New Ireland Review*, 30, no. 4 (Dec. 1908), p 195. For a discussion of this in a British context see Constance Rover, *Women's suffrage and party politics in Britain, 1866–1914* (London, 1967).
43 *IC*, 9 Aug. 1913.
44 Ibid., 29 Nov. 1913.
45 See above, p 9.
46 This was the pseudonym of Elizabeth A.M. McCracken (*c.* 1865–1944). This Belfast author of various suffrage pamphlets was a former unionist supporter who joined the IWSS and later the WSPU. Her husband, George McCracken, was the solicitor who defended suffragettes during their trials in Belfast in 1914.
47 *IC*, 21 June 1913.
48 Ibid., 24 Jan. 1914.
49 Ibid., 23 Aug. and 13 Dec. 1913. McCracken and Mellone's propaganda work was accredited with setting a positive example for all Irish suffragists (ibid., 21 June 1913).
50 Frederick Ryan, 'The suffrage tangle', *Irish Review* (Sept. 1912), p 346.
51 Memoirs of Marie A. Johnson, 29 Jan. 1972 (National Library of Ireland [hereafter NLI], Ms. 21194 (I)).
52 Ibid.
53 Some of this correspondence, dated July 1912, is reproduced in Rosemary Cullen Owens, *Did your granny have a hammer? A history of the Irish suffrage movement, 1876–1922* (Dublin, 1985).
54 Margaret McCoubrey (1880–1955); Originally from Glasgow, McCoubrey came to Belfast in 1905. She was active in the suffrage movement from 1910 and pioneered the open-air campaign of the IWSS. She later became involved in the WSPU's Ulster campaign and in September 1914 became honorary secretary of the IWFL's Ulster Centre. She was a pacifist and anti-militarist and became the general secretary of the Co-operative Guild. In 1920 she was elected as a Labour councillor for Dock Ward in Belfast (Kate Newmann, *A dictionary of Ulster biography* [Belfast, 1993], p 152, and Elizabeth Hutchinson, 'Reminiscence' (n.d.). 'Reminiscence' was written by Margaret McCoubrey's daughter. I am grateful to Dr Myrtle Hill for giving me a copy of this unpublished typescript).

55 *IC*, 25 Jan. 1913.
56 Ibid., 15 Feb. 1913.
57 Ibid.
58 Taped interview with Miss Margaret Robinson on suffrage activity in Belfast, 1975 (PRONI, TP. 35). Robinson was born in Banbridge, Co. Down, in 1876. She was the secretary of Belfast's IWSS, before joining the Belfast branch of the WSPU in 1913. In Nov. 1911 she was imprisoned in Holloway for two months with Dr Elizabeth Bell, also of Belfast's IWSS, for breaking windows during a suffragette demonstration in London.
59 *IC*, 9 Aug. 1913.
60 Ibid., 6 Sept. 1913.
61 *The Times*, 1 December 1911. F.G. Banbury, Walter Long, Austen Chamberlain, Arnold Ward, Helmsley and F.E. Smith signed this letter.
62 *IC*, 17 May 1913.
63 Maria Luddy, *Hanna Sheehy Skeffington* (Cork, 1995), cited p 19.
64 Transcript of interview with Monsignor A. Ryan from 'By the Way' BBC broadcast, 3 Jan. 1981 (PRONI, T.3600/2).
65 Carson also received a deputation from the Belfast branch of the Women's Social and Political Union in Mar. 1914 which is discussed later in this chapter.
66 *Votes for Women*, *c*. 1914 (PRONI, T. 3259/2/5). Carson was personally opposed to women's suffrage and on one occasion this led him to publicly humiliate a suffragette chained outside his London home. Anticipating the so-called 'demands of nature' Carson instructed his butler to empty a jug of water where the woman was chained and 'having heard the pointed and irreverent comments of the crowd which soon collected . . . the suffragette soon unchained herself and shamefacedly made off' (H. Montgomery Hyde, *Carson: The life of Sir Edward Carson, Lord Carson of Duncairn* (London, 1953), p 368).
67 *IC*, 4 Jan. 1913.
68 *Northern Whig*, 24 Aug. 1912.
69 *IC*, 31 Jan. 1914.
70 Beth McKillen, 'Irish feminism and national separatism, 1914–1923', *Eire-Ireland*, 17 (Fall and Winter 1982), pp 52–67, 72–90.
71 See chapter II for an analysis of women's participation in unionism.
72 *IC*, 6 Sept. 1913.
73 Ibid., 22 June 1912.
74 Ibid., 20 Oct. 1912. The IWSS heckled the Belfast covenant processions.
75 Ibid., 8 Mar. 1913.
76 Ibid., 2 Aug. 1913.
77 This was the only Irish branch of the Anti-Suffrage League.
78 Diary of Ruby Carson, 16 Oct. 1918 (PRONI, D. 1507/B/38).
79 Diary of Cecil Craig, 1 Jan. 1910 (PRONI, D. 1415/B/37).
80 Edith, 7th Marchioness of Londonderry, 1878–1959. See chapter II for an analysis of her involvement in unionist politics.
81 Edith Londonderry, *Women's indirect influence and its effect on character: Her position improved by the franchise, morally and materially* (n.p., 1909) (PRONI, D.3099/3/25).
82 *The Times*, 1 Apr. 1912. This letter was written in response to the anti-suffrage views expounded by Sir Almroth Wright on women's 'natural' unsuitability to vote. Wright was a distinguished bacteriologist at St Mary's Hospital in London and the author of *The unexpurgated case against woman suffrage* (London, 1913).
83 *The Times*, 1 Apr. 1912.
84 *IC*, 20 Sept. 1913.
85 Ibid., 27 Sept. 1913.
86 Ibid.
87 Ibid., 22 Nov. 1913. There is no evidence in unionist records to support the Northern Committee of the IWSF's claim.
88 Ibid., 20 Sept. 1913.
89 Ibid.
90 Ibid., 18 Oct. 1913.

91 Ibid., 7 Feb. 1914.
92 Ibid., 9 May 1914.
93 Ibid., 14 Feb. 1914.
94 Ibid., 1 Nov. 1913.
95 Ibid., 23 Aug. 1913. McCracken's article was subsequently reproduced and distributed in pamphlet form amongst unionist women in Belfast. This was later interpreted as a possible cause for the unionists' suffrage pledge of September 1913. This, however, seems most unlikely.
96 Ibid., 14 Feb. 1914.
97 Ibid., 11 Apr. 1914.
98 E. S. Pankhurst, *The suffragette movement: An intimate account of persons and ideals* (London, 1977, reprint of orig. ed., London, 1931), p 548.
99 Ryan, 'The suffrage tangle', p 346. Militancy remained such a contentious issue that in 1919 Dora Mellone ignored the militant campaign in a series of articles which she published in the *Common Cause* on fifty years of the Irish suffrage movement. This led the *Irish Citizen* to brand her 'the Irish ostrich' (*IC,* Mar. 1919).
100 Hanna Sheehy Skeffington, 'The women's franchise movement – Ireland', *Irish Review* (July 1912), pp 226–7.
101 Owens, *Smashing Times*, p 71 and Pankhurst, *The suffragette movement*, p 548.
102 This occurred on 16 November 1912.
103 *IC*, 15 Mar. 1913.
104 Ibid., 26 Apr. 1913.
105 Ibid., 23 Aug. 1913
106 Ibid., 13 Sept. 1913.
107 Ward, 'Suffrage first', pp 28–9.
108 Dorothy Evans (1889–1944) (*Dorothy Evans and the Six Point Group* [London, *c.* 1945], p 71 [Fawcett Library, London, 305. 406041]). I am grateful to Catriona Beaumont for sending me this information.
109 The WSPU announced their arrival in Ulster in the pages of the *Irish Citizen* by including a statement within the IWSS's weekly report (*IC*, 13 Sept. 1913).
110 *IC*, 7 June 1914.
111 Robina Gamble to Margaret Robinson, 16 Apr. 1913 (PRONI, T.3259/1/7).
112 Mrs Heron to Margaret McCoubrey, 29 Apr. [*c.* 1914] (PRONI, T.3259/1/6).
113 *IC*, 20 Sept. 1913.
114 Ibid.
115 Leah Levenson and Jerry H. Natterstad, *Hanna Sheehy Skeffington: Irish feminist* (Syracuse, 1986), p 29.
116 *IC*, 13 Sept. 1913. In line with these sentiments the *Irish Citizen* opposed the establishment of the English-based organisation the Men's Political Union in Belfast (*IC*, 21 Feb. 1914).
117 Ibid., 20 Sept. 1913.
118 *Northern Whig*, 14 Apr. 1914. James Craig thanked the IWSF for this affirmation. In June 1914 the Northern Committee of the IWSF published a letter in the press to James Craig which reiterated their 'entire confidence in the [suffrage] promise given by your council' (*Belfast News-Letter*, 3 June 1914).
119 Hutchinson, 'Reminiscence', p 10. For a discussion of this in a British context see Brian Harrison, *Peaceable kingdom: Stability and change in modern Britain* (Oxford, 1982), pp 27–8.
120 Taped interview with Robinson on suffrage activity in Belfast (PRONI, TP. 35).
121 Memoirs of Marie Johnson (NLI, Ms. 21194 (I)).
122 *IC*, 27 July 1912. Sandra Stanley Holton records the WSPU's regular usage of past revolutionary movements in 'In sorrowful wrath: Suffrage militancy and the romantic feminism of Emmeline Pankhurst', in Harold L. Smith (ed), *British feminism in the twentieth century* (Aldershot, 1990), pp 7–24.
123 *IC*, 12 Apr. 1913.
124 Ibid., 5 July 1913.
125 Sheehy Skeffington, 'The women's franchise movement', p 225.
126 *The Suffragette*, 29 May 1914.
127 Pankhurst, *The suffragette movement*, pp 547–8.

128 *IC*, 6 June 1914.
129 Ibid., 11 Oct. 1913. This was a quote from Mrs Chambers of Belfast's IWSS.
130 *Belfast Evening Telegraph*, 14 Mar. 1914.
131 This meeting was to be addressed by Emmeline Pankhurst, but her imprisonment in England for militant activities prevented this. However, Flora Drummond, another prominent member of the WSPU, replaced her. This perhaps signifies the importance of the meeting.
132 *IC*, 18 Apr. 1914.
133 Diary of Cecil Craig, 3 June 1914 (PRONI, D. 1415/B/37).
134 Ibid.
135 See appendix B for details of the WSPU's Ulster campaign.
136 See Andrew Rosen, *Rise up women! The militant campaign of the Women's Social and Political Union, 1903–1914* (London and Boston, 1974).
137 Pankhurst, *The suffragette movement*, p 549.
138 Memoirs of Marie Johnson (NLI, Ms 21194 (I)).
139 *IC*, 29 Dec. 1913.
140 *Belfast News-Letter*, 12 Feb. 1912.
141 Diary of Lilian Spender, 6 June 1914 (PRONI, D.1633/2/19). Lady Lilian Spender (1890–1960), wife of Wilfred Spender, permanent secretary to the Northern Ireland Ministry for Finance and head of the Northern Ireland Civil Service, 1924–44.
142 *Belfast News-Letter*, 1 June 1914.
143 *IC*, 13 June 1914. Sir Edward Carson was addressing this meeting.
144 Pankhurst, *The suffragette movement*, p 549.
145 Memoirs of Marie Johnson (NLI, Ms 21194 (I)).
146 *IC*, 27 June 1914. A magistrate cautioned those involved and deemed this attack a regrettable misunderstanding. This led the *Citizen* to conclude that the underlying assumption was that the attack would have been justified if the women had been suffragettes.
147 Diary entry of Lilian Spender, 10 Apr. 1914 (PRONI, D.1633/2/19).
148 Murphy, *The women's suffrage movement*, p 150.
149 Diary of Lilian Spender, 31 July 1914 (PRONI, D. 1633/2/19).
150 A.E. Metcalfe, *Women's efforts: A chronicle of British women's fifty years' struggle for citizenship, 1865–1914* (Oxford, 1917), p 333.
151 *IC*, 1 Apr. 1914. See also *Belfast Evening Telegraph*, 8 Apr. 1914, and Crown Files at Assize and Commission (Belfast Petty Sessions), The King v. Dorothy Evans and Madge Muir (Noxious Things and Explosives) (PRONI, BELF 1/1/2/45/8).
152 See appendix B for details of subsequent suffragette arrests and trials.
153 Small received a two-month sentence for breaking windows at unionist headquarters in Belfast's Old Town Hall. She eventually secured her unconditional release by hunger striking. Considerable debate was prompted by the application of the Cat and Mouse Act and Miss Houston, a member of the IWFL in Dublin, broke windows in College Green post office in sympathy with Mabel Small and in protest against the barbarity of this legislation. Houston was subsequently imprisoned for a month (information compiled from *IC*, May 1914).
154 *IC*, 22 Aug. 1914. This was in line with the Pankhursts' autocratic control of the WSPU.
155 Ibid., 20 Feb. 1915.
156 Ibid., 10 May 1913.
157 Taped interview with Margaret Robinson (PRONI, TP. 35).
158 Margaret MacCurtain, 'Women, the vote and revolution', in Margaret MacCurtain and Donnacha O Corrain (eds), *Women in Irish society: The historical dimension* (Dublin, 1987), p 52.
159 Dorothy Evans opposed the WSPU's pro-war stance, remaining avowedly anti-militarist throughout the war. She stayed in Belfast until 1915 when she returned to England. From 1921 she was a member and honorary secretary of the feminist organisation, the Six Point Group. Throughout the 1920s she unsuccessfully contested parliamentary seats for Labour. Evans also initiated the Women for Westminster movement to train women as councillors and MPs. Lilian Metge remembered her as 'independent, fearless . . . carrying with her an atmosphere of

liberty so infectious that she infused all . . . a modern Winged Victory'. Hanna Sheehy Skeffington alleged that 'in organising the North (chiefly Belfast) she [Evans] did splendid work, understanding the psychology of the people' (information compiled from *Dorothy Evans and the Six Point Group*, pp 66, 71) (Fawcett Library, London, 305.406041).

160 *IC*, 12, 26 Sept. and 3 Oct. 1914. None of the politicians accepted the Ulster Centre's invitation.
161 Ibid., 24 Oct. 1914.
162 Ibid., 23 Jan. 1915.
163 Ibid., 6 Mar. 1915.
164 For instance, in 1917 Louie Bennett of the Irish Women's Workers' Union edited the *Citizen* when Hanna Sheehy Skeffington was in America.
165 Francis Sheehy Skeffington was killed in 1916. See Luddy, *Hanna Sheehy Skeffington*, pp 28–9.
166 See Martin Pugh, 'Politicians and the woman's vote, 1914–18', *History*, 59 (1974), pp 358–74. Britain was amongst nineteen European and American countries to promote women's suffrage as a reward for war work in the period 1915 to 1922.
167 Morgan, *Suffragists and liberals*, p 7.
168 Martin Pugh, *Women and the women's movement in Britain, 1914–59* (London, 1992), p 42.
169 Diary of Ruby Carson, 12 Jan. 1918 (PRONI, D. 1507/C/4).
170 *IC,* July 1918.
171 See McKillen, 'Irish feminism', pp 72–90.
172 *IC*, Nov. 1918.
173 Ibid., Dec. 1918.
174 Ibid., Feb. 1920.
175 See chapter III for an analysis of nationalist women.
176 *IC*, Oct. 1919.
177 Ibid., 9 Jan. 1915.
178 Richard Dawson Bates to Theresa Londonderry, 21 Aug. 1916 (PRONI, D. 2846/1/7/9). McMordie was appointed to the council two years later in 1918. See chapter V for an analysis of women in local government and chapter VI for an assessment of McMordie's parliamentary career.
179 See chapter VI for an analysis of women MPs in the parliament of Northern Ireland, 1921 to 1940.
180 Draft conclusions of Northern Ireland cabinet meeting, 12 June 1924 (PRONI, CAB 4/116/4).
181 See chapters III and VI for an analysis.
182 Crissie M. Doyle, *Women in ancient and modern Ireland* (Dublin, 1917), p 3.
183 Caroline E. Stephen, 'Women and politics', *The Nineteenth Century and After,* 71 (Feb. 1907), p 231.

CHAPTER TWO

1 *Darlington and Stockton Times*, 22 Nov. 1913 (PRONI, D. 2846/1/2/7). Extract from an address made to a meeting of women unionists by Theresa, Dowager Marchioness of Londonderry (1856–1919). Theresa was the eldest daughter of Charles Talbot, 19th Earl of Shrewsbury and a Conservative MP. In 1875 she married Charles Stewart Vane-Tempest, a unionist MP for Co. Down from 1878 to 1884, where his family owned a 50,000-acre estate. Charles was the Irish lord lieutenant from 1886 to 1889, president of the Ulster Unionist Council and a member of the House of Lords from 1884 until his death in 1915. Theresa was vice-president of the UWUC from 1911 to 1913 and president from 1913 to 1919. She was also a Primrose League Dame and was appointed to the Senate of The Queen's University of Belfast in 1909. She moved to London in 1917. Theresa is recognisable as Lady Roehampton in Vita Sackville West's novel, *The Edwardians* (London, 1930).

2 Edith Londonderry, *Woman's indirect influence, and its effect on character: Her position improved by the franchise morally and materially* (n.p., 1909) (PRONI, D. 3099/3/6/2). Edith, 7th Marchioness of Londonderry (1878–1959), married Theresa Londonderry's son Charles in 1889, a unionist MP for Maidstone from 1906 to 1915, Northern Ireland Minister for Education from 1921 to 1925 and leader of the Northern Ireland Senate from 1921 to 1926. Charles was appointed 1st Commissioner of Works in the British cabinet in 1928 and, due to Edith's influence with the Labour Prime Minister, Ramsay MacDonald, he was appointed as the Secretary of State for Air from 1931 to 1935. In 1935 Charles was appointed Lord Privy Seal and leader of the House of Lords. Edith was a vice-president of the UWUC from 1919 to 1959. In 1915 she established the Women's Legion, an organisation designed to train women to replace men on active military service. She was awarded a DBE for this work in 1917 and this was changed to a military award in 1918. She was the first woman to receive this honour. Edith also promoted the Ulster linen and lace-making industries and ran an embroidery school from Mount Stewart, the family's estate in Co. Down.

3 See Alvin Jackson, 'Unionist myths, 1912–85', *Past and Present*, 136 (1992), pp 165, 184; Patrick Buckland, 'Irish unionism and the new Ireland', in D.G. Boyce (ed), *Revolution in Ireland, 1879–1923* (Dublin, 1988), pp 71–90, and James Loughlin, *Ulster unionism and British national identity since 1885* (London and New York, 1995).

4 This is with the exception of Nancy Kinghan, *United we stood: The story of the Ulster Women's Unionist Council, 1911–74* (Belfast, 1975). This is the official history of the Ulster Women's Unionist Council. Kinghan was the UWUC's organising secretary from 1938 to 1971. For a detailed analysis of the UWUC see also Diane Urquhart, 'The Ulster Women's Unionist Council, 1911–40' (unpub. MA diss., The Queen's University of Belfast, 1991), and '"The female of the species is deadlier than the male"? The Ulster Women's Unionist Council, 1911–40', in Janice Holmes and Diane Urquhart (eds), *Coming into the light: The work, politics and religion of women in Ulster, 1840–1940* (Belfast, 1994), pp 93–125.

5 See above, chapter I, for an analysis of Isabella Tod's involvement in the Ulster suffrage movement and chapters IV and V for her involvement in the campaigns to admit women to poor law and local government administration. In 1888 the Women's Liberal Federation was split by political deliberations over Home Rule. Members opposing this legislation, like Isabella Tod, left the federation to establish the Women's Liberal Unionist Association. This association had 15,000 members in fifteen branches, including a Belfast branch, by the 1890s (see Patricia Hollis, *Ladies elect: Women in English local government, 1865–1914* [Oxford, 1987], p 62, and Jane Rendall, *Equal or different: Women's politics, 1800–1914* [London, 1987].

6 Maria Luddy, 'Isabella M.S. Tod', in Mary Cullen and Maria Luddy (eds), *Women, power and consciousness in nineteenth-century Ireland* (Dublin, 1995), cited p 221.

7 I am grateful to Noel Armour for this information.

8 Isabella Tod to Hugh de Fellenberg Montgomery, 12 Oct. 1892 (PRONI, D. 627/428/196).

9 Lady Ewart was the wife of Robert, 3rd Baronet of Glenmachen. Margaret Byers was the founder of Victoria College, Belfast, and a prominent member of Belfast Ladies' Institute, which campaigned for women's educational reform. Byers was also an active suffragist and temperance worker. Lady Edith Dixon (DBE) was the wife of Sir Thomas, 2nd Baronet of Ballymenoch, the high sheriff for Antrim in 1912 and Down in 1913.

10 *Report of the general meeting of 12,000 delegates at the Ulster convention* (Belfast, 1892) (F.J. Bigger collection, Central Library, Belfast, Q. 126), p 104.

11 Peter Gibbon, *The origins of Ulster Unionism: The formation of popular Protestant politics and ideology* (Manchester, 1975), p 135. For further details on this event see Gordon Lucy (ed), *The great convention: The Ulster unionist convention of 1892* (Lurgan, 1995).

12 *Londonderry Sentinel*, 21 Mar. 1893, reprinted in Maria Luddy, *Women in Ireland, 1800–1918: A documentary history* (Cork, 1995), p 323. The wives of fifteen clergy signed this letter: eight Church of Ireland, five Presbyterian, one Methodist and one Congregationalist.

13 Violet Hobhouse (née McNeill) (1864–1902) combined an interest in Irish culture and language with fervent unionist sympathies. The exact date of her tour is unknown, but her death in 1902 dates this activity either to the first or second Home Rule crisis (Kate Newmann, *A dictionary of Ulster biography* [Belfast, 1993], p 109).
14 Lucy, *The great convention*, pp 55–6.
15 Alvin Jackson, 'Unionist politics and Protestant society in Edwardian Ireland', *History Journal*, 33, no. 4 (June 1990), p 852.
16 Luddy, *Women in Ireland*, cited p 324.
17 Ross was a unionist MP for Londonderry city from 1892 to 1895. Ulster women signatories numbered 19,632 (Kinghan, *United we stood*, p 8).
18 Patrick Buckland, *Irish unionism: A documentary history, 1885–1923* (Belfast, 1973), p 143. The IUA Ladies' Committee sent 12,000–20,000 papers per week from its central office in Dublin in 1893. This organisation co-operated with the UWUC during the third Home Rule crisis. For example, English delegates from the Women's Amalgamated Unionist and Tariff Reform Association were shown the south and west of Ireland by members of the IUA Ladies' Committee and then around 'the prosperous loyalist district in the North East by way of contrast' by members of the UWUC (Minute book [hereafter MB] UWUC standing committee, 17 July 1911 (PRONI, D. 2688/1/3)).
19 Mrs Georgina Stewart, president of the IUA Ladies' Committee in Dublin, to Lady Louisa Antrim, Apr. 1893 (PRONI, D. 2977/39). Louisa was the daughter of Lieutenant-General Honourable Charles Grey and niece of 3rd Earl Grey. She married the 6th Earl of Antrim in 1895. She was a Lady of the Bedchamber to Queen Victoria and Queen Alexandra. The family seat was Glenarm Castle in Co. Antrim.
20 A total of 70,000 Irish women's signatures were collected.
21 Mrs Sawyers to Lady Antrim, 20 May 1893 (PRONI, D. 2977/39).
22 Jane Macaulay to Lady Antrim, n.d. [1893] (PRONI, D. 2977/39).
23 C.J. Stannus to Lady Antrim, 24 May 1893 (PRONI, D. 2977/39). She was the mother of Louisa Stannus, a member of Lisburn's board of guardians from 1911 and deputy vice-chair of the board from 1913 to 1932. See chapter IV for an analysis of the work of women poor law guardians.
24 C.J. Stannus to Lady Antrim, 6 June 1893 (PRONI, D. 2977/39).
25 G.E. O'Neill to Lady Antrim, n.d. [1893] (PRONI, D. 2977/39).
26 Louise O'Neill to Lady Antrim, 19 May 1893 (PRONI, D. 2977/39).
27 Eleanor Archdale to Hugh de Fellenberg Montgomery, 17 Nov. 1893 (PRONI, D. 627/428/223). This organisation was possibly formed as part of a network of Unionist Clubs which were established by Lord Templetown throughout provincial towns in Ulster in 1893 (A.T.Q. Stewart, *The Ulster crisis: Resistance to Home Rule, 1912–14* [London, 1967], p 31).
28 MB North Tyrone Women's Unionist Association [hereafter WUA], 1907 (PRONI, D. 1098/2/1/1). It is possible that this association was established in response to the formation of the Ulster Unionist Council in 1905 to co-ordinate the activities of male unionists.
29 Mary Anne was the fourth daughter of the Earl of Howe. She married James Hamilton, the 2nd Duke of Abercorn, in 1869. He was a unionist MP for Co. Donegal from 1860–1880 and the chief spokesman for Ulster unionism in the House of Lords from 1895. The family's seat was Baronscourt, Co. Tyrone. Mary Anne served as first president of the UWUC from 1911 to 1913. She died in 1929. Walter Long was appointed unionist leader in 1906.
30 MB North Tyrone WUA, 28 May 1907 (PRONI, D. 1098/2/1/1).
31 Ibid. The last minutes, dated 29 Oct. 1907, give no indication of whether this body continued to be politically active.
32 Philippa Levine, *Feminist lives in Victorian England: Private roles and public commitment* (Oxford, 1990), p 29.
33 R.E. Quinault, 'Lord Randolph Churchill and Home Rule', in Alan O'Day (ed), *Reactions to Irish nationalism* (Dublin, 1987), pp 323–4.
34 Rosalind, the only daughter of the 4th Earl of Lucan, married James, the 3rd Duke of Abercorn, in 1894. He was a unionist MP for Londonderry city from 1900 to 1913, lord lieutenant for Co. Tyrone 1913 to 1953, a member of the Northern

Ireland Senate and governor of Northern Ireland from 1922 to 1945. Rosalind was a vice-president of the UWUC from 1914 to 1919 and president from 1919 to 1922. She died on 18 Jan. 1958.

35 Ian Colvin, *The life of Lord Carson* (3 vols, London, 1934), iii, cited p 40. Ruby, daughter of Colonel Stephen Frewen of Somerset. In September 1914 she married Sir Edward Carson, later Lord Carson of Duncairn, who had been widowed in April 1913. Ruby was a vice-president of the UWUC from 1914 until her death in 1966. She was widowed in 1935.

36 Leaflet by Thomas Moles on the presentation made to Carson by the UUC's standing committee, June 1925 (PRONI, D. 1507/3/8/1), p 114.

37 Diary of Ruby Carson, 2–3 Feb. 1918 (PRONI, D. 1507/C/4).

38 *Belfast Telegraph*, 19 Oct. 1923.

39 Lilian Spender was born in 1880, the daughter of Rosser Dean of London. She married Wilfrid Spender in 1913. Her husband re-raised and commanded the UVF in 1920 and served as permanent secretary to the Northern Ireland Ministry for Finance and head of the Northern Ireland civil service from 1925 to 1944. The Spenders left Ireland in 1955 to live in England. Lilian Spender was widowed in 1960. Cecil Craig was born in 1883, the only child of Sir Daniel Tupper, an officer in the king's household. In 1905 she married James Craig, later 1st Viscount of Craigavon and the first Prime Minister of Northern Ireland. She was the UWUC's president from 1923 to 1942, a vice-president from 1912 to 1923 and from 1942 until her death in 1960. She was nominated for a DBE by Winston Churchill in 1940 and was widowed in November of that year.

40 St John Ervine, *Craigavon: Ulsterman* (London, 1949), p 108.

41 Londonderry, *Woman's indirect influence.*

42 Leonore Davidoff, *The best circles: Society, etiquette and the season* (London, 1973), p 16. Dowagers, like Theresa Londonderry, exercised the ultimate authority in social circles.

43 Edith, 7th Marchioness of Londonderry, *Retrospect* (London, 1938), p 173. For instance, the agreement of April 1911 to organise unionist propaganda was named the Londonderry House Agreement, as this was where the majority of negotiations had taken place.

44 Mary Anne, 2nd Duchess of Abercorn, to Hugh de Fellenberg Montgomery, 29 Dec. 1891 (PRONI, D. 627/428/10).

45 Lilian Spender to Wilfrid Spender, 29 June 1916 (PRONI, D. 1295/17/2).

46 Ibid., 2 Nov. 1917 (PRONI, D. 1295/17/3).

47 Diary of Cecil Craig, 9 Mar. 1922 (PRONI, D. 1415/B/38).

48 Queen Victoria to Hariot Dufferin, 30 Apr. 1886 (PRONI, D. 1231/G/11/4). Hariot, the 5th Dowager of Dufferin and Ava, was born in 1843, the eldest daughter of Archibald Rowan-Hamilton of Killyleagh Castle in Co. Down. She married Frederick, 1st Marquis of Dufferin and Ava, of Clandeboye estate, Co. Down, in 1862. She was a vice-president of the UWUC from 1921 to 1936. She was awarded freedom of the city of Belfast in 1912 and a DBE in 1917. She accompanied her husband in his appointments as Governor General, to Canada from 1872 to 1878, viceroy of India from 1884 to 1888, ambassador to Russia from 1879, Turkey from 1881 to 1882, Italy from 1888 to 1889 and France in 1892. Hariot wrote several accounts of their travels and also established a successful charity to fund the medical training of women in India.

49 See, for example, Arthur Bigge's letter to Theresa Londonderry, 22 Jan. 1914 (PRONI, D. 2846/1/5/1–9).

50 James Craig to Theresa Londonderry, 12 Mar. 1915 (PRONI, D. 2846/1/3/6). Edith Wheeler was the UWUC's honorary secretary from 1911 to 1912; Julia McMordie was a vice-president of the UWUC from 1919 until her death in 1941 and Dehra Chichester-Clarke (later Parker) was a vice-chairman of the council from 1918 to 1930. Both McMordie and Parker were later elected as unionist members of the Northern Ireland parliament. See chapter VI for an analysis of women in the parliament of Northern Ireland from 1921 to 1940.

51 Political notes of Theresa Londonderry, 10 Aug. 1915 (PRONI, D. 3084/C/B/1/3), and diary extract, 5 Dec. 1918 (PRONI, D. 3084/C/B/1/14).

52 Anne de Courcy, *Circe: The life of Edith, Marchioness of Londonderry* (London, 1992), cited p 36.
53 Edmund Gosse to Theresa Londonderry, 12 May 1910 (PRONI, D. 2846/2/26).
54 H. Montgomery Hyde, *Carson: The life of Sir Edward Carson, Lord Carson of Duncairn* (London, 1953), cited p 125.
55 Ian Colvin, *The life of Lord Carson* (3 vols, London, 1936), ii, p 443.
56 Notes of H. Montgomery Hyde on a conversation with Mrs St George Robinson, sister of Edward Carson, 22 July 1950 (PRONI, D. 3084/H/3/9).
57 Montgomery Hyde, *Carson*, ii cited p 297. Theresa felt that if Carson had been properly approached he would have accepted the leadership of the Conservative Party in 1911.
58 The council was established following a proposal by Edith Mercier Clements that was seconded by Lady Cecil Craig. Clements was the UWUC's assistant honorary treasurer from 1911 to 1920. She was appointed vice-chair in 1920, but died later in the same year.
59 The association of some women with the UWUC was solely titular. For instance, only six of the twenty-three women mentioned above regularly attended meetings: Theresa Londonderry; Lady Wilhelmina Anderson, the wife of Sir Robert, 1st Baronet of Belfast and lord mayor of the city from 1908 to 1909; Lady Ewart; Lady Paula Jaffe, the wife of Sir Otto Jaffe, lord mayor of Belfast in 1899 and from 1904 to 1905 and president of the Ulster Reform Club in 1905; Lady Dixon and Lady Dunleath (DBE), the wife of 2nd Baron of Ballywalter. Lady Beatrice Macnaghten was the wife of the Honourable Sir Francis, 8th Baronet of Bushmills, and Dowager Lady Matilda Clanmorris was the wife of 5th Baron of Clanmorris.
60 The only untitled vice-president was Mrs Julia McMordie. She was a unionist member of the Northern Ireland parliament from 1921 to 1925. See chapter VI for an analysis of her career.
61 The first Home Rule bill was defeated in the Commons in June 1886. The second bill was defeated in the Lords in Sept. 1893.
62 Jackson, 'Unionist myths', p 165.
63 MB Lurgan WUA, 13 May 1911 (PRONI, D. 3790/4).
64 Ibid.
65 Jean Victor Bates, *Sir Edward Carson: Ulster leader* (London, 1921), p 6. Bates published a number of articles on unionism in English and American journals. In 1917 her articles in the *Morning Post* were commended by Carson as being 'excellently well done and should bring home to the people over here some of the things they are apt to forget'. He also suggested that these should be collected together and published in pamphlet form (Edward Carson to Richard Dawson Bates, 13 Aug. 1917 [PRONI, D. 1507/A/24/15–16]). Jean Bates also interviewed journalists encouraging them to write features on unionism and offered to pen articles in Carson's name (Jean Bates to Edward Carson, 17 Oct. 1919 [PRONI, D. 1507/A/31/30]).
66 Bates, *Sir Edward Carson*, p 8.
67 *New Zealand Herald*, 21 Nov. 1929 (PRONI, D. 1415/A/28).
68 *Belfast News-Letter*, 19 Jan. 1912.
69 James Winder Good, *Ulster and Ireland* (Dublin and London, 1919), p 290.
70 *Belfast News-Letter*, 24 Jan. 1911.
71 Diary of Lilian Spender, 22 Mar. and 5 June 1914 (PRONI, D. 1633/2/19).
72 Good, *Ulster and Ireland*, p 290.
73 Ronald McNeill, *Ulster's stand for union* (London, 1922), pp 38, 113.
74 Good, *Ulster and Ireland*, p 290.
75 The records of the Association of Loyal Orangewomen of Ireland are not yet open to researchers. The Orange Order was revived in 1885 in response to Gladstone's conversion to Home Rule (Stewart, *The Ulster crisis*, p 31).
76 The female member listed was Mrs Burnside, a housewife of 12 Mountjoy Gardens in Belfast (Roy Allen, *A place of honour, an account of the Orange Order in Ballynafeigh: The first one hundred years, 1887–1987* [Belfast, 1987], p 37).
77 *Ulsterwoman, a journal for union and progress*, no. 1, 12 July 1919 (PRONI, D. 2688/1/10).

78 A.R. Sibbett, *Orangeism in Ireland and throughout the empire* (2 vols, London, 1939), ii, p 612.
79 M.W. Dewar et al, *Orangeism: A new historical appreciation* (Belfast, 1967), p 160. The close ties between these two bodies are also referred to by Allen, *A place of honour*, p 31.
80 *Belfast Evening Telegraph*, 12 July 1912. Branches of the Association of Loyal Orangewomen were also established in America and Canada.
81 Good, *Ulster and Ireland*, p 292.
82 *Belfast News-Letter*, 22 Sept. 1913, and *Darlington and Stockton Times*, 22 Nov. 1913. In comparison to the UWUC, Cumann na mBan's total membership peaked in 1919 with 4,425 members (David Fitzpatrick, 'The geography of Irish nationalism, 1910–21', in C.H. Philpin (ed.), *Nationalism and popular protest in Ireland* [Cambridge, 1987], pp 421–2). Approximately 1,000 women in Ulster were members of suffrage societies (*IC*, 30 May 1914).
83 For a detailed analysis of the UWUC's work see Urquhart, 'The Ulster Women's Unionist Council', pp 27–52.
84 MB UWUC, 30 Apr. 1912 (PRONI, D. 1098/1/1), and Kinghan, *United we stood*, p 20. This petition was presented to the House of Commons by Sir John Lonsdale on 11 June 1912.
85 *Belfast News-Letter,* 28 July 1913.
86 *UWUC Annual Report* [hereafter AR], 1913 (PRONI, D. 2688/1/3).
87 Male covenant figure from Stewart, *The Ulster crisis*, p 65. Women's declaration figure from UWUC executive committee minutes [hereafter ECM], 16 Jan. 1913 (PRONI, D. 1098/1/1). There were female majorities in sixteen of the twenty-nine areas of Ulster where signatures were collected for the covenant and declaration.
88 Buckland, *Irish unionism, 1885–1923*, cited p 329.
89 *UWUC Year Book* (Belfast, 1920) (PRONI, D. 2688/1/9).
90 Diary of Cecil Craig, 17 Jan. 1913 (PRONI, D. 1415/B/38). In May 1916 Theresa also 'abused' Edward Carson's wife, Ruby, because the unionist's second-in-command, James Craig, occasionally spoke to Winston Churchill, who supported Home Rule (Diary of Ruby Carson, 24 May 1916 [PRONI, D. 1507/C/2]).
91 *IC*, 9 May 1914.
92 Thousands of Ulster women received first-aid and nursing instruction from 1913 to 1914. During the First World War many women who had been trained for the UVF nursed at the front.
93 Mrs Young and Mrs Casement both took five bundles of arms to Galgorm in Co. Antrim and Mrs Gibson took an unknown quantity of arms to Lisfallon (Buckland, *Irish unionism, 1885–1923*, p 250).
94 Stewart, *The Ulster crisis*, p 203.
95 Ervine, *Craigavon*, p 263.
96 Diary of Lilian Spender, 6 May 1914 (PRONI, D. 1633/2/19).
97 MB UWUC advisory committee, 3 Feb. 1914 (PRONI, D. 2688/1/5).
98 Ibid., 9 June 1914 (PRONI, D. 2688/1/5). The stance taken by those opposing the UWUC's constituency campaign was possibly caused by problems experienced in April 1914, when the UWUC wanted a pledge that their workers would not be used as clerks or messengers in Scottish constituencies, but would conduct constructive electioneering work by canvassing voters of doubtful political persuasion (ibid., 6 Apr. 1914 [PRONI, D. 2688/1/3]).
99 Theresa Londonderry to Edward Carson, 10 June 1914 (PRONI, D. 1507/A/6/5).
100 Diary of Lilian Spender, 14 Feb. 1936 (PRONI, D. 1633/2/36). The Comforts for the Ulster Division Fund was chaired by Rosalind, 3rd Duchess of Abercorn. Lilian Spender was honorary secretary and Ruby Carson was honorary treasurer of the fund. This organisation worked in close co-operation with the Ulster Gift Fund.
101 Ibid., 6 May and 15 Sept. 1914 (PRONI, D. 1633/2/19).
102 Lilian Spender to Wilfred Spender, 9 May 1917 (PRONI, D. 1295/17/3).
103 Diary of Ruby Carson, 24 Feb. 1918 (PRONI, D. 1507/C/4).
104 MB UWUC advisory committee, 14 May 1914 (PRONI, D. 2688/1/5).
105 Ibid., 18 Apr. 1917 (PRONI, D. 2688/1/7).
106 Edith Wheeler to Theresa Londonderry, 8 July 1916 (PRONI, D. 2846/1/8/39).

107 Edith Mercier Clements to Theresa Londonderry, 19 July 1916 (PRONI, D. 2846/1/8/48).
108 Edith Wheeler to Theresa Londonderry, 16 Aug. 1916 (PRONI, D. 2846/1/8/43).
109 Hugh de Fellenberg Montgomery to Mrs M.W. Sinclair, 20 Sept. 1916 (PRONI, D. 627/429/66).
110 *Northern Whig*, 7 Apr. 1919.
111 Rory Fitzgerald, 'Ulster women against Home Rule: The role of the Ulster Women's Unionist Association in the Home Rule crisis, 1911–14' (unpub. BA diss., University of Ulster, 1989), p 5. By 1914 there were 371 Ulster Clubs, which collectively represented the grassroots of unionist organisation (Patrick Buckland, *Irish unionism: Ulster unionism and the origins of Northern Ireland, 1886–1922* [Dublin, 1973], p 47).
112 Alvin Jackson, 'Irish unionism, 1905–21', in Peter Collins (ed), *Nationalism and unionism: Conflict in Ireland, 1885–1921* (Belfast, 1994), p 42.
113 Rosalind, 3rd Duchess of Abercorn, to Edward Carson, 10 Oct. 1916 (PRONI, D. 1507/A/19/9).
114 Theresa Londonderry to Edward Carson, 18 Jan. 1918 (PRONI, D. 1507/A/26/8).
115 Edith Wheeler to Theresa Londonderry, 20 June 1918 (PRONI, D. 1507/A/28/9).
116 Ibid.
117 MB UWUC, 4 June 1918 (PRONI, D. 2688/1/7). Edith Wheeler was responsible for this document, which was entitled 'What is the position of the UWUC'. For further details see Urquhart, 'The Ulster Women's Unionist Council', pp 64–5, and 'The female of the species is more deadlier than the male', pp 106–7.
118 See, for example, Rosalind, 3rd Duchess of Abercorn, to Edward Carson, 10 Oct. 1916 (PRONI, D. 1507/A/19/9), cited above.
119 Edward Carson to Theresa Londonderry, 4 Sept. 1918 (PRONI, D. 2846/1/1/1–158).
120 Richard Dawson Bates to Edward Carson, 8 Oct. 1918 (PRONI, D. 1505/A/28/43).
121 Ibid.
122 Richard Dawson Bates to Theresa Londonderry, 18 June 1918 (PRONI, D. 1507/A/28/5).
123 By 1918 the UUC had 432 members. The UWUC's representation on the UUC was not increased until 1944, when each local women's unionist association could return six representatives.
124 *UUC AR*, 1919 (PRONI, D. 972/17).
125 Ronald McNeill to Theresa Londonderry, 23 June 1918 (PRONI, D. 2846/1/8/53).
126 UWUC miscellaneous papers, 27 Feb. 1929 (PRONI, D. 2688/1/10).
127 Richard Dawson Bates to Theresa Londonderry, 29 June 1918 (PRONI, D. 2846/1/8/70/A). As the papers of the Association of Loyal Orangewomen are not yet open to researchers, it is not known whether Bates' attempt to induce Theresa Londonderry to join the association was successful.
128 *Northern Whig*, 20 May 1921.
129 *Belfast News-Letter*, 25 May 1925.
130 Winifred Campbell, 'Down the Shankill', *Ulster Folklife*, 22 (1976), p 21.
131 UWUC ECM, 1 Mar. 1921 (PRONI, D. 1098/1/2). I have found no other references concerning either the work or aims of the Women's Advisory Council.
132 *Northern Whig*, 7 Feb. 1921.
133 Ibid.
134 See chapter VI for an assessment of their careers.
135 UWUC ECM, 18 Mar. 1919 (PRONI, D. 1098/1/2). The minutes of the executive committee of the UWUC record that in 1920 seven women came forward as unionist candidates in the poor law elections. The UWUC interviewed all seven candidates and agreed to pay the election expenses of three women (UWUC ECM, 1 June 1920 [PRONI, D. 1098/1/2]).
136 See chapters IV and V for an analysis of women poor law guardians and local government councillors.
137 Buckland, *Irish unionism, 1885–1923*, p 418.
138 Furthermore, in 1923 a joint meeting of male and female unionists in Portadown was addressed by James and Cecil Craig (Diary of Cecil Craig, 20 Oct. 1923 [PRONI, D. 1415/A/38]).

139 MB Mid Armagh Men's Unionist Association (PRONI, D. 1327/23/4A).
140 *Northern Whig*, 5 Apr. 1928. Mrs Ainsworth Barr (CBE) was honorary treasurer of the UWUC from 1920 to 1930, a vice-chair from 1923 to 1925 and from 1933 until her death in 1947.
141 *Northern Whig*, 20 May 1921.
142 *Belfast News-Letter*, 11 Jan. 1929.
143 Edith, 7th Marchioness of Londonderry, typescript of article entitled 'Armistice Day, 1932' (PRONI, D. 3099/3/25).
144 *Belfast News-Letter*, 10 May 1929.
145 Ibid.
146 Diary of Cecil Craig, 14 May 1929 (PRONI, D. 1415/A/38). She first issued an electoral appeal to women in 1925.
147 For instance, in 1925 Craig gave a £100 donation from an unnamed unionist supporter to the UWUC for executing the best work for the unionist cause (UWUC ECM, 1 Apr. 1925 [PRONI, D. 1098/1/2]). In Nov. 1933 and Mar. 1938 Craig gave £500 of his own money to the UWUC (UWUC ECM, 18 Jan. 1933 and 2 Mar. 1939 [PRONI, D. 1098/1/2]).
148 In 1931 the UWUC's executive committee and annual meeting agreed to send a representative to meetings of this body (UWUC MB, 27 Jan. 1931 [PRONI, D. 1098/1/3]).
149 Figure compiled from *UUC Year Book* (Belfast, 1923) (PRONI, D. 1327/20/1/1). Those appointed included Miss Leah Garratt, the Grand Secretary and later Grand Mistress of the Association of Loyal Orangewomen. Other female delegates were active in government: Dehra Parker and Julia McMordie were both members of the Northern Ireland parliament; Mrs Jessie Kydd was a local councillor and Mrs Margaret Gilliland and Mrs Minnie McCutcheon were both poor law guardians. Several titled women were also appointed: Ladies Allen, Kennedy, Anderson, Dunleath and Dixon. In one instance a husband and wife were both nominated, the Webbs of Randalstown, who represented Antrim's unionist association.
150 For instance, in 1934 female representation was 20 per cent. Figure compiled from *UUC Year Book* (Belfast, 1934) (PRONI, D. 1327/20/1/8).
151 *Belfast News-Letter*, 7 Nov. 1930.
152 *Belfast Telegraph*, 12 Aug. 1925. Mrs Dixon, later Lady Glentoran, was a vice-chair of UWUC from 1912 to 1930 and vice–president of the organisation from 1930 to 1964.
153 MB St Anne's WUA, 17 Oct. 1919 (PRONI, D. 2688/2/1).
154 *Belfast Telegraph*, 18 Feb. 1932.
155 MB North Down WUA, 11 Dec. 1925 (PRONI, D. 2688/3/1).
156 *Belfast News-Letter*, 8 Oct. 1930.
157 The journal was published from Oct. 1925 to June 1927.
158 For a discussion of this in a British context, see Gail Braybon, *Women workers in the first world war: The British experience* (London, 1981).
159 *Ulsterwoman, a journal of union and progress*, no. 1, 12 July 1919. This was the predecessor of the UWUC's publication, *Northern Ireland, home and politics, a journal for women*. *Ulsterwoman* was published until Aug. 1920.
160 Mr J. Johnston, MP, addressing the annual meeting of Lurgan and North Armagh WUA, as reported in the *Lurgan Mail*, 5 Apr. 1930.
161 *Belfast Telegraph*, 27 Oct. 1937.
162 Extract from Cecil Craig's address to the annual meeting of the UWUC (*Northern Whig*, 9 May 1930).
163 Diary of Lilian Spender, 19 Mar. 1921 (PRONI, D. 1633/2/24) and 4 Dec. 1921 (PRONI, D. 1633/2/25).
164 *Belfast News-Letter*, 8 Dec. 1921.
165 *Daily Herald*, 22 Apr. 1926.
166 This was acknowledged in the *Morning Post*, 31 Oct. 1924.
167 *Belfast News-Letter*, 22 Jan. 1927.
168 From 25 to 29 Nov. 1933 in the Oldpark and Duncairn districts of Belfast and in the Mourne area of Co. Down.
169 *Daily Mail*, 20 Jan. 1938.

170 Diary of Cecil Craig, 9 Dec. 1940 (PRONI, D. 1415/B/38).
171 Jonathan Bardon, *A history of Ulster* (Belfast, 1992), p 552.
172 Diary of Cecil Craig, 9 Dec. 1940 (PRONI, D. 1415/B/38).
173 See PRONI, D. 3099/3/13/1–153 and D. 3099/3/15/1–91.
174 Samuel Hoare to Edith Londonderry, 22 Apr. 1936 (PRONI, D. 3099/3/15/54).
175 de Courcy, *Circe*, cited p 168.
176 *UWUC AR*, 1924, (PRONI, D. 2688/1/9).
177 H. Montgomery Hyde, *The Londonderrys: A family portrait* (London, 1979), cited p 159.
178 Ibid.
179 Ibid.
180 de Courcy, *Circe*, p 231.
181 Edith Londonderry to Helen McLean, 31 Oct. 1931 (PRONI, D. 3099/8/36). McLean was the UWUC's organising secretary.
182 *UWUC AR*, 1922 (PRONI, D. 2688/1/9). Women appointed under the Ulster scheme were to act as telephonists, telegraphists, nurses, cooks, policewomen and searchers to deal with women suspected of carrying arms or documents.
183 Notes on the Ulster Women's Volunteer Association, 20 July 1922 (PRONI, FIN 18/2/56). The association had offices at King's Chambers in Belfast.
184 Ibid., 1 July 1922 (PRONI, FIN 18/2/78).
185 *Sunday Chronicle*, 10 Apr. 1938.
186 *Northern Ireland. Home and politics. A journal for women*, 1, no. 1, Feb. 1926.

CHAPTER THREE

1 *Irish News*, 29 Mar. 1905. Poem taken from an article by 'Celestine' on Irish womanhood.
2 Jonathan Bardon, *A history of Ulster* (Belfast, 1992), pp 443, 496.
3 D. George Boyce, *Nationalism in Ireland* (3rd ed, London and New York, 1995), pp 401–2.
4 I am grateful to Dr Eamon Phoenix for this information.
5 In her biography of her father, Nora Connolly O'Brien makes one of the few references to nationalist women electioneering in Ulster, noting that she canvassed for nationalist candidates in Belfast in 1914 (Nora Connolly O'Brien, *James Connolly: Portrait of a rebel father* [Dublin, 1975, reprint of orig. ed. Dublin, 1935], p 118).
6 Motto of the monthly Belfast publication, *Shan Van Vocht* [hereafter *SVV*]. Shan Van Vocht personified Ireland as a poor old woman. It was also the title of a popular nationalist song written in 1796 to commemorate the French fleet's departure for Ireland.
7 Charlotte Eaton, 'Ethna Carbery – poet of the Celts', *Catholic World*, 121 (Apr.-Sept. 1925), p 325.
8 Kathleen Tynan, 'Ethna Carbery: An Irish singer' *Catholic World*, 109 (July 1919), p 481.
9 Eaton, 'Ethna Carbery', pp 325–6. Alice Milligan (1866–1953) was born in Omagh, Co. Tyrone. Her family was Protestant and middle class and she was privately educated at Methodist College, Belfast, and the Ladies' Department of King's College, London. Milligan, who often wrote under the pseudonym of Iris Olkryn, was an acclaimed poet, Irish language enthusiast and playwright. Anna Johnston (1864–1902) was born in Ballymena, Co. Antrim. Johnston was an accomplished poet and popular short story writer. Many of her works were written under the pseudonym of Ethna Carbery. She married the Donegal writer, Seamus MacManus, shortly before her death in 1902. Milligan and Johnston were introduced to one another by W.B. Yeats.
10 *Northern Patriot* [hereafter *NP*], 1, no. 1, 15 Oct. 1895. The Henry Joy McCracken Literary Society was established in Belfast in 1895. The society financed the publication of the *Northern Patriot* with the intention of keeping the

paper independent of any political faction. Milligan and Johnston resigned from its editorship as a result of an unspecified disagreement concerning the maintenance of the paper's non-party affiliation. The *Northern Patriot* continued publication but because of competition from *Shan Van Vocht* it was forced to reduce its price and finally ceased publication in November 1897.

11 Ibid.

12 Samuel Levenson, *James Connolly: A biography* (London, 1973), p 50. Ernest established this association after Alice encouraged her brother to meet James Connolly.

13 Sheila Turner Johnston, *Alice: The life of Alice Milligan* (Omagh, 1994), p 96.

14 Ibid., p 136.

15 Tynan, 'Ethna Carbery', p 480.

16 Eaton, 'Ethna Carbery', p 328.

17 Tynan, 'Ethna Carbery', pp 481–2.

18 Richard Harp, 'The *Shan Van Vocht* and Irish nationalism', *Eire-Ireland*, 24 (1989), p 47.

19 *SVV*, 4, no. 2, 6 Feb. 1899.

20 Ibid.

21 Ibid., 1, no. 13, 8 Jan. 1897.

22 Ibid., 1, no. 9, 4 Sept. 1896.

23 Ibid., 1, no. 10, 2 Oct. 1896.

24 Ibid., 2, no. 3, 12 Mar. 1897.

25 Ibid.

26 The Ulster executive operated in conjunction with a provisional committee in Dublin. The Dublin committee was initiated by the Irish Republican Brotherhood. Milligan refused to comply with W.B. Yeats' request to postpone the centenary celebrations in Belfast because of his concerns about detracting attention from his first theatre production in the city (Harp, 'The *Shan Van Vocht*', p 51).

27 Bridhid Mhic Sheain, 'Glimpses of Erin. Alice Milligan: poet, Protestant, patriot', *Fortnight* (supplement), 326 (Mar. 1994), p 20.

28 *SVV*, 2, no. 7, 5 July 1897.

29 See Timothy O'Keefe, 'The 1898 efforts to celebrate the United Irishmen: The '98 centennial', *Eire-Ireland*, 23, no. 2 (1988) pp 51–73.

30 It is unclear whether branches of this organisation were established outside the province, as both *Shan Van Vocht* and the nationalist press refer only to its Ulster activities.

31 *NP*, 1, no. 12, 9 Oct. 1896. Margaret T. Pender, née O'Doherty, born in Co. Antrim in 1865. She was a popular poet and writer. Her novels included *A tale of Ulster in '98* (Belfast, 1898). She succeeded Alice Milligan as president of the Belfast branch of the Nationalist Association of Irishwomen.

32 Ibid.

33 Ibid., 2, no. 15, 29 Jan. 1897. These aims were previously highlighted in *SVV*, 1, no. 4, 3 Apr. 1896.

34 Ibid., 1, no. 3, 21 Dec. 1895. This was the last edition of the *Northern Patriot* edited by Milligan and Johnston.

35 For instance, sixty members of the National Association of Irishwomen travelled to Ballycarry in Co. Antrim to decorate the grave of the 1798 veteran, Willie Nelson (Mhic Sheain, 'Glimpses of Erin', p 17).

36 *SVV*, 2, no. 11, 1 Nov. 1897.

37 Ibid.

38 Ibid., 2, no. 10, 4 Oct. 1897.

39 Ibid. The circular was signed by Alice Milligan, Anna Johnston, Margaret Pender, Mrs B. O'Malley, Mrs J. McCauley and Marjorie Johnston in Belfast, Mrs Margaret McCullough in Moneyrea and Mrs Kenny and Mrs Fottrell in Dublin.

40 Ibid., 2, no. 10, 4 Oct. 1897.

41 *Irish News*, 14 Mar. 1898.

42 *SVV*, 2, no. 10, 4 Oct. 1897.

43 Margaret Ward, *Unmanageable revolutionaries: Women and Irish nationalism* (Dingle, 1983), p 48.

44 Tynan, 'Ethna Carbery', p 482.
45 Elbridge Colby, 'Ethna Carbery: A woman who loved Ireland', *Catholic University Bulletin*, 20 (1914), p 533.
46 Eaton, 'Ethna Carbery', p 326.
47 Bulmer Hobson, *Ireland: Yesterday and tomorrow* (Tralee, 1968), p 2. Hobson was personally acquainted with both Milligan and Johnston.
48 Maud Gonne MacBride, *A servant of the queen* (London, 1974), p 176.
49 Maria Luddy, *Women in Ireland, 1800–1918: A documentary history* (Cork, 1995), cited p 304.
50 Jenny Wyse Power, 'The political influence of women in modern Ireland', in W.G. Fitzgerald (ed), *The voice of Ireland* (Dublin, 1924), p 159.
51 Ward, *Unmanageable revolutionaries*, p 41.
52 Flann Campbell, *The dissenting voice* (Belfast, 1991), p 365. There were an estimated 100,000 members of the Gaelic League throughout Ireland.
53 Roger Blaney, 'The Irish language in Ulster from the 1890s to the present day', in Eamon Phoenix (ed), *A century of northern life: The Irish News and one hundred years of Ulster history, 1890s–1990s* (Belfast, 1995), p 172.
54 John Harbinson, *The dynamics of cultural nationalism: The Gaelic revival and the creation of the Irish nation state* (London, 1987), p 166.
55 A.E. Cleary, 'The Gaelic League, 1893–1919', *Studies*, 8 (1919), p 404.
56 Tom Garvin, *Nationalist revolutionaries in Ireland, 1858–1928* (Oxford, 1987), cited p 86.
57 Helen Macnaghten to Anne Richardson, *c.* 1910 (PRONI, D. 1006/3/2/24). Helen Macnaghten became very involved in promoting the Irish language on Rathlin Island, Co. Antrim. She lived at Runkerry House in Bushmills, Co. Antrim, and co-founded Bushmills Suffrage Society with her sister, Edith. Her mother, father and sister Edith were all poor law guardians; see chapter IV for an analysis. Though resident in London, Anne Richardson's family home was Moyallen House in Gilford, Co. Down.
58 Ibid., *c.* 1910 (PRONI, D. 1006/3/2/43).
59 Milligan did not accept this nomination as a result of increasing family commitments caused by the failing health of her mother (Johnston, *Alice: The life of Alice Milligan*, p 115).
60 Blaney, 'The Irish language in Ulster', p 175.
61 Margaret Dobbs was born in Dublin in 1873. She lived most of her life in Cushendun, Co. Antrim, and remained active on the Glenarrif *feis* committee until her death in 1961. She also became a member of Cumann na mBan (Kate Newmann, *A dictionary of Ulster biography* [Belfast, 1994], p 65). The *feis* was held on land belonging to Ada McNeill, an active member of the Gaelic League and sister of Ronald McNeill, a unionist MP. He had little sympathy with Ada's political interests. For instance, he referred to a meeting of several hundred Protestant nationalists held in Ballymoney on 24 October 1913, which included his sister on the platform, as a 'little handful of cranks' (J.R.B. McMinn, 'The Ballymoney meeting of 1913: A nationalist mirage?', *The Glynns, Journal of the Glens of Antrim Historical Society*, 12 (1984), cited p 37).
62 Power, 'The political influence of women', p 159.
63 Helen Macnaghten to Anne Richardson, *c.* 1910 (PRONI, D. 1006/3/2/24).
64 Garvin, *Nationalist revolutionaries*, cited p 84. This description is taken from the *Belfast News-Letter*, 28 May 1904.
65 Hyde and many moderates resigned from the league as a result of this resolution. The league remained in existence, though was less active in Ulster than throughout the remaining three provinces. It has been estimated that the league's frequency in Ulster, measured per 10,000 inhabitants, was 4.5, compared to 11 in Leinster, 16 in Munster and 16 in Connacht (David Fitzpatrick, 'The geography of Irish nationalism, 1901–21', in C.H.E. Philpin (ed), *Nationalism and popular protest in Ireland* [Cambridge, 1987], p 421).
66 R.F. Foster, *Modern Ireland, 1600–1972* (London, 1988), p 432.
67 Eamon Phoenix, *Northern nationalism: Nationalist politics, partition, and the Catholic minority in Northern Ireland, 1890–1940* (Belfast, 1994), pp 3, 406.

68 There was a central Belfast Ladies' Branch and a John Dillon Ladies' Branch in the Ballymacarrett area of South Belfast. It is unclear whether any other branches were established.
69 See, for example, *Irish News*, 29 Mar. 1905 and 7 June 1905.
70 Ibid., 12 June 1905.
71 Ibid., 7 June 1905.
72 Ibid.
73 Ibid., 29 Mar. 1905.
74 Ibid., 26 Oct. 1914.
75 Ibid.
76 Ibid.
77 Bardon, *A history of Ulster*, p 408.
78 For an analysis of the Catholic Church's role in Ulster see Mary Harris, *The Catholic Church and the foundation of the Northern Irish state* (Cork, 1993).
79 Phoenix, *Northern nationalism*, p 4.
80 *Hibernian Journal* [hereafter *HJ*], 6, no. 9, Feb. 1917. The *Hibernian Journal* was established in 1907.
81 Ibid., 17, no. 11, Nov. 1936.
82 Ibid., 2, no. 5, July 1915.
83 Phoenix, *Northern nationalism*, cited p 281.
84 *HJ*, 4, no. 3, Mar. 1923.
85 Ibid., 7, no. 1, Jan. 1925. Only five branches of the Ladies' Auxiliary were in existence at this time in the Irish Free State (ibid.).
86 Ibid., 17, no. 1, Jan. 1936.
87 *Irish News*, 7 Dec. 1918.
88 Ibid., 9 Dec. 1918.
89 Ibid.
90 *HJ*, 5, no. 3, Mar. 1924.
91 Ibid., 5, no. 3, Aug. 1915.
92 Ibid.
93 Ibid., 3, no. 14, Dec. 1914. Members of the Ladies' Auxiliary worked in conjunction with the Catholic Truth Society, the St Vincent de Paul Society and various female religious orders engaged in philanthropy.
94 Ibid., 5, no. 2, July 1915.
95 *IC*, 5 Oct. 1912.
96 *HJ*, 8, no. 2, July 1918.
97 Ibid., 8, no. 9, Feb. 1919.
98 Ibid.
99 Ibid., 1, no. 1, Sept. 1919.
100 Ibid., 1, no. 3, Nov. 1919.
101 Ibid.
102 Phoenix, *Northern nationalism*, p 121.
103 *HJ*, 10, no. 1, Jan. 1929.
104 For instance, cookery, housewifery, sewing, Irish language and dancing, drill, and choral and drama classes were listed as suitable activities for branches of the Ladies' Auxiliary (ibid., 6, no. 9, Feb. 1917).
105 Ibid., 9, no. 1, Jan. 1928.
106 Ibid., 12, no. 7, July 1931.
107 Ibid., 18, no. 8, Aug. 1937.
108 Ibid.
109 Brian Farrell, 'Markievicz and the women of the revolution', in F.X. Martin (ed), *Leaders and men of the Easter rising: Dublin 1916* (Dublin, 1967), cited p 230.
110 The Patriotic Treat Committee was organised to counter the children's treat that was held to commemorate Queen Victoria's Irish visit. The Treat Committee catered for 30,000 children in Dublin. For an analysis of this committee, see Ward, *Unmanageable revolutionaries*.
111 MacBride, *A servant of the queen*, p 291. In December 1902 Inghinidhe na hÉireann joined Cumann na hGeadheal, a federation of nationalist organisations which included women on its executive.

112 *Bean na hÉireann*, no. 18, 1910.
113 Ward, *Unmanageable revolutionaries*, p 104.
114 *Bean na hÉireann*, no. 21, 1911.
115 Inghinidhe na hÉireann was absorbed into Cumann na mBan in May 1915.
116 *Constitution and rules of Cumann na mBan*, *c.* 1914 (PRONI, D. 1507/A/10/5). Cumann na mBan established branches from March 1914. A total of sixty-three branches were set up by October of that year, including some in England.
117 C.H. Fallon, *Soul of fire: A biography of Mary MacSwiney* (Cork and Dublin, 1963), p 20.
118 Margaret Ward, *In their own voice: Women and Irish nationalism* (Dublin, 1995), cited pp 38–40.
119 Ibid., cited p 40.
120 *Constitution and rules of Cumann na mBan*, *c.* 1914 (PRONI, D. 1507/A/10/5).
121 Ward, *Unmanageable revolutionaries*, p 106.
122 Nora Connolly continued to be politically active after her father was executed in 1916. In 1918 she campaigned for Sinn Féin and was imprisoned during the war of independence. From 1921 she was treasurer of the Socialist Party of Ireland and with Peader O'Donnell organised the Republican Congress Organising Bureau, which aimed to provide a socialist solution to the national question and build on the working-class radicalism of the 1932 outdoor relief protests in Belfast. She also served three terms as a senator and died in 1981.
123 Connolly O'Brien, *James Connolly*, p 172.
124 Winifred Carney (1888–1943), secretary to James Connolly and ardent suffragist. Carney was imprisoned at Aylesbury following her arrest during the 1916 rising. She stood unsuccessfully as a Sinn Féin candidate in Belfast in 1918. Following her defeat she concentrated on working for the Transport and General Workers' Union in Belfast. She became a member of the Northern Ireland Labour Party in the 1920s.
125 Lil Conlon, *Cumann na mBan and the women of Ireland, 1913–25* (Kilkenny, 1969), pp 1–2.
126 See above for an analysis of Dobbs' involvement in the Gaelic League.
127 Connolly O'Brien, *James Connolly*, p 205. Cathal McDowell of the Irish Volunteers taught rifle practice to the Belfast branch of Cumann na mBan.
128 Nora Connolly O'Brien, *We shall rise again* (London, 1981), p 11.
129 Connolly O'Brien, *James Connolly*, p 205.
130 Ibid., pp 205–6.
131 Figures from Beth McKillen, 'Irish feminism and national separatism, 1914–23', *Eire-Ireland*, 17 (Fall/Winter 1982), pp 64–5. In 1916, on receipt of Eoin MacNeill's countermanding order to the Irish Volunteers in Ulster, the Connolly sisters and five other members of Cumann na mBan journeyed to Dublin to inform James Connolly that northern members of the volunteers were prepared to fight in the rising. These women became the first female couriers active in the rising.
132 *Cumann na mBan annual convention report*, 28–29 Sept. 1918 (NLI, P. 2188).
133 Fitzpatrick, 'The geography of Irish nationalism', pp 421–2. In Fitzpatrick's estimation all republican associations, including Cumann na mBan, were weakest in Ulster in comparison with the rest of the country. However, figures given at the annual Cumann na mBan convention in 1921 reveal that the organisation was weak in both Ulster and Connacht, with 93 branches and 46 branches respectively. The organisation had 118 branches in Leinster and 375 in Munster (*Cumann na mBan annual convention report*, 22–3 Oct. 1921 [NLI, P. 2188]).
134 *Cumann na mBan annual convention report*, 22–23 Oct. 1921 (NLI, P. 2188).
135 Ward, *In their own voice*, cited p 79.
136 Ibid., cited p 86.
137 *Irish News*, 5 Dec. 1918.
138 Helga Woogan, 'Winnie Carney: A silent radical' (West Berlin, 1983), p 12. I am grateful to Dr Margaret Ward for sending me this unpublished typescript. See chapter I for an analysis of Marie Johnson's involvement in the Ulster suffrage movement.
139 Ulster's proportion of delegates attending the 1921 convention represented 12 per cent of the total (*Cumann na mBan annual convention report*, 22–23 Oct. 1921 [NLI, P. 2188]).
140 Ward, *Unmanageable revolutionaries*, p 173. This breakaway group did not actively support the IRA.

141 *Cumann na mBan*, 2, no. 1, Feb. 1925. This was the official paper of the organisation, first published in 1922 for four months, but temporarily suspended because of Cumann na mBan's involvement in the civil war. It was revived in 1925.
142 Ibid.
143 Ward, *Unmanageable revolutionaries*, p 247.
144 Ibid., p 222.
145 Unlike Cumann na mBan, Mna na Phoblachta recognised the authority of Dáil Éireann (Ward, *In their own voice*, p 160).
146 Harris, *The Catholic Church*, p 265.
147 Phoenix, *Northern nationalism*, cited p 281.
148 Boyce, *Nationalism in Ireland*, p 403.
149 Phoenix, *Northern nationalism*, cited p 374.
150 In addition to abolishing PR, the Northern Ireland government also altered local government boundaries in 1924 (Paul Bew, Peter Gibbon and Henry Patterson, *Northern Ireland, 1921–94: Political forces and social classes* [London, 1995], p 17).
151 Northern Ireland House of Commons debates, vol XIII, cols 2890–2, 15 Nov. 1927. See chapter VI for an analysis of the introduction of equal suffrage in 1928.

CHAPTER FOUR

1 Extract from a poem by E. Fortescae Moresby in *IC*, 29 Nov. 1913.
2 The poor law was introduced to Ireland in 1838 with the original aim of providing indoor relief for the destitute poor. The pressure that the Great Famine placed on this system led to outdoor relief being granted to the able-bodied in times of exceptional distress from 1847. Ireland was divided into 137 administrative unions, twenty-seven of which, providing accommodation for 20,550 paupers, were located in Ulster. Boards of guardians were originally under the control of Poor Law Commissioners, but this responsibility was transferred to the Local Government Board in 1872 and to the Northern Ireland Ministry for Home Affairs in 1921.
3 In order to gain an insight into women's work in this sphere of municipal government approximately 170 minute books, each of between 300 and 600 pages in length, of Ballymoney, Belfast, Lisburn and Londonderry boards of guardians have been assessed.
4 *Fermanagh Times*, 10 Sept. 1896.
5 See chapter I for an analysis of the IWSLGA. In 1896 the IWSLGA had a total of forty-four members. The passage of two pieces of legislation relating to women's municipal rights, the Poor Law Guardians (Ireland) (Women) Act of 1896 and the 1898 Local Government (Ireland) Act, stimulated interest in the organisation and by 1904 the association had nearly 400 members (Marie O'Neill, 'The Dublin Women's Suffrage Society and its successors', *Dublin Historical Record*, 38, no. 4 [1984–5], p 130). The English equivalent of the IWSLGA was the Association for Promoting the Return of Women as Poor Law Guardians, established in 1881.
6 For an analysis of Tod's involvement in the suffrage campaign and unionist politics see chapters I and II.
7 Isabella Tod, 'Municipal franchise for women in Ireland', *Englishwoman's Review*, 170 (15 July 1887), p 289.
8 Isabella Tod, 'The place of women in the administration of the Irish poor law', *Englishwoman's Review*, 103 (15 Nov. 1881), p 487.
9 Tod, 'Municipal Franchise' p 290.
10 Poor law work has also been described as 'domestic economy on a larger scale' (Patricia Hollis, *Ladies' elect: Women in English local government, 1865–1914* [Oxford, 1987], p 230).
11 Tod, 'The place of women', p 486.
12 *IWSLGA Annual Report* [hereafter *AR*], 1904 (NLI, I. 3996 i 3), p 11.
13 Virginia Crossman, *Local government in nineteenth-century Ireland* (Belfast, 1994), cited p 55.
14 R.C. Owens, *Did your granny have a hammer? A history of the Irish suffrage movement, 1876–1922* (Dublin, 1985), p 4. Under this legislation Irish women possessed one advantage over the electorate in England, as lodgers were still disenfranchised under English municipal provisions.

15 Anna Haslam, 'Women poor law guardians in Ireland', *Englishwoman's Review*, no vol noted (15 Oct. 1896), p 256.

16 Ibid., p 257. The Belfast press did not cover this meeting.

17 *Belfast Evening Telegraph*, 6 Apr. 1899. A total of thirty-one candidates stood in Belfast in this election. Four of the seven female candidates were successful: Jane Payne, Dupre Fennell, Lizzie Carson and Emily Callwell. Florence Clark was returned unopposed to the Belfast guardians. The trade unionist, Mary Galway, as well as Sarah Thompson and Kate Megahy, were all defeated by male candidates. The latter two were former guardians. Kate Megahy had been the first female guardian in Belfast and was described as 'the pioneer of the ladies' movement at the Board' (*Belfast Evening Telegraph*, 5 Apr. 1899). Megahy was co-opted back onto Belfast's board of guardians in Nov. 1900 and in the next triennial election of 1902 she topped the polls in Clifton ward by a large majority.

18 Ibid., 4 June 1902.

19 Martin Pugh, *Women and the women's movement in Britain, 1914–1959* (Hampshire, 1992), p 57.

20 A total of 260 women were elected as local government councillors and poor law guardians in Ulster in the period 1896 to 1940. In Ulster the majority (66 per cent) of women guardians were married, 32 per cent were single and for 2 per cent their marital status was not stated. See chapter V for an analysis of women local government councillors.

21 *Fermanagh Times*, 10 Sept. 1896. Martin was the daughter of the Presbyterian minister of Lisbellaw and was described as 'a worthy and respected member' of her father's congregation (ibid.).

22 The total number of poor law guardians in Ulster was 879 (*Ulster Year Book* [Belfast, 1932], p 265).

23 Patricia Hollis, 'Women in council: Separate spheres, public space', in Jane Rendall (ed), *Equal or different: Women's politics, 1800–1914* (Oxford, 1987), pp 192–213.

24 Table 2 is compiled from the minute books of twenty-seven boards of guardians situated in Ulster (PRONI, BG I–XXVII). The 1899 election was the first in which women stood as candidates. Each subsequent year marks the date of the triennial poor law election. Ø denotes that a minute book was not received by PRONI, – denotes that no women were listed. Note that for Ballymoney the 1936 figure refers to office bearers only, as the membership of the board was not listed, and that the 1939 figure is for 1941, as the minute books for 1937–40 were not received by PRONI.

25 Minute book [hereafter MB] of Lisburn board of guardians [hereafter BG], 18 Jan. 1910, 26 July and 23 Aug. 1921 (PRONI, BG XIX/A/121 and BG XIX/A/132).

26 MB Lisburn BG, 31 Dec. 1912 (PRONI, BG XIX/A/123). Barbour resigned because of ill health. This appeal was ineffective, because Jacob Cuthbert was co-opted in her place (ibid., 22 Apr. 1913 [PRONI, BG XIX/A/124]).

27 Ibid., 24 Sept. 1929 (PRONI, BG XIX/A/136). In 1930 Dr Quin was finally appointed as medical officer for Lisburn dispensary district (ibid., 30 Nov. 1930).

28 Lady Frances Macnaghten, the wife of Lord Justice Macnaghten and the mother of Edith and Helen, the founders of Bushmills Suffrage Society. Lord Macnaghten and Edith also served as poor law guardians in Ballymoney and Belfast respectively. Helen was an active member of the Gaelic League, see chapter III for an analysis of her activities.

29 Compiled from annual lists of office bearers on boards of guardians in *Thom's directory of Ireland* (44 vols, Dublin, 1896–1940).

30 MB Belfast BG, 9 June 1908 (PRONI, BG VII/A/81). She was deputy vice-chairman from 1908 to 1910 and 1912 to 1916 and later served as vice-chairman, 1916 to 1918.

31 Ibid., 10 June 1918 (PRONI, BG VII/A/99).

32 Mrs Montgomery accepted the chairmanship of Ballymoney board in 1940.

33 From 1910 to 1937.

34 From 1898 to 1920.

35 From 1899 to 1938.

36 From 1908 to 1930.

37 MB Lisburn BG, 4 Jan.–19 Dec. 1916 (PRONI, BG XIX/A/127).

38 Ibid., 27 May 1930 (PRONI, BG XIX/A/136). Five male guardians attended no meetings in the same period.
39 MB Belfast BG, 20 Oct. 1903 (PRONI, BG VII/A/72) and 13 Dec. 1927 (PRONI, BG VII/A/118).
40 E.P. Hennock, 'Finance and politics in urban local government in England, 1835–1900', *Historical Journal*, 6, no. 2 (1963), p 224.
41 Anon., 'The work of women as poor law guardians', *Westminster Review*, 123 (1885), reprinted in Patricia Hollis, *Women in public: Documents of the Victorian women's movement 1850–1900,* (London, 1979), pp 247–8.
42 Ministry of Home Affairs for Northern Ireland, local government inquiry into the administration of Belfast union, proceedings 2 Dec. 1938 to 2 Jan. 1939 (PRONI, HA 63/3), p 750. As a result of this inquiry Belfast workhouse was placed under the control of two commissioners, Henry Diamond and Dr L.D. Graham.
43 Ibid., proceedings 19 Nov. to 2 Dec. 1938 (PRONI, HA 63/1), p 743.
44 *Belfast and Ulster directory* (Belfast, 1923).
45 Brian Harrison, 'Philanthropy and the Victorians', *Victorian Studies*, 9 (June 1966), pp 353–74.
46 MB Lisburn BG, 22 Jan. 1929 (PRONI, BG XIX/A/136).
47 In 1919 Coleman's son was infected by the scarlet fever epidemic and she was prohibited from nursing him at home unless she closed her shop and workroom. Financially unable to do this because her husband could not work, she was obliged to admit her child to Belfast Infirmary (Ministry of Home Affairs for Northern Ireland, local government inquiry into the administration of Belfast union, proceedings 19 Nov. to 2 Dec. 1938 [PRONI, HA 63/1], p 743).
48 Jessica Gerard, 'Lady bountiful: Women of the landed classes and rural philanthropy', *Victorian Studies*, 30 (Winter 1987), p 190.
49 Ronald G. Walton, *Women in social work* (London and Boston, 1975), p 78.
50 For details on the work of these organisations see Alison Jordan, *Who cared? Charity in Victorian and Edwardian Belfast* (Belfast, 1992).
51 Maria Luddy, 'Women and charitable organisations in nineteenth-century Ireland', *Women's Studies International Forum*, 11, no. 4 (1988), pp 301–5, and Mary McNeill, *The life and times of Mary Ann McCracken, 1770–1866: A Belfast panorama* (Belfast, 1988, reprint of orig. ed. Belfast, 1960), pp 257–60.
52 In closer knit rural communities with a smaller network of leisured middle-class women to participate in work of this kind, it appears that visiting was conducted informally and often on an individual basis.
53 Diary of Reverend A. McIntyre, 1853–56 (PRONI, D. 1558/2/3). I am grateful to Cathy Hurst for this information.
54 Maria Luddy, *Women and philanthropy in nineteenth-century Ireland* (Cambridge, 1995), p 199.
55 Mary Clancy has also identified the importance of philanthropy in encouraging women in Galway to come forward as poor law candidates in 'On the "Western outpost": Local government and women's suffrage in Co. Galway, 1898–1918', in Gerard Moran (ed), *Galway: History and society. Interdisciplinary essays on the history of an Irish county* (Dublin, 1996), pp 562–3.
56 Reverend John Redmond, *Church, state and industry in East Belfast, 1827–1929* (Belfast, 1961), p 91.
57 See Arabella Fennell, *Letters on primary education* (Belfast, 1905).
58 MB Belfast BG, 26 Mar. 1929 (PRONI, BG VII/A/21).
59 MB Lisburn BG, 24 Aug. 1909 (PRONI, BG XIX/A/120). Although the child's mother named Stannus as legal guardian, the adoption was not sanctioned, as the woman's husband claimed custody.
60 In 1933 her sister, Rosa Towers, joined Josephine O'Neill, deputy vice-chairman of Londonderry board from 1914 to 1937. Following the death of Josephine O'Neill in 1937, another sister, Binnie, was co-opted in her place.
61 See chapter I for an analysis of female guardians in the suffrage movement.
62 MB Lisburn BG, 2 Oct. 1900 (PRONI, BG XIX/A/105). In the four unions under analysis, no suffrage motions were ever put to the boards for discussion.
63 In England poor law electoral contests also remained low key and many seats were uncontested (Hollis, 'Women in council', p 210).

64 *Belfast Evening Telegraph*, 6 Apr. 1899.
65 Ibid., 4 June 1902.
66 Ibid.
67 MB UWUC executive committee, Mar. 1920 (PRONI, D. 1098/1/2) and 6 May 1930 (PRONI, D. 1098/1/3). See chapter II for an analysis of women's involvement in unionist politics.
68 See chapter III for an analysis of women's involvement in northern nationalism.
69 M.A. Crowther, *The workhouse system, 1834–1929* (London, 1981), pp 75–6.
70 Tod, 'The place of women', p 486.
71 IWSLGA, 'Suggestions for intending women workers under the Local Government Act, 1901' (Dublin, 1901) (NLI, P. 790 (1)), p 6.
72 Hollis, 'Women in council', p 202.
73 MB Belfast BG, 4 May and 14 Sept. 1897 (PRONI, BG VII/A/61).
74 Ibid., 26 July 1898 (PRONI, BG VII/A/62).
75 See MB Londonderry BG, 1899 (PRONI, BG XXI/A/25), and MB Lisburn BG, 1899 (PRONI, BG XIX/A/104).
76 MB Lisburn BG, 1902 (PRONI, BG XXI/A/107).
77 MB Ballymoney BG, 1899 (PRONI, BG V/A/72) and 1901 (PRONI, BG V/A/76).
78 MB Londonderry BG, 12 Jan. 1924 (PRONI, BG XXI/A/35).
79 Ibid., 14 July 1934 (PRONI, BG XXI/A/37).
80 MB Ballymoney BG, 1 Aug. 1901 (PRONI, BG V/A/75). Londonderry BG, 23 Feb. 1907 (PRONI, BG XXI/A/ 29) and 27 Jan. 1912 (BG XXI/A/31). Morris was unsuccessful.
81 See MB Belfast BG, 1906–40 (PRONI, BG VII/A/108–42), and MB Lisburn BG, 13 Feb. 1934 (PRONI, BG XIX/A/138). Beattie campaigned from 1928 to 1934. In 1931 a home was established in Belfast, but Beattie remained dissatisfied, as it only catered for educable children.
82 MB Lisburn BG, 19 Dec. 1899 (PRONI, BG XIX/A/104).
83 MB Londonderry BG, 19 Jan. 1901 (BG XXI/A/26).
84 MB Belfast BG, 4 May 1897 (PRONI, BG VII/A/61).
85 MB Londonderry BG, 12 Jan. 1901 (PRONI, BG XXI/A/26).
86 In Londonderry the circular was given to Margaret Gilliland and Josephine O'Neill, who were poor law guardians and members of the local committee of the Women's National Health Association (MB Londonderry BG, 2 Nov. 1912 [PRONI, BG XXI/A/31]).
87 Boards of guardians resented having to finance out-relief payments. This was especially apparent in Belfast, where demands were greatest due to the industrial composition of the city's workforce. During the economic depression of the 1930s Belfast guardians became involved in serious disputes with the Northern Ireland Ministry for Home Affairs and the board's decision to temporarily halt payments to those who had been in receipt of relief payments for over six months caused serious riots in the city during October 1932 (Angela Clifford, *The poor law in Ireland* [Belfast, 1983], p 2).
88 MB Lisburn BG, 19 Dec. 1899 (PRONI, BG XIX/A/104).
89 Ibid., 9 Apr. 1918 (PRONI, BG XIX/A/129).
90 Ministry of Home Affairs for Northern Ireland, local government inquiry into the administration of Belfast Union, proceedings of 2 Dec. 1938 to 2 Jan. 1939 (PRONI, HA 63/1), p 745.
91 MB Londonderry BG, 18 Feb. 1933 (PRONI, BG XXI/A/37).
92 MB Belfast BG, 6 June 1935 (PRONI, BG VII/A/133).
93 The appointment of three male guardians in Londonderry in 1925 to investigate cases of unmarried mothers maintained in the workhouse was exceptional (MB Londonderry BG, 6 June 1925 [PRONI, BG XXI/A/35]).
94 Michael Farrell, *The poor law and the workhouse in Belfast, 1838–1948* (Belfast, 1978), pp 74–5. By 1913 there were 205 illegitimate births per annum in Belfast workhouse (MB Belfast BG, 7 Jan. 1913 [PRONI, BG VII/A/91]).
95 MB Londonderry BG, 31 Oct. 1936 (PRONI, BG XXI/A/37).
96 Ibid., 15 June and 8 Mar. 1901 (PRONI, BG XXI/A/26).
97 Ibid., 31 Oct. 1936 (PRONI, BG XXI/A/37).
98 MB Lisburn BG, 29 Aug. 1905 (PRONI, BG XIX/A/114).
99 MB Belfast BG, 20 Feb. 1899 (PRONI, BG VII/A/63).

100 MB Lisburn BG , 8 Mar. 1910 (PRONI, BG XIX/A/121).
101 MB Ballymoney BG, 26 Apr. 1900 (PRONI, BG V/A/74). The female members of Londonderry board were formed into a ladies' committee to procure clothing for children being sent to national schools in 1900 (MB Londonderry BG, 24 Mar. 1900 [PRONI, BG XXI/A/26]).
102 See MB Belfast BG, 1904 (PRONI, BG VII/A/74), 1907 (PRONI, BG VII/A/80) and 1910 (PRONI, BG VII/A/86).
103 In the late nineteenth century Belfast's Women's Temperance Association established a committee for boarded out infants in its girls' home (Maria Luddy, 'Isabella M.S. Tod', in Maria Luddy and Mary Cullen (eds), *Women, power and consciousness in nineteenth-century Ireland* [Dublin, 1995], p 211).
104 M.E. Rose, *The English poor law, 1780–1930* (Newton Abbot, 1971), p 190. The first boarding out scheme was introduced in Bethnal Green union in 1869 (ibid.).
105 For a full analysis of the passage of this legislation see Joseph Robins, *The lost children: A study of charity children in Ireland, 1700–1900* (Dublin, 1980).
106 Suzanne Day, 'The workhouse child', *Irish Review*, 2, no. 16 (June 1912), p 171.
107 In 1908 James Cherry unsuccessfully tried to join Belfast's boarding out committee. It remained an all-female body (MB Belfast BG, 16 June 1908 [PRONI, BG VII/A/81]).
108 Isabella Tod, 'Boarding-out of pauper children', *Statistical and Social Inquiry Society of Ireland Journal*, 7, no. 5 (Aug. 1878), p 298.
109 MB Lisburn BG, 13 Nov. 1906 (PRONI, BG XIX/A/116).
110 Ibid.
111 Ibid., 1 Jan. 1907.
112 Ibid.
113 In 1925 in response to protests from the members of Lisburn's boarding out committee the board agreed to lend a car to enable the women to visit children throughout the union (MB Lisburn BG, 23 June 1925 [PRONI, BG XIX/A/135]).
114 For instance, Mrs Macartney of Lissanoure Castle and Mrs Leslie, wife of the High Sheriff for Co. Antrim, both served on Ballymoney's boarding out committee from 1906 (MB Ballymoney BG, 14 June and 29 Nov. 1906 [PRONI, BG V/A/86]).
115 Ibid., 15 July 1909 (PRONI, BG V/A/89), and MB Clogher BG, 10 June 1930 (PRONI, BG IX/A/79).
116 MB Belfast BG, 9 June and 22 Dec. 1908 (PRONI, BG VII/A/82).
117 Ibid., 21 Aug. 1906 (PRONI, BG VII/A/76).
118 MB Lisburn BG, 27 May 1930 (PRONI, BG XIX/A/136).
119 In the four boards under analysis male guardians occasionally employed workhouse children, but they rarely fostered children.
120 In 1905 the cost of a single passage to Canada was estimated at £8.10*s* 0*d*.
121 MB Belfast BG, 4 June 1901 (PRONI, BG VII/A/67).
122 MB Lisburn BG, 21 Feb. 1911 (PRONI, BG XIX/A/122).
123 MB Belfast BG, 2 July 1901 (PRONI, BG VII/A/66).
124 Belfast's boarding out committee was still campaigning for this legislative reform in 1935.
125 MB Ballymoney BG , 8 July 1909 (PRONI BG V/A/89).
126 MB Lisburn BG, 3 Sept. 1912 (PRONI, BG XIX/A/123). The Local Government Board later recommended that relieving officers already employed by the guardians act as visitors (ibid., 26 Nov. 1912).
127 MB Belfast BG, 2 July 1901 (PRONI, BG VII/A/66).
128 Ibid., 2 Jan. 1904 (PRONI, BG VII/A/73). Interestingly none of the female guardians introduced this motion to the board, as Mr Adams presented the motion.
129 Dympna McLoughlin, 'Workhouses and Irish female paupers, 1840–70', in Maria Luddy and Cliona Murphy (eds), *Women surviving* (Dublin, 1990), p 122.
130 MB Belfast BG, 5 Dec. 1905 (PRONI, BG VII/A/76).
131 MB Lisburn BG, 15 Jan. 1918 (PRONI, BG XIX/A/129).
132 MB Londonderry BG, 29 Jan. 1910 (PRONI, BG XXI/A/30).
133 MB Belfast BG, 4 June 1901 (PRONI, BG VII/A/67).
134 Ibid., 14 Jan. 1911 (PRONI, BG VII/A/87).
135 Henry Miller, 'The administration of the poor laws in Ireland till 30 Nov. 1921: and in Northern Ireland from 1 Dec. 1921 till present date [1942]' (unpub. MCSc. diss., The Queen's University of Belfast, 1942), no page references are included.

136 MB Londonderry BG, 17 Mar. 1900 (PRONI, BG XXI, A/26). This comment was prompted by Morris complaining to the National Society for the Prevention of Cruelty to Children about the treatment afforded to children in the workhouse infirmary.
137 Ibid., 16 June 1900 (PRONI, BG XXI/A/26).
138 Ibid., 7 Sept. 1907 (PRONI, BG XXI/A/ 29). Her husband was also forced to leave this meeting.
139 Ibid., 14 Jan. 1905 (PRONI, BG XXI/A/28).
140 Ibid., Sept. 1907 to May 1908 (PRONI, BG XXI/A/29). The trial was held in Dublin on 2 May 1908. Morris continued to disrupt meetings and, when appointed to the visiting committee, she often produced separate reports.
141 Ministry of Home Affairs for Northern Ireland local government inquiry, proceedings, 2 Dec. 1938 to 2 Jan. 1939 (PRONI, HA 63/3), p 745. After this event the workhouse clerk always accompanied the female guardians of Belfast board on their visits.
142 Ibid.
143 MB Belfast BG, 4 May 1897 (PRONI, BG VII/A/61).
144 Ibid., 26 June 1900 (PRONI, BG VII/A/65).
145 Ibid., 11 Dec. 1900 (PRONI, BG VII/A/66).
146 This was noted as the motto of Esther McDonnell, a poor law guardian in Belfast (ibid., 15 Oct. 1929 [PRONI, BG VII/A/122]).
147 Ibid., 23 May 1924 (PRONI, BG VII/A/111).
148 Ibid., 10 June 1926 (PRONI, BG VII/A/115).
149 Ibid., 7 Dec. 1926 (PRONI, BG VII/A/116). She was a guardian from 1921 to 1926 and resigned 'owing to home arrangements' (ibid.).
150 Ibid., 13 Dec. 1927 (PRONI, BG VII/A/118). McDonnell was elected in 1924, but chose not to stand in the next triennial election of 1927.
151 MB Lisburn BG, 26 Nov. 1929 (PRONI, BG XIX/A/136). She was chairman from 1913 to 1920.
152 Ibid., 11 Apr. 1933 (PRONI, BG XIX/A/137).
153 MB Belfast BG, 6 June 1934 (PRONI, BG VII/A/131).
154 MB Lisburn BG, 10 Mar. 1925 (PRONI, BG XIX/A/135). This dispute was solved by a male member of the board lending his car to the lady visitors (ibid., 23 June 1925).
155 MB Belfast BG, 3 Dec. 1929 (PRONI, BG VII/A/122).
156 MB Lisburn BG, 19 June 1918 (PRONI, BG XIX/A/128).
157 Gilbert Slater, 'The relief of the poor', in H.J. Laski, W.I. Jennings and W.A. Robson (eds), *A century of municipal progress, 1835–1935* (London, 1935), p 355.

CHAPTER FIVE

1 J. E. M. Brownlow, 'Women's work in local government' (1911), reprinted in Patricia Hollis, *Women in public: The women's movement, 1850–1900.* (London, 1979), p 274.
2 John Webb, *Municipal government in Ireland: Mediaeval and modern* (Dublin, 1918), pp 278–9.
3 William Johnston also introduced the Poor Law (Ireland) (Women) Act to parliament in 1896. The Municipal Corporations (Ireland) Act of 1887 was introduced in response to Belfast Corporation's plans for an extensive and costly drainage scheme that would substantially increase the city's rates. To qualify under the 1887 legislation, householders had to be resident within a seven-mile radius of Belfast borough for a year. As a result of considerable parliamentary opposition, this legislation was only applied to Belfast and women remained excluded from the municipal franchise throughout the rest of the country until 1898. (Virginia Crossman, *Local government in nineteenth-century Ireland* [Belfast, 1994], pp 83–4).

4 See chapter I for an analysis of Tod's involvement in the suffrage campaign and chapter II for her involvement in unionist politics.
5 Crossman, *Local government*, p 85.
6 Isabella M. S. Tod, 'Municipal franchise for women in Ireland', *The Englishwoman's Review*, 70, 15 July 1887, p 291. In 1894 women were admitted to the municipal electorate in Blackrock and Kingstown (Rosemary Cullen Owens, *Smashing times: A history of the Irish women's suffrage movement, 1889–1922* [Dublin, 1984], p 25).
7 This bill was withdrawn as a result of impending parliamentary dissolution (Crossman, *Local government*, p 85).
8 *IWSLGA Annual Report* [hereafter *AR*], 1896 (NLI, I 3996 i 3), p 7.
9 Ibid., 1898, p 7.
10 See chapter I and Marie O'Neill, 'The Dublin Women's Suffrage Society and its successors', *Dublin Historical Record*, 38, no. 4 (1984–5), pp 126–40.
11 *IWSLGA AR*, 1898 (NLI, I. 3996 i 3), p 7. No details concerning personnel or activities are contained in this report.
12 Ibid.
13 *IWSLGA AR*, 1896 (NLI, I. 3996 i 3), p 3. Johnston provides another example of support for unionism and women's suffrage not being wholly incompatible with one another.
14 Ibid., 1902, pp 7–8.
15 Crossman, *Local government*, cited p 95. The IWSLGA were supported by the Women's Liberal Unionist Association in England and by the Scottish Women's Liberal Federation (ibid.).
16 County boroughs possessed the same powers as county councils and urban district councils, but remained independent of county council authority (*Ulster Year Book* [Belfast, 1947], p 29).
17 Crossman, *Local government*, p 93. All rural district councillors also served as poor law guardians. Where a poor law union cut across county boundaries, or where both urban and rural district councils were elected for one locality, separate poor law elections continued to be held for guardians representing urban areas (John Muldoon, *A guide to Irish local government* [Dublin, 1898], p 21).
18 Anna Haslam, 'Irishwomen and the Local Government Act', *The Englishwoman's Review*, 15 Oct. 1898, reprinted in Maria Luddy, *Women in Ireland, 1800–1918: A documentary history* (Cork, 1995), p 294.
19 Ibid.
20 *IWSLGA AR*, 1910 (NLI, I 3996 i 3), p 11.
21 Ibid., 1911, p 13.
22 Helen Blackburn, *Women's suffrage: A record of the women's suffrage movement in the British Isles* (New York, 1971, reprint of orig. ed., London, 1902), p 216.
23 Statistics compiled from *Thom's directory* (42 vols, Dublin, 1898–1940).
24 This statement refers to the period 1896 to 1940. Because of the very small number of female urban district, county, borough and county borough councillors, tables have not been compiled. A statistical analysis is given in the text.
25 See chapter IV for an analysis of female poor law guardians.
26 The respective figures for female rural district councillors was 1.35 per cent and for female urban district councillors was 0.94 per cent. Annually there were 698 rural district councillors, 348 urban district councillors, 100 county borough councillors, 82 borough councillors and 174 county councillors in Ulster (*Ulster Year Book* [Belfast, 1932], p 265).
27 Table 4, is compiled from minute books of thirty-two rural district councils in Ulster, 1899–1940. 1899 was the first municipal election in which women stood as candidates. Ø denotes that a minute book was not received by PRONI, / denotes that members were not individually listed, – denotes that no women were listed.
28 Down and Londonderry.
29 The following urban district councils situated in Ulster had female members: Ballymena, Banbridge, Cookstown, Donaghadee, Dromore, Limavady, Portrush, Portadown and Warrenpoint.
30 MB Coleraine Urban District Council, 30 Jan. 1920 (PRONI, LA 25/2CA/10). In 1921 Kydd agreed to accept this position and raised no objection when she was subsequently re-appointed from 1923 to 1927.

31 MB Portrush Urban District Council, 22 June 1911 (PRONI, LA 65/2CA/3).
32 *IC*, 3 Jan. 1914.
33 This resolution was adopted by the council (MB Portrush Urban District Council, 2 Oct. 1911 [PRONI, LA 65/2CA/3]).
34 *IC*, 3 Jan. 1914.
35 Of the thirty-three women who served as county, county borough and urban district councillors, eleven also held the position of poor law guardian. Rural district councillors were automatically appointed as poor law guardians.
36 See chapter VI for an analysis of the parliamentary careers of Dehra Parker, Julia McMordie and Margaret Waring.
37 *IC*, 18 Jan. 1913.
38 Ibid.
39 See chapters II and III for an analysis.
40 There were female electoral majorities in Antrim, Armagh, Down and Londonderry.
41 *IC*, Jan. 1920.
42 Ibid., Feb. 1919. This was a front-page article.
43 MB UWUC executive committee, 18 Mar 1919 (PRONI, D. 1098/1/2).
44 Minutes of UWUC AM, 26 Jan. 1932 (PRONI, D. 1098/1/3).
45 *IC*, Feb. 1919.
46 Ibid., Jan. 1920.
47 This is similar to women joining boards of guardians' boarding out committees before standing for election or being co-opted as poor law guardians. See chapter IV for an analysis of boarding out work.
48 MB Armagh County Council, 27 Mar. 1925 (PRONI, LA 2/2GA/16).
49 MB Antrim County Council, 17 June 1924 (PRONI, LA 1/2GA/25).
50 See MB Limavady Rural District Council, 1933 (PRONI, LA 45/2FA/8).
51 Brownlow, 'Women's work in local government', reprinted in Hollis, *Women in public*, pp 273–4.
52 *IC*, 18 Jan. 1913.
53 MB Armagh County Council, 6 June 1933 (PRONI, LA 2/2GA/25).
54 Following her co-option, Bessie Quin had to prove her capabilities as a councillor, as in 1925 she was only appointed to the tuberculosis committee and not to the other four committees of which her husband had been a member. By 1927 she was a member of these committees and also served as the council's representative on Queen's University Senate. The council's chairman commended her interest in the affairs of the locality, which was 'equally as keen as that of her late husband . . . [she] has brought to the meetings of the Council clear thinking and keen intelligence' (MB Armagh County Council, 7 June 1927 [PRONI, LA 2/2GA/19]).
55 Ibid., 10 June 1936 (PRONI, LA 2/2GA/28).
56 Hillsborough Rural District Council, 4 June 1920 (PRONI, LA 37/2FA/7). No explanation was given for Keightley's defeat.
57 Alice Young was the eldest daughter of Lord Chief Justice Macnaghten. Her sisters, Ethel and Helen, founded Bushmills Suffrage Society. Her mother, father and younger sister, Ethel, all served as poor law guardians. In 1893 Alice married Rt Hon William Young of Galgorm Castle, Co. Antrim. Alice Young was also a well-known photographer (see B.M. Walker, *Shadows on glass: A portfolio of early Ulster photography* [Belfast, 1976]). She was described as a 'breathless individual . . . clever and interesting' (Diary of Lilian Spender, 17 May 1928 [PRONI, D. 1633/2/31]).
58 From 1911 Lilly Ann Barr regularly topped the poll in Ballymena's Market Ward in the triennial municipal elections.
59 Robertson remained a rural district councillor until the end of the period under analysis (PRONI, LA 45/2FA/7–10).
60 *Irish News*, 31 May 1902.
61 Richard Dawson Bates to Edward Carson, 23 Jan. 1920 (PRONI, D. 1507/A/33/20).
62 Michael Farrell, *Northern Ireland: The Orange state* (London, 1976), p 85.
63 Lord Snell, 'The town council', in H.J. Laski, W.I. Jennings and W.A. Robson (eds), *A century of municipal progress, 1835–1935* (London, 1935), p 78.
64 Royal assent was withheld from this bill for several months. The redrafting of local electoral boundaries, due to the introduction of single-seat constituencies, meant that the 1923 elections were postponed until 1924 (Farrell, *Northern Ireland*, p 84).

65 This is in the period up to 1940.
66 MB Downpatrick Rural District Council, 10 June 1924 (PRONI, LA 30/2FA/18). It is difficult to assess the number of unionist and nationalist councillors because newspaper coverage of election results was sporadic and the minute books of local councils do not list the party affiliation of individual members. Moreover, from the late 1920s the press rarely commented on local government contests or recorded municipal electoral results (Ian Budge and Cornelius O'Leary, *Belfast: Approach to crisis: A study of Belfast politics, 1613–1917* (London and Basingstoke, 1973), p 185).
67 Diary of Lilian Spender, 1 Dec. 1923 (PRONI, D. 1633/2/26).
68 Farrell, *Northern Ireland*, p 85.
69 Crossman, *Local government*, cited p 84.
70 *IWSLGA AR*, 1898 (NLI, I 3996 i 3), p 6.
71 *IWSLGA, Suggestions for intending women workers* (Dublin, 1901) (NLI, P. 790 (1)), p 7.
72 See chapter VI for an analysis of Parker's parliamentary career.
73 Dehra Parker, 'Women in local government work', *Northern Ireland. Home and politics. A journal for women*, 2, no. 3, Apr. 1927.
74 Electoral manifestos of various unionist candidates standing in the Pottinger ward of Belfast, 15 Jan. 1926 (PRONI, D.1327/16/1/5). Julia McMordie was successfully elected.
75 A similar division of council work on the basis of gender has been identified in an English context. See Patricia Hollis, 'Women in council: Separate spheres, public space', in Jane Rendall (ed), *Equal or different: Women's politics, 1800–1914* (Oxford, 1907), p 204.
76 Unlike boards of guardians, all councillors were appointed to finance committees. This was presumably a result of the greater control which municipal councils had over rate collection and expenditure.
77 MB Armagh County Council, 15 May 1928 (PRONI, LA 2/2GA/19).
78 Ibid., 15 Apr. 1930 (PRONI, LA 2/2GA/21).
79 Ibid.
80 This resolution was sent to the Northern Ireland parliament and Ministry for Finance (MB Lisburn Rural District Council, 23 Apr. 1935 [PRONI, LA 47/2FA/13]).
81 MB Portrush Urban District Council, 23 Jan. 1914 (PRONI, LA 65/2CA/4).
82 MB Ballymena Urban District Council, 1 Jan. 1917 (PRONI, LA 14/2CA/3).
83 This resolution was forwarded to the Ministry for Home Affairs (MB Armagh County Council, 1 Dec. 1926 [PRONI, LA 2/2GA/18]).
84 MB Portrush Urban District Council, 4 Dec. 1916 and 1 Jan. 1917 (PRONI, LA 65/2CA/4–5).
85 Ibid., 4 Mar. 1907 (PRONI, LA 65/2CA/2).
86 MB Coleraine Urban District Council, 10 Oct. 1922 (PRONI, LA 25/2CA/12).
87 MB Strabane Rural District Council, 9 Mar. 1937 (PRONI, LA 67/2FA/26).
88 MB Lisburn Rural District Council, 28 Apr. 1925 (PRONI, LA 47/2FA/9).
89 Ibid., 23 June and 25 Aug. 1925 (PRONI, LA 47/2FA/9).
90 Ibid., 13 Mar. 1928 (PRONI, LA 47/2FA/10).
91 Ibid., 26 June 1936 (PRONI, LA 47/2FA/13).
92 MB Ballymena Rural District Council, 4 July 1936 (PRONI, LA 15/2FA/36).
93 MB Portrush Urban District Council, 7 Oct. 1907 (PRONI, LA 65/2CA/2).
94 Ibid., 2 Dec. 1907.
95 Ibid., 3 Aug. 1909 (PRONI, LA 65/2CA/3). In a similar vein, Minnie Beattie successfully proposed that the district medical officers implement the duties prescribed under the Public Health Act's diphtheria immunisation provisions in Lisburn (MB Lisburn Rural District Council, 28 July 1936 [PRONI, LA 47/2FA/13]).
96 MB Portrush Urban District Council, 4 May 1908 (PRONI, LA 65/2CA/3).
97 MB Lisburn Rural District Council, 25 Mar. 1930 [PRONI, LA 47/2FA/11].
98 This deputation was successful (ibid., 27 Sept. and 22 Nov. 1938 [PRONI, LA 47/2FA/13]).
99 Ibid., 28 Nov. 1939 (PRONI, LA 47/2FA/14).
100 MB Strabane Rural District Council, 11 Aug. 1925 and 8 Mar. 1938 (PRONI, LA 67/2FA/20 and LA 67/2FA/26).

101 MB Irvinestown Rural District Council, 21 June 1939 (PRONI, LA 39/2FA/21).
102 MB Armagh County Council, 27 Mar. 1925 (PRONI, LA 2/2GA/16).
103 Ibid., 31 Mar. 1925.
104 *IC*, Feb. 1920.
105 MB Armagh County Council, 10 June 1937 (PRONI, LA 2/2GA/28).
106 Snell, 'The town council', pp 74–5.
107 From 1920 to the end of the period under analysis.
108 From 1899 to 1927 and from 1924 to the end of the period under analysis.
109 MB Lisburn Rural District Council, 6 June 1934 (PRONI, LA 47/2FA/9).
110 MB Armagh County Council, 10 Jan. 1939 (PRONI, LA 2/2GA/30).
111 MB Portrush Urban District Council, 8 Sept. 1919 (PRONI, LA 56/2CA/5).
112 There were only a few exceptions. For example, Lilly Ann Barr, the only female member of Ballymena Urban District Council, was not included in the council's all-male delegation to attend a meeting of the Women's National Health Association in Dublin in 1908 to discuss treatment for consumptives (MB Ballymena Urban District Council, 5 Oct. 1908 [PRONI, LA 14/2CA/2]) and Minnie Beattie made no response when Antrim County Council refused to allocate funding to the Society for the Prevention of Venereal Disease in 1931 (MB Antrim County Council, 23 June 1931 [PRONI, LA 1/2GA/32]).
113 Edith, Marchioness of Londonderry, *Retrospect* (London, 1938), p 144.

CHAPTER SIX

1 Extract from Rosalind, 3rd Duchess of Abercorn's address to a female unionist demonstration in Belfast (*Northern Whig*, 20 May 1921). She was president of the UWUC from 1919 to 1922.
2 The three female MPs were: Dehra Parker (1882–1963), MP for Londonderry from 1921 to 1929 and for South Londonderry from 1933 to 1960. In 1901 she married Colonel Robert Chichester, a unionist MP, but she was widowed in 1921. In 1928 she married Admiral Henry Wise Parker and her second married name is used throughout this chapter. In 1929 Parker stood down in favour of her son-in-law, James Chichester-Clarke, who was elected unopposed as a unionist member for the constituency of South Londonderry. Following his death in March 1933, Dehra Parker retook her seat. Julia McMordie (1860–1941), MP for South Belfast from 1921 to 1925. Her late husband, the Rt Hon James McMordie, had been an MP for East Belfast and Lord Mayor of Belfast five times from 1910 to 1914. Margaret Waring, born in 1887, was an MP for Iveagh in County Down from 1929 to 1933. Northern Irish figure calculated from Sidney Elliot, *Northern Ireland parliamentary election results, 1921–72* (Chichester, 1973), p 118.
3 British figure calculated from Martin Pugh, *Women and the women's movement in Britain, 1914–59* (London and Hampshire, 1992), p 159. A total of thirty-six women sat in the imperial parliament in the period 1919 to 1939 (Brian Harrison, 'Women in a men's house: The women MPs, 1919–45', *Historical Journal*, 29, no. 3 [1986], p 623). In the period 1922 to 1937, ten women were elected to Dáil Éireann (Mary Clancy, 'Aspects of Women's Contribution to the Oireachtas Debate in the Irish Free State, 1922–37', in Maria Luddy and Cliona Murphy (eds), *Women surviving* [Dublin, 1989], pp 231–2).
4 A total of nine women were elected to the Northern Ireland parliament from 1921 to 1972: Mrs L.I.M. Calvert [Independent] 1945–53; Mrs A. Dickson [Unionist] 1969–72; Dr E. Hickey [Independent] 1949–58; Mrs J. McMordie [Unionist] 1921–25; Mrs D. McNabb [Unionist] 1953–69; Miss B. Maconachie [Unionist] 1953–69; Mrs S.M. Murnaghan [Liberal] 1961–69; Dame Dehra Parker [Unionist] 1921–29 and 1933–60 and Mrs M.A. Waring [Unionist] 1929–33 (Elliot, *Northern Ireland parliamentary election results*, p 126).
5 Northern Ireland figure calculated from Elliot, *Northern Ireland parliamentary election results*, p 118 In Britain women represented 3.2 per cent of the total candidature from 1918 to 1945 (figure calculated from Pugh, *Women and the women's movement*, p 159).

6 Temperance supporters stood for election in 1929 under the auspices of the Local Optionist Party. They contested two seats in the Victoria and St Anne's constituencies of Belfast and one seat in Larne (see Jonathan Bardon, *A history of Ulster* [Belfast, 1992], p 511).
7 Elliot, *Northern Ireland parliamentary election results*, p 45.
8 Ibid., p 36.
9 See chapter I for an analysis of this in municipal elections.
10 See chapter V for an assessment of women's reluctance to stand as candidates in municipal elections.
11 Pugh, *Women and the women's movement*, p 190.
12 See chapters III and V for an analysis of the impact of this disillusion amongst northern nationalist women.
13 Pugh, *Women and the women's movement*, p 165.
14 McMordie served as a councillor and later as an alderman on Belfast's Corporation until 1930. She held the position of high sheriff until 1930 (*Thom's directory* [Dublin, 1920–30]).
15 Dehra Parker was a rural district councillor from 1920 to 1933 and from 1936 until the end of the period under analysis (MB Magherafelt Rural District Council, 1920–40 [PRONI, LA 53/2FA/19–42]). She served as a poor law guardian from 1920 until the end of the period under analysis and held the position of chairman of the board of guardians from 1924 to 1927 (MB Magherafelt Board of Guardians, 1920–40 [PRONI, BG 23/A/69–86]).
16 Pugh, *Women and the women's movement*, p 166.
17 Dehra Parker and Julia McMordie were vice-chairmen of the Ulster Women's Unionist Council from 1918 to 1930 and 1911 to 1919 respectively. McMordie was a vice-president of this organisation from 1919 to 1941.
18 *IC*, Sept. 1918.
19 Ibid.
20 Ibid., Nov. 1918.
21 Northern Ireland House of Commons debates [hereafter NI HOC], vol II, cols 372–3, 5 Apr. 1922.
22 Ibid., vol III, col 664, 2 May 1923. Julia McMordie was informed that no special provision was required, as the term 'inspector' had been changed to include both sexes.
23 Ibid., vol II, cols 372–3, 5 Apr. 1922.
24 Ibid., cols 694–5, 26 May 1922.
25 Harrison, 'Women in a men's house', pp 636–40, and Pugh, *Women and the women's movement*, p 194.
26 NI HOC, vol II, cols 506–7, 16 May 1922.
27 Ibid., col 673, 2 May 1923.
28 Ibid., col 664. A female school inspector had already been appointed.
29 Martin Wallace, *Northern Ireland: Fifty years of self-government* (Newton Abbot, 1971), pp 121–2.
30 NI HOC, vol IV, col 543, 3 Apr. 1924.
31 This was possibly because of McMordie's age, as she was sixty-five in 1925. However, she remained an alderman in Belfast Corporation until 1930 and a vice-president of the Ulster Women's Unionist Council until her death in 1941.
32 NI HOC, vol XI, cols 647–8, 18 June 1929. Negotiations to establish a special school for mentally handicapped children in Northern Ireland were in progress at this time.
33 Ibid., col 656.
34 She addressed the house on the following occasions: 18 June 1929, 25 June 1929 and 26 Nov. 1929. Ibid., vol XIII, col 14, 3 Mar. 1931.
35 Ibid., col 16.
36 Ibid., cols 15–16.
37 Ibid., col 15.
38 Ibid., cols 15–16.
39 Ibid., col 17.
40 Ibid., col 2907, 17 Dec. 1931.
41 She was awarded a DBE in 1949. Parker also served as chair of the Northern Ireland Health Services Board and president of the Council for the Encouragement of Music

and the Arts. She resigned from politics in June 1960 because of ill health. It has been claimed that she ensured that her parliamentary seat went to her grandson, James Chichester-Clarke, that Terence O'Neill should succeed Brookeborough as the Prime Minister of Northern Ireland and that he should in turn should be succeeded by her grandson, Chichester-Clarke (Art Byrne and Sean McMahon, *Great Northerners* [Swords, 1991], p 195).

42 NI HOC, vol I, cols 352–3, 1 Dec. 1921.

43 Ibid.

44 Ibid., col 356.

45 Ibid., col 389.

46 Ibid., vol III, cols 248–9, 21 Mar. 1923.

47 Ibid., vol XXIII, col 1673, 25 June 1940. Parker was opposing a nationalist proposal to establish all-party government in Ulster.

48 The Conservative MP Florence Horsburgh was the first women to perform this duty in the imperial parliament in 1936 (Pamela Brookes, *Women at Westminster: An account of women in the British parliament, 1918–66* [London, 1967], p 115).

49 NI HOC, vol IV, col 10, 11 Mar. 1924.

50 Ibid., vol VIII, col 916, 27 Apr. 1927.

51 Ibid., vol VI, cols 133–4, 21 Apr. 1925.

52 Ibid., vol XIII, col 4116–18, 8 December 1927. Major Shillington proposed an alternative vote in support of the government, which was passed by 25 to 12 votes (ibid.). Joseph Devlin, representing West Belfast, and Thomas McAllister, MP for Antrim, were the first nationalist members to enter the Commons in 1925 (Bardon, *A history of Ulster*, p 510).

53 NI HOC, vol X, col 1160, 21 Mar. 1929.

54 Ibid., vol XVII, col 135, 22 Nov. 1934. In the following year Parker stated: 'the ordinary Members of this House . . . have a very great responsibility. That responsibility is not just towards their constituents or towards any particular section of the community; it is towards the welfare of the whole Province' (ibid., col 1740, 16 May 1935).

55 Ibid., col 137, 22 Nov. 1934.

56 Ibid., vol II, col 270, 28 Mar. 1922. This bill was annually renewed until 1925, when it was renewed for a five-year period. In 1933 it was instituted as a permanent part of the Northern Ireland legal system.

57 Ibid., col 590, 26 Apr. 1923. This was passed as an appendage to the 1923 Education Act.

58 Ibid., vol VII, cols 1014–15, 5 May 1926.

59 The government appointed commissioners to discharge the functions of these local authorities (Bardon, *A history of Ulster*, pp 499–500).

60 NI HOC, vol II, cols 1046–8, 17 Oct. 1922.

61 Ibid., vol XVII, col 1575, 18 Apr. 1935. The unionist government alleged that the dissolution of nationalist local authorities and the abolition of PR were in response to near 'wartime conditions' in the province and threatened to resign when royal assent was withheld from this bill for two months (Bardon, *A history of Ulster*, p 500).

62 NI HOC, vol XIII, col 2886, 15 Nov. 1927. The measure was defeated on its second reading by twenty-five votes to fourteen. It was ordered to be read in the House in six months' time.

63 Ibid., vol XIII, cols 2903–07.

64 Ibid., cols 2903–04.

65 Ibid., col 2911.

66 This act enfranchised women aged twenty-one and over, who were resident in Northern Ireland for a period of three years, the owner or occupier of lands or premises valued at least £5 or business premises of the value of £10, who were married to a man qualified to exercise the local government franchise or were graduates of the Queen's University of Belfast.

67 NI HOC, vol IX, col 2830, 31 Oct. 1928.

68 Ibid., col 2843.

69 Ibid., cols 2843–46.

70 Parker's speech was reprinted in the UWUC's publication, *Northern Ireland. Home and politics. A journal for women*, 2, no. 3, Apr. 1927.
71 NI HOC, vol XVII, col 1183–6, 3 Apr. 1935.
72 The Minister for Education, the 7th Marquis of Londonderry, opposed this on the basis that it was unnecessary 'in view of the strides that women have made in the recent past and the position to which they have attained through their own merits' (ibid., vol III, col 518, 25 Apr. 1923).
73 Ibid., col 734, 8 May 1923. Mr Megaw, the parliamentary secretary to the Ministry for Home Affairs, assured Morrison and Parker that this question would be considered. Parker raised this question again in November (ibid., col 2074, 16 Nov. 1923).
74 Ibid., vol IV, col 267, 20 Mar. 1924.
75 Ibid., col 734, 7 May 1924. The 1924 Illegitimate Children Act was supplemented by the passage of the Legitimacy Act of 1928 that allowed a child to be legitimised by the subsequent marriage of its parents.
76 Ibid., col 1231, 20 Oct. 1925.
77 Ibid., vol III, col 82, 13 Mar. 1923.
78 Harrison, 'Women in a men's house', cited p 642.
79 NI HOC, vol III, cols 198–9, 20 Mar. 1923. The proposed increase in the age of consent was defeated.
80 Ibid., vol XVII, cols 1183–6, 3 Apr. 1935. To support her argument Parker cited the work of female JPs in England who administered the Married Women's Desertion Act of 1886, the Illegitimate (Affiliation Order) Act of 1924 and cases dealing with assaults on children (ibid.).
81 Ibid., cols 540–4, 12 Dec. 1934.
82 Ibid., cols 1183–6, 3 Apr. 1935.
83 Ibid., vol XV, col 1517, 10 May 1933.
84 Ibid., vol VI, cols 1382–3, 20 Oct. 1925.
85 Ibid., vol IXX, col 1938–39, 13 Oct. 1937.
86 Parker stated that she received several appeals from farmers in her constituency asking for help. She quoted the following extract from one letter which she received to the Commons: 'We have no one to help us but you, and you have never failed us' (ibid., vol VI, col 1468, 22 Oct. 1925).
87 Ibid., cols 376–7, 5 May 1925.
88 Ibid., cols 397–8. For an example of the hostility between Henderson and Parker, see ibid., vol XVI, cols 1397–8, 3 May 1934.
89 Ibid., vol VI, cols 397–8, 5 May 1925.
90 Ibid., col 1468, 22 Oct. 1925.
91 Ibid., col 134, 21 Apr. 1925.
92 Ibid., vol IX, cols 2053–4, 22 May 1928. Parker regularly raised the Bann drainage issue in the Commons. See, for example, ibid., vol XV, col 2022, 3 Oct. 1933, and vol XVII, col 1241, 16 Apr. 1935.
93 Ibid., vol VI, cols 279–82, 29 Apr. 1925.
94 Ibid., vol XVI, col 1750, 17 May 1934.
95 Ibid., vol XVII, cols 2363–66, 12 June 1935.
96 Ibid., vol XVII, cols 540–4, 12 Dec. 1934.
97 Ibid., vol XVI, col 2443, 9 Oct. 1934.
98 Ibid., col 2248.
99 Ibid., col 2247.
100 Ibid.
101 Ibid., cols 2611–15, 16 Oct. 1934.
102 Ibid., vol IV, col 490, 2 Apr. 1924.
103 Ibid., vol XVI, cols 1512–3, 9 May 1934.
104 Several British women had been appointed to cabinet: Margaret Bonfield was parliamentary secretary at the Ministry of Labour in 1924 and Minister of Labour from 1929 to 1931; Susan Lawrence was parliamentary secretary at Education in 1924 and at the Ministry of Health 1929 to 1931 and the Duchess of Atholl was parliamentary secretary at Education from 1924 to 1929 (Pugh, *Women and the women's movement*, p 203).

105 NI HOC, vol XXI, col 568, 30 Mar. 1938.
106 Ibid., vol XXII, col 1023, 20 Apr. 1939.
107 Ibid., vol XXIII, cols 1295–6, 29 May 1940.
108 Ibid., col 1480, 11 Oct. 1938.
109 J.A. Oliver, *Working at Stormont* (Dublin, 1974), p 81.
110 *Belfast News-Letter*, 5 Mar. 1929.
111 G.C. Duggan, *Northern Ireland: Success or failure* (Dublin, 1950), p 28.
112 Ibid.
113 Dehra Parker to St John Irvine [*c.* 1945] (PRONI, CAB 94/16/1). I am grateful to Gill McIntosh for drawing my attention to this letter. Parker was appointed Minister for Health and Local Government in 1949.
114 Ibid.
115 Harrison, 'Women in a men's house', p 363.
116 Duggan, *Northern Ireland: Success or failure*, p 28.
117 NI HOC, vol IXX, col 217, 9 Mar. 1937. The Labour MP John Beattie made this comment.
118 *Belfast News-Letter*, 2 Nov. 1929.

CONCLUSION

1 Vera Brittain, *Lady into woman: A history of women from Victoria to Elizabeth II* (London, 1953), p 29.
2 Ibid., p 42.
3 Paula Baker, 'The domestication of politics: Women in American political society, 1780–1920,' *American Historical Review*, 89, no. 3 (June 1984), p 463.
4 Maria Luddy, *Women in Ireland: 1800–1918: A documentary history* (Cork, 1995), cited pp 287–8.
5 Hariot, 1st Marchioness of Dufferin and Ava, speech entitled 'Women's opportunities at church work', n. d., [*c.* 1920–36] (PRONI, D. 1231/G/13/25). She was a UWUC vice-president from 1921 to 1936.
6 Ibid.
7 Basil Brooke to J. Beattie, 10 Sept. 1943, Cabinet secretariat files, 2nd series (Ministry of Labour and Health and Social Services) (PRONI, CAB 9C/50/1).
8 Ibid. Sample letter to conference delegates from Ernest Bevin, Aug. 1943 (PRONI, CAB 9C/50/1).
9 *Northern Ireland. Home and Politics. A journal for women*, 2, no. 3, Apr. 1927.
10 *An Phoblacht*, 25 June 1932.
11 Jane Lewis (ed), *Labour and love: Women's experience of home and family, 1850–1940* (Oxford, 1986), cited p 19.

APPENDICES

1 Compiled from the *Irish Citizen*; Rosemary Cullen Owens, *Smashing Times: A history of the Irish women's suffrage movement, 1889–1922* (Dublin, 1984), and Cliona Murphy, *The women's suffrage movement and Irish society in the early twentieth century* (Hemel Hempstead, 1989).
2 Compiled from the *Irish Citizen; Northern Whig; Belfast News-Letter;* Andrew Rosen, *Rise up women! The militant campaign of the Women's Social and Political Union, 1903-14* (London and Boston, 1974), and A.E. Metcalfe, *Woman's effort: A chronicle of British women's fifty years' struggle for citizenship, 1865–1914* (Oxford, 1917).

Bibliography

PRIMARY SOURCES

Belfast Central Library

Papers of F.J. Bigger.

National Library of Ireland

Papers of Bulmer Hobson (Ms. 13161).
Papers of Joseph McGarrity (Ms. 17539).
Papers of Eoin McNeill (Ms. 10882).
Papers of Hanna Sheehy Skeffington (Ms. 24090, 24092, 21194).

Omagh Public Library

Obituaries of Alice Milligan.

Public Record Office of Northern Ireland

Northern Ireland Government papers
Board of Guardian Minutes, 1896–1940 (BG 1–27).
Crown Files at Assize and Commission, 1914 (BELF 1).
Local Authority Minutes, 1898–1940 (LA 1–69).
Papers of the Assistant Under Secretary's Office, 1920–1921 (AUS 1).
Papers of the Department of Prime Minister, 1934 (PM 2).
Papers of the Ministry of Education for Northern Ireland, 1938–1940 (ED 32/A).
Papers of the Ministry of Home Affairs for Northern Ireland, 1938–1939 (HA 63).
Papers of the Northern Ireland Cabinet, 1924, 1935, 1943 (CAB 4, CAB 9).

Private papers
Papers of Lady Louisa Antrim (D. 2977).
Papers of Lady Cynthia Brookeborough (D. 3004).
Papers of Lord Edward and Lady Ruby Carson (D. 1507).
Papers of Lord James and Lady Cecil Craig (D. 1415).
Papers of Charlotte Despard (D. 2479, D.3987).

Papers of Hariot, Marchioness of Dufferin and Ava (D. 1231).
Papers of Elinor Gardner (D. 2548).
Papers of Cahir Healy (D. 2991).
Papers of Dorothy Holmes (T. 2948).
Papers of Margaret Houston (T. 2879).
Papers of H. Montgomery Hyde (D. 3084).
Papers of Mrs W. Leeper (D. 3741).
Papers of Theresa, Marchioness of Londonderry (D. 2846).
Papers of Edith, Marchioness of Londonderry (D. 3099).
Papers of Helen Macnaghten (D. 1006/3).
Papers of Ronald and Ada McNeill (D.2661).
Papers of Hugh de Fellenberg Montgomery (D. 627).
Papers of Helen Richardson (D. 2362/5).
Papers of Thomas Sinclair (D. 1961).
Papers of Lady Lilian Spender (D. 1295, D. 1633).
Papers of Mrs F. Waring (D. 3783).
Taped interview with Margaret Robinson, 1975 (TP. 35).

Political organisation papers
Miscellaneous papers relating to women's suffrage (T. 2125, T. 3259, T. 3600).
Papers of Ballycastle Women's Unionist Association (D. 2688/5).
Papers of Central Women's Section of the Northern Ireland Labour Party (D. 3311).
Papers of Dunmurry Women's Unionist Association (D. 1460).
Papers of East Antrim Women's Unionist Association (D. 1332).
Papers of Lurgan Women's Unionist Association (D. 3790).
Papers of North Down Women's Unionist Association (D. 2688/3).
Papers of North Tyrone Women's Unionist Association (D. 1098/2).
Papers of St Anne's Women's Unionist Association (D. 2688/2).
Papers of South Belfast Women's Unionist Association (D. 2688/4).
Papers of Ulster Unionist Council (D. 1327).
Papers of Ulster Women's Unionist Council (D. 1098/1, D. 2688/1).

Victoria College, Belfast

Papers of Belfast Ladies' Institute.

Printed sources

Bean na hÉireann
Belfast Evening Telegraph
Belfast News-Letter
Belfast Telegraph

Burke's Peerage (London, 1921, 1939)
Cumann na mBan
Dod's Peerage (London, 1921)
Evening Standard
Fermanagh Times
Hibernian Journal
Irish Citizen
Irish News
Irish Times
Londonderry Sentinel
Lurgan Mail
Morning Post
Northern Ireland. Home and politics. A journal for women
Northern Ireland House of Commons Debates (1921–1940)
Northern Patriot
Northern Whig
Reports of Cumann na mBan (NLI, P. 2188, P. 2119)
Reports of Irish Women's Suffrage and Local Government Association (NLI, I. 3996, P. 790)
Reports of Irish Workhouse Association (NLI, P. 2467, Ir. 94108)
Thom's directory of Ireland (Dublin, 1896–1940)
Proceedings of the Ulster Unionist Convention (Belfast, 1892)
Report of the Ulster Unionist Convention (Belfast, 1892)
Shan Van Vocht
Sunday Chronicle
The Times
Ulster Gazette
Ulsterwoman. A journal for union and progress

SECONDARY SOURCES

Books

Adam, Ruth, *A woman's place, 1910–1975* (London, 1975).
Akenson, D.H., *Education and enmity: The control of schooling in Northern Ireland, 1920–1950* (Belfast, 1973).
Akinson, Diane, *The suffragettes in pictures* (London, 1996).
Alexander, Sally, *Becoming a woman and other essays in nineteenth and twentieth century feminist history* (London, 1994).
Allen, Roy, *A place of honour, an account of the Orange Order in Ballynafeigh: The first one hundred years, 1887–1987* (Belfast, 1987).
Anderson, B.S., and Zinsser, J.P., *A history of their own* (2 vols, London, 1990).

Angerman, A., et al (eds), *Current issues in women's history* (London, 1989).

Atholl, Duchess of, *Women and politics* (London, 1931).

Banks, Olive, *Faces of feminism* (Oxford, 1981).

—— *The biographical dictionary of British feminists, 1900–1945* (vol 2, Hemel Hempstead, 1990).

—— *The politics of British feminism, 1918–1970* (Aldershot, 1993).

Bardon, Jonathan, *A history of Ulster* (Belfast, 1992).

Barrington, Ruth, *Health, medicine and politics in Ireland, 1900–1970* (Dublin, 1987).

Bartley, Paula, *The changing role of women, 1815–1914* (London, 1996).

Barton, Brian, *Northern Ireland in the Second World War* (Belfast, 1995).

Bates, Jean Victor, *Sir Edward Carson: Ulster leader* (London, 1921).

Baxter, Sandra, and Lansing, Marjorie, *Women and politics* (revised ed, Michigan, 1983).

Beard, M.R., *Women as a force in history: A study of traditions and realities* (New York, 1946).

Beckett, J.C, and Glasscock, R.E. (eds), *Belfast: The origins and growth of an industrial city* (London, 1967).

Beddoe, Deirdre, *Discovering women's history* (London, 1983).

—— *Back to home and duty: Women between the wars, 1918–1939* (London, 1989).

Bell, S.G., and Offen, K.M., *Women, family and freedom, 1880–1950* (vol 2, Stanford, 1983).

Bew, Paul, Gibbon, Peter, and Patterson, Henry, *Northern Ireland, 1921–1994: Political forces and social classes* (London, 1995).

Biggs-Davidson, J., and Chowdharay-Best, G., *The cross of St Patrick: The Catholic unionist tradition in Ireland* (Kensal, 1984).

Birrell, Derek, and Murie, Alan, *Policy and government in Northern Ireland* (Dublin, 1980).

Blackburn, Helen, *Women's suffrage: A record of the women's suffrage movement in the British Isles* (New York, 1971, reprint of orig. ed, London, 1902).

Blackburne, E.O., *Illustrious Irishwomen* (2 vols, London, 1877).

Blain, Virginia, Clements, Patricia, and Grundy, Isobel (eds), *The feminist companion to literature in English* (London, 1990).

Bleakley, David, *Saidie Patterson: Irish peacemaker* (Belfast, 1980).

Blease, W.L., *The emancipation of English women* (New York, 1977).

Bock, Gisela, and James, Susan (eds), *Beyond equality and difference: Citizenship, feminist politics and female subjectivity* (London and New York, 1992).

Bolt, Christine, *The women's movements in the United States and Britain from the 1790s to the 1920s* (London and New York, 1993).

Bourke, Joanna, *Husbandry to housewifery* (Oxford, 1993).

Boxer, Marilyn J., and Quataert, Jean H. (eds), *Connecting spheres: Women in the western world, 1500 to present* (Oxford and New York, 1987).

Boyce, D.G., *Nationalism in Ireland* (3rd ed, London and New York, 1995).

Boyd, Andrew, *The rise of the Irish trade unions, 1729–1970* (Ireland, 1986, reprint of orig. ed, Tralee, 1972).

Boyle, J.W., *The Irish labor movement in the nineteenth century* (Washington, 1988).

Brady, A.M., and Cleeve, Brian, *A biographical dictionary of Irish writers* (Mullingar, 1985).

Brady, Anna, *Women in Ireland: An annotated biography* (Connecticut, 1988).

Brady, Ciaran (ed), *Interpreting Irish history* (Dublin, 1994).

Branca, Patricia, *Silent sisterhood: Middle-class women in the Victorian home* (London, 1975).

Braybon, Gail, *Women workers in the First World War: The British experience* (London, 1981).

—— and Summerfield, Penny, *Out of the cage: Women's experiences in two world wars* (London, 1987).

Bridenthal, Renate, and Koonz, Claudia (eds), *Becoming visible: Women in European history* (Boston, 1977).

Brittain, Vera, *Lady into woman: A history of women from Victoria to Elizabeth II* (London, 1953).

Brookes, Pamela, *Women at Westminster: An account of women in the British parliament, 1918–66* (London, 1967).

Buckland, Patrick, *Irish unionism: The Anglo-Irish and the new Ireland, 1885–1922* (Dublin, 1972).

—— *Irish unionism: Ulster unionism and the origins of Northern Ireland, 1886–1922* (Dublin, 1973).

—— *Irish unionism: A documentary history, 1885–1923* (Belfast, 1973).

—— *Lord Craigavon* (Dublin, 1980).

—— *The factory of grievances: Devolved government in Northern Ireland, 1921–1939* (Dublin, 1987).

Budge, Ian, and O'Leary, Cornelius, *Belfast: Approach to crisis: A study of Belfast politics, 1613–1917* (London, 1973).

Burke, Helen, *People and poor law in nineteenth century Ireland* (Dublin, 1987).

Burke, Peter (ed), *New perspectives on historical writing* (Cambridge, 1991).

Burns, Dawson, *Temperance in the Victorian age* (London, 1897).

Byrne, Art, and McMahon, Sean, *Great northerners* (Swords, 1991).

Caine, Barbara, *Victorian feminists* (Oxford, 1992).

Campbell, Flann, *The dissenting voice: Protestant democracy in Ulster from plantation to partition* (Belfast, 1991).

Campbell, Kate (ed), *Critical feminism* (Buckingham and Philadelphia, 1992).
Carroll, B.A., *Liberating women's history* (London, 1976).
Clarke, Kathleen, *Revolutionary woman: An autobiography, 1878–1972* (Dublin, 1991).
Clear, Caitriona, *Nuns in nineteenth century Ireland* (Dublin and Washington, 1987).
Clifford, Angela, *The poor law in Ireland* (Belfast, 1983).
Collins, John, *Local government* (2nd ed, Dublin, 1963).
Colvin, Ian, *The life of Lord Carson* (vols 2–3, London, 1934, 1936).
Concannon, Helena, *Women of ninety-eight* (Dublin, 1919).
Conlon, Lil, *Cumann na mBan and the women of Ireland, 1913–1925* (Kilkenny, 1969).
Connolly, James, *The re-conquest of Ireland* (Belfast and Dublin, 1972, reprint of orig. ed, Dublin, 1915).
Corelli, Marie, *Free opinions freely expressed on certain phases of modern social life and conduct* (London, 1905).
Cosgrove, Art (ed), *Marriage in Ireland* (Dublin, 1985).
Cott, N.E., *The grounding of modern feminism* (London and New Haven, 1986).
Coulter, Carol, *The hidden tradition: Feminism, women and nationalism in Ireland* (Cork, 1993).
Cousins, J.H. and M.E., *We two together* (Madras, 1950).
Coxhead, Elizabeth, *Daughters of Erin; Five women of the Irish renascence* (London, 1965).
Crawford, F.H., *Guns for Ulster* (Belfast, 1947).
Cronin, Sean, *Irish nationalism* (Dublin, 1980).
Crosby, Christina, *The ends of history: Victorians and 'The woman question'* (London and New York, 1991).
Crossman, Virginia, *Local government in nineteenth-century Ireland* (Belfast, 1994).
Crowther, M.A., *The workhouse system, 1834–1929* (London, 1981).
Cullen, Mary (ed), *Girls don't do honours: Irish women's education in the nineteenth and twentieth centuries* (Dublin, 1987).
—— and Luddy, Maria (eds), *Women, power and consciousness in nineteenth-century Ireland* (Dublin, 1995).
Currell, M.E., *Political women* (London, 1974).
Curtin, Chris, Jackson, Pauline, and O'Connor, Barbara (eds), *Gender in Irish society* (Galway, 1987).
Dancyger, Irene, *A world of women: An illustrated history of women's magazines* (Dublin, 1978).
Davidoff, Leonore, *The best circles: Society, etiquette and the season* (London, 1973).
Davies, N.Z., and Farge, Arlette (eds), *A history of women in the west* (vol 3, London and Massachusetts, 1993).

de Beauvoir, Simone, *The second sex* (London, 1972, reprint of orig. ed in translation, London, 1953).

de Courcy, Anne, *Circe: The life of Edith, Marchioness of Londonderry* (London, 1992).

Devlin, Paddy, *Yes, we have no bananas: Outdoor relief in Belfast, 1920–1939* (Belfast, 1981).

Day, S.R., *The amazing philanthropists* (London, 1916).

Dewar, M.W., Brown, J., and Long, S.F., *Orangeism: A new historical appreciation* (Belfast, 1967).

Dicey, A.V., *Letters to a friend on votes for women* (London, 1909).

Donovan, Katie, Jeffares, A.N., and Kennelly, Brendan, *Ireland's women: Writings past and present* (Dublin, 1994).

Doyle, Crissie M., *Women in ancient and modern Ireland* (Dublin, 1917).

Dudley Edwards, Owen, et al, *Celtic nationalism* (London, 1968).

Duggan, G.C., *Northern Ireland: Success or failure* (Dublin, 1950).

Duke, L.L. (ed), *Women in politics: Outsiders or insiders?* (New Jersey, 1993).

Elliot, Sidney, N*orthern Ireland parliamentary election results, 1921–1972* (Chichester, 1973).

Ehreneich, Barbara, and English, Deirdre, *For her own good: 150 years of the experts advice to women* (London, 1979).

Elshtain, J.B., *Women and war* (New York, 1987).

Ervine, St John, *Craigavon: Ulsterman* (London, 1949).

Evans, Mary (ed), *The woman question* (2nd ed, London, 1994).

—— and David Morgan, *Work on women* (London and New York, 1979).

Fallon, C.H., *Soul of fire: A biography of Mary MacSwiney* (Cork and Dublin, 1963).

Farrell, Michael, *Northern Ireland: The Orange state* (London, 1976).

—— *The poor law and the workhouse in Belfast, 1838–1948* (Belfast, 1978).

Fennell, Arabella, *Letters on primary education* (Belfast, 1905).

Ferris, Mary, et al, *Women's voices: An oral history of women's health in Northern Ireland, 1900–1990* (Dublin, 1992).

Fischer, G.V., *Journal of women's history: A guide to periodical literature* (Indianapolis, 1992).

Fitzpatrick, David (ed), *Ireland and the First World War* (Dublin, 1986).

Follis, B.A., *A state under siege: The establishment of Northern Ireland, 1920–1925* (Oxford, 1995).

Forster, Margaret, *Significant sisters: The grassroots of active feminism, 1839–1939* (London, 1984).

Foster, R.F., *Modern Ireland, 1600–1972* (Dublin, 1988).

Fox, R.M., *Louie Bennett* (Dublin, 1957).

—— *Rebel Irishwomen* (Dublin and Cork, 1935).

Fox-Genovese, Elizabeth, *Feminism without illusions* (London and Carolina, 1991).

Fraser, Derek (ed), *The new poor law in the nineteenth century* (London, 1976).

Friedan, Betty, *The feminine mystique* (London, 1963).

Gailey, Andrew, *Ireland and the death of kindness: The experience of constructive unionism, 1890–1905* (Cork, 1987).

Gallagher, Frank, *The indivisible island: The history of the partition of Ireland* (London, 1957).

Gardiner, Juliet (ed), *What is history today . . . ?* (Hampshire, 1989, reprint of orig. ed, Hampshire, 1988).

Garvin, Tom, *Nationalist revolutionaries in Ireland, 1858–1928* (Oxford, 1987).

Gaskell, Ernest, *Ulster leaders: Social and political* (London, 1914).

Genet, Jacqueline (ed), *The big house in Ireland: Reality and representation* (Dingle, 1991).

Gibbon, Peter, *The origins of Ulster unionism: The formation of popular Protestant politics and ideology* (Manchester, 1975).

Githens, M., Norris, P., and Lovenduski, J., *Different roles, different voices: Women and politics in the United States and Europe* (New York, 1994).

Good, James Winder, *Ulster and Ireland* (Dublin and London, 1919).

—— *Irish unionism* (Dublin and London, 1920)

Gould, Michael, *The workhouses of Ulster* (Belfast, 1983).

Gray, John, *City in revolt: James Larkin and the Belfast dock strike of 1907* (Belfast, 1985).

Gray, Tony, *The Orange Order* (London, 1972).

Greer, Margaret, *An outline of Ireland's story* (London, 1914).

Hamilton, C.J., *Notable Irishwomen* (Dublin, n.d.).

Harbinson, J.F., *The Ulster Unionist Party, 1882–1973, its development and organisation* (Belfast, 1973).

Harris, Mary, *The Catholic Church and the foundation of the Northern Irish state* (Cork, 1993).

Harrison, Brian, *Separate spheres: The opposition to women's suffrage in Britain* (London, 1978).

Hartman, M.S., and Banner, Lois (eds), *Clio's consciousness raised: New perspectives on the history of women* (New York, 1974).

Harvey, A.D., *Collision of empires: Britain in three world wars, 1793–1945* (London, 1992).

Haste, Cate, *Rules of desire: Sex in Britain: World War One to the present* (London, 1992).

Haverty, Anne, *Constance Markievicz* (London, 1988).

Hayley, Barbara, and McKay, Enda (eds), *Three hundred years of Irish periodicals* (Mullingar, 1987).

Helferty, Seamus, and Refausse, Raymond, *Directory of Irish archives* (Dublin, 1988).

Hellerstein, E.O., Hume, L.P., and Offen, K.M. (eds), *Victorian women* (Brighton, 1981).

Higonnet, M.R., Michel, S., and Weitz, M.C. (eds), *Behind the lines: Gender and the two world wars* (London and New Haven, 1987).

Hill, Myrtle, and Pollock, Vivienne, *Image and experience* (Belfast, 1993).

Hobsbawm, Eric, and Ranger, Terence (eds), *The invention of tradition* (Cambridge, 1983).

Hobson, Bulmer, *Ireland: Yesterday and tomorrow* (Tralee, 1968).

Hoff, Joan, and Coulter, M. (eds), *Irish women's voices: Past and present* (Indiana, 1995).

Holcombe, Lee, *Victorian ladies at work* (Newton Abbot, 1973).

—— *Wives and property: Reform of the married women's property law in nineteenth-century England* (Toronto and Buffalo, 1983).

Hollis, Patricia, *Women in public: The women's movement, 1850–1900* (London, 1979).

—— *Ladies elect: Women in English local government, 1865–1914* (Oxford, 1987)

Holmes, Janice, and Urquhart, Diane (eds), *Coming into the light: The work, politics and religion of women in Ulster*, 1840–1940 (Belfast, 1994).

Hoppen, K.T., *Elections, politics and society in Ireland, 1832–1885* (Oxford, 1984).

Hume, David, *For Ulster and her freedom: The story of the April 1914 gunrunning* (Lurgan, 1989).

Hutchinson, John, *The dynamics of cultural nationalism: The Gaelic revival and the creation of the Irish nation state* (London, 1987).

Hutton, Sean, and Stewart, Paul (eds), *Ireland's histories* (London, 1991).

Hyde, H. Montgomery, *Carson: The life of Sir Edward Carson, Lord Carson of Duncairn* (London, 1953).

—— *The Londonderrys: A family portrait* (London, 1979).

Hyland, Aine, and Milne, Kenneth, *Irish educational documents* (vol 1, Dublin, 1987).

Innes, C.L., *Women and nation in Irish literature and society, 1800–1935* (Hemel Hempstead, 1993).

Jackson, T.A. *The Ulster Party: Irish unionists in the House of Commons, 1884–1911* (Oxford, 1989).

—— *Sir Edward Carson* (Dublin, 1993).

Jalland, Patricia, *The liberals and Ireland: The Ulster question in British politics to 1914* (Brighton, 1980).

—— *Women, marriage and politics, 1860–1914* (Oxford, 1986).

Jaquette, J.S. (ed), *Women in politics* (London and New York, 1974).

Johnson, D.S., *The inter-war economy in Ireland* (Ireland, 1985).

Johnston, Sheila Turner, *The harper of the only God: Alice Milligan, selected poems* (Omagh, 1984).

—— *Alice: The life of Alice Milligan* (Omagh, 1994).

Jones, Mary, *These obstreperous lassies: A history of the Irish Women Workers' Union* (Dublin, 1988).

Jordan, Alison, *Margaret Byers: Pioneer of women's education and founder of Victoria College, Belfast* (Belfast, 1992).

—— *Who cared? Charity in Edwardian and Victorian Belfast* (Belfast, 1992).

Kamm, Josephine, *Rapiers and battleaxes: The women's movement and its aftermath* (London, 1966).

Kanner, Barbara (ed), *The women of England from Anglo-Saxon times to the present* (London, 1980).

Kelleher, Margaret, and Murphy, James H. (eds), *Gender perspectives in nineteenth-century Ireland: Public and private spheres* (Dublin, 1997).

Kelly, Joan, *Women, history and theory* (London and Chicago, 1984).

Kennedy, Dennis, *The widening gulf: Northern attitudes to the independent Irish state, 1919–1949* (Belfast, 1988).

Kinghan, Nancy, *United we stood: The story of the Ulster Women's Unionist Council, 1911–1974* (Belfast, 1975).

Kleinberg, S.J. (ed), *Retrieving women's history: Changing perceptions of the role of women in politics and society* (Oxford, 1988).

Laffan, Michael, *The partition of Ireland, 1911–1925* (Dublin, 1983).

Laski, H.J., Jennings, W.I., Robson, W.A. (eds), *A century of municipal progress, 1835–1935* (London, 1935).

Lee, J.J., *Modernisation of Irish society, 1848–1918* (Dublin, 1973).

—— *Ireland, 1912–1985: Politics and society* (Cambridge, 1989).

Lerner, Gerda, *The majority finds its past: Placing women in history* (London, 1979).

—— *The creation of patriarchy* (vol 1, London and New York, 1986).

—— *The creation of feminist consciousness* (Oxford and New York, 1993).

Levenson, Leah, and Natterstad, Jerry H., *Hanna Sheehy Skeffington: Irish feminist* (Syracuse, 1986).

Levenson, Samuel, *James Connolly: A biography* (London, 1973).

Levine, Philippa, *Feminist lives in Victorian England: Private roles and public commitment* (Oxford, 1990).

Lewenhak, Sheila, *Women and trade unions* (London, 1977).

Lewis, Jane, *Women in England: Sexual divisions and social change, 1870–1950* (London, 1984).

—— (ed), *Labour and love: Women's experience of home and family, 1850–1940* (Oxford and New York, 1986).

—— *Before the vote was won: Arguments for and against women's suffrage* (London and New York, 1987).

—— *Women and social action in Victorian and Edwardian England* (Aldershot, 1991).

Linklater, Andro, *An unhusbanded life. Charlotte Despard: Suffragette, socialist and Sinn Féiner* (London, 1980).

Londonderry, Edith, Marchioness of, *Retrospect* (London, 1938).
Loughlin, James, *Gladstone, Home Rule and the Irish question, 1882–1883* (Dublin, 1986).
—— *Ulster unionism and British national identity since 1885* (London and New York, 1995).
Lucy, Gordon (ed), *The Ulster covenant: A pictorial history of the 1912 Home Rule crisis* (Ulster, 1989).
—— *The great convention: The Ulster unionist convention of 1892* (Lurgan, 1995).
Luddy, Maria, *Hanna Sheehy Skeffington* (Cork, 1995).
—— *Women and philanthropy in nineteenth-century Ireland* (Cambridge, 1995).
—— *Women in Ireland, 1800–1918: A documentary history* (Cork, 1995).
—— and Cliona Murphy (eds), *Women surviving: Studies in Irish women's history in the nineteenth and twentieth centuries* (Dublin, 1989).
Lyons, F.S.L., *Ireland since the famine* (London, 1971).
—— *Culture and anarchy in Ireland, 1890–1939* (Oxford, 1979).
Lytton, Constance, and Warton, Jane, *Prisons and prisoners: The stirring testimony of a suffragette* (London, 1988, reprint of orig. ed, London, 1914).
MacBride, Maud Gonne, *A servant of the queen* (London, 1974).
McCarthy, Charles, *Trade unions in Ireland, 1894–1960* (Dublin, 1977).
MacCurtain, Margaret, and O'Corrain, Donnacha (eds), *Women in Irish society: The historical dimension* (Dublin, 1987).
—— and O'Dowd, Mary (eds), *Women in early modern Ireland* (Edinburgh, 1991).
MacKnight, Thomas, *Ulster as it is* (2 vols, London, 1896).
MacManus, Francis (ed), *The years of the great test, 1926–1939* (Dublin, 1967).
McNeill, Mary, *The life and times of Mary Ann McCracken, 1770–1866: A Belfast panorama* (Belfast, 1988, reprint of orig. ed, Belfast, 1960).
McNeill, Ronald, *Ulster's stand for union* (London, 1922).
Madden-Simpson, Janet (ed), *Woman's part: An anthology of short fiction by and about Irish women, 1890–1960* (Dublin, 1994).
Maher, Liam, *Temperance in Ireland* (Dublin, 1959).
Maltby, Arthur, *The government of Northern Ireland, 1922–1972: A catalogue and breviate of parliamentary papers* (Dublin, 1974).
Mangan, Henry (ed), *Poems by Alice Milligan* (Dublin, 1954).
Mann, Jean, *Women in parliament* (London, 1962).
Mansergh, Nicholas, *The government of Northern Ireland* (London, 1936).
—— *The Irish question, 1840–1921* (3rd ed, London, 1975).
Marjoribanks, Edward, *The life of Lord Carson* (vol 1, London, 1932).
Martindale, Hilda, *Women servants of the state, 1870–1938* (London, 1938).

Marwick, Arthur, *Women and war, 1914–1918* (London, 1977).
Masterman, N. (ed), *Chalmers on charity* (Westminster, 1900).
Maxwell, Henry, *Ulster was right* (London, 1933).
Messenger, Betty, *Picking up the linen threads: A study of industrial folklore* (Belfast, 1980, reprint of orig. ed, London and Texas, 1978).
Metcalfe, A.E., *Women's efforts: A chronicle of British women's fifty years' struggle for citizenship, 1865–1914* (Oxford, 1917).
Middleton, Lucy, *Women in the labour movement* (London and New Jersey, 1977).
Miller, D.W., *Queen's rebels: Ulster loyalism in historical perspective* (Dublin, 1980).
Milotte, Mike, *Communism in modern Ireland* (Dublin, 1984).
Mitchell, Arthur, and O'Snodaigh, Padraig (eds), *Irish political documents, 1869–1916* (Dublin, 1989).
Morgan, Austen, *Labour and partition: The Belfast working class, 1905–1923* (London, 1991).
Morgan, David, *Suffragists and liberals: The politics of woman suffrage in England* (Oxford, 1975).
Muldoon, John, *A guide to Irish local government* (Dublin, 1898).
Mulvihill, Margaret, *Charlotte Despard: A biography* (London, 1989).
Munck, Ronnie, and Rolston, Bill, *Belfast in the thirties* (Belfast, 1987).
Murphy, Cliona, *The women's suffrage movement and Irish society in the early twentieth century* (Hemel Hempstead, 1989).
Nelson, Sarah, *Ulster's uncertain defenders* (Belfast and New York, 1984).
Newmann, Kate, *A dictionary of Ulster biography* (Belfast, 1993).
Niven, Richard, *Orangeism as it was and is* (Belfast, 1910).
Noble, Iris, *Emmeline and her daughters: The Pankhurst suffragettes* (Folkestone, 1974).
Nolan, J.A., *Ourselves alone: Women's emigration from Ireland, 1885–1920* (Kentucky, 1989).
Norman, Diana, *Terrible beauty: A life of Constance Markievicz, 1868–1927* (London, 1987).
O'Brien, Nora Connolly, *James Connolly: Portrait of a rebel father* (Dublin, 1975, reprint of orig. ed, Dublin, 1935).
—— *We shall rise again* (London, 1981).
Ó Broin, Leon, *Revolutionary underground: The story of the Irish Republican Brotherhood, 1858–1924* (Dublin, 1976).
O'Connor, Emmet, *A labour history of Ireland, 1824–1960* (Dublin, 1992).
O'Connor, John, *The workhouses of Ireland* (Dublin, 1995).
O'Day, Alan, *Reactions to Irish nationalism* (Dublin, 1987).
O'Dowd, Mary, and Wichert, Sabine (eds), *Chattel, servant or citizen: Women's status in church, state and society* (Belfast, 1995).
O'Neill, Marie, *From Parnell to de Valera: A biography of Jennie Wyse Power, 1858–1941* (Dublin, 1991).

O'Neill, W.L., *The woman movement: Feminism in the United States and England* (London, 1969).
O Tuama, Sean (ed), *The Gaelic League idea* (Cork and Dublin, 1972).
Offen, Karen, Roach Pierson, Ruth, and Rendall, Jane (eds), *Writing women's history* (London, 1991).
Oliver, J.A., *Working at Stormont* (Dublin, 1974).
Orr, Philip, *The road to the Somme: Men of the Ulster Division tell their story* (Belfast, 1987).
Owens, Rosemary Cullen, *Smashing times: A history of the Irish women's suffrage movement, 1889–1922* (Dublin, 1984).
—— and Andree Sheehy Skeffington, *Votes for women* (Dublin, 1975).
Pankhurst, E.S., *The suffragette movement: An intimate account of persons and ideals* (London, 1977, reprint of orig. ed., London, 1931).
Patterson, Henry, *Class conflict and sectarianism: The Protestant working class and the Belfast labour movement, 1868–1920* (Belfast 1980).
Perrot, Michelle (ed), *Writing women's history* (Oxford 1992).
Pethick-Lawrence, Emmeline, *My part in a changing world* (London, 1938).
Phoenix, Eamon, *Northern nationalism: Nationalist politics, partition and the Catholic minority in Northern Ireland, 1890–1940* (Belfast, 1994).
—— (ed), *A century of northern life: The Irish News and one hundred years of Ulster history, 1890s–1990s* (Belfast, 1995).
Prochaska, F.K., *Women and philanthropy in nineteenth-century England* (Oxford, 1980).
Pugh, Martin, *The Tories and the people, 1880–1935* (Oxford, 1985).
—— *Women and the women's movement in Britain, 1914–1959* (London, 1992).
Purvis, June (ed), *Women's history: Britain, 1850–1945* (London, 1995).
Raeburn, Antonia, *The suffragette view* (London, 1976).
Ramelson, Marian, *The petticoat rebellion: A century of struggle for women's rights* (London, 1972).
Randell, Victoria, *Women and politics: An international perspective* (2nd ed, London, 1987).
Ranney, Austin, *Pathways to parliament: Candidate selection in Britain* (London and Melbourne, 1965).
Redmond, John, *Church, state and industry in East Belfast, 1827–1929* (Belfast, 1961).
Rendall, Jane (ed), *The origins of modern feminism: Women in Britain, France and the United States, 1780–1860* (London, 1985).
—— *Equal or different: Women's politics, 1800–1914 (Oxford, 1987)*
Robb, J.H., *The Primrose League, 1883–1906* (New York, 1968).
Roberts, Elizabeth, *Women's work, 1840–1940* (Hampshire, 1988).
Robins, Joseph, *The lost children: A study of charity children in Ireland, 1700–1900* (Dublin, 1980).
—— *Fools and mad: A history of the insane in Ireland* (Dublin, 1986).

Rooke, Patrick, *Women's rights* (London, 1972).

Rose, Catherine, *The female experience: The story of the woman movement in Ireland* (Galway, 1975).

Rose, M.E., *The English poor law, 1780–1930* (Newton Abbot, 1971).

Rosen, Andrew, *Rise up women! The militant campaign of the Women's Social and Political Union, 1903–1914* (London and Boston, 1974).

Rosenbaum, Simon (ed), *Against Home Rule: The case for union* (London, 1912).

Rosenberg, Rosalind, *Beyond separate spheres: Intellectual roots of modern feminism* (London and New Haven, 1982).

Rover, Constance, *Women's suffrage and party politics in Britain, 1866–1914* (London, 1967).

—— *Love, morals and the feminists* (London, 1970).

Rowbotham, Sheila, *Hidden from history: Three hundred years of women's oppression and the fight against it* (London, 1974).

Rubinstein, David, *Before the suffragettes: Women's emancipation in the 1890s* (Brighton, 1986).

Ryan, W.P., *The Irish literary revival* (New York, 1970, reprint of orig. ed, London, 1895).

Sawyer, Roger, *We are but women: Women in Ireland's history* (London, 1993).

Scott, Joan Wallach, *Gender and the politics of history* (Sussex and New York, 1988).

Shanks, A.N., *Rural aristocracy in Northern Ireland* (Aldershot, 1988).

Shiman, Lilian Lewis, *Women and leadership in nineteenth-century England* (London, 1992).

Shkolnik, E.S., *Leading ladies: A study of eight late Victorian and Edwardian political wives* (London and New York, 1987).

Sibbett, A.R., *Orangeism in Ireland and throughout the Empire* (2 vols, London, 1939).

Sinclair, Betty, *Ulsterwomen and the war* (Belfast, 1942).

Smiley, P.K., *The peril of Home Rule* (London, 1911).

Smith, Harold L. (ed), *British feminism in the twentieth century* (Aldershot, 1990).

Smyth, Ailbhe, *Irish women's studies reader* (Dublin, 1993).

Soldon, N.C., *Women in British trade unions, 1874–1976* (Dublin, 1978).

Spender, Dale, (ed), *Man made language* (London and Boston, 1980).

—— *Men's studies modified: The impact of feminism on the academic disciplines* (Oxford, 1981).

—— *For the record: The making and meaning of feminist knowledge* (London, 1985).

Stacy, Margaret, and Price, Marion, *Women, power and politics* (London and New York, 1981).

Stead, W.T., *The centenary of 1798 and its bearing on the practical politics of to-day* (London, 1898).

Stewart, A.T.Q., *The Ulster crisis, 1912–1914* (London, 1967).

—— *Edward Carson* (Dublin, 1981).

Strachey, Ray, *The cause: A short history of the women's cause in Great Britain* (Bath, 1974, reprint of orig. ed, London, 1928).

Summers, Anne, *Angels and citizens: British women as military nurses, 1854–1914* (London, 1988).

Thompson, William, *Appeal to one half of the human race, women, against the pretensions of the other half, men, to retain them in political, and thence in civil and domestic slavery* (London, 1983, reprint of orig. ed, Great Britain, 1825).

Tickner, Lisa, *The spectacle of women: Imagery of the suffrage campaign, 1907–1914* (London, 1989).

Tong, Rosemary, *Feminist thought* (London, 1994).

Tosh, John, *The pursuit of history* (2nd ed, London and New York, 1991).

Tuttle, Lisa, *Encyclopaedia of feminism* (London, 1986).

Travers, Patrick, *Settlements and divisions: Ireland, 1870–1922* (Dublin, 1988).

Tweedy, Hilda, *A link in the chain: The story of the Irish Housewives Association, 1942–1992* (Dublin, 1992).

Vallance, Elizabeth, *Women in the house: A study of women members of parliament* (London, 1979).

Van Voris, Jacqueline, *Constance de Markievicz in the cause of Ireland* (Massachusetts, 1967).

Vicinus, Martha, *Suffer and be still: Women in the Victorian age* (London, 1973).

—— *Independent women: Work and community for single women, 1850–1920* (London, 1985)

Walker, B.M., *Shadows on glass: A portfolio of early Ulster photography* (Belfast, 1976).

—— *Ulster politics: The formative years, 1868–1886* (Belfast, 1989).

Walker, G.S., *The politics of frustration: Harry Midgely and the failure of labour in Northern Ireland* (Manchester, 1985).

Wallace, Martin, *Northern Ireland: Fifty years of self-government* (Newton Abbot, 1971).

Walton, R.G., *Women in social work* (London and Boston, 1975).

Ward, Margaret, *Unmanageable revolutionaries: Women and Irish nationalism* (Dingle, 1983).

—— *Maud Gonne: Ireland's Joan of Arc* (London, 1990).

—— *In their own voice: Women and Irish nationalism* (Dublin, 1995).

Webb, John J., *Municipal government in Ireland: Mediaeval and modern* (Dublin, 1918).

Webb, Sidney and Beatrice, *English poor law policy* (London, 1910).

—— *English poor law history* (London, 1963, reprint of orig. ed, London, 1929).

Wilson, Thomas (ed), *Ulster under Home Rule* (London, 1955).
Wollstonecraft, Mary, *A vindication of the rights of women* (New York, 1989, reprint of orig. ed, London, 1792).
Wright, Sir Almroth E., *The unexpurgated case against woman suffrage* (London, 1913).
Wuthrow, Robert, *Cultural analysis* (London, 1984).

Articles and pamphlets

Armstrong, D.L., 'Social and economic conditions in the Belfast linen industry, 1850–1900', *Irish Historical Studies*, 7, no. 28 (Sept. 1951), pp 235–69.
Ballard, Linda-May, '"Just whatever they had handy." Aspects of childbirth and early child-care in Northern Ireland, prior to 1948', *Ulster Folklife*, 31 (1985), pp 59–72.
Baker, Paula, 'The domestication of politics: Women and American political society, 1780–1920', *American History Review*, 89, no. 3 (June 1984), pp 620–47.
Bew, Paul, 'A Protestant parliament and a Protestant state: Some reflections on government and minority in Ulster, 1921–1943', Art Cosgrove and J.I. McGuire (eds), *Parliament and community* (Belfast, 1981), pp 237–48.
Blewett, Neal, 'The franchise in the United Kingdom, 1885–1918', *Past and Present*, 32, no. 4 (1965), pp 27–56.
Boran, Marie, 'Politics of revolution: Local government in Ireland during the Anglo-Irish war', *Cathair na Mart*, 8 (1988), pp 100–8.
Bourke, Joanna, 'The best of all Home Rulers: The economic power of women in Ireland, 1800–1914', *Irish Economic and Social History*, 18 (1991), pp 34–47.
Bourque, J.C., and Grossholtz, Jean, 'Politics an unnatural practice: Political science looks at female participation', *Politics and Society*, 4, no. 2 (Winter, 1974), pp 225–66.
Boyce, D.G., 'British Conservative opinion and the Ulster question, and the partition of Ireland, 1912–1921', *Irish Historical Studies*, 17, no. 65 (Mar. 1970), pp 89–112.
Boyle, J.W., 'The Belfast Protestant Association and the Independent Orange Order, 1901–1910', *Irish Historical Studies*, 13, no. 50 (Sept. 1962), pp 117–52.
Breatnach, Eileen, 'Women and higher education in Ireland, 1879–1914' *Crane Bag*, 4, no. 1 (1980), pp 47–54.
Buckland, Patrick, 'The unity of Ulster unionism, 1886–1939', *History*, 60 (1975), pp 211–23.
—— *The Northern Ireland question, 1886–1986* (London, 1987).
—— 'Irish unionism and the new Ireland', in D.G. Boyce (ed), *Revolution in Ireland, 1879–1923* (Dublin, 1988), pp 71–90.

—— 'Carson, Craig and the partition of Ireland, 1912–1921', in Peter Collins (ed), *Nationalism and unionism: Conflict in Ireland, 1885–1921* (Belfast, 1994), pp 75–89.

Buckley, A.D., '"On the club": Friendly societies in Ireland', *Irish Economic and Social History*, 14 (1987), pp 39–58.

Caine, Barbara, 'Feminism, suffrage and the nineteenth-century English women's movement', *Women's Studies International Forum*, 5, no. 6 (1982), pp 537–50.

Campbell, Winifred, 'Down the Shankill', *Ulster Folklife*, 22 (1976), pp 1–33.

Clancy, Mary, 'On the "Western outpost": Local government and women's suffrage in Co. Galway, 1898–1918' in Gerard Moran (ed), *Galway: History and society: Interdisciplinary essays on the history of an Irish county* (Dublin, 1996), pp 557–87.

Cleary, A.E., 'The religious aspect of women's suffrage', *Irish Review*, 3, no. 33 (Nov. 1913), pp 479–84.

—— 'The Gaelic League, 1893–1919', *Studies*, 8 (1919), pp 398–408.

Colby, Elbridge, 'Ethna Carbery: A woman who loved Ireland', *Catholic University Bulletin*, 20 (1914), pp 533–40.

Collier, J.F., 'Women in politics', in M.Z. Rosaldo and Louise Lamphere (eds), *Women in culture and society* (Stanford, 1974), pp 89–96.

Concannon, Helena, 'The Ethna Carbery country', *Catholic Bulletin*, 18, no. 8 (1928), pp 876–80.

Conway, T.G., 'Women's work in Ireland', *Eire-Ireland*, 7 (1972), pp 10–27.

Cullen, Mary, 'Women, history and identity', *Maynooth Review*, 6, no. 1 (May 1980), pp 65–79.

—— 'How radical was Irish feminism between the 1860s and 1920?', in P.J. Corish (ed), *Radicals, rebels and establishments* (Belfast, 1985), pp 185–201.

—— 'History women and history men: The politics of women's history', in Daltun O'Ceallaigh (ed), *Reconsiderations of Irish history and culture* (Dublin, 1994), pp 113–33.

Daly, M.E., 'Women in the Irish workforce from pre-industrial to modern times', *Saothar*, 7 (1981), pp 74–82.

Daly, Miriam, 'Women in Ulster', in Eiléan Ní Chuilleanáin (ed), *Irish women: Image and achievement* (Dublin, 1985), pp 51–66.

Darcy, R., 'The election of women to Dail Eireann: A formal analysis', *Irish Political Studies*, 3 (1988), pp 63–76.

Davin, Anna, 'Imperialism and motherhood', *History Workshop*, 5 (Spring, 1978), pp 9–65.

Davis, Tricia, et al, 'The public face of feminism: Early twentieth-century writings on women's suffrage', in Richard Johnson et al (eds), *Making history* (London, 1982), pp 303–24.

Day, S.R., 'The crime called out-door relief', *Irish Review*, 2, no. 14 (Apr. 1912), pp 73–80.

—— 'The workhouse child', *Irish Review*, 2, no. 16 (June, 1912), pp 169–79.

de Bhaldraithe, Eoin, 'Mixed marriages and Irish politics: The effect of Ne Temere', *Studies*, 77 (1988), pp 284–99.

Brun, Bairbre de, 'Women and imperialism in Ireland', *Women's Studies International Forum*, 11, no. 4 (1988), pp 323–28.

Dodd, J.T., 'Women as justices of the peace', *Contemporary Review*, 112 (1917), pp 320–27.

Charlotte Eaton, 'Ethna Carbery: Poet of the Celts', *Catholic World*, 121 (Apr.-Sept. 1925), pp 321–33.

Evans, R.J., 'Women's history: The limits of reclamation', *Social History*, 5, no. 2 (May 1980), pp 273–81.

—— 'The history of European women: A critical survey of recent research', *Journal of Modern History*, 52, no. 4 (Dec. 1980), pp 656–75.

Fanning, J.R., 'The Unionist Party in Ireland, 1906–1910', *Irish Historical Studies*, 15, no. 58 (Sept. 1966), pp 147–71.

Farrell, Brian, 'Markievicz and the women of the revolution', in F.X. Martin, (ed), *Leaders and men of the Easter Rising: Dublin 1916* (London, 1967), pp 227–38.

Fitzpatrick, David, 'The geography of Irish nationalism 1910–21', in C.H.E. Philpin, (ed), *Nationalism and popular protest in Ireland* (Cambridge, 1984), pp 403–39.

—— 'The modernization of the Irish female', in P. O'Flanaghan, K. Whelan, and P. Ferguson, (eds), *Rural Ireland, 1600–1900* (Cork, 1987), pp 162–80.

—— 'A share of the honeycomb: Education, emigration and Irishwomen', in Mary Daly, and David Fitzpatrick (eds), T*he origins of popular literacy in Ireland: Language change and educational development, 1700–1920* (Dublin, 1990), pp 167–188.

—— 'Women, gender and the writing of Irish history', *Irish Historical Studies*, 27, no. 107 (May 1991), pp 267–73.

Fox-Genovese, Elizabeth, 'Placing women's history in history', *New Left Review*, no. 133 (May-June 1982), pp 5–29.

Foy, Michael, 'Ulster unionist propaganda against Home Rule, 1912–1914', *History Ireland*, 4, no. 1 (Spring 1996), pp 49–53.

Gallagher, Anita, 'Nationalism in East Down', in David Fitzpatrick (ed), *Ireland and the First World War* (Dublin, 1986), pp 90–108.

Gardiner, Francis, 'Political interest and participation of Irish women, 1922–1992: The unfinished revolution', *Canadian Journal of Irish Studies*, 18, no. 1 (July 1992), pp 15–39.

Garvin, Tom, 'Priests and patriots: Irish separatism and fear of the modern, 1890–1914', *Irish Historical Studies*, 25, no. 97 (May 1986), pp 67–81.

Gerard, Jessica, 'Lady bountiful: Women of the landed classes and rural philanthropy', *Victorian Studies*, 30 (Winter 1987), pp 183–210.

Glandon, V.E., 'The Irish press and revolutionary Irish nationalism, 1900–1922', *Eire-Ireland*, 16 (1981), pp 21–33.

Hannam, June, 'Women and politics', in June Purvis (ed), *Women's History: Britain, 1850–1945* (London, 1995), pp 217–45.

Harp, Richard, 'The *Shan Van Vocht* and Irish nationalism', *Eire-Ireland*, 24 (1989), pp 42–52.

Harrison, Brian, 'Philanthropy and the Victorians', *Victorian Studies*, 9 (June 1966), pp 353–74.

—— 'For church, queen and family: The Girls' Friendly Society, 1874–1920', *Past and Present*, 61 (Nov. 1973), pp 107–38.

—— 'The act of militancy: Violence and the suffragettes, 1904–1914', in Brian Harrison, *Peaceable Kingdom: Stability and change in modern Britain* (Oxford, 1982), pp 26–81.

—— 'Women's suffrage at Westminster, 1886–1928', in Michael Bentley and John Stevenson (eds), *High and low politics in modern Britain* (Oxford, 1983), pp 80–122.

—— 'Women in a men's house: The women MPs, 1919–45', *Historical Journal*, 29, no. 3 (1986), pp 623–54.

Haslam, Anna, 'Women poor law guardians in Ireland', *The Englishwoman's Review*, no vol noted (15 Oct. 1896), pp 256–8.

Hazelkorn, Ellen, 'The social and political views of Louie Bennett, 1870–1956', *Saothar*, 13 (1988), pp 32–45.

Hearne, Dana, 'The Irish Citizen, 1914–1916: Nationalism, feminism and militarism', *Canadian Journal of Irish Studies*, 18, no. 1 (July 1992), pp 1–14.

Heatley, Fred, 'The York Street Co-operative Women's Guild, 1913–1921', *North Belfast History Magazine*, 2 (1986), pp 21–4.

Hennock, E.P., 'Finance and politics in urban local government in England, 1835–1900', *Historical Journal*, 6, no. 2 (1963), pp 212–25.

Himmelfarb, Gertrude, 'Some reflections on the new history', *American History Review*, 94, no. 3 (June 1989), pp 661–70.

Holton, S.S., '"In sorrowful wrath": Suffrage militancy and the romantic feminism of Emmeline Pankhurst', in H.L. Smith (ed), *British feminism in the twentieth century* (Aldershot, 1990), pp 7–24.

Innes, C.L., 'A voice in directing the affairs of Ireland: *L'Irlande Libre, The Shan Van Vocht and Bean na h-Éireann*', in Paul Hyland and Neil Sammells (eds), *Irish writing: Exile and subversion* (London, 1991), pp 146–58.

Jackson, T.A., 'Unionist history', *Irish Review*, 7–8 (Autumn 1989–Spring 1990), pp 58–66, 62–9.

—— 'Unionist politics and Protestant society in Edwardian Ireland', *Historical Journal*, 33, (1990), pp 839–66.

—— 'Unionist myths, 1912–1985', *Past and Present*, 136 (Aug. 1992), pp 164–85.

—— 'Irish unionism, 1905–1921' in Peter Collins (ed), *Nationalism and unionism* (Belfast, 1994), pp 35–46.

Johnson, D.S., 'The Belfast boycott, 1920–1923', in J.M. Goldstrom and L.A. Clarkson (eds), *Irish population, economy and society* (Oxford, 1981), pp 287–307.

Kelly, Vivien, 'Irish suffragettes at the time of the Home Rule crisis', *History Ireland*, 4, no. 1 (Spring, 1996), pp 33–8.

Kent, S.K., 'The politics of sexual difference: World War One and the demise of British feminism', *Journal of British Studies*, 27 (July 1988), pp 232–53.

Kerber, L.K., 'Separate spheres, female worlds, woman's place: The rhetoric of women's history', *Journal of American History*, 75, no. 1 (June, 1988) pp 9–39.

Laski, Marghanita, 'Domestic life', in Simon Nowell-Smith (ed), *Edwardian England, 1901–1914* (Oxford, 1964), pp 139–212.

Lerner, Gerda, 'Placing women in history', in B.A. Carroll (ed), *Liberating women's history: Theoretical and critical essays* (Illinois, 1976), pp 357–67.

Lewis, Jane, 'Beyond suffrage: English feminism in the 1920s', *Maryland Historian*, 6, no. 1 (1975), pp 1–17.

—— 'In search of real equality: Women between the wars', in Frank Gloversmith (ed), *Class, culture and social change* (Brighton, 1980), pp 208–39.

Liddington, Jill, 'Rediscovering suffrage history', *History Workshop*, 4 (1977), pp 192–202.

Longley, Edna, 'The rising, the Somme and Irish memory', in Mairin Ni Dhonnchadha, and Theo Dargan, (eds), *Revising the rising* (Londonderry, 1991), pp 29–49.

Luddy, Maria, 'Irish women and the Contagious Diseases Acts, 1864–1886', *History Ireland*, 1, no. 1 (Spring, 1993), pp 32–4.

—— 'Women and charitable organisations in nineteenth century Ireland', *Women's Studies International Forum*, 2, no. 4 (1988), pp 301–5.

—— 'Women and politics in nineteenth-century Ireland', in Gialanella Valiulis and Mary O'Dowd (eds), *Women and Irish history: Essays in honour of Margaret MacCurtain* (Dublin, 1997), pp 89–108.

McCartney, Donal, 'Hyde, D.P. Moran, and Irish Ireland', in F.X. Martin (ed), *Leaders and men of the Easter Rising: Dublin 1916* (London, 1967), pp 43–54.

McClelland, Aiken, 'The later Orange Order', in T.D. Williams (ed), *Secret societies in Ireland* (Dublin, 1963), pp 126–37.

McCraith, L.M., 'Irishwomen and their vote', *New Ireland Review*, 30 (Dec. 1908), pp 193–8.

MacDonagh, Thomas, 'The best living Irish poet (Alice Milligan)', *Irish Review*, 4, no. 41 (Sept.–Nov. 1914), pp 287–93.

McDowell, R.B., 'The landed classes and the professions', in T.W. Moody and J.C Beckett (eds), *Ulster since 1800* (London, 1957), pp 99–109.

McKillen, Beth, 'Irish feminism and national separatism, 1914–1923', *Eire-Ireland*, 17 (Fall Winter 1982), pp 52–67, 72–90.

McMinn, J.R.B., 'Presbyterianism and politics in Ulster, 1871–1906', *Studia Hibernica*, 21 (1981), pp 127–46.

—— 'Liberalism in north Antrim, 1900–1914', *Irish Historical Studies*, 23, no. 89 (May 1982), pp 17–29.

—— 'The myth of "Route" liberalism in Co. Antrim, 1869–1900', *Eire-Ireland*, 17, no. 1 (Spring, 1982), pp 137–49.

—— 'The Ballymoney meeting of 1913: A nationalist mirage?', *The Glynns*, 12 (1984), pp 34–9.

Mhic Sheain, Bridhid, 'Glimpses of Erin. Alice Milligan: Poet, Protestant, patriot', *Fortnight* (supplement), no. 236 (Mar. 1994), pp 1–26.

Manning, Maurice, 'Women in Irish national and local politics, 1922–1977', in Margaret MacCurtain and Donnacha O'Corrain (eds), *Women in Irish society* (Dublin, 1978), pp 92–102.

Meehan, Helen, 'Ethna Carbery: Anna Johnston McManus', *Donegal Annual*, 45 (1993), pp 55–65.

Missing pieces (Dublin, 1983).

Mitchell, Susan, 'The petticoat in politics', in W.G. Fitzgerald (ed), *The voice of Ireland* (Dublin, 1924), pp 164–66.

Mogey, John, 'Social relations in rural society', in T.W. Moody, and J.C. Beckett (eds), *Ulster since 1800* (London, 1957), pp 71–9.

More missing pieces (Dublin, 1985).

Morrissey, Hazel, 'Betty Sinclair: A woman's fight for socialism', *Saothar*, 9 (1983), pp 121–132.

Mullin, Molly, 'Representations of history, Irish feminism, and the politics of difference', *Feminist Studies*, 17, no. 1 (Spring, 1991), pp 29–50.

Murphy, Cliona, 'Suffragists and nationalism in early twentieth century-Ireland', *History of European Ideas*, 16, no. 4 (1993), pp 1009–15.

—— 'Women's history, feminist history or gender history', *Irish Review*, 12 (Spring–Summer, 1992), pp 21–6.

Newberry, J.V., 'Anti-war suffragists', *History*, 62 (1977), pp 411–25.

—— 'Feminist consciousness and the First World War', *History Workshop*, 23 (Spring, 1987), pp 81–101.

Nic Shuibhne, Marie, 'Women pioneers', *Wolfe Tone Annual* (1944–1945), pp 21–3.

O'Brien, Gerard, 'A question of attitude: Responses to the new poor law in Ireland and Scotland', in Rosalind Mitchinson and Peter Roebuck (eds), *Economy and society in Scotland and Ireland*, 1500–1939 (Edinburgh, 1988), pp 160–70.

O'Cleirigh, Nellie, 'Lady Aberdeen and the Irish connection', *Dublin Historical Record*, 39 (Dec. 1985–Sept. 1986), pp 28–32.

O'Delaney, Barry, 'Cumann na mBan', in W.G Fitzgerald (ed), *The voice of Ireland* (Dublin, 1924), pp 162–3.
O'Driscoll, Finbarr, 'Equal rights for women in higher education: A forgotten aspect of the Royal University', *Irish Educational Studies*, 6, no. 2 (1986–1987), pp 39–55.
O'Hegarty, P.S., 'Obituary of Alice L. Milligan', *Dublin Magazine*, 28, no. 4 (Oct.-Dec. 1953), p 45.
O'Keefe, Timothy, 'The 1898 efforts to celebrate the United Irishmen: The '98 centennial', *Eire-Ireland*, 23, no. 2 (1988), pp 51–73.
O'Neill, Marie, 'The Ladies' Land League', *Dublin Historical Record*, 25, no. 4 (1982), pp 122–33.
—— 'The Dublin Women's Suffrage Society and its successors', *Dublin Historical Record*, 38, no. 4 (1984–1985), pp 126–40.
Owens, Rosemary Cullen (ed), 'Votes for ladies, votes for women: Organised labour and the suffrage movement, 1876–1922', *Saothar*, 9 (1983), pp 32–47.
—— *Did your granny have a hammer? A history of the Irish suffrage movement, 1876–1922* (Dublin, 1985).
Park, Jihang, 'The British suffrage activists of 1913: An analysis', *Past and Present*, 120 (Aug. 1988), pp 147–62.
Phoenix, Eamon, 'Northern nationalists, Ulster unionists and the development of partition, 1900–1921', in Peter Collins (ed), *Nationalism and unionism* (Belfast, 1994), pp 107–22.
Power, Jenny Wyse, 'The political influence of women in modern Ireland', in W.G. Fitzgerald (ed), *The voice of Ireland* (Dublin, 1924), pp 158–61.
Pugh, Martin, 'Politicians and the woman's vote, 1914–1918', *History*, 59 (1974), pp 358–74.
—— *Women's suffrage in Britain, 1867–1928* (London, 1980).
Quinault, R.E., 'Lord Randolph Churchill and Home Rule', in Alan O'Day (ed), *Reactions to Irish nationalism* (Dublin, 1987), pp 319– 45.
Roberts, D.A., 'The Orange Order in Ireland: A religious institution?', *British Journal of Sociology*, 22 (1971), pp 269–82.
Rodner, W.S., 'Leaguers, covenanters, moderates: British support for Ulster, 1913–1914', *Eire-Ireland*, 17, 3 (1982), pp 68–85.
Ross, J.F.S., 'Women and parliamentary elections', *British Journal of Sociology*, 4, no. 1 (1953), pp 14–24.
Rowan, Caroline, 'Women in the Labour Party, 1906–1920', *Feminist Review*, no. 12 (Oct. 1982), pp 74–91.
Ryan, Frederick, 'The suffrage tangle', *Irish Review* (Sept. 1912), pp 346–51.
Ryan, Louise, 'The *Irish Citizen*, 1912–1920', *Saothar*, 17 (1992), pp 105–11.
—— 'Women without votes: The political strategies of the Irish suffrage movement', *Irish Political Studies*, 9 (1994), pp 119–39.
Savage, D.C., 'The origins of the Ulster Unionist Party, 1885–1886', *Irish Historical Studies*, 12, no. 47 (May 1961), pp 185–208.

Scott, J.W., 'Women in history: The modern period', *Past and Present*, 101, no. 98 (1983), pp 141–57.

—— 'Gender: A useful category of historical analysis', *American Historical Review*, 91, no. 5 (Dec. 1986), pp 1053–75.

—— 'History in crisis? The others' side of the story', *American Historical Review*, 94, no. 3 (June 1989), pp 671–92.

Shannon, C.B., 'Ulster liberal unionists and local government reform, 1885–1898', *Irish Historical Studies*, 18, no. 71 (Mar. 1973), pp 407–23.

Sheehan, Aideen, 'Cumann na mBan policies and activities', in David Fitzpatrick (ed), *Revolution? Ireland, 1917–1923* (Dublin, 1990), pp 88–97.

Sheehy Skeffington, Hanna, 'The women's franchise movement – Ireland', *Irish Review* (July 1912), pp 225–7.

—— 'Women and politics', *The Bell*, 7, no.2 (Nov. 1943), pp 143–48.

Sheppard, M.G., 'The effects of the franchise provision on the social and sex composition of the municipal electorate, 1882–1914', *Society for the Study of Labour History Bulletin*, 45, (Autumn, 1982), pp 19–25.

Smith, B.G., 'The contribution of women to modern historiography in Great Britain, France and the United States, 1750–1940', *American History Review*, 89, no. 3 (June 1984), pp 709–32.

Smith-Rosenberg, Carroll, 'Politics and culture in women's history', *Feminist Studies*, 6, no. 1 (Spring, 1980), pp 55–64.

Stephen, Caroline E., 'Women and politics', *The Nineteenth Century and After*, 71 (Feb. 1907), pp 227–36.

Stephens, Laura, 'An Irish workhouse', *New Ireland Review*, 13 (May 1900), pp 129–34.

Summers, Anne, 'A home from home: Women's philanthropic work in the nineteenth century', in Sandra Burman (ed), *Fit work for women* (London, 1979), pp 33–63.

Stubbs, J.O., 'The unionists and Ireland, 1914–1918', *Historical Journal*, 33, 4 (1990), pp 867–93.

Te Brake, J.K., 'Irish peasant women in revolt: The Land League years', *Irish Historical Studies*, 28, no. 109 (May 1992), pp 63–80.

Thane, Pat, 'Women and poor law in Victorian and Edwardian England', *History Workshop*, 6 (Autumn, 1978), pp 29–51.

Thompson, Dorothy, 'Women and nineteenth-century radical politics: A lost dimension', in Juliet Mitchel and Ann Oakley (eds), *The rights and wrongs of women* (Middlesex, 1976), pp 112–38.

Tod, I.M.S., 'Boarding-out of pauper children', *Statistical and Social Inquiry Society of Ireland Journal*, 7, 5 (Aug. 1878), pp 293–9.

—— 'The place of women in the administration of the Irish poor law', *The Englishwoman's Review*, 103 (15 Nov. 1881), pp 481–89.

—— 'Women and the new franchise bill: A letter to an Ulster member of parliament' (Mar. 1884), reprinted in Jane Lewis (ed), *Before the vote*

was won: Arguments for and against women's suffrage (London and New York, 1987), pp 396–403.
—— 'Municipal franchise for women in Ireland', *The Englishwoman's Review*, 170 (15 July 1887), pp 289–91.
Tynan, Kathleen, 'Ethna Carbery: An Irish singer', *Catholic World*, 109 (July 1919), pp 477–86.
—— 'A trumpet call to Irish women', in W.G. Fitzgerald (ed), *The voice of Ireland* (Dublin, 1924), pp 170–74.
Vickery, Amanda, 'Golden age to separate spheres? A review of the categories and chronology of English women's history', *Historical Journal*, 36, no. 2 (1993), pp 383–414.
Walker, B.M., 'The Irish electorate, 1868–1915', *Irish Historical Studies*, 18, no. 71 (Mar. 1973), pp 359–406.
Walker, G.S., 'The Northern Ireland Labour Party in the 1920s', *Saothar*, 10 (1985), pp 19–27.
Walsh, Oonagh, 'Testimony from imprisoned women', in David Fitzpatrick (ed), *Revolution? Ireland, 1917–1923* (Dublin, 1990), pp 69–86.
Ward, Margaret, 'Feminism in Northern Ireland: a reflection', *Honest Ulsterman*, 83 (Summer, 1987), pp 59–70.
—— 'Marginality and militancy: Cumann na mBan, 1914–1936', in Austen Morgan, and Bob Purdie (eds), *Ireland: Divided nation. Divided class* (London, 1980), pp 96–110.
—— 'The Ladies' Land League', *Irish History Workshop*, no. 1 (1981), pp 27–53.
—— '"Suffrage first – above all else!" An account of the Irish suffrage movement', *Feminist Review*, 10 (Feb. 1982), pp 21–36.
—— 'Women in Irish history', *Terence MacSwiney memorial lectures* (London, 1986), pp 67–80.
—— *The missing sex: Putting women into Irish history* (Dublin, 1991).
—— 'The league of women delegates and Sinn Féin, 1917', *History Ireland*, 4, no. 3 (Autumn, 1996), pp 37–41.
Whitford, F.J., 'Joseph Devlin', *Threshold*, 1, no. 2 (1957), pp 24–33.
Whyte, J.H., 'How much discrimination was there under the unionist regime, 1921–1968?', in Tom Gallagher and James O'Connell (eds), *Contemporary Irish studies* (Manchester, 1983), pp 1–35.

Theses

Fitzgerald, Rory, 'Ulster Women against Home Rule: The role of the Ulster Women's Unionist Association in the Home Rule crisis, 1911–1914' (unpub. BA diss., University of Ulster, 1989).
Foy, M.T., 'The Ancient Order of Hibernians: An Irish political-religious pressure group, 1884–1975' (unpub. MA diss., The Queen's University of Belfast, 1976).

—— 'The Ulster Volunteer Force: Its domestic development and political importance'(unpub. PhD diss., The Queen's University of Belfast, 1986).

Hamill, Jonathan, 'Women in the Belfast textile operatives, 1890–1939' (unpub. PhD diss., The Queen's University of Belfast, 1999).

Harbinson, J.F., 'A history of the Northern Ireland Labour Party, 1891–1949' (unpub. MSc diss., The Queen's University of Belfast, 1966).

Miller, Henry, 'The administration of the poor laws in Ireland till 1921; and in Northern Ireland from 1921, till the present [1942]' (unpub. MCSc. diss., The Queen's University of Belfast, 1942).

Paisley, Ian, Jnr., 'The political career of Dame Dehra Parker' (unpub. MA diss., The Queen's University of Belfast, 1994).

Percy, C.A., 'Women's constructions of feminism in Northern Ireland' (unpub. PhD diss., The Queen's University of Belfast, 1994).

Phoenix, Eamon, 'The nationalist movement in Northern Ireland, 1914–1928' (unpub. PhD diss., The Queen's University of Belfast, 1983).

Ross, E.M., 'Women and poor law administration, 1857–1909' (unpub. MA diss., University of London, 1956).

Walker, L.E., 'The women's movement in England in the late nineteenth and early twentieth centuries' (unpub. PhD diss., University of Manchester, 1984).

Index